Islands of Identity

History-writing and identity formation in five island regions in the Baltic Sea

Samuel Edquist & Janne Holmén

©The Authors

Södertörn University
SE-141 89 Huddinge

www.sh.se/publications

Cover photograph: Jonas Mathiasson
Cover Design: Jonathan Robson
Layout: Per Lindblom & Jonathan Robson

Printed by Elanders, Stockholm 2015

Södertörn Academic Studies 59
ISSN 1650-433X

ISBN 978-91-86069-98-8

Contents

Preface	7
History-writing and identity formation in five island regions in the Baltic Sea	
JANNE HOLMÉN	9
The islands	10
Identities and islands	14
History-writing and identity	22
The Baltic islands as regions	25
The geography of history	28
Strange exceptions or illustrative examples?	29
Research questions and primary sources	31
Works cited	36
In the shadow of the Middle Ages? Tendencies in Gotland's history-writing, 1850–2010	
SAMUEL EDQUIST	39
The questions and the literature	43
Methods and primary sources	44
Gotland history-writing analysed	57
The medieval narrative, *c*.1850–1975	59
Cession to Sweden	83
The folklore narrative, *c*.1850–1975	89
Nature and history united	94
Modern history-writing, *c*.1975 onwards	94
The two dominant narratives	111
The third narrative	120
The implications of the dominant medieval narrative	124
References	126

Åland—navigating between possible identities,
1852–2012
JANNE HOLMÉN   143

   Methods, sources and earlier research   144
   The character of Åland   160
   Prehistory and the early Middle Ages   182
   Swedish rule, Russian rule   197
   Autonomy   213
   The development of Ålandic history-writing   232
   References   236

Saaremaa and Hiiumaa—revolutionizing identities
in Baltic German, national Estonian, and Soviet histories,
1827–2012
JANNE HOLMÉN   243

   Earlier research   245
   The character of Saaremaa and Hiiumaa   255
   Ancient and medieval history   266
   The Danish, Swedish, and Russian periods   275
   The tumultuous twentieth century   287
   The Saaremaa uprising in 1919   287
   Conclusions   302
   References   307

Bornholmian history-writing
JANNE HOLMÉN   313

   Earlier research on Bornholmian history-writing   315
   Methods and sources   319
   Authors and funders   320
   The character of the Bornholmians   324
   Ancient and medieval history   346
   Early modern Bornholm   355
   Isolation, integration, alienation   364
   Conclusions   378
   References   383

Comparative conclusions—general lessons regarding
islandness and collective identities
JANNE HOLMÉN   387

    The rise of regional history, 1804–2013   387
    Wars and uprisings   390
    The Baltic as a front line   392
    Security as the root of identity   393
    The social roots of regional identity   394
    Geography and identity   395
    Differences and divisions within the islands   397
    Free and egalitarian islanders?   400
    Regional identity, a threat to national unity?   401
    The complementarity of islandness   403
    Common heritage, invented traditions—
    or geography?   405
    The relationship between islandness
    and regional identity on the Baltic islands   411
    Works cited   412

Preface

The project *Islands of Identity* was started on 1 January 2009 by Samuel Edquist, Janne Holmén, and Erik Axelsson. Our initial plan was to divide the work of the project equally, but as Samuel and Erik were simultaneously engaged in other projects, Janne gradually took over a larger part. In the finished book, Janne has written the introduction, the conclusion, and the sections on Åland, Saaremaa and Hiiumaa, and Bornholm. Samuel has written the section about Gotland, while Erik Axelsson has been project leader and initiated a survey of Bornholmian sources that turned out to be a highly valuable basis for Janne's continued research about the island. All three of us have read and commented upon the draft book in its entirety. We—Samuel and Janne—would like to thank Erik for his contributions and enthusiastic companionship.

In the course of the project we have received invaluable help from many scholars, librarians, and others knowledgeable about regional history, of whom we can mention only a few by name. Kenneth Gustavsson and Dan Nordman have given valuable comments on the essay on Ålandic history-writing. Professor Nils Erik Villstrand contributed with insights into the general state of regional history-writing in Finland. Katrin Aar at the Archival Library in Kuressaare was of great help in finding sources from Saaremaa, and Olavi Pesti and Marika Mägi have commented on the essay about Saaremaa. Geltmar von Buxhöwden was of help in unravelling the biographical and genealogical information about the history writers and historical figures from the Buxhöwden family. The director of Hiiumaa museum, Helgi Põllo, has been of great help in many ways, and Vello Kaskor has also read the essay about Hiiumaa.

Ann Vibeke Knudsen, former director of Bornholm's museum, was of great help in the project's initial stages. The Bornholmian archaeologist Finn Ole Sonne Nielsen provided valuable input regarding Bornholm's older history. Karin Larsen at the Centre for Regional and Tourism Research has also read the essay about Bornholm, and honoured us with an invitation to publish an article about our project in the anthology *From One Island to Another*. Olof Hansson and Lars Hermanson are to be thanked for their valuable comments on the Gotland essay. Professor Torkel Jansson in Uppsala has given valuable feedback on large portions of the manuscript.

Parts of the manuscript have been presented at seminars at the Institute of Contemporary History at Södertörn University and at the Department of History at Uppsala University. The Publication Committee at Södertörn University has also been of great help in seeing the book to print.

The project has been represented at several seminars, conferences, and workshops: 'Katoaako kansallinen identiteetti' in Helsinki in 2009; 'Islands of the world' on Bornholm in 2010; 'Shared past—conflicting histories' in Turku in 2011; 'Öande och öighet', arranged by Owe Ronström in Stockholm in 2012; and the Swedish History Days conference in Mariehamn in 2012.

Ålands kulturstiftelse provided financial support for Janne's initial studies on Åland.

Finally, we would like to thank the Foundation for Baltic and East European Studies, which has financed our research project and has displayed great flexibility in accommodating the changes we have been forced to make in the project's original timetable.

History-writing and identity formation in five island regions in the Baltic Sea

Janne Holmén

The sea creates distance to the mainland, providing islands with 'natural boundaries'; simultaneously, it functions as a route of communication with foreign shores. Political changes may shift the balance between the separating and the connecting properties of the sea. For example, the collapse of the Iron Curtain after 1989 helped the Baltic Sea regain its position as a link between peoples instead of a moat separating them. Our aim is to investigate how the geographic situation of islands—isolation in combination with potentially far-reaching waterway connections—affects the formation of identities in interplay with political changes and cultural processes. We investigate if and how a regional island identity is expressed in regional history-writing from the large islands in the Baltic Sea during the nineteenth and twentieth centuries, with particular focus on how it related to other sub-national, national, and regional identities. History-writing is strongly linked to the formulation of collective identities. Quite a lot of historiographical research has been committed to asking how historians, by writing about 'their' past, have constructed national identities, but thus far the emergence of regional identities has been less studied.

In this research project, we have chosen historical works produced or initiated *on* Baltic islands, in the assumption that the islanders in those books are making a statement about where they come from, who they are, where they have their loyalties, and with what historical periods, peoples, and realms they identify. It must be emphasized that the views on history and identity that are revealed in these sources are the ones held by a regional intellectual elite, who were attempting to influence popular sentiment on the islands. Thus we do not attempt to investigate views of history at the grassroots level, for which ethnological or folkloric sources would have been more appropriate, or to describe the progress of the academic discourse about the islands' history. That said, the regional history-writing which we investigate has of course developed in interplay with both popular and academic understandings of history, and often these categories are to some extent amalgamated.

The islands selected for the studies are Gotland, the Åland Islands, Hiiumaa, Saaremaa, and Bornholm. Janne Holmén has conducted the studies of Åland, Saaremaa and Hiiumaa, and Bornholm; Samuel Edquist, the study of Gotland. Where called for, we have elected to describe the five islands as island regions, a choice of terminology that reflects that they all have secondary islands, and that all of them are geographic entities that surpass the merely local scale—they are past or present provinces or counties, not parishes or other small communities. Thus this in an investigation of *regional* history-writing and regional identity; *local* is a term that we reserve for history-writing and identity formation in the parishes, towns, and secondary islands which together constitute island regions.

The islands

The world's islands are not evenly distributed. Since the last Ice Age, the process of post-glacial isostatic uplift has produced a disproportionally large number of islands in coastal waters between 58°N and 66°N.[1] The islands selected for the present project are all situated in this zone, so in that respect they are 'typical' islands. The northerly and coastal position of the typical island implies that it can often be reached on foot—across the ice in wintertime, that is. This is especially true in the brackish Baltic Sea, which freezes more easily than the saltier oceans. Åland, Hiiumaa, and Saaremaa are connected to the mainland by an ice sheet in normal winters, Gotland and Bornholm are not.

In spite of their relative geographical and cultural proximity to one another, the islands in the Baltic Sea provide a rich variation in geographical, historical, and political parameters relevant to the construction of local and regional identities: remoteness from the mainland, fragmentation of the archipelago, previous affiliations with foreign countries,

---

[1] Depraetre & Dahl 2007, 70–1, 76–7.

linguistic differences to the mainland, and current or historical political autonomy.

Relief map of the Baltic Sea. Source: Wikimedia Commons, edited by Janne Holmén.

The Swedish island of Gotland at 3,000 km² is the largest of all the Baltic islands, and has a population of some 57,000. Administratively, Gotland, together with a few smaller islands, has been one of Sweden's 21 counties (*län*). Gotlands län consisted of only one municipality (*kommun*), which was also called Gotland. On 1 January 2011, Gotland's county and municipality merged to become Region Gotland. The island was also one of Sweden's 25 historical provinces (*landskap*). Today, the Gotlanders generally consider themselves Swedes, but the medieval language of Gotland is considered by linguists to have been distinct from Swedish. Before the fourteenth century, Gotland was largely autonomous, with only loose ties to the Swedish kingdom. However, in 1361, Gotland was attached to the Danish realm, and a period of economic stagnation began. In 1645, Gotland was handed over to Sweden.

Åland is an autonomous province (*landskap*) of Finland, the main island of Fasta Åland being situated 70 km from the Finnish mainland and 36 km from the Swedish mainland. However, Fasta Åland is connected to mainland Finland by an archipelago with the highest density of islands found anywhere in the world.[2] The Åland Islands number nearly 7,000 islands larger than 0.25 ha, 60 of them populated; include the smaller islands, and the total figure reaches 27,000, with a land area of 1,552 km². Åland had 28,500 inhabitants on 31 December 2012, and is the only one of the Baltic islands studied here with an increasing population. The official language on Åland is Swedish, the mother tongue of 90 per cent of Åland's and 5 per cent of Finland's population.[3] Åland and Finland were integral parts of Sweden until 1809, when they came under Russian sovereignty. In the autumn of 1917 a movement began on Åland which sought secession from Finland—which then still belonged to Russia—and union with Sweden. When Finland gained its independence in December that year it attempted to assert its control of Åland, which caused a conflict with Sweden about the sovereignty of the islands. To appease the Ålanders, Finland offered them autonomy. The League of Nations granted Finland sovereignty over Åland in 1921, on the condition that the language and culture of the inhabitants were safeguarded. The Åland Islands were duly granted autonomy in line with the Finnish suggestion.

Saaremaa is an Estonian county (*maakond*). In addition to the main island of Saaremaa and adjacent small islands, Saare County comprises the sizeable island of Muhu and more distant Ruhnu in the Bay of Riga. Covering some 2,922 km², the county has a total population of 34,527, down from around 40,000 in the early 1990s. Today, 98% of the inhabitants of Saaremaa and Hiiumaa speak Estonian, but German, the language of the landed aristocracy and the merchants of the town of Arensburg (present-day Kuressaare), was common until the Second

[2] Depraetre & Dahl 2007, 71.
[3] ÅSUB 2012.

World War, and the island of Ruhnu once had a Swedish-speaking population that fled the island for Sweden during the Second World War. Saaremaa was invaded by German crusaders in 1227, and the island, like Hiiumaa immediately to the north, was divided between the Brothers of the Sword (from 1237 the Livonian Order) and the bishopric of Ösel–Wiek, which also comprised present-day Läänemaa on the mainland. In 1559 Saaremaa passed to Denmark, which in turn handed the island over to Sweden in 1645. In 1710 Russian troops gained control of the island, and it remained part of the Russian Empire until the end of the First World War, when Estonia gained its independence after a short German occupation. Kuressaare/Arensburg is situated on the southern coast of Saaremaa and has had good connections to Riga, which was the centre of Livonia. The distance from the southern tip of the Sõrve peninsula to Latvia is less than 30 km. Saaremaa constitutes 6.5% of Estonia's land area and is home to 2.6% of the country's population. In the present investigation that makes it the largest island relative to its mainland, although Gotland is larger in absolute terms. Prior to the Second the Second World War, 60,000 people, 5% of the country's total, lived on Saaremaa.[4]

With a land area of 1,023 km², Hiiumaa is the smallest of the island regions investigated in this project. Moreover, it largely consists of wetlands and other uncultivable areas, which has meant that throughout history it has had a relatively small population. Hiiumaa was probably populated from Saaremaa and Sweden in the thirteenth century. The proportion of Swedish peasants was greater than on Saaremaa, and they remained a large community until the end of the eighteenth century. Hiiumaa was also under Swedish rule longer than Saaremaa, from 1563 to 1710. Like Saaremaa, the island suffered heavy population losses during the Second World War. The population is still decreasing, and in 2012 it had dipped to 9,984. Kärdla on Hiiumaa did not officially become a town until 1938, and it was not until 1946, when Hiiumaa became a separate county, that Kärdla replaced Haapsalu on the mainland as the administrative centre of the island. By that time Estonia had become a Soviet republic, and the Estonian islands remained affected by travel restrictions until Estonia regained its independence in 1992.

Bornholm is part of Denmark, and has been so with a few interruptions since the late tenth century. The island has been much contested,

---

[4] The population statistics for Saaremaa and Hiiumaa were gathered from the Statistics Estonia database <http://pub.stat.ee> for 2012.

however. In the Middle Ages it was the scene of a power struggle between the Danish king and the archbishops of Lund in Skåne. From 1525 until 1575 it was leased to the Hanseatic city of Lübeck, and in 1658 it was ceded to Sweden. An uprising in December that year brought the island back under the control of the Danish king; however, Skåne and the rest of eastern Denmark were permanently lost to Sweden, which meant that Bornholm found itself 135 km distant from Denmark proper, with Sweden a mere 35 km away. From 1940 to 1945 the island, like the rest of Denmark, was under German occupation. In contrast to the rest of the country, Bornholm also experienced a year of Soviet occupation from May 1945 until April 1946. Unlike the other islands in this study, Bornholm has several urban centres which were established back in the Middle Ages. The total population of the island today is 41,000, and it is steadily shrinking.[5] Bornholm is the only area in Denmark labelled a *regionskommune* (regional municipality) as of 1 January 2003, when the island's five municipalities were merged with Bornholm's *amt* (county) after a referendum. When Denmark abandoned the system of *amter* in favour of regions on 1 January 2007, Bornholm became part of Region Hovedstaden.

Identities and islands

The fact that affiliations with nations, regions, ethnic groups, or social classes can be overlapping and intertwined makes collective identities hard to study. Different academic disciplines have their own ways of approaching the questions of identity formation. In this study we will combine two of these perspectives: the field of island studies (sometimes 'nissology' or 'islandology') and the study of the uses of history. Island studies focus on the geographical dimension, with the central debate within this field being whether the surrounding sea promotes the formation of a common identity among islanders by clearly delimiting and secluding their island. Scholars interested in the use of history, meanwhile, tend to be more concerned with cultural and historical factors, and in general consider identity a cultural product of quite recent fabrication. Most scholars believe groups form collective identities by

---

[5] Statistics Denmark, <http://www.dst.dk/en/Statistik/emner/befolkningogbefolkningsfremskrivning/folketal.aspx>.

selectively remembering historical or mythological events that promote cohesion, while forgetting other events that do not serve this purpose. Opponents of the view that national identities might entirely be explained as recent constructions are also primarily concerned with cultural factors. The most prominent example is Anthony D. Smith's theory of 'ethnies'. Although Smith acknowledges the importance of recent nation-building processes, he suggests that modern national identity has been formed around a pre-existing kernel, an original ethnic group who share a common culture.[6] However, we would argue that a combination of historical and geographical perspectives can deepen any understanding of collective identities. To that end, we set out to demonstrate why islands offer a particularly good set of samples for our exploration of the links between identity, geography, and history.

The origin and meaning of collective identities

The term 'identity' has a history stretching back to ancient Greece and Aristotle, but according to the political scientist W. J. M. Mackenzie it was not fully developed in the sense of collective or political identity before the publication of Lucian Pye's *Aspects of Political Development* in 1966, even though it had occasionally been used in its present meaning by historians and other scholars in the first half of the twentieth century.[7] Mackenzie is of the opinion that the concept of 'collective political identity' evolved in the American academic community from the mid 1950s, prompted by an acute awareness of decolonization. Lucian Pye outlined six crises that a society had to overcome before it could become a modern nation-state, the first of them 'the identity crisis':

> The first and most fundamental crisis is that of achieving a common sense of identity. The people in a new state must come to recognize their national territory as being their true homeland, and they must feel as individuals that their own personal identities

---

[6] Smith 1986.
[7] Mackenzie 1978, 19, 30–1. The coinage 'national identity' in 1966 is illustrated by its first occurrences in the Nordic languages in the years 1967–9. In Estonian, the term 'rahvuslik identiteet' had made a brief appearance in 1965—referring to black Americans—but it did not surface again until Estonia achieved independence from the Soviet Union in 1992 (Wahlbäck 1967, 35; Helsinki-Seura 1968, 41; Haugen 1966, 24; Udenrigspolitiske selskab 1969, 30; Sögel 1965, 19; Õispuu 1992). Google book-search was used to chart the history of terms, which, although far from perfect, gives a general picture of a word's history.

are in part defined by their identification with their territorially delimited country. In most of the new states traditional forms of identity ranging from tribe to caste to ethnic and linguistic groups compete with the sense of larger national identity.[8]

Thus, the concept of collective identities has its origin in the study of national identity. However, it is not only on a national level that individuals might feel identification with a place and its inhabitants. Although the traditional identities that Pye mentions are not primarily territorial, old and new nation-states alike have to compete with local and regional identities on many different levels—village, parish, county, and so on. In this study, we use the term 'region' for geographic entities directly under the national level.

The concept of local identity was already being used by the American social worker Robert Archey Woods back in 1898, referring to districts in New York:

> The reestablishment of a degree of local self-government in this great district is positively necessary, not only for the political training of citizens, but for securing the local identity and local loyalty out of which the feeling of social responsibility springs. American democracy does not contemplate the formation of vast, sprawling, formless masses of population governed from a single centre.[9]

Thus Woods saw a direct link between local identity, democratic participation, and social responsibility. Although they did not use the term identity, the contemporary local heritage movement in the Nordic countries had similar ideas about the virtue of cultivating a knowledge of and affinity for one's local community. Woods's view that civic activity is an efficient way of forming a local identity is today shared by many scholars. For example, it has inspired attempts to strengthen local self-government in Poland, where border changes and population movements following the Second World War have resulted in weak local identities in western regions such as Lower Silesia, where most of the population lack roots in the area. However, the effects of these reforms are disputed.[10]

---

[8] Pye 1966, 63.
[9] Woods 1898, 307.
[10] Kurantowicz 2001, 188 ff.

Often, regional identities operate in harmony with national identity; as the examples above illustrate, they can even be seen as a building blocks for a functioning national democracy. In these cases, local history-writing is not trying to tear down the national historical narrative, only to reassert the region's position within it. For example, regional historians in Sweden have often tried to place the cradle of the Swedish kingdom in their own *landskap*. The home region is seen as the origin, the heart, or the most important part of the nation, not as something distinctly different from it. However, regional identities can also come to rival national identities. A strong regional identity might appear to be the more natural community than the nation-state, in some extreme cases even leading to demands for independence and the formation of a new nation-state—the point where regionalism turns into nationalism. European separatist movements, including Scottish, Flemish, Basque, and Catalan parties, have their own group in the European Parliament, the European Free Alliance (EFA). Of the five islands in this research project, only Åland has a political party, Ålands Framtid, which favours independence and is a member of the EFA.[11]

Sharp borders and strong identities?

It has been argued that islands have an exceptional ability to instil a sense of local or regional identity in their inhabitants. Geographers, social scientists, anthropologists, and political scientists tend to concur that island populations share a sense of belongingness and affinity that is a direct consequence of 'islandness', the specific isolation and boundedness that is so characteristic of islands.[12] The term islandness is used in preference to the pejorative 'insularity', but it also implies that local identity is not only quantitatively stronger on islands than in mainland communities, but also that it is qualitatively different—it includes the awareness of being an islander, secluded with your fellow islanders at some distance from the rest of the world.[13]

In the last decades of the twentieth century, 'island studies' emerged as a distinct field of research. Political scientists and geographers wanted to investigate the specific social, economic, and political conditions that were linked the geographical condition of islandness. Investigations of the

---

[11] EFA homepage.
[12] For example, White 1995, 4; Olausson 2007, 29; Hay 2006, 22; Royle 2001, 11; Baldacchino 2004, 272–3.
[13] Conklin 2007.

connection between geography and politics had been common in the first half of the twentieth century, then labelled geopolitics. Most of the geopoliticians had little interest in islands, preoccupied as they were with the power struggles between great powers. However, the Swedish political scientist Rudolf Kjellén argued that the sea was the best possible border, and that the insular state therefore was the ideal. Notably, he stressed that the role of the border was not to protect the state as a shell. Rather, it had to be a compromise between boundary and channel of communication, and the sea offered the best combination of those properties. Of course, the location of a given island affected the extent to which the surrounding sea provided protection and communication. While Kjellén considered Great Britain's location to be almost perfect, he was of the opinion that New Zealand was too isolated from the viewpoint of efficient communications.[14] Similarly, in his great work on the Mediterranean in sixteenth century, the French historian Fernand Braudel concluded that islands are isolated only as long as they are outside the normal sea routes; when integrated into the trade routes they become actively involved in the dealings of the outside world. As a consequence, islands might be both far ahead and far behind general history, torn between archaism and innovation.[15]

By recognizing the dual nature of islands' boundaries, Kjellén and Braudel touched on a subject that has become one of the major themes in the field of island studies: the question whether islands should primarily be considered isolated or connected. Erik and Thomas Clarke have described the relationship between isolation and connection as one of complementarity, borrowing a term from quantum physics. Quoting Niels Bohr, they claim that to do it justice, an island 'needs to be described as both isolated and connected, for the two "are equally necessary for the elucidation of the phenomena" '.[16]

According to Pete Hay, the idea that islands are secluded worlds does not find much favour in contemporary island studies. Instead of being seen as a sharp border, the shoreline is described as a 'shifting liminality' or a 'permeable membrane'. To Hay's mind, the current line is that 'connectedness describes the island condition better than isolation'. Because of their small hinterlands, islands are forced to trade in order to

[14] Kjellén 1916, 54 ff.
[15] Braudel 1976, 150.
[16] Clarke & Clarke 2009, 316.

get access to vital goods; the smaller the island, the more dependent it is on trade.[17]

The dependence on trade when it comes to the Baltic region is illustrated by the fact that its smaller and more marginal islands were not permanently populated before the mainland cities, primarily Stockholm and Tallinn, emerged in the thirteenth century, providing islanders with the markets from which they could get grain in exchange for their fish and butter. This was true for the Stockholm, Turku, and Åland archipelagos right up to the twentieth century, and in older times for most of Fasta Åland and Hiiumaa as well, since these islands had even less agricultural land in the past. (The process of post-glacial isostatic uplift has slowly increased the area of arable land; islands that are now suitable for farming were in the Middle Ages still reliant on pasture and fishing.)

While the image of islands as delimited by sharp borders lends itself to the hypothesis that islanders acquire a strong local identity, the fact that islands can be highly dependent on trade also has consequences for the formation of identity. It is a common assumption that collective identity is formed in confrontation with other groups. Islanders who are too isolated might not even be aware of their own islandness. Godfrey Baldacchino claims that localism might have been a way for elites on autonomous islands to explain their relationship to the mainland, his point being that 'The conception and expression of island identity ... are part of an ongoing dialectic between the geographic and the political'. He also underlines that islandness is relational: 'an island's administration might be seen to act as a "mainland" by the inhabitants of outlying islands, enhancing the latter's sense of island identity.'[18]

Most island jurisdictions consist of more than one island—they are to some extent archipelagic. That is something of a corrective to the notion that islands have natural boundaries and sharp edges, and it means that the identity-shaping power of islands might have a divisive influence within island jurisdictions. All the islands in this study are in fact accompanied by smaller inhabited islands. Fasta Åland is surrounded by a heavily fragmentized archipelago, consisting of about 27,000 islands, of which 60 are inhabited, while Bornholm only has the small Ertholmene

[17] Hay 2006, 4–5.
[18] Baldacchino 2004, 273–4.

archipelago (Christansø and some adjacent islands).[19] Based on the main island's size relative to its archipelago's land area, a classification into monoinsular (100%), quasi-monoinsular (>90%), multi-insular (>50%), and archipelagic (<50%) has been proposed. Secessionist tendencies have been seen in the last few decades in archipelagic and multi-insular states.[20] According to this model, Åland is multi-insular, while the other islands in the study are quasi-monoinsular. Of the five island regions studied, Saare County has the largest single secondary island, Muhu, with an area of 201 km^2 (compared to Saaremaa's 2,673 km^2) and 5.5 per cent of the county's total population. Since the focus of this research project is history-writing concerning entire island regions, we will not examine in detail the history-writing and identity formation on secondary islands. However, since the potentially divisive properties of multi-insularity—and the effect that this might have had on the formation of regional identity—has to be kept in mind, the existence of secondary island history-writing will be briefly surveyed.

Edward Warrington and David Milne have assembled research results from several disciplines to suggest a typology of island governance. They identify seven different types—civilization, fief, fortress, refuge, settlement, plantation, and entrepôt—all of which they claim are linked to a particular identity. The 'island civilization' is the most unusual; in modern times it comprises only Britain and Japan. As it refers to really large and populous islands with an influence in world politics, the category is not applicable to the Baltic islands. The 'fief' includes islands that are heavily exploited by a colonial power or domestic elite. The islands' identity is torn between a dominating defensive traditionalism and a radical utopian minority, both of which help counteract the formation of nationalism. Warrington and Milne mention Haiti as a modern example.[21] Hiiumaa and Saaremaa shared similarities with the fief up until the end of the First World War. The 'fortress' is generally a small island, such as Malta, used by a larger power to control trade routes and communications. Its identity is affected by the foreign garrison because of the influx of foreign lifestyles, religions, and customs. Islanders can choose to

---

[19] The figure for the Åland Islands is the official one given by Statistics Åland; however, such figures should always be handled with caution, given that they are dependent on the minimum size of the entity one chooses to define as an island.
[20] Depraetere & Dahl 2007, 101–102.
[21] Warrington & Milne 2007, 404

adapt to, absorb, or oppose the foreign influences.[22] All of the islands in this study have at times had the character of fortresses. The 'refuge' is an isolated sanctuary such as Taiwan or Cuba, whose identity is characterized by defining itself against an empire. The islanders are highly nationalistic, but at the same time seek international recognition.[23] This description fits the Ålandic self-image as the last, threatened refuge of pure Swedishness in Finland, an attitude which is prevalent at least at a rhetorical level.

While the fief, the fortress, and the refuge are quite rare in global terms, Warrington and Milne's three remaining types are more common. The 'settlement' and the 'plantation' are different kinds of European colonies in the third world.[24] While these two types bear little resemblance to the islands in the Baltic Sea, Warrington and Milne claim that Åland is a representative of the last category—the 'entrepôt'. This kind of island has the same favourable location as the fortress, but is able to use it for its own benefit. The entrepôt is characterized by 'investment finance, entrepreneurial flair as well as a legal, regulatory, and dispute-resolution regime that facilitates market transactions and innovation by minimizing cost and risk'. Singapore, the Channel Islands, Åland, and Mauritius are examples drawn from different regions. Warrington and Milne claim that these islands are paradoxically characterized by 'a conservative ethos and a modern lifestyle, valuing individual well-being as well as social conformism, safeguarding democratic formalities while promoting strong, hierarchical leadership'. The entrepôt attracts immigrants, and functions as a melting pot, so favouring assimilation. Unlike other types of islands, it exploits externally induced change and subordinates it to local direction. According to Warrington and Milne, it is the economic success of the entrepôt that makes it an attractive model for other islands, rather than its sovereignty or democracy per se.[25]

One branch of island studies has investigated representations of islands. While these studies are often focused on how outsiders have objectified islands or how they have functioned as metaphors in fiction,[26]

---

[22] Warrington & Milne 2007, 406.
[23] Warrington & Milne 2007, 407–408.
[24] Warrington & Milne 2007, 410, 413.
[25] Warrington & Milne 2007, 413 ff., quotes at 413 and 414.
[26] For example, Edmond & Smith 2003; Gillis 2004.

some have also addressed islanders' self-representation and its importance for their construction of a common identity. Alex Law describes a particular brand of island nationalism, which 'derives its force not only from land-based "roots" but also from the imaginary relationship of the collective group to the sea and the coastline'. He argues that the history of the Royal Navy's dominance of the seas as well as the concept of an 'island race' have been important factors in the creation of British island nationalism, but that they—and with them the sense of a unified Britishness—are now slipping away.[27]

History-writing and identity

Towards the end of the twentieth century, increasing numbers of scholars in various disciplines turned their attention to the uses of history. History can be used by different actors—historians, politicians, journalists, writers, or the public—for different purposes, for example to create meaning or legitimacy or to handle a changing world.[28] As early as 1874, Friedrich Nietzsche had identified three types of uses of history: the monumental, the antiquarian, and the critical. He argued that if these three were in balance, life could be enhanced. The monumental use of history can be described as the construction of myths; the antiquarian use attempts to preserve the past; while the critical use of history is linked to the need to criticize the past.[29]

If we use Nietzsche's terminology, the recent wave of investigations into the uses of history which took off in the 1980s has been a critical use of history.[30] It has targeted earlier generations of historians, accusing them of having been involved in the monumental use of history, producing myths used in the construction of national identities. In 1983, *The Invention of Tradition*, edited by Eric Hobsbawm and Terence Ranger, illustrated how

---

[27] Law 2005, 267, 270, 275, quote at 267.
[28] Nora 1984–1992; Lowenthal 1985; Samuel 1994–8; Eriksen 1999; Aronsson 2004.
[29] Nietzsche 2008. The Swedish historian Benny Jacobsson (2008), in his study of identity in Västergötland in 1646–1771, used a tripartite division of regional identity based on Nietzsche's categories.
[30] A search for the term 'national identity' using Google Ngram Viewer shows that its use, which had increased steadily during the 1960s and 1970s, took off dramatically in the mid 1980s, following the publication of the below-mentioned books. Probably this development was also spurred by the rise of nationalist movements in many countries in the Eastern Bloc.

national traditions that were perceived as ancient in fact were deliberate inventions, often not more than a few decades old.[31] The same year, Benedict Anderson claimed that nations were imagined political communities. The modern nation was too large for its citizens to have ever been in direct contact with one another, but they still shared a sense of community. According to Anderson, it was modern print capitalism that had enabled the formation of these imagined communities. To explain the formation of several separate national identities with one and the same language—as, for example, in Latin America—Anderson referred to the existence of old administrative units. The importance of these initially quite arbitrarily constructed regions grew with time, as their centres were separated by vast geographic distances, and officials were bound to make careers within the same unit, forming an imagined community together with their fellow climbers on the career ladder.[32]

Anders Linde-Laursen, who has studied how national borders and national differences between Sweden and Denmark were formed, is of the opinion that 'The relation between nation-building and spatial limits on geographic movement is one of the most central points of Anderson's *Imagined communities*', but that this aspect of his work is less known than the concept of imagined communities and the emphasis on print capitalism.[33] Whether or not Anderson himself would view his work in that light, it is interesting to note that he describes the first translation of *Imagined communities*—into Japanese in 1987—as an attempt by two of his former students to 'help in the paedagogical struggle against Japanese insularity'.[34]

It was 1983 that also saw the publication of Ernest Gellner's *Nations and nationalism*, in which he argued that nationalism was a consequence of the division of labour in industrial societies. New generations were no longer socialized by the local community, but by the national education system. Gellner argued that such a system constitutes a pyramid, at the top of which are the universities, which train the educators of primary schoolteachers. He claimed that such a pyramid was the minimum size

[31] Hobsbawm & Ranger 1983.
[32] Anderson 1983; Anderson 2006, 52.
[33] Linde-Laursen 1995, 1143.
[34] Andersson 2006, 211.

for a functioning political unit, and that sub-units of society were no longer capable of social reproduction.[35]

Gellner's argument offers little prospect for the survival of regional identities in the industrial age. The islands in our study are not large enough to sustain the whole pyramid, although an attempt was made with an independent university college on Gotland in 1998–2013.[36] However, we believe that regional history-writing might offer an alternative avenue for the social reproduction of units too small to sustain their own teacher training courses. In fact, several of the islands studied in our research project have at times produced regional school textbooks, incorporating regional history-writing. As of 1991, Åland has had an independent school system, regulated by separate laws and curricula, and can in that respect be compared to a nation-state. However, its teachers are trained at Swedish or Finnish universities—a reflection of Gellner's claim that a modern state below a certain size has to be parasitic on its neighbours.[37]

Gellner was also of the opinion that in industrial societies 'There is very little in the way of any effective, binding organization at any level between the individual and the total community', which leaves little room for strong regional identities; however, he acknowledges that there might be obstacles to the entropy that eradicates all differences within the nation, mentioning genetic and cultural factors such as race and religion.[38] In those terms, this study can be described as an attempt to determine whether a geographical factor—islandness—can also be considered an obstacle to social entropy.

However, not all researchers who participated in this wave of scholarly activity shared the idea that national identities are predominantly recent, constructed, and imagined. Anthony D. Smith is of the opinion that nation-building requires the pre-existence of a core 'ethnie', which shares a common denomination, an origin myth, a common history, a distinct common culture, a territory, and a sense of solidarity. It should be noted that Smith is not a perennialist in the sense that he considers nations as necessary and constant, but he believes they are formed around certain old, recurring myths and symbols.[39]

---

[35] Gellner 1983, 34.
[36] This was a consequence of a decentralization and subsequent recentralization of Sweden's system of higher education.
[37] Gellner 1983, 48.
[38] Gellner 1983, 63 ff., quote at 63.
[39] Smith 1986; Smith 2000: 62 ff.

Local and regional identity has often been thought to be less imagined and more genuine than national identity. After all, in the much smaller local community, people have greater opportunity to meet one another in person. It might be argued that this aspect of the local community is imposed if they are islanders: since the sea restricts travel to a certain extent, their daily encounters with other people are more likely to be restricted to members of the local community than would be the case if the border had not been there. However, the Swedish historian Peter Aronsson believes that this view of how local identity is formed is romanticized. Narratives might be mediated in a different way in the local community than on a national or regional level, oral traditions being more important in smaller communities, but identity is still constructed through narratives. In addition, local narratives are also dispersed in print, just like national history-writing.[40] It is for this reason that we have chosen regionally produced historical publications as the primary source material for this study.

The Baltic islands as regions

Identity can be formed on many different levels: village, municipality, region, nation, Europe, 'Western culture', and so on. The islands examined in this study are best described as regions, defined as the territorial level directly under the state, although some of the islands have at times been part of larger regions. According to Peter Aronsson, in order for the identity of a region to be widely known (which does not necessarily mean that its inhabitants share a strong sense of regional identity) it needs to be discernable, have a name, and be symbolized by institutions. He holds that the medieval Swedish *landskap* (provinces, among them Gotland and Åland) fulfilled these criteria before they were integrated into the nation-state. Administrative divisions were often made to overcome these potentially dangerous, armed, and independent jurisdictions.[41] Saaremaa was an Estonian *maakond*, while Bornholm was a Danish *amt*, both terms best translated as 'county'. Hiiumaa formed part of Lääne County until 1946, when the island became a county in its own right. Back in 1634 the old

---

[40] Aronsson 2004, 133.
[41] Aronsson 2004, 134.

Swedish *landskap* had been replaced by *län* (counties) as the most important administrative units, most often with different borders. Finland replaced its *län*, a survival from the Swedish period, with regions on 1 January 2010, but Åland, as an autonomous province, was not affected by the reform. In Estonia the old term *maakond* was reinstated in 1990, but the borders followed the divisions of the Soviet era, and they are not identical to the historical Estonian provinces. Denmark replaced thirteen *amter* with five regions on 1 January 2007.

It is interesting to note that while administrative borders have shifted on the mainland, the islands have in general retained or regained their status as administrative units. Perhaps the islands' isolation from the mainland as well as the perceived 'naturalness' of their borders have helped protect the old counties. Gotland is today a Swedish region; until 1 January 2011 it was a *län* (county), which uniquely was identical with Gotlands *kommun* (municipality). Åland was from 1634 to 1918 part of Åbo och Björneborgs län on the Finnish mainland. The creation of Ålands län in 1918 was part of an initially failed attempt by the Finnish authorities to thwart the islanders' demands for unification with Sweden by giving Åland autonomy. In 1922, after the League of Nations had granted Finland sovereignty over Åland in exchange for autonomy, Landskapet Åland was introduced as the name for the new self-governing region. However, the state of Finland still used the term Ålands län to describe the regional functions that were kept under government control. The provincial government on Åland opposed the use of the term Ålands län, which was finally abandoned when Finland's *län* were replaced by regions on 1 January 2010. Meanwhile, of the islands in the study, Bornholm has been most affected by the recent redrawing of regional borders. In 1662, Hammershus len (county) was transformed into Bornholms amt (county). It was the only *amt* whose borders were not altered in the reforms of 1793 and 1970, but Bornholm was affected when Denmark replaced its *amter* with larger regions on 1 January 2007. Regardless of the distance, Bornholm is now one of 29 *kommuner* (municipalities) within Region Hovedstaden, the region of the Danish capital Copenhagen. However, because of its special geographic situation, Bornholm has retained the title *regionskommune*, or regional municipality, introduced on 1 January 2003 following a referendum in 2001 that favoured the amalgamation of the five municipalities on the island. The Bornholmian *regionskommune* has some privileges that elsewhere in Denmark are associated with the regions, such as its own *vækstforum* (growth forum) for regional economic development.

It has been suggested that the percentage its islands contribute to the land area of a country might provide a measure of its island interests and concerns. Using that measure, Denmark's island interests, with 33.9 per cent of its land area being islands, are second only to Malaysia's among mainland states.[42] In addition, the majority of Denmark's population live on islands.[43] However, such 'island interests' do not seem to have been a priority for the civil servants who drew up the borders of the new regions, neither was the supposed distinctness and naturalness of coastline borders. Of Denmark's five regions, none covers an entire island, although Region Zealand has borrowed its name from one. However, the country's archipelagic nature is reflected in the fact that Statistics Denmark since 1901 has kept population records per island—with the country's only mainland, the Jutland Peninsula, being listed as one of the islands.

The fact that most Danes live on islands does not necessarily mean that they identify themselves as islanders. Baldacchino stresses that an island identity has a constructed dimension, being are formed, intentionally or subconsciously, by 'confronting a depository of knowledge and shared history … of an island to that of a, typically larger, possibly global, community or threat'.[44] Against that, geographers have noticed that regions that are peripheral and have a distinct shape are easier to recognize than others. For example, few people fail to identify Florida, Texas, California, and Maine.[45] These states are in the corners of the country, and their borders are to a large extent shoreline. It might be argued that islands meet the criteria for being easily recognizable better than most other regions. However, it is ironic that in Gould and White's study, Hawaii, like Alaska, was not included at all—apparently as being too peripheral to fit on the map. Although the main topic of their work *Mental maps* is spatial perception, the authors never reflect on the fact that they have themselves consistently excluded two American states.

Of the islands in the Baltic Sea, Bornholm is the island that is most often omitted or misplaced on national maps, a fact much criticized by

---

[42] Depraetere & Dahl 2007, 100–101.
[43] Statistics Denmark, <http://www.statistikbanken.dk/BEF4>, accessed 4 January 2013.
[44] Baldacchino 2004, 273.
[45] Gould & White 1986, 87.

regional writers.[46] On the Åland Islands, monolingually Swedish, grievances do not so much concern the fact that the islands are occasionally left out as that they are sometimes labelled with their Finnish name, Ahvenanmaa.

The geography of history

In this research project we have combined the geographical perspective prevalent in island studies with a political and historical approach. By so doing, we have sought fresh insights into two entrenched theoretical conflicts: the question of whether islands should be considered isolated and secluded, or connected to a far-reaching oceanic network of communication; and whether collective identities can be constructed at will using a toolbox of history and mythology, or whether they have to be based on an existing sense of affinity.

A historical dimension opens up many possibilities in the field of island studies. Primarily, the historiographical investigation has utilized source material that enables us to investigate how identity has evolved on the islands over the two centuries that we are concerned with, adding empirical flesh to the theoretical bones of the earlier discussions. However, a historical approach might also help develop the theoretical discussion. It is hard to argue against the fact the islands have a secluded, insular quality about them, but at the same time there is no doubt that the sea can also function as a connective medium. We will address how different historical circumstances affect the balance between the divisive and the connective natures of the sea surrounding the islands. For example, how did wars and border changes affect the islanders' opportunities and propensity to connect with the surrounding world? It is in answering such questions that we can chart the ways in which island identity formation has manifested itself during periods of seclusion and during periods of high interconnectedness.

An island studies perspective also promises to be fruitful in the field of historical consciousness studies. While acknowledging that alongside a common culture, a common territory is crucial to the formation of a collective identity, most scholars have still focused almost entirely on the

---

[46] For example, Bøggild 2004, 16–17.

cultural dimension. In this collection of island case studies, we will illustrate how geography influences the development of political history in a way that affects the formation of regional identities, and ultimately how, under certain historical circumstances and in certain geographic locations, regional identities take shape, are reshaped—or do not take shape at all.

Strange exceptions or illustrative examples?

The perhaps most renowned comparative investigation of nationalism is Miroslav Hroch's *Social preconditions of national revival in Europe*. There he investigates the social and geographical origins of the nationalist movements in several European countries, among them Finland and Estonia. One might believe that his work would give us an insight into the national sentiments on Åland, Hiiumaa, and Saaremaa in the nineteenth century; however, in the maps depicting the territorial distribution of the Finnish and Estonian national movements, all three islands are omitted. Hroch mentions that the Estonian islands were the least nationally active areas in the country, and presumably omitted Åland for much the same reason.[47]

Although the low nationalist activity on the islands is an interesting phenomenon which deserves to be investigated, it does not in itself explain why the islands were omitted from the maps. As the example of Peter Gould and Rodney White shows, islands are both easily identified and easily overlooked. Does this mean that our study is nothing more than a filling in of the last exotic blank spots on a map of collective identities, charting the exceptional remnants wisely omitted by earlier researchers who have focused on more relevant historical currents? We would argue not, and that our study of exceptions will lead to a better understand of general trends.

Identity is a vague, evasive concept that is difficult to study, not least because of the multitude of collective identities that a single individual might express under different circumstances. On a local and regional level the problem is further complicated by an overlap of areas. For example, administrative units such as the Swedish counties (*län*) do not correspond

---

[47] Hroch 1985, 73, 83. The coastal Finnish island of Kimito is included on the map since it was the home of at least four leading patriots.

with the old Swedish provinces (*landskap*), which are still more important carriers of identity. The problem is simplified when we choose to study island regions: their borders have remained largely unchanged for centuries. This means that in the case of islands, the borders of historical regions better correspond to modern administrative units than is the case with mainland regions.

The idea that studies of islands offer a chance to simplify complex problems is widespread, especially in the fields of biology and anthropology in which islands are seen as 'natural laboratories'. Charles Darwin, Alfred Russell Wallace, Margaret Mead, and Bronisław Malinowski are examples of scientists who have benefited from island observations in their development of general theories.[48] Similarly, the purpose of the present study is not only to learn about the formation of identities on five Baltic islands, but also to learn from these islands about the formation of regional identities in general.

Just like islands, all geographic regions are to varying degrees isolated from and connected to the surrounding world, that degree being determined by historical and political forces that are likely to affect the formation of identities within the regions. It is not because the forces in play are fundamentally different on islands that we have chosen to study them; it is because the action of general forces are more clearly discernible in the extreme conditions of the islands, and therefore more easily studied.

The metaphor of islands as laboratories should not be taken too far, of course. It must be borne in mind that all islands are unique, and that islands as a group—and groups of islands—do have unique properties that have to be taken into consideration.[49] In looking at Baltic island identities and history-writing, one would expect to find some features that are unique to each of the islands, some that are common to islands in similar situations, some that are shared by all islands, and some that might reasonably be found in mainland regions too. The extent to which our findings can be generalized to other regions will only be decided by further research, however.

---

[48] Royle 2007, 50–1.
[49] Baldacchino 2004, 277–8.

Research questions and primary sources

The main methodological problem in a qualitative text analysis is selection, especially when the source material is as vast as it is in this study. This investigation has required selections on three levels. First we narrowed down which islands to investigate; then we selected which books should be considered regional history-writing from these islands; and finally we selected themes from the books that are strongly linked to expressions of collective identity, themes that have since determined the disposition of this book.

Geography was of help in the first selection. The Baltic Sea contains seven large islands, here described as island regions, and together these islands make up the B7 Baltic Islands network.[50] Of these, we selected five to study—Gotland, Åland, Hiiumaa, Saaremaa, and Bornholm—all of which are, or in the case of Bornholm have until recently been, independent administrative units directly under the level of the state. Rügen and Öland, which are not studied in the project, are part of Kalmar län and Landkreis Vorpommern–Rügen respectively.

In order to determine which texts should be used as source material, we needed to define the concept 'regional history-writing'. In this study, it refers to publications that were either written by current or former inhabitants of the islands, or which were published with the help of institutions based on the islands. Regarding content, regional history-writing is defined as the history that covers an entire island region, and not only single municipalities, towns, or smaller islands that are part of the island region. Works that treat the islands as part of a larger region have also been left out. For example, Hiiumaa was until recently often included in works about Lääne County, to which the island belonged administratively until after the Second World War, but these books cannot be considered part of a process to build a separate Hiiu identity.

We have focused on historical non-fiction, leaving literary accounts of the islands' history to one side. Books about folkloric descriptions of the islands' past have also been excluded, such as the Saaremaa legends about the giant 'Suur Tõll'. We have included the historical parts of multi-disciplinary works which describe an island's geography, nature, society, and history. These works, for example, have been the most common form

---

[50] With the exception of Rügen, these islands' history has been described by Sørensen 1992.

of historical synthesis about Saaremaa in the twentieth century, and they are usually dominated by history-writing with shorter chapters on other subjects. For Gotland and Bornholm these works are so numerous that a selection has been necessary.

Our aim has also been to include all books published since the turn of the nineteenth century that meet our criteria for regional history-writing. We have met with varying degrees of success for the different islands, and it is always possible that the occasional work has escaped our efforts to identify them all. We have not attempted to include all the articles published in regional newspapers or periodicals, as this would have made the source material too vast to handle, and the core themes and arguments in these articles are generally represented in the books we have studied. Normally, the authors of the most important books, such as Marius Kofoed Zahrtmann on Bornholm and Matts Dreijer on Åland, were also the most prolific writers of articles. However, in some instances we have turned to articles to deepen our understanding, to trace how the description of certain themes developed over time, or to enable comparisons of themes that are treated in books about some islands but only in articles about others.

In spite of our efforts to define regional history-writing clearly, there are of course many books that are borderline cases. This is especially the case for Gotland, where the line between national and regional history-writing almost disappeared in the twentieth century, and hence Samuel Edquist discusses the very specific methodological problems in his essay on the island. The selection has been inclusive rather than exclusive, and since most of the books published about the islands' history have a substantial degree of involvement by writers or institutions from the islands, only a limited number of works have been left out—mainly those concerned with military history, such as events on Bornholm or Saaremaa during the Second World War.

A case could be made for a narrower selection, of course. Would not the essence of regional identity be better studied if the borderline cases were left out? For example, does the volume on Åland's nineteenth century in the series *Det åländska folkets historia* (2006), written by three professional historians from mainland Finland and Sweden, really represent regional Ålandic history-writing? In this case we would argue that it does, since their choice of topic was decided by the body that commissioned the book, Ålands kulturstiftelse (the Åland Cultural Foundation). More importantly, if the foundation had thought the three historians might produce a view of history which was unacceptable, they would not have given them the commission in the first place. Two decades earlier it would have been unthinkable for the Foundation to contract professional historians with a critical view of the island's established regional history-writing. The first volumes in the series represent a view of history that differed substantially from the one held by academic researchers on the mainland. Thus the choice of writers in itself represented an important shift in the Ålandic view of history, and it is important that our selection of sources makes it possible to identify and analyse such changes.

One could also argue that the financial conditions for sponsoring and publishing books regionally differ from island to island, with Åland and Gotland today having the best resources and Hiiumaa the smallest. However, these financial differences mirror the different islands' abilities to exert regional influence over how their histories are written. It is therefore only to the good that our selection of sources reflects these differences.

The islands and the books duly selected, the critical task remained: the analysis of how the view of history they convey was linked to collective identities. The source material amounts to tens of thousands of pages. This made necessary a selection of themes to structure and categorize the material, which in turn has helped us to draw conclusions, and enables us to present them in a convincing, understandable, and digestible manner to the reader.

The existing literature provided us with just such a structure for the investigation, for we have used the conclusions of earlier researchers and theorists about the aspects of history that are commonly employed in the construction of collective identities, looking for the parallels with our sources. This basic framework has naturally been complemented with additional categories, describing the themes we have found in our sources, but which were unknown to earlier research.

Earlier researchers, then, have outlined the two major avenues by which collective identities are constructed: by the maintenance of borders against 'the other', or by nourishing central symbols and myths within the group. We have found it useful to consider both approaches, so that the way in which boundaries were created is analysed as a process parallel to—and in interplay with—the invention of a common historical past.

One central question regarding the construction of boundaries is the islands' relations with other geographically defined communities. We investigate how regional history-writing portrays the relationship between the islands and the nations and nation-states of the Baltic region, and which supranational or transnational communities the islands have excluded or included in their histories. Examples of this are given in the essays about Åland's borders and Bornholm's relationship with Denmark, Skåne, and Sweden.

The islands' history-writing can also be analysed in terms of myths or narratives that define the community by specifying its temporal and geographical origins. Such myths highlight certain historical events or figures, and there might be references to past glories or declines.[51] We have investigated which parts of the past have been included in the regional narratives, and which have been 'forgotten'. Island-specific myths, such as the uprising on Bornholm in 1658, are considered, but so is the degree to which the islands' history-writing includes national myths—such as the Schleswig wars—in their narratives.

Another area of analysis is how the island communities' temporal and geographical origins are described. Is there, for instance, a conflict between 'ethnic' origin myths, focusing on the history of a people, and 'geographical' origin myths, which put place at the centre of history?[52] Previous research indicates that ethnic myths of origin are more persistent in a regional context than on the national level, at least during the latter part of the twentieth century.[53] We consider whether this is the case on the large Baltic islands.

Further insight is lent by comparisons of the different islands. All the islands studied in this project have been part of the Swedish kingdom for longer or shorter periods. Bornholm, Saaremaa, and Gotland have all belonged to the Danish realm, and some Ålandic history writers until recently claimed that their island also experienced a Danish period in the early Middle Ages, although this theory has now been discounted. Åland, Saaremaa, and Hiiumaa have been part of the Russian Empire, and all five islands have felt the presence of Russian or Soviet troops, albeit very briefly in the case of Gotland. We compare the islands' commemoration of their Swedish, Danish, and Russian experiences, and analyse what the

---

[51] Smith 1999, 62–8.
[52] For this discussion, see, for example, Nordlund 2001.
[53] Wallette 2004, 313 ff.

similarities and differences might tell us about the relationship between regional and national identities.

We have also used the islands' geographic locations as a parameter for a comparative analysis. For example, Åland and Bornholm are both located between two nation-states and two languages, and we consider how regional history-writing deals with this fact. The geographical perspective does need to be combined with a historical point of view, of course. In the cases of Bornholm and Åland, it must be remembered that their intermediary locations are the consequence of historical events; before Denmark lost Skåne in 1658 and Sweden lost Finland in 1809, the islands were not peripheral border regions but more centrally located provinces.

Finally we also address the question of whether internal divisions within the island regions can be discerned in regional history-writing, and, if so, how they have been treated during different periods. Was there a tendency to downplay internal divisions as the formation of a regional identity gained momentum, for example?

The islands' regional history-writing has been treated separately in four essays. In the first essay, Samuel Edquist analyses Gotlandic history-writing. Janne Holmén's three essays are devoted to Åland, Saaremaa and Hiiumaa (because of their many similarities, treated together), and Bornholm. Specific methodological problems related to the individual islands are addressed at the beginning of each essay. Each essay can be read separately as a historiographical case study of the given island's regional history-writing: each considers how regional history-writing has evolved on that particular island since the early nineteenth century, and what this can tell us about the emergence and development of a regional island identity; each considers its island's history-writing thematically through a qualitative text analysis; and each essay ultimately speaks to uses of history. The concluding essay takes this a step further, using the geographical perspective of island studies to compare the conclusions reached in the individual case studies. By making generalizations based on how historical and geographical circumstances in interplay have shaped the regional identities on the islands in our study, we attempt to complement the previous theories of identity formation.

Our source material is mainly written in Danish, Swedish, Estonian and German, and a few authors describe the language they have used as Bornholmian. Quotes are given in English in the text and in the original language in the footnotes. Titles of books which are mentioned in the text are given in an English translation in the list of references.

Works cited

Anderson, Benedict (1983), *Imagined Communities. Reflections on the Origin and Spread of Nationalism* (London: Verso).
— (2006), *Imagined Communities. Reflections on the Origin and Spread of Nationalism*. Revised edition (London: Verso).
Aronsson, Peter (1995), *Regionernas roll i Sveriges historia* (ERU-rapport 91; Stockholm: Fritzes).
— (2004), *Historiebruk. Att använda det förflutna* (Lund: Studentlitteratur).
ÅSUB (2012), *Åland in Figures* (Mariehamn: Åland Islands Statistical Agency), <http://www.asub.ax/files/alsiff2012_en.pdf>.
Baldacchino, Godfrey (2004), 'The Coming of Age of Island Studies', *Tijdschrift voor economische en sociale geografie*, 95/3.
— (2007) (ed.), *A World of Islands. An Island Studies Reader* (Charlottetown: Institute of Island Studies).
Böggild, Hansaage (2004), *Gyldendals bog om Bornholm* (Copenhagen: Gyldendals).
Braudel, Fernand (1976), *The Mediterranean and the Mediterranean World in the age of Philip II*, i (New York: Harper).
Callard, Keith B. (1959), *Political Forces in Pakistan, 1947–1959* (New York: Institute of Pacific Relations).
Clarke, Erik & Clarke, Thomas L. (2009), 'Isolating connections – connecting isolations', *Geografiska Annaler: Series B, Human Geography*, 91 (4): 311–23.
Conklin, Philip (2007), 'On Islanders and Islandness', *Geographical Review*, 97 (2): 191–201.
Depraetere, Christian & Dahl, Arthur L. (2007), 'Locations and Classifications', in Baldacchino 2007.
Edmond, Rod & Smith, Vanessa (2003) (eds.), *Islands in History and representation* (London: Routledge).
EFA, <www.e-f-a.org>, 11 November 2011.
Eriksen, Anne (1999), *Historie, minne og myte* (Oslo: Pax Forlag).
Geary, Patrick J. (2002), *The myth of nations: The medieval origins of Europe* (Princeton: PUP).
Gellner, Ernest (1983), *Nations and Nationalism* (Oxford: Blackwell).
Gerner, Kristian & Karlsson, Klas-Göran (2002), *Nordens medelhav. Östersjöområdet som historia, myt och projekt* (Stockholm: Natur & Kultur).
Gillis, John (2004), *Islands of the Mind: How the Human Imagination Created the Atlantic World* (New York: Palgrave Macmillan).

Gould, Peter & White, Rodney (1986), *Mental maps* (2nd edn., London: Routledge).
Hagerman, Maja (2006), *Det rena landet. Om konsten att uppfinna sina förfäder* (Stockholm: Prisma).
Haugen, Einar Ingvald (1966), *Riksspråk og folkemål: norsk språkpolitikk i det 20. århundre* (Oslo: Universitetsforlaget).
Hay, Pete, (2006), 'A Phenomenology of Islands', *Island Studies Journal*, 1 (1): 19–42.
Helsinki-seura (1968) *Helsinki-seuran vuosikirja*. Helsinki: Helsinki-seura
Hobsbawn, Eric J. & Ranger, Terence (1983) (eds.), *The invention of tradition* (Cambridge: CUP).
Hornborg, Erik (1945), *Kampen om Östersjön till slutet av segelfartygens tidevarv* (Stockholm: Bonnier).
Hroch, Miroslav (1985), *Social preconditions of national revival in Europe* (Cambridge: CUP).
Jacobsson, Benny (2008), *Den sjunde världsdelen. Västgötar och Västergötland 1646-1771. En identitetshistoria* (Stockholm: Stockholms Universitet, Institutionen för litteraturvetenskap och idéhistoria).
Kjellén, Rudolf (1916), *Staten som lifsform* (Politiska handböcker 3; Stockholm: Geber).
Klinge, Matti (1995), *Östersjövärlden* (Helsinki: Otava).
Kurantowicz, Eva (2001), 'Local Identity of Small Communities. Continuity or Change', in Michael Schemmann & Michal Bronn (eds.), *Adult Education and Democratic Citizenship IV* (Cracow: Impuls), 187–94.
Law, Alex (2005), 'Of Navies and Navels: Britain as Mental Island', *Geografiska Annaler, Series B, Human Geography* (Special Issue: Islands: Objects of Representation), 87 (4): 267–77.
Linde-Laursen, Anders (1995), 'Small differences, large issues: the making and remaking of a national border', in V. Y. Mudimbe (ed.), *Nations, identities, cultures* (Durham: Duke University Press).
Lowenthal, David (1985), *The Past is a Foreign Country* (Cambridge: CUP).
Mackenzie, William James Millar (1978), *Political identity* (Manchester: MUP).
Nietzsche, Friedrich (2008), *On the use and abuse of history for life* (Gloucester: Dodo).
Nora, Pierre (1984–92) (ed.), *Les lieux de mémoire* (7 vols., Paris: Gallimard).
Nordlund, Christer (2001), *Det upphöjda landet. Vetenskapen, landhöjningsfrågan och kartläggningen av Sveriges förflutna, 1860–1930* (Umeå: Kungl. Skytteanska Samfundet).
Õispuu, S. (1992) (ed.), *Eesti ajalugu: ärkamisajast kuni tänapäevani* (Tallinn: Koolibri).
Olausson, Pär M. (2007), *Autonomy and Islands: A Global Study of the Factors that Determine Island Autonomy* (Turku: Åbo Akademi University Press).

Pye, Lucian (1966), *Aspects of Political Development. An analytic study* (Boston: Little, Brown).
Royle, Stephen A. (2001), *A Geography of Islands. Small island insularity* (London: Routledge).
— (2007), 'Definitions & Typologies', in Baldacchino 2007.
Samuel, Raphael (1994–8), *Theatres of memory* (2 vols., London: Verso).
Smith, Anthony D. (1986), *The Ethnic Origins of Nations* (Oxford: Basil Blackwell).
— (1999), *Myths and Memories of the Nation* (New York: OUP).
— (2000), *The Nation in History: Historiographical Debates About Ethnicity and Nationalism* (Hannover, NH: University Press of New England).
Sørensen, Søren (1992), *Öarna i Österjön: Förr och nu* (Visby: Gotlands fornsal i sambarbete med Nordens institut på Åland).
Statistics Denmark, <http://www.dst.dk/en/Statistik/emner/befolkning-og-befolkningsfremskrivning/folketal.aspx>, 5 May 2012.
— <http://www.statistikbanken.dk/BEF4>, 4 January 2013.
Statistics Estonia, <http://pub.stat.ee>, 5 May 2012.
Udenrigspolitiske selskab (1969), *Fremtiden: Tidsskrift for international orienteering*, 24.
Wahlbäck, Krister (1967), *Från Mannerheim till Kekkonen* (Stockholm: Aldus/Bonnier).
Wallette, Anna (2004), *Sagans svenskar. Synen på vikingatiden och de isländska sagorna under 300 år* (Malmö: Sekel).
Warrington, Edward & Milne, David (2007), 'Island Governance', in Baldacchino 2007.
White, Geoffrey M. (1995), *Identity through history: Living stories in a Solomon Islands society* (Cambridge: CUP).
Woods, Robert A. (1898), *The City Wilderness: A Settlement Study* (Boston: Houghton Mifflin).
Zander, Ulf (2001), *Fornstora dagar, moderna tider: Bruk av och debatter om svensk historia från sekelskifte till sekelskifte* (Lund: Nordic Academic Press).

In the shadow of the Middle Ages? Tendencies in Gotland's history-writing, 1850–2010

Samuel Edquist

Previous research on history-writing and other forms of the use of history has so far to a large extent analysed national and ethnic identities and their formation through narratives of the past.[1] Other territorial identity projects have been less studied, relatively speaking. Still, the importance of the past is just as obvious in local, regional, and supranational identity projects.[2] The latter have largely used similar mechanisms as those used in the nationalist projects, at least on the discursive level. Not only do geographical and contemporary cultural aspects delineate the regional 'us', but, more than that, do so by telling and retelling a common narrative about the past. 'We' have always lived here, 'we' have shared a common destiny down the centuries.

In this study, I will analyse regional identity construction on Gotland. Gotland is the largest of all the Baltic islands, with a population of some 57,000 and a land area of 3,000 km². It is one of Sweden's twenty-five historical provinces (*landskap*), and constitutes a separate county (*län*). The province of Gotland also includes some smaller islands. The only inhabited one is Fårö, a separate parish at Gotland's north-eastern edge, with some 550 inhabitants and a land area of 114 km². Some of the uninhabited islands—Gotska Sandön, Stora Karlsö, and Lilla Karlsö—have nevertheless played a role in regional topography and history-writing, thanks to their distinctive landscape and as somewhat exotic places where historical events of the more curious and thrilling kind have taken place.[3]

---

[1] Among numerous examples, see, for example, T. Eriksen 1993; Fewster 2006.
[2] Aronsson 2004, 133–43.
[3] Källgård 2005, 206 ff.

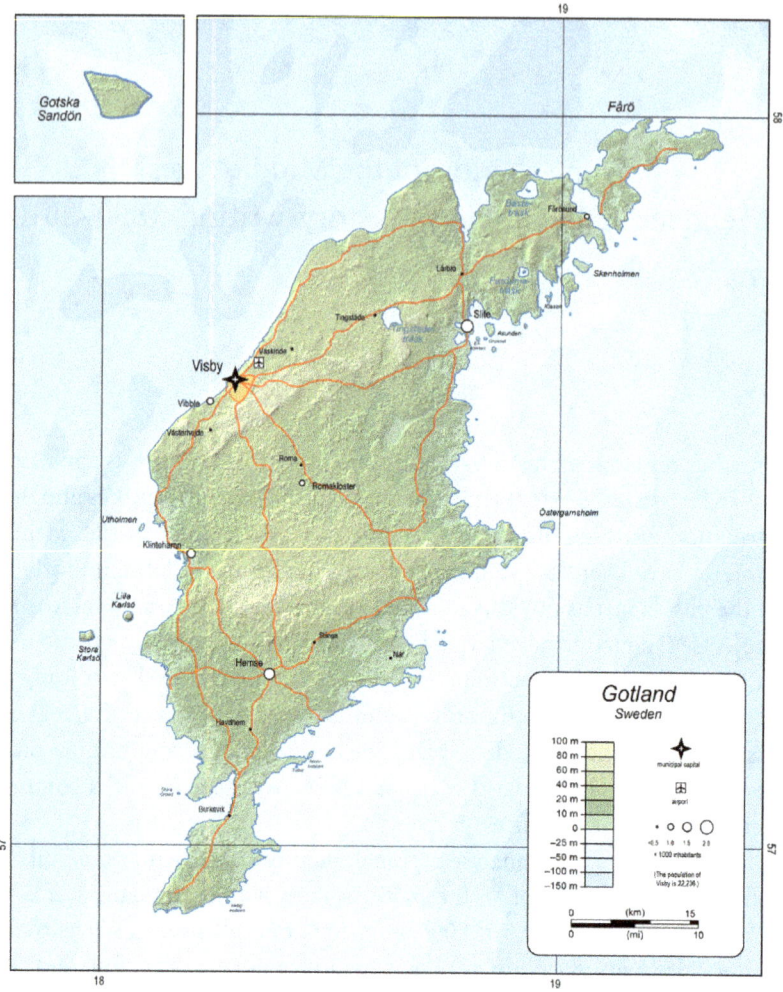

Topographic map of Gotland. Source: Wikimedia Commons

It has often been rightly said that Swedishness was created by explicitly adding together its constituent provinces. The clearest example of this is the central plot of Selma Lagerlöf's schoolbook *Nils Holgersson's wonderful journey through Sweden* (1906–1907) where each province is added to the next. Their regional particularities are only beneficial at the national level—Sweden becomes a collection of provincial characteristics.[4] Thus, the provinces have generally *not* been viewed as anti-national in Sweden.

[4] Arcadius 1997, 32–8; Jönses 1999.

It should be noted that regional identity in Sweden has been almost totally centred on the historical provinces (*landskap*)—even though they lost their administrative status in the seventeenth century. Since that time, the counties (*län*) have been the essential administrative regional units, with separate government representatives. In the 1860s, the so-called county councils (*landsting*) were created, a form of municipal government that to this day is responsible for healthcare, local transport, and so on. The county councils are in most cases geographically identical with the counties. In recent years, some county councils have been merged into regions (*regioner*), and at time of writing there are plans to redraw the administrative map of Sweden once again, this time merging more counties into larger regions. However, this on-going development will not change the historical provinces, which remain the focus of cultural identities (although there are a couple of notable exceptions).[5] Still, the relations between provinces and the administrative units are hard to study in the case of Gotland, where province, county, and even municipality include exactly the same territory.[6]

Some of the Swedish provinces have a stronger identity than others. In many cases, it exists in parallel to a strong connection to the national identity. Not least, Uppland and Dalarna have (in different ways) been singled out as symbols of the true Swedishness. Uppland has been hailed as the cradle of the ancient Swedish kingdom, the seat of Sweden's archbishop, and (a part of) the capital. Dalarna has played the role of the home of the true, nationally minded Swedish peasantry. When Sweden was threatened, the peasants of Dalarna to a man marched to the rescue of the Swedish freedom, according to nineteenth- and early twentieth-century nationalist Swedish history-writing, especially in the narratives about the uprisings of Engelbrekt Engelbrektsson, Sten Sture, and Gustav Eriksson (later King Gustav I Vasa) against the Danish-led Kalmar Union in the fifteenth and sixteenth centuries.[7] Today, the sort of history-writing

[5] The names of the two northernmost counties—Västerbotten and Norrbotten—are generally used for their respective inlands, even though that is the province of Lapland. As a matter of fact, two Swedish counties (*län*) have taken the names of historical provinces since the 1990s: Kopparbergs län was renamed Dalarnas län, and Skåne län resulted from the unification of Malmöhus län and Kristianstads län.
[6] In 1971, Gotland's various municipalities were centralized into one: Gotlands kommun (Gotland Municipality). As a result, the hitherto separate Gotland County Council was dissolved. In 2011, the municipality of Gotland changed its name from Gotlands kommun to Region Gotland.
[7] Edquist 2004; Rosander 1993.

that focuses on distant political developments is less common. Even so, Dalarna is still a symbol of a vague Swedishness in folklore and traditions. The Dalecarlians are seen as sturdy and steadfast, and 'Swedish' folk culture is often stereotypically located to Dalarna.

Some other Swedish provinces, where the regional identities are particularly cultivated, have a more problematic relationship with the Swedish national state. Skåne, Jämtland, and Gotland all to some degree breed a sort of partial independence towards the rest of Sweden, rooted in the fact that they stood outside the Swedish realm in the past. In the case of Skåne, it is strongly emphasized that the province was part of Denmark until 1658, and that in many ways it still has a culture and traditions that makes it somewhat different from the rest of Sweden.[8] Jämtland also became part of Sweden in the seventeenth century, and there is a strong notion that there was once a medieval, democratic, peasant state there, independent of both Norway and Sweden.[9]

Finally, Gotland is perhaps the most 'different' Swedish province. Even though, with a few exceptions, Gotlanders identify themselves as Swedes, the islanders have a strong regional identity. One reason for this is the obvious geographical distinctness: it can only be reached by air or by sea— the ferry crossing to the mainland takes around three hours. But perhaps the most distinct nucleus of Gotlandic regional identity is its history. Before the fourteenth century, Gotland was largely autonomous, with only a loose connection to the Swedish kingdom. After 1361, Gotland was attached to Denmark, and a period of economic stagnation ensued. In 1645, Gotland passed to Sweden.

As we shall see, this otherness is often used as a positive mark of the island. In history-writing, Gotland has often been treated as something peculiar, not least thanks to its history.[10] The flourishing city of Visby is often singled out as one of the key ports of the Baltic Sea from the twelfth to the fourteenth century. Concerning even earlier eras, there is a strong notion that Gotland was an independent republic, governed by free and equal peasants who were engaged in long-distance trade, especially to the east. The ancient Gotlanders or Gutes (*gutar*) are usually described as a nation of their own, separate from the mainland Swedes (*svear*) and Geats (*götar*), and with their own language.

---

[8] F. Persson 2008.
[9] Häggström 2000.
[10] Lagerlöf 2005, 139–40.

The questions and the literature

The broad outlines of Gotland's history-writing are quite well known; the more detailed nuances, not so. I wish to shed further light on some of the more important ones. How did regional self-perception change in the nineteenth and twentieth centuries? To what extent was there a wish to mark Gotland's distance from the rest of Sweden? And were there any attempts to link Gotland to other geographical entities in and around the Baltic Sea instead?

When dealing with islands, the recent advent of 'island studies' or 'nissology' should be mentioned.[11] Much of that research focuses on discourses and metaphors, stressing that islands are more metaphors than reality, and that these discursive structures to a large extent frame our understanding of islands, whether from within or outside.[12] For example, in the eighteenth century there was a shift in understanding from seeing islands as symbols of cooperation and sources for new futures and utopias, to the still dominant discourse that islands are remote, exotic, isolated, and alienated.[13] However, the present study's main concerns, from an analytical point of view, are regionalism and the uses of history. It is highly probable that an island such as Gotland forms a more distinct regional identity thanks to its relative isolation, and that makes it suitable for a study of the relations between region and nation.

Earlier research has to some extent analysed Gotlandic regional identity, primarily in connection to its folkloric aspects such as *gotlandsdricka* (a malted beer) and *varpa* (a stone-throwing game reminiscent of boules).[14] The ethnologist Owe Ronström has in a number of works studied the different 'mindscapes' of Gotlandic identity, especially focusing on their everyday use in society.[15] In doing so, he has studied the present-day use of medieval history, something that has also been analysed in a couple of monographs about Visby's annual Medieval Week.[16] Carina Johansson has studied the iconic images of contemporary Visby, which concentrate

---

[11] For example, Baldacchino 2008; Baldacchino 2007.
[12] For example, Fletcher 2008. For a critical view, which stresses the physical reality of islands that should not be shadowed, see Hay 2006, 29–30.
[13] Ronström 2009, 168–9.
[14] For example, Salomonsson 1979; Yttergren 2002.
[15] Especially Ronström 2008.
[16] Gustafsson 1998; C. Johansson 2000c; Gustafsson 2002a; Gustafsson 2002b; Sandström 2005.

entirely on its medieval heritage, leaving the vast majority of its people and history in shadow.[17] There are even more studies on the effects of the discourses of the tourist industry—all serving to create a widespread image of Gotland as something exotic, where the peculiarities of the island's nature and historical monuments are the most mentioned.[18]

Thanks to especially Johansson and Ronström, the historiography and heritage construction of Visby is fairly well known. There are also a number of studies of individual historiographers, such as Per Arvid Säve and the like, who have been influential in creating a Gotlandic historical narrative.[19] The island's heritage institutions have also produced history about themselves.[20]

The anthology *Kulturarvets betydelse* (2000) analyses present-day heritage projects and the general public's reactions to them, covering the Medieval Week, the Bunge Museum, the Bläse Limeworks Museum, and other places.[21] There are also some studies of the academic narratives about Gotland, where Nanoushka Myrberg criticizes on-going tendencies to overestimate the 'uniqueness' of Iron Age and medieval Gotland—a tendency that sits well with tourist interests, for which it is important to show a glorious and spectacular past. The uniqueness of Gotland rather lies in the fact that so much of its built heritage still survives, for example its medieval churches.[22]

Thus, Gotland's history-writing has only been partially analysed, and it is my purpose in this essay to shed further light on its general tenor.

Methods and primary sources

Gotland has a rich vein of history-writing—the most of all the Baltic islands, in fact. Thus, there are a vast amount of sources available for

---

[17] C. Johansson 2009; see also C. Johansson 2006.
[18] See Rossipal 1996 for a study of (predominantly mainland Swedish) informants' associations with the word 'Gotland'.
[19] Gislestam 1975 (from Strelow to Carl Johan Bergman); see also Körner 1984, 10 ff.; and Nerman 1945 (concerning Gotland's prehistory). Further, there are articles about individual writers: Gerentz 1989 on Richard Steffen; and Palmenfelt 1993 on Säve (with précis of Säve's description of Gotland's history, 53 ff.); see also Lindquist et al. 1992.
[20] *Gotlands turistförening 75 år* (1971); Kronborg Christensen & Smitterberg 2007.
[21] Johansson et al. 2000.
[22] Myrberg 2008.

study, since the books and articles on Gotland's history can be numbered in thousands. For centuries, there has been a separate history-writing tradition on or about Gotland.[23] The main bulk of this history-writing has been produced since the late nineteenth century, a time that has seen a large number of monographs published on Gotland's history. Dozens of these are general descriptions of Gotland's general history, while a great deal has been written about more specific topics.

At Almedalsbiblioteket—Gotland's main library—there is a particular collection of *Gotlandica*, that is to say literature from or about Gotland. A part of this, also called Gotlandica, is now a separate sub-database of the national *Libris* database, organised by Kungliga Biblioteket (the National Library of Sweden in Stockholm). I extracted all 4,253 titles that were part of the latter collection on a certain date: 20 March 2010. Even so, some cases were found where 'obvious' titles that *should* be part of the Libris Gotlandica had been left out.

That quantity of literature is easily sufficient to create a good picture of the writings on Gotlandic society and history. A large portion of the Libris Gotlandica consists of books and articles on everyday politics, healthcare, geology, and so on.[24] At the beginning of my research, I planned to apply quantitative analyses to the different texts by marking them according to themes, chronological scope, and so forth. However, I realized that it would be too big a task for this relatively limited study. Still, the Gotlandica collection has proved an important step in narrowing down the potential source material.

The most important material for this study are the books about Gotland that deal with the island as a whole, and that are not limited to some specific subject or historical period. Even so, I have also used a lot of other texts as well, in order to complement the main source material. Even so, because of the limits of the study, there are important books and authors that are not represented, especially from the academic field of history-writing.[25] Sometimes the Gotland books are explicitly historical in character, and, where not, they generally include chapters on Gotland's history. There are different categories of Gotland books, some being

---

[23] Gislestam 1975; see also Sjöberg 1963, foreword.
[24] Existing bibliographical works have also been helpful, for example, Bergh, Engeström & Rydberg 1991.
[25] For example, works by the likes of the archeologist Nils Lithberg, the philologist Herbert Gustavson, the teacher and amateur historian Åke G. Sjöberg, and the church historian Sven-Erik Pernler.

schoolbooks, and others having been produced by learned societies or for the benefit of tourists. Some were written by academics, some by journalists, and still others by educationists. I will briefly present the major groups of authors and types of historical works concerning Gotland, and, in some cases, their relative chronological importance from the nineteenth century to the present day.

Gotland's history-writing before the nineteenth century falls outside the scope of this study. However, some of those texts have been central to the island's historical consciousness into our own day, since they are continuously quoted and discussed. That is definitely the case with *Gutasaga*—a short supplement in a fourteenth-century manuscript of *Gutalagen*, the medieval Gotland law book. Probably composed in the thirteenth or early fourteenth century, *Gutasaga* starts with a highly mythical description of the genesis of Gotland and its first inhabitants: Þieluar (in modern Swedish Tjelvar or Thjelvar) and his descendants. It continues that Gotland became overpopulated, whereupon a proportion of the people had to emigrate. *Gutasaga* also explains how Gotland became part of the Swedish kingdom, and how it was Christianized.[26]

In the sixteenth century, the Gotlandic priest Nicolaus Petreius (Niels Pedersen) wrote a Latin chronicle connecting the Goths of the Roman epoch with the Gutes of Gotland.[27] Another work of history, the *Cronica Guthilandorum* or *Den Guthilandiske cronica* by Hans Nielsson Strelow, published in Danish in 1633, rapidly gained iconic status in Gotlandic historiography, not least concerning the medieval history of the island. Strelow today is generally considered to be highly tendentious, but he obviously used sources that have since disappeared.[28] Another early text is Haquin Spegel's *Rudera Gothlandica* (1683).[29] The authors of the seventeenth century often relied on *Gutasaga*, which was regarded as an important state document. Among the Danes (Strelow) and the Swedes (Johan Hadorph), Þieluar was claimed to have come from Skåne and Östergötland respectively, in order to prove Gotland's correct national affiliation.[30]

---

[26] For the text with commentary, see Lindkvist 1983. The name *Gutasaga* is not original; the philologist Carl Säve invented it in the nineteenth century.
[27] *Fornvännen* 104 (2009), 226–7.
[28] Körner 1991.
[29] There were also attempts to identify ancient Atlantis with Gotland; see Sjöberg 1963, 7.
[30] Gardell 1987, 11–12.

The pioneers

The nineteenth century is sometimes called 'the century of history'.[31] The growth of nationalism and other territorial identity projects brought with them an interest in the origins of nations and ethnic communities, and the historical consciousness as a whole was part of a new framework of consciousness, a modern spirit which evolved in the wake of the American and French revolutions and the dissolution of the feudal system.[32]

There was a wave of interest not only in the history of states and nations, but also in the 'genuine' popular culture. In the surviving remnants of an old, 'real' folk culture, untouched by modernity and the emerging industrial society, the true essence of the people was to be found. This romantic interest in 'the people' was in the beginning almost exclusively organized by educated and/or wealthy townspeople. Gotland was no exception.

In the nineteenth century, there were a number of domestic Gotlandic 'amateur historians' who were deeply engaged in the project of strengthening the historic consciousness of the island. In many ways, it was they who founded the modern tradition of Gotlandic history-writing. The foremost of these pioneers were all schoolteachers: Per Arvid Säve (1811–1877), Carl Johan Bergman (1817–1895), and Alfred Theodor Snöbohm (1819–1901). While Snöbohm was a rural elementary schoolteacher, Säve and Bergman both worked at the Visby gymnasium, whose staff in the mid nineteenth century played a crucial role in Gotland's cultural life, far beyond the walls of the school.[33]

Per Arvid Säve was raised in an educated family in Visby.[34] His interests were cultural history and gathering various legends and myths in the countryside, many of which dealt with past event in Gotland's history. Most of them were not published in his own lifetime, so they did not influence history-writing directly.[35] However, Säve's other writings had a

---

[31] M. Persson 2007, 95.
[32] Berman 1982; Nordin 1989; Anderson 1991; Hobsbawm 1992.
[33] Palmenfelt 1993, 37–95; Bohman 1992.
[34] His brother, the philologist Carl Säve, was also an important figure in Gotland's intellectual life. He was a professor at Uppsala University, and edited *Gutalagen*, published in 1859, coining the term *Gutasaga* in the process (Gislestam 1992, 22; Palmenfelt 1993, 38 ff.).
[35] Palmenfelt 1992a, 62–3. They were published in Gustavson & Nyman 1959–60 and Gustavson & Nyman 1961.

vast influence from the very first. His many 'sagas' were mostly ethnological studies, sometimes using legends and stories he collected—and they mainly dealt with Gotland's relatively recent past. The saga concept had a wide meaning for Säve, including tales from the past, his own memories, and information from the literature. The term saga was directly taken from the Norse tradition.[36] They were largely addressed to an audience on the mainland—only 'Hafvets och fiskarens sagor' (1880) was first published on Gotland.[37]

Among Carl Johan Bergman's works on Gotland's history, one can mention the short general history *Gotlands geografi och historia i lättfattligt sammandrag* (1870); the compilation of shorter essays, *Gotländska skildringar och minnen* (1882); and a book on Visby (1885). All these works were ran to several editions.

Alfred Theodor Snöbohm is best known for his general work about Gotland, *Gotlands land och folk* (1871). It was one of the earliest books on Gotland's entire history, ensuring him a high status in the historiographical tradition of Gotland ever since.

The Friends of Gotland's Antiquities

Gotlands Fornvänner (the Friends of Gotland's Antiquities) was an association founded in 1874 on the initiative of Per Arvid Säve and other influential local intellectuals. The following year, they founded a museum dedicated to Gotland's cultural history, Gotlands fornsal (lit. the Hall of Gotland's Antiquities), situated in the centre of Visby.[38] Gotlands fornsal is today Gotlands Museum, the official regional museum. The initiative and ideas behind it were typical of the age, when the rise of regional museums and a folk revival were seen in Sweden as elsewhere.[39]

Säve wanted the museum to be a folkloric collection of the Gotlander's culture. However, in the early twentieth century, the centre of gravity in the activities of Gotlands fornsal shifted to the prehistoric and medieval

---

[36] Nyman 1992, 33.
[37] English translations of the titles of published works are given in the list of works cited. Säve's sagas were *Skogens sagor* (1866), *Strandens sagor* (1873), *Handelns och näringarnas sagor* (1876, partly published), *Åkerns sagor* (1876), *Gutarnas forn- och framtidssaga* (1878), *Hafvets och fiskarens sagor* (1880), *Jaktens sagor* (1940) (Palmenfelt 1992b; Palmenfelt 1993, 49–50).
[38] Palmenfelt 1993, 71; <http://www.gotlandsmuseum.se/om-museet>.
[39] Salomonsson 1992; Nyman 1992.

periods. In 1910, Gotlands Fornvänner was transformed into a *fornminnesförening* (antiquarian society)—in order to get government funding it was obliged to be responsible for Gotland's antiquities. A number of sites and buildings were donated to Gotlands fornsal, and Gotlands Fornvänner today still owns a large number of buildings all over the island. A great many excavations around Visby also highlighted the emphasis on older history.[40] Since 1929, the Friends of Gotland's Antiquities have published an influential annual journal, *Gotländskt Arkiv* ('Gotlandic Archive'), which is partly learned, partly popular in character. Articles on archaeology are especially common.

In many ways, the nineteenth-century pioneers created what one might call a dominant Gotlandic historiography that has survived to today, albeit with many internal differences and contradictions. It has been reproduced in various regional books and articles, by prominent history-producing institutions as well as by independent actors, firmly in the grip of the dominant discourse or ideology. There are some recurrent topics in the island's regional history-writing. From the very start there has been a division between an internal, 'agrarian' discourse, focusing on the local cultural history of later centuries, and an externally oriented 'medieval' narrative, concentrating on the island's more distant glory days. It is these details that I will now unravel.

The local heritage movement

As we have seen, 'pioneers' such as Säve and Bergman largely concentrated their efforts on Gotland's cultural history, rooted in a Romantic notion of the countryside and its people. Folk culture was vanishing, and the feeling was that it had to be saved, at least by identifying what still remained and getting it down on paper.

In the late nineteenth century, a great many people joined in the work of this folk revival, intent on saving and cultivating the old ways. For example, Mathias Klintberg (1847–1932), a teacher at Visby Gymnasium, was passionately interested in Gotlandic peasant culture, and was a keen collector of local dialects. Among his works we find *Spridda drag ur den gotländska allmogens lif* (1914).[41]

---

[40] 'Föreningen Gotlands fornvänners fastigheter' 1998; Mattias Legnér, lecture given to the Per Arvid Säve-symposiet at Gotlands museum, 28 September 2011.
[41] Klintberg 1914; see also the posthumous Klintberg & Hedin 1983.

A central figure in this was Theodor Erlandsson (1869–1953), an elementary schoolteacher. He has been called 'Gotland's Hazelius', after the Swedish folklorist Arthur Hazelius, who founded Skansen, Stockholm's famous outdoor museum, in 1891. Erlandsson set up something similar, an open-air history museum in Bunge in the north-east of the island, in 1907.[42] At the same time, the focus of Gotlands fornsal's activities shifted to the Middle Ages, as we have seen. Thus, some kind of a division of labour was created between Gotlands fornsal and initiatives such as Erlandsson's, which were predominantly organized in the countryside.

Erlandsson also wrote a number of books on various aspects of Gotlandic folklore, not least the three volumes with the typical title *En döende kultur: bilder ur gammalt gotländskt allmogeliv* (1923–46).[43] Furthermore, he collected what could be called contemporary folklore, for example in a 1928 book of stories about Gotlanders who had left the island to go to sea or to countries far away.[44] Last but not least, Erlandsson also wrote a general history of Gotland for the young, *Gotland, dess historia och geografi i lättfattligt sammandrag för fosteröns barn och ungdom* (1900).

In the same epoch, the island's local heritage movement was established. The two first local heritage organizations were founded in 1918, and in 1936, Gotlands Hembygdsförbund (the Gotland Heritage Association) was founded. The latter today is an umbrella organization for 73 local heritage associations and 31 other associations on the island.[45] From 1979, it has issued the journal *Från Gutabygd* ('From Guteland').

The local heritage movement is responsible for a vast amount of local history-writing, but typically about a certain parish or village. There are also many amateur historians writing this kind of history, for which there is a flourishing market on Gotland, as well as in the rest of Sweden.

Professional historians

The scholarly history-writing about Gotland—long produced on the mainland of Sweden—was not slow to single out the island as unique. For example, in the historian Hans Hildebrand's *Svenska folket under hednatiden* (1866, 2nd edn. 1872), there was a specific chapter covering Gotland.

---

[42] Gislestam 1996.
[43] Erlandsson 1923; Erlandsson 1935; Erlandsson 1946.
[44] Erlandsson 1928. Another work by Erlandsson was the historical novel *Farmannasagor* about Gotland in the Middle Ages (Erlandsson 1949).
[45] Norrby 1986; <http://www.hembygd.se/gotland>.

In the twentieth century, Swedish archaeological research, conducted by mainland institutions such as the universities of Uppsala and Stockholm, used Gotland more than any other Swedish region as a research field. To some extent, this was also the case with studies of medieval art and architecture, thanks to Gotland's rich built heritage, especially its churches. Out of the 95 churches on the island in the keeping of the Church of Sweden, 92 are medieval.[46] There are many reasons for this interest in Gotland, but an obvious case is the fact that the historic monuments on the island have been much better preserved than on the mainland (partly thanks to long periods of economic stagnation and a fairly low increase in population).[47]

Many of the prominent scholars who have worked on Gotland's history have been archaeologists, including Birger Nerman (1888–1971), John Nihlén (1901–1983), and Mårten Stenberger (1898–1973), or medieval historians such as Hugo Yrwing (1908–2002). There have also been many art historians, especially those specializing in the Middle Ages, for example Johnny Roosval (1879–1965) and Bengt G. Söderberg (1905–1985). Many of the academic researchers also worked up general histories of Gotland; Söderberg wrote many books on Gotland's history, for example.

At least in the beginning, most of the academics who specialized in Gotland were born and raised on the mainland. Some of them worked for a time on Gotland, for example at Gotlands fornsal in the case of Stenberger (1934–45), or bought holiday homes on the island, as Roosval did.[48] Some were born Gotlanders, but moved to the mainland in order to get an academic position, while maintaining their research interests in their native island; early examples are Carl Säve (1812–1876), a professor in Uppsala, and Söderberg, who got his doctoral degree in Stockholm.

With time, native Gotlanders became more prominent among the experts on the island.[49] In later years it has become possible to find work as a researcher on the island: the department of archaeology at Stockholm University had a branch in Visby, and in 1998 the independent Högskolan på Gotland (Gotland University College) was founded, although in 2013

---

[46] Lagerlöf et al. 1971, 16.
[47] Jonsson & Lindquist (1987) 2002, 9–10.
[48] The so-called Villa Muramaris in Visby: <http://www.muramaris.se>.
[49] For example, the historians Carl Johan Gardell and Jens Lerbom and the ethnologists Ulf Palmenfelt and Owe Ronström.

it lost its independence, and as Campus Gotland became part of Uppsala University.

Popular works

In the late nineteenth century, tourists began flooding to Gotland. That was helped by initiatives mainly by Visby traders all of whom were members of the influential society De Badande Vännerna (DBW, 'The Bathing Friends'), founded in 1814. DBW had organized schools, a bank, and a botanical garden in Visby, and not least, has been an arena for networking among men of economic or cultural influence on the island. That there was an organized ferry service between Gotland and the mainland from the 1860s was, of course, an important requisite for this development.[50] In the tourist discourse, Gotland, and especially Visby, was depicted in exotic terms. Its medieval ruins and historic monuments were no longer considered an environmental problem, but instead something to romanticize and preserve.[51] In the 1920s and 1930s, tourism was given another boost, partly on the initiative of the shipping company, Gotlandsbolaget, and its long-time director Carl Ekman, or 'Gotlandskungen', 'The King of Gotland'. The Swedes—who had more leisure time, and by the 1930s a fortnight's holiday by law—were to get to know Gotland. Roses were planted in the old town of Visby to make it more picturesque. The tourist posters displayed the slogan that would become so well known: Visby was the 'city of roses and ruins'.[52]

The tourist industry had been organized by a variety of associations. In 1896, Gotlands turistförening (Gotland's Tourist Association) was founded. Today it continues to publish brochures and even books on Gotland's history. Some have been quite 'touristic', with extensive advice on accommodation and eating, while others are more standard textbooks on Gotland's nature, culture, and history, such as historian Carl Johan Gardell's *Gotlands historia i fickformat* (1987).[53]

Svenska Turistföreningen (STF, the Swedish Touring Club), founded in 1885, has also promoted Gotland's tourism and history with different types of texts, publishing yearbooks about the island (1940 and 1966), as

---

[50] *Gotlands turistförening 75 år* (1971), 4; Bohman 1985; Rossipal 1994.
[51] Grandien 1974, 200 ff., 207, 214; Gustafsson 2002a, 64 ff.; Gustafsson 2002b, 37–8.
[52] 'Rosornas och ruinernas stad'; Svahnström 1984, 13, preface by Bo Grandien; Svensson 1998, 14.
[53] Gardell 1987; for the GTF, see *Gotlands turistförening 75 år* (1971).

well as many travel books that have run to several editions. The latter were largely written by two of the leading figures of Gotland's modern history-writing tradition: Söderberg and the artist Maj Wennerdahl (b. 1939). Among their products are general introductions, as well as shorter tourist guides and more essayistic books.[54]

Guidebooks have been published by many different bodies: national and Gotland tourist associations, conservation authorities, the municipalities, and so on. Another one of Söderberg's books, *Strövtåg i Gotlands historia* (1971), published by the local publishing company Gotlandskonst, is typical of the genre. It presents the history of Gotland in a geographical disposition, dealing with events in the past in different parts of the island, brought together as a route for the tourist to follow.[55]

There have also been books for visitors written by individuals.[56] Some of these Gotland books are of a more personal character, being largely essays such as Lisbeth Borger-Bendegard's *Kära Gotland! En personlig kärleksförklaring* (1993).[57] A related category are the coffee-table books, which primarily consist of pictures and photographs, generally of 'typically' Gotlandic things such as *rauks* (sea stacks), churches, and limekilns.[58] Some of the older ones were published as part of larger national series. The publishing company Allhem in Malmö, for example, produced a number of folio-sized books on different Swedish provinces, presenting their history in pictures. Gotland got its book in 1959: *Gotland – ett bildverk* with an accompanying text by Söderberg.[59] Another phenomenon in the mid twentieth century was the 'book film', a large picture book presented in strict chronological order like pages in a newspaper, mostly covering themes such as the labour movement and the temperance movement, and Gotland's recent history got its share in *Från fars och farfars tid: en bokfilm om gutarnas ö* (1959) and *Från fars och min tid: en bokfilm om Gotland 1915–1970* (1972).[60]

---

[54] For a general introduction, see B. Söderberg 1948. For brief tourist guides, see Nihlén 1930; B. Söderberg 1949; Hamberg 1970. For collections of essays, see B. Söderberg 1975; Wennerdahl 1985.
[55] B. Söderberg 1971.
[56] For example, Carlén 1862.
[57] See also Lundqvist & Lundqvist 1972.
[58] For example, Laago & Sjöstrand 1995.
[59] Gotland – ett bildverk (1959).
[60] *Från fars och farfars tid: en bokfilm om gutarnas ö* (1959); *Från fars och min tid: en bokfilm om Gotland 1915–1970* (1972).

Yet another genre is what might be called 'saga books'. They are collections of essays that deal with myths and stories—the 'sagas'. Among them, real historical events are mixed with legends—from *Gutasaga* to the sort Per Arvid Säve collected in the nineteenth century. An early example is Bergman's *Gotländska skildringar och minnen* (1882), and later ones are Nihlén's *Sagornas ö: Sägner och sagor från Gotland* (1928), as well as two subsequent books in the same series, Söderberg's *Gotlands sällsamheter – sagor och sannsagor från gutarnas ö* (1975) and Wennerdahl's *Sällsamheter på Gotland* (1985).

In recent decades, national popular education societies and local heritage associations have issued a large number of books concerned with different provinces. Among them, of course, are some covering Gotland. The largest popular education organization, Arbetarnas Bildningsförbund (ABF, the Workers' Educational Association), has published three different books on Gotland, all written by amateurs, through its publishing company Brevskolan (later Bilda). The first one was the aptly named *Gotland* (1981), written by Janne Werkelin (b. 1948). Ulf Bergqvist and Maj Wennerdahl wrote *Gotland: den förhäxade ön* (1987) where the latter wrote the sections on Gotland's history. Wennerdahl's portions of that book were the basis for the third book, again entitled *Gotland* (2001).[61]

Other organizations have contributed to the list of publications. *Gotland* (1981) by the journalist Stig Arb (1928–2003) was part of a series of province books produced by Riksförbundet för hembygdsvård (the national association for the preservation of the local heritage movement),[62] and *Gotland – navet i havet* (1994) by Stig Jonsson (1927–2010)— also a journalist and a local politician—was said to have been written at the behest of 'various educational organizations'.[63]

The dividing line between the different types of author and entity as I have described them here is only for the sake of discussion. In reality, it was not that strict. Many academics, Nihlén, Roosval, and Söderberg among them, wrote popular histories of the island. There are also some general but somewhat more academic works, such as the anthologies *Historia kring Gotland* (1963) and *Gutar och vikingar* (1983). The latter was explicitly about the Viking Age, but the former, typically, was about

---

[61] Werkelin 1981; Bergqvist & Wennerdahl 1987; Wennerdahl 2001.
[62] Arb 1981, 5.
[63] S. Jonsson et al. 1994, 5 ('på uppmaning av olika studieorganisationer').

the Middle Ages, even though the title gives the impression that it is a general history.

Last but not least, the largest history work ever published about Gotland was issued in 1945, celebrating the third centenary of Sweden's possession of the island: the two-volume *Boken om Gotland*, with over 1,100 pages and almost 50 articles by the leading experts of the day about Gotland's history and contemporary society. The archaeologist Mårten Stenberger covered Gotland's prehistory, and scholars such as Sture Bolin, Elias Wessén, Sune Lindqvist, and Adolf Schück other aspects of Gotland's oldest past. In the second volume, the bulk of authors were amateurs—mainly teachers. Typically, only 2 of the 32 authors were women (the historian Toni Schmid on monasteries, and Ulla Melin on Gotland's crafts).

Schoolbooks

There are also a number of school textbooks on Gotland's history. Erlandsson's *Gotland, dess historia och geografi* (1900), mentioned earlier, was followed by four further editions, the last in 1946. Another, *Gotland: läsebok för skola och hem*, came in 1924, edited by Johannes Linnman. Intended to be read 'in the home', it was a compilation of shorter essays, poems, and accounts of the island's history and nature.[64] In the later twentieth century, more schoolbooks followed.[65] In the 1990s, Lars Olsson (b. 1933) and Roger Öhrman (b. 1937) wrote *Gotland: förr och nu* (1993, 2nd edn. 1996), the latter being responsible for the historical sections. At the same time, Öhrman was also writing an ambitious history book about Gotland, *Vägen till Gotlands historia* (1994, 'The road to Gotland's history'), published by Gotlands Fornvänner in collaboration with a local publishing company that specializes in school textbooks.[66] Öhrman had earlier written about Gotland's history in a brief essay about Visby, and a shorter schoolbook in the 1980s.[67] Otherwise, he has written a great deal about local Gotlandic history, especially a series of books about the area around Slite in the north-east of the island. Olsson, meanwhile, has

---

[64] The book was published in an Uppsala publishing house's Hembygdsböckerna series, which covered most of the Swedish historic provinces (*landskap*), issued in 1918–48.
[65] Uhr 1957.
[66] Öhrman 1994; Olsson & Öhrman 1996.
[67] Öhrman 1973; Funck et al. 1984.

written another textbook on Gotland, *Efter Tjelvar* (2003), intended for young schoolchildren.[68]

Gotlanders or mainlanders

What differences have existed between the descriptions written by authors based on Gotland, and those written on the mainland in Swedish nation-state context? Is it at all possible to make such a distinction? Many prominent writers down the years have been scholars who themselves come from the mainland, while native Gotland 'patriots', such as Per Arvid Säve, by studying at mainland universities have been educated into a shared National Romantic tradition, which they later adapted to conditions as they found them on their home island.

The academic or literary histories, produced by scholars and museum professionals, were often written by mainlanders, even though they frequently had some form of anchoring on Gotland by residence or work. Among the non-academics, their Gotland origins played a larger part. It would be difficult to distinguish the historiography between the one produced by mainlanders and the one written by Gotlanders. Thus, there is no clear border between local Gotlandic history-writing and mainland history-writing about the island.

A special category among the Gotland authors are the *sommargotlänningar* or 'summer Gotlanders', a term used for those mainland Swedes who spend time on Gotland (mainly in the summer), having bought houses there.[69] They are much in evidence in Visby as well as in the countryside. The most famed summer Gotlanders were Olof Palme and Ingmar Bergman, who both had houses on Fårö.[70] Among the Gotland authors, we have already noted the example of Johnny Roosval, and later examples are Stig Arb (1928–2003) and the journalist Lisbeth Borger-Bendegard.[71]

---

[68] L. Olsson 2003a, with four accompanying booklets covering Visby and different parts of the island (L. Olsson 2003b, 2003c, 2003d, 2003e).
[69] The term has 6,310 Google hits (22 November 2011). The Öland equivalent, '*sommarölänning*', with 8,190 hits, is even more common, while similar terms include '*sommarskåning*' (180 hits), '*sommarupplänning*' (0), '*sommarsörmlänning*' (5), '*sommarstockholmare*' (86), '*sommarjämte*' (9), '*sommarvärmlänning*' (30), '*sommarvästgöte*' (0), '*sommarhallänning*' (341), '*sommarsmålänning*' (8), and '*sommarspanjor*' (2).
[70] Other famous summer Gotlanders include the politician Ingvar Carlsson.
[71] Arb 1981, preface; Borger-Bendegard 1993.

As Owe Ronström pointed out, however, the distinction between mainlanders and Gotlanders is an important factor in Gotland's regional consciousness and self-image. The fact that the island's ruling elite when it comes to industry and government has long consisted of incomers has added to the common impression that Gotland is somewhat inferior.[72] Leif Yttergren has also noted that Gotland's regional identity is almost solely centred on cultural concerns, not political ones, which makes it very different to, say, Åland. Yttergren finds one reason for this in the fact that the separate Gotlandic identity is strongest in the countryside, which in turn has been weak in political and economic matters.[73]

Gotland history-writing analysed

I will begin the analysis of the treatment of the island's past in Gotland publications by sorting out the main narratives, of which there are two principle strands: Gotland's medieval glory and, mainly concerning more recent centuries, its cultural history.

In many of the Gotland history books, there is a noticeable quantitative predominance of older history, especially the Iron Age (c.500 BC–AD 1050) and the Middle Ages (c.1050–1520) see Appendix 1, which gives the number of pages of history of various epochs in fifteen typical Gotland books). This is what I would term the *medieval narrative*, which is most pronounced when Gotland is presented to a wider readership, whether in mainland Sweden or abroad. It amounts to the official historiography.[74] Typical examples are the works of Bengt G. Söderberg, whose books have a marked concentration on the Middle Ages. For him, the period before 1361 was the obvious 'age of greatness' for Gotland. He pointed out that it was its medieval history that attracted tourists to the island in the mid twentieth century.[75]

One of the reasons for this was that a large proportion of the academic experts on Gotland were archaeologists. Medieval art history is another such field with a concentration of specialist expertise, partly explaining why the 'official history' of Gotland in many respects is centred on

---

[72] Ronström 2008, 176 ff.
[73] Yttergren 2002, 16–17.
[74] See also Yttergren 2002, 29; Bohman 1990, 187.
[75] B. Söderberg 1949, 40 ('Storhetstiden'), 93–4.

prehistory and the Middle Ages. The largest number of scholars and experts specialize in those areas.

The oldest history books from the nineteenth century, such as those by Snöbohm and Bergman, were rather detailed when it came to the 'dark' period of Gotland's history—that is between 1361 and 1645. However, this cannot in any way be explained as reflecting a more positive view of the period. Instead, a more probable explanation is that those history books to a large extent leaned on known sources and historical accounts, and for the late Middle Ages and the early modern period there were simply more facts known. Not least, there were Strelow's often-cited seventeenth-century histories, which were very detailed about these epochs. Later on, knowledge of the history of the earlier periods has increased, thanks to the voluminous archaeological research on the island.

A more 'indigenous' tradition in Gotlandic history-writing mostly emanated from the folklore movement. There, the cultural history of the island stands in focus, especially the Gotland of peasants in the seventeenth to nineteenth centuries. I would call this the *folklore narrative.*

Between the medieval and folklore narratives stands a 'modernist' narrative, which is more concerned with the modern age, but still deals extensively with social and political matters. It is not specifically folklore-oriented. The more modern the history, the more likely it will cover subjects such as the industrialization of Gotland, or migrations within Gotland, immigration, emigration, and the like. Such topics might be most interesting for those already 'inside', but apparently are not considered something for tourists or outsiders, being thought typical for *any* province or local community in Sweden or elsewhere. It does not distinguish Gotland from the rest.

This modernist stream of narratives is thus more focused on other areas of Gotland's history, and more targeted at a Gotland audience. Of the voluminous *Boken om Gotland* (1945), with the break between its volumes falling in 1645, the second volume which covers the period 1645–1945 is the longer of the two. Normally that would be the case if we were looking at a national Swedish history, or even other provinces' histories. The first volume, ending in 1645, also deals to a relatively large extent with topics such as the peasants' history and internal territorial divisions, more typical of traditional local history.[76]

---

[76] Steffen 1945a; Berg 1945; Svahnström 1945.

Otherwise, an emphasis on more recent periods of history is obvious in schoolbooks and other books addressed to a local audience, examples being Roger Öhrman's *Vägen till Gotlands historia* (1994) and Stig Jonsson's *Gotland – navet i havet* (1994). The former includes a longish section on modern society and history, with topics such as the demographic development of the twentieth century and modern political history.[77] Meanwhile, as we will see, while 'indigenous' Gotlandic history-writing has had much to say about recent centuries in the island's development, the 'external' or tourist discourse, in focusing on prehistory and the Middle Ages, is often sketchy when it comes to later periods.

The medieval and folklore narratives, as well as the alternative modernist narrative focusing on modern Gotland, should be seen as centres of gravity; there are few books that exclusively belong to this or that narrative. For example, the medieval and folklore narratives can co-exist in the same book, even if one of them usually is the stronger. In the following, I will describe the main subjects in Gotlandic history-writing. I have divided the material chronologically, so that texts from the period that ended in the 1970s are considered first, followed by developments in history-writing from the 1970s to the present day, the reason for this choice of watershed being that until the 1970s there was a 'classic' Gotlandic history-writing, which is fairly easy to summarize despite its many guises, but after that, the situation became a little more complex and history-writing more diverse. Within these two main chronological sections, I first deal with the main topics of the medieval narrative, and then with the ways other aspects of Gotland's past have been treated.

The medieval narrative, c.1850–1975

An important element in chronological narratives is the attempt to establish origins. Origins can be of different kinds: the origins of the country itself, the origins of a certain cultural trait, or the origins of its people. This is central to most history-writing when it comes to identity production, and it is of course also the case with Gotland.[78]

---

[77] Öhrman 1994; S. Jonsson et al. 1994, 92–6; see also Uhr 1957, for although it covers the standard ground, with its emphasis on Gotland's long history and an extended description of Visby, modern Gotland with its agriculture and industry dominates the text.

[78] Edquist 2009, 28–31 and literature cited there.

The impact of Gutasaga

The fact that, in *Gutasaga*, Gotland has its own origin myth dating from the Middle Ages—the only Swedish province to do so—has unsurprisingly facilitated the development of a Gotlandic historical consciousness in modern times. Several elements in *Gutasaga* have been central in the narrative of Gotland's history up to the present day—despite the fact that its content was certainly suited to the need in the thirteenth and fourteenth centuries to emphasize Gotland's relative independence from the Swedish kingdom. Regardless of whether the elements in the story were taken as true or not, they have at least been discussed. This particularly applies to the treaty with the Swedes and the sections on Christianity. The fact that there are very few written sources for Gotland's history before the twelfth century has obviously made *Gutasaga* all the more important.

Gutasaga tells how the first humans came to the island, which until then sank into the sea by day and rose out of it by night. First came Þieluar (Tjalvar), whose son Hafþi (Havde) and his wife Huita Stierna (Vitastjerna) were the ancestors of the Gutes. The couple's sons Guti (Gute), Graipr (Graip), and Gunfiaun (Gunnfjaun) partitioned the island between themselves. Some time after that, the island became overpopulated, at which point every third Gute, chosen by lot, was forced to emigrate. They first resisted, barricading themselves in Torsborg—usually identified with the Iron Age fortress of Torsburgen. After that, they went to Fårö, and from there to Hiiumaa, up the River Daugava, and so to Greece (Byzantium).

In the nineteenth century, *Gutasaga* was still being treated as an accurate source regarding Þieluar and his descendants. In Alfred Theodor Snöbohm's *Gotlands land och folk* (1871), they were described as the very first Gotlanders. They were supposed to have come from the south along with the Geats (*götarna*, who were at that time seen as equating to the Goths, *goterna*) in the dim and distant past.[79]

Towards the end of the nineteenth century, source criticism led to a more jaundiced view of these strongly mythical elements in the opening of *Gutasaga*. It was claimed that there was *perhaps* a glimpse of historical truth in the narrative of emigration in *Gutasaga*, a memory of the Gutes'

---

[79] Snöbohm 1871, 73–8; see also Säve & Bergman 1858, 3; Carlén 1862, 40; Bergman 1870, 53–4. At the same time, Odin was still generally viewed as a historical king of Sweden (Edquist 2009, 132).

participation in the great migrations.⁸⁰ However, many authors continued to use the origin story in *Gutasaga* for its educational value. In Carl Johan Bergman's *Gotländska skildringar och minnen* (1882), it was stressed that Þieluar symbolized hard work, and that the account of the treaty between Gotland and the Swedes called to mind the island's bonds with the rest of Sweden.⁸¹ Another example is Theodor Erlandsson's *Gotland – dess historia och geografi för fosteröns barn och ungdom* (1900), where 'real' history was interwoven with stories from *Gutasaga*, which were printed in a different font size and style.⁸²

Well into the twentieth century, some researchers tried to rehabilitate *Gutasaga* as a historical source, especially concerning later developments such as the migration myth. But above all, the elements of *Gutasaga* have continued to be widely used, especially in more essayistic forms of history-writing, as a form of aesthetic decoration. An example is the archaeologist Mårten Stenberger's account of the island's prehistory in the book on Gotland by the Swedish Tourist Association (STF) in 1940. There, he finished his account of the first inhabitants of the island after the ice melted with the words: 'Thjelvar [Þieluar] must have been that old.'⁸³ It was also not surprising that the extensive coffee-table book *Gotland – ett bildverk* (1959) began with *Gutasaga* in its entirety. In the accompanying text by Bengt G. Söderberg, *Gutasaga* was repeatedly cited as a kind of interesting spice.⁸⁴ It has a particularly prominent place in the 'saga' books, being the oldest of the Gotlandic legends.⁸⁵

Ethnic origins

What then of the ethnic origins of the present-day Gotlandic population—the Gutes? In the nineteenth century, in Sweden as in most other European countries, there was a growing tendency to emphasize that most Europeans were of the Indo-European family of peoples, originally sharing the same language, religion, and race. The Indo-Europeans—with subgroups such as the Latin peoples, the Greeks, the Slavs, the Celts, and

---

⁸⁰ Bergman/Rosman 1898, preface, v, 85–6 (in this case, Rosman's posthumous edition, which claimed that the parts on the oldest history had been totally rewritten).
⁸¹ Bergman 1882, 1–9.
⁸² Erlandsson 1900, 5 ff.; Erlandsson 1920.
⁸³ Stenberger 1940, 55 ('Så gammal måste Thjelvar vara').
⁸⁴ *Gotland – ett bildverk* (1959), 7–10, 90, 131–2; see also, for example, B. Söderberg 1949, 8 ff.; Uhr 1957, 6.
⁸⁵ B. Söderberg 1975, 6 ff.

the Germanic peoples—were supposed to have immigrated to Europe long before the birth of Christ. This was also the time when the prehistoric epoch was divided into the Stone, Bronze, and Iron Ages, and the transitions between these periods were long explained by population changes.[86]

By the mid nineteenth century, this explanation of ancient history was on the point of being generally accepted among educated people. One of its chief representatives in Sweden, Hans Hildebrand, stated that the theory of immigration in *Gutasaga* was mythical and not true, but he also claimed that the Gutes (*gutarna*) were a Germanic people distinct from the Geats (*götarna*) and Swedes (*svearna*) on the mainland.[87] Thus, it was only natural that this form of explanation also informed contemporary history-writing by those based on Gotland. In Snöbohm's *Gotlands land och folk* (1871), the difference is made between Geatic (*Götiska*) and Germanic (*Germaniska*) peoples. However, they were all members of a large 'Indo-Germanic ... ur-tribe', who celebrated fire, just as Gutes in later periods did. The Gutes—a specific tribe among the Geats—were said to have immigrated from the south a few centuries before Christ. In Bergman's *Gotlands geografi och historia i lättfattligt sammandrag* (1870), the Germanic Gutes (*Gutarna)* were claimed to have entered Gotland at roughly the same time as its tribesmen, the Geats (*Göterna*), immigrated to the southern part of mainland Sweden. They both came from the Black Sea, although it was hard to tell when.[88]

Per Arvid Säve claimed that the Gutes (*gutarna*) came to Gotland with the Iron Age; they pushed aside the more raw and uncivilized tribes of the Stone and Bronze Ages. He depicted the Gutes in a way typical of the time, in a Social Darwinist, highly ethnocentric manner with racialist overtones: 'the blue-eyed and fair-haired *Gutes* of Geatic kin, who were more cultivated, used tools of bronze, iron, etc.'[89] Erlandsson claimed in 1900 that the Germanic Gutes had moved to Gotland at the beginning of the Iron Age, around the beginning of our era.[90]

---

[86] Edquist 2012.
[87] Hildebrand 1872, 195, 197; for ethnicity, see also Hildebrand 1866, 69–70.
[88] Snöbohm 1871, 76 ff., quote at 78 ('Indo-germaniska ... urstam'); Bergman 1870, 53–4.
[89] Säve 1979c (1880), 7–8, 16 ('de blåögda ljushåriga *gutarna* av götisk folkätt, vilka hade högre odling, brukade don av brons, järn o.s.v.'); Säve 1980 (1876), 35 ff.; Säve 1983, 12; see also Palmenfelt 1993, 53 ff.
[90] See, for example, Erlandsson 1900, 5; Erlandsson 1920, 5.

There were also supposed to have been migrations in the opposite direction. Even as late as the mid twentieth century, researchers such as Söderberg and Stenberger claimed that the Goths had emigrated from Scandinavia—probably including Gotland—towards the Black Sea in the first centuries of our era.[91]

Trading on the age of greatness

The golden age of Gotland's past has long been placed in the Middle Ages, when the island was said to have been a largely independent state that controlled the Baltic trade, bringing riches to the island, and not least enabling Visby to be a wealthy centre of commerce. The medieval paradigm of Gotlandic history-writing means that these topics dominate representations of the past. Sometimes the history-writing about Gotland's Middle Ages was rather 'dry' and antiquarian in character,[92] but often it had an explicit purpose: to let the Gotland of today bask in its glorious past.

'Gotland's age of greatness' was the name given to the two centuries after the introduction of Christianity in Alfred Theodor Snöbohm's *Gotlands land och folk* (1871). That was also a 'golden age', when the country 'enjoyed the blessings of peace and liberty'.[93] Snöbohm emphasized, however, that *Gutasaga* spoke of Gutnish (related to the prehistoric and medieval *Gutes*) commercial expeditions back in pagan times, stretching back to the days when the 'Geatic tribes' had migrated to the north.[94] Snöbohm claimed that there was an extraordinary thirst for freedom on Gotland, which he connected with its position in the middle of the sea and the tradition of trading voyages:

> The sea creates daring and freedom-loving men, for the open sea is the home of the brave and free. This love of the open sea with its fresh life of adventure has in the Gutnish people preserved that strong love of freedom and independence, which has made the

---

[91] Stenberger 1940, 64 ff.; Stenberger 1945b, 79; B. Söderberg 1949, 26.
[92] For example, Lindström 1892 and 1895, works by an amateur historian (a retired paleontologist) with no evident interest in conjuring up character or interest.
[93] Snöbohm 1871, 105 (ch. 5) ('Gotlands storhetstid', 'guldålder', 'njöt fredens och frihetens välsignelser').
[94] Snöbohm 1871, 91 ('Götiska stammar').

independent Gutnish yeomen, the proud Gutnish Vikings—the free sons of the sea—unwilling to submit to the will of a lord.[95]

Even though the Gotlanders had signed a treaty with the Swedish kingdom, according to *Gutasaga*, Gotland remained virtually independent until the thirteenth and fourteenth centuries. Gotlandic histories regularly stress this independence and its importance for Gotland's central position in the medieval Baltic. This narrative has been reproduced in most of the history-writing, with the exception of more recent academic studies, which often question older romanticizing ideas.

The medieval glory of Gotland can be said to have rested on two pillars: economic conditions, and socio-political circumstances. Gotland was not only a centre of trade, making the island rich; it was an independent, peasant-dominated republic. These two topics have been combined in various ways. Nineteenth-century writers were not slow to emphasize the importance of trade in the history of Gotland—striking, when one considers that this was a time when state and politics otherwise dominated history-writing. The island was then a waypoint on the trade route between East and West, Carl Johan Bergman stressed in 1858.[96] This explanation was also the norm in mainland historiography of the time: Hans Hildebrand, for example, wrote in 1872 that Gotland had been the mercantile centre of the Nordic countries long before the Viking Age.[97] Theodor Erlandsson also stressed that the Gutes very early on had gathered 'extraordinary riches' and came in contact with the Romans, Greeks, and Arabs—more or less by themselves, since they were de facto independent from the Swedes. And the highlight was the period 1000–1361: 'The age of greatness'.[98] Similar formulations about Gotland as a major hub of Baltic trade were the rule during the early twentieth century too.[99] Usually said to span roughly the twelfth to fourteenth centuries, many also argued that Gotland took a leading role in the region in the

---

[95] Snöbohm 1871, 91 ('Hafvet uppammar djerfva och frihetsälskande män, ty det fria hafvet är de tappres och fries hem. Det har varit denna kärlek till det fria hafvet med dess friska äfventyrarelif, som hos Gutafolket underhållit den starka kärlek till frihet och oberoende, som vållat att de sjelfständige gutniske odalmännen, de stolte gutniske vikingarne – hafvets fria söner – ej velat underkasta sig en herrskares vilja').
[96] Säve & Bergman 1858, 2–3; see also Bergman 1870, 56–7.
[97] Hildebrand 1872, 195, 197.
[98] Erlandsson 1900, 5–6 ('enastående rikedom', 5), 11 ('Storhetstiden'); Erlandsson 1920, 5–6, 12.
[99] Bergman/Rosman 1898, 92; Roosval 1926, 8

Viking Age or even earlier. For example, when the art historian Johnny Roosval wrote a tourist guide to Gotland's historic remains, published in 1926, he said that in the later Iron Age Gotland had played the leading part 'in the all-Nordic culture'.[100]

In the inter-war period, there was an increasing interest in the remains of what was considered to be Gutnish equivalents to other trading towns around the Baltic, such as Birka, Hedeby, Wolin, and Truso. At Västergarn, money was given in 1932 by Gotlandsfonden (a foundation started in 1925 using Wilhelmina von Hallwyl's donation to Gotlands Fornvänner to strengthen Gotland's heritage) for excavations in the area, which were resumed later in the twentieth century.[101]

The image of this golden age was not unambiguous, however. Per Arvid Säve's description of these times almost amounts to alternative history-writing. The age was entirely bloody and dark, he wrote. *Strandens sagor* (1873) describes Gotland's relations with surrounding societies as a catalogue of violence, brutality, and war, stretching well into Säve's own age: he uses examples from the Viking Age, the Middle Ages, and the sixteenth and seventeenth centuries. Gotland's neighbours were brutish, but the Gutes themselves were no better. Their culture was shaped by the violent peoples from the far shores of the Baltic, but also by the sea itself—'their mother, the stormy sea'.[102] This had turned the Gutes into 'a true sea people'; often every second farmer son went to sea, fishing or setting sail for distant parts.[103] They ruthlessly robbed and looted visiting seamen or ships that ran aground, showing no mercy. Time itself was the explanatory factor for Säve, who used the term 'the ages of darkness'.[104] The 'old times' were 'evil times', with no society to speak of and a great deal more wilderness.[105] In his final words, though, Säve underlined that these dark times had been replaced with something

---

[100] Roosval 1926, 8 ('i den all-nordiska kulturen').
[101] <http://www.gotlandsfonden.se/>; Floderus 1934; Nerman 1934; Lamm 1980.
[102] Säve 1979b (1873), 166 ('sin moder, det stormfulla havet, av vars grundlynne och danad deras väsende är sammanblåst').
[103] Säve 1979b (1873), 169 ('ett sannskyldigt sjöfolk').
[104] Säve 1979b (1873), 172–3, quote at 172 ('mörkrets tidsåldrar'). For examples, see Säve 1979b (1873), 176–7 (Fårö farmers killing others on Gotska Sandön), 177–8 (robbers on Stora Karlsö), 178 ff.
[105] Säve 1979b (1873), 159 ff., quote at 159 ('De gamla tiderna voro allestädes onda tider, ty samhälle fanns ej, eller var det en vildmark').

better, and that the inhabitants of the more central parts of Gotland never took part in such sea robbery.[106]

It should be noted that this narrative was not in the least disparaging of the other, more romanticizing accounts of Gotland's past that were produced in Säve's own time. The positive and negative aspects of the distant past complemented one another—a tendency not unique to Gotland. Pre-Christian religion and culture, for example, were generally depicted in both dark and bright colours at the same time. It was barbaric, brutal, and dark, but, equally, it was something national and Germanic.[107]

Independent Gutes

Generally speaking, Gotland's history-writing has identified the Gutnish farmers as the driving force in the Gotlandic trade. Thus, there is an obvious link between the image of Gotland as a strong and wealthy trade centre, and that of Gotland as an independent peasant republic.

Above all, it has been constantly stressed that Gotland in its golden age was in most practical affairs a politically independent entity, even though it was formally attached to the Swedish kingdom. To explain the nature of the link to Sweden, *Gutasaga* has been the main source. There, the story of the great emigration was followed by a description of how Gotland was linked to the Swedish kingdom, the result of a treaty in pagan times, when Gotland's representative Avair Strabain from the parish of Alva secured military support from the Swedes in return for an annual tribute. This narrative has constantly been used and discussed in Gotlandic historiography. The actual story of Avair Strabain tended to be taken as true, above all when pushing the idea that the union with the Swedes was mutual: the Gutes voluntarily entered into the treaty, and afterwards they could concentrate on their mainly peaceful endeavours, while benefitting from the military protection provided by the Swedes.[108] The upshot was that it made Gotland in effect 'a free and independent country, a small state of its own', in the words of Snöbohm.[109] Virtually all the history-writing, as we shall see, says that

---

[106] Säve 1979b (1873), 211.
[107] See Wickström 2008.
[108] Säve & Bergman 1858, 3–4; Bergman 1870, 54; Thordeman 1944, 12 ff.; Schück 1945, 180–1.
[109] Snöbohm 1871, 94 ff., quote at 96 ('ett fritt och sjelfständigt land, en liten egen stat'); Erlandsson 1900, 7, 13–14 is similar; see also Bergman/Rosman 1898, 87. In Schück 1940, 80, 83–4, 89, another theory is added—that the treaty with the Swedes in the

Gotland was basically independent until the late thirteenth century, when Swedish influence grew.

Thus Bergman stressed that 'the island had its independent constitution, its own rulers or judges, and was thus only a protectorate under Sweden'. He also gave the example of the Gotlanders making treaties with Henry the Lion, the mighty duke of Saxony and Bavaria in the mid twelfth century.[110] Bengt G. Söderberg, meanwhile, said that the voluntary union with the Swedes was one of the most important events in the history of Gotland, and accentuated the division of labour between the warlike Swedes and peaceful Gutes. It is made into something natural and extra-historical. Incorporation into the Swedish kingdom was rational for the Gotlanders; it was 'a Gotlandic strategy of trade politics' to buy peace in exchange for military protection.[111] The depiction of Avair Strabain—one among the most credible in *Gutasaga*, according to Söderberg—'is also consistent with the ancient Gotlandic attitude and mentality: rather appeal to the silver-scales than the sword'.[112]

The differences between the interpretations have generally concerned the actual date of the treaty with the Swedes. In the nineteenth century, the treaty was generally thought to have been agreed in the Viking Age.[113] That interpretation has also been the most common in the twentieth century. However, in the 1920s, another opinion emerged, which has had quite a few followers. The philologist and archaeologist Birger Nerman linked the story in *Gutasaga* about an ancient emigration with the union with the Swedes. Nerman is mainly known for his thesis that the Swedish kings of the largely mythical dynasty of the Ynglings—Aun, Egil, and Adils—were historical figures during the fifth and sixth centuries, and that they had been buried in the famous 'royal mounds' at Gamla Uppsala. Nerman wrote a series of popular historical works based on his research, and it seems that his theories (as well as similar ones put forward by his

---

twelfth and thirteenth centuries was part of a strategy to counter the German presence in Visby.
[110] Bergman 1870, 54 ('ön hade sin sjelfständiga författning, sina egna styresmän eller domare, och var sålunda endast ett skydds-land under Sverige'), 58.
[111] B. Söderberg 1949, 36 ('ett gotländskt handelspolitiskt drag').
[112] B. Söderberg 1949, 35-6, quote at 36 ('står också i samklang med forntida gutnisk inställning och mentalitet: hellre vädja till silvervågen än till svärdet'); B. Söderberg 1957, 31 is similar; *Gotland - ett bildverk* (1959), 131-2; B. Söderberg 1975, 228-9 (quote at 229).
[113] Snöbohm 1871, 95 (late tenth century); see also Thordeman 1944, 12 ff., who chooses not to guess when it could have happened.

colleagues) of an ancient Swedish empire with roots deep in the Iron Age had a substantial impact in Sweden, not least outside academia.[114]

Nerman devoted considerable attention to Gotland. He began his research career in the 1910s by studying the island's Iron Age, when he established radical changes in the archaeological material from the sixth century. In a paper from 1923, he came to the conclusion—by linking *Gutasaga*, Rimbert's *Vita Anskarii*, and Wulfstan of Hedeby's often-cited travel account from the ninth century—that a large number of Gotlanders must have emigrated to areas east of the Baltic in about AD 500. Shortly afterwards, Gotland was incorporated into the Swedish kingdom. Nerman was inclined to take traditionally disputed written sources as gospel, if he could link them to archaeological evidence. The case of *Gutasaga* was yet another 'example of how saga traditions, which have long been regarded as historically worthless' were found to contain historical truth when matched with the archaeological material.[115]

Some researchers followed Nerman's reasoning, for example fellow archaeologist John Nihlén, as will be seen. Other colleagues of Nerman's such as Sune Lindqvist, however, did not embrace the theory that *Gutasaga* could be interpreted as meaning that the Swedes had conquered the Gutes in the sixth century.[116] Nerman's emigration theory was then thoroughly criticized in 1943 by the historian Lauritz Weibull, who argued that the story in *Gutasaga* about overpopulation, drawing lots, and emigration was a typical ancient and medieval learned tradition. Elements of the story could even be found in Herodotus, Weibull claimed.[117] Lauritz Weibull and his brother Curt were forceful advocates of a more telling criticism of literary sources for prehistoric and medieval events, which meant that they rejected the possibility to say almost anything of certainty about Swedish political history before the eleventh century. However,

---

[114] Edquist 2009, 132–3; Edquist 2012, 45 ff.
[115] Nerman 1923, 71 ('exempel på, hur sagotraditioner, som länge betraktats som historiskt värdelösa').
[116] Instead, Lindqvist pointed out that Gotland later was a rival to Birka (*Fornvännen* 28 (1933), 187, review). The argument that the emigration story in *Gutasaga* reflected true events around AD 500 was believed to be probable by, for example, Wessén 1943, 299–300. See also Tiberg 1944.
[117] Weibull 1943. In the anthology *Historia kring Gotland* (Sjöberg 1963), Nerman took the opportunity to defend his old argument (Nerman 1963), which was printed next to a reprint of Weibull's original article.

many archaeologists, with Nerman in the forefront, continued to use such methods for decades to come.[118]

In general, subsequent academic history-writing has generally been very sceptical of the theories of a Gutnish emigration during the Migration Period, even if Mårten Stenberger and Elias Wessén referred to this interpretation in *Boken om Gotland* without overt criticism.[119] There are, however, other elements of Nerman's research on Gotland that have been more long-lasting, primarily his account of the supposedly Gutnish and Swedish colonies in present-day Latvia in the seventh and eighth centuries, to which I will return later.

Nerman's view that Gotland's incorporation into the Swedish kingdom came as early as the sixth century did find some followers. Drawing on a different selection of new research findings, Richard Steffen claimed in 1943 and 1945 (*Boken om Gotland*) that it was beyond doubt that the island had been conquered or at least invaded by the Swedes, specifically those from Uppland, in the late sixth century, and that there were clear similarities between the Mälaren culture and the new Gotlandic culture after that.[120]

A peasant democracy

One of the most enduring ideas about Gotland's golden age is that there must have been an egalitarian and democratic agrarian society—a 'peasant republic'. That view was based mainly on *Gutalagen* and the absence of an aristocracy and direct royal control. Alfred Theodor Snöbohm, in *Gotlands land och folk* (1871), described pre-Christian Gotland (as well as the rest of Scandinavia) as a 'pure democracy' in which 'the people themselves possessed the power and the government, and exercised it'. This free independence continued after Christianization, and lasted into the thirteenth century.[121]

Bergman wrote of 'a republic of free peasants'.[122] Not surprisingly, Erlandsson was at pains to point out that the Gutes who plied the trade routes over the Baltic Sea were all country-dwellers: it was peasants who

---

[118] Edquist 2009, 132–3; Edquist 2012, 44–5 and literature cited there.
[119] See, for example, Stenberger 1945b, 93–4; Wessén 1945a, 153–4.
[120] Steffen 1943, 49 ff (he did not mention Nerman, though); Steffen 1945a, 226.
[121] Snöbohm 1871, 85 ('ren demokrati', 'folket sjelft innehade makten och styrelsen samt utöfvade den'), 116 ff.
[122] Bergman/Rosman 1898, 90 ('en republik af fria bönder').

led the Gotlandic trade republic.[123] Gunnar Jonsson argued in the STF yearbook of 1940 that, because of the island's 'popular constitution', the free, equal men 'regardless of barriers and decrees by lords' could conduct trade.[124] In *Boken om Gotland* (1945), its trade and peasant society were accentuated in the foreword: 'that impressive breed of merchant farmers … virtually controlled the trade of the Baltic Sea and Russia'.[125]

Similar descriptions of the socio-political conditions in medieval Gotland were the rule.[126] Bengt G. Söderberg underlined medieval Gotland as a continuation of the prehistoric societal order.[127] It was 'a virtually autonomous state, a kind of peasant republic' with 'a free peasant population that had given themselves a social structure and laws'—'a democracy without a concentration of power in any single hand'.[128] This was in tune with the then prevalent view in Sweden, where the medieval provincial laws were considered to reflect an ancient legal system with roots in a pre-Christian yeoman democracy.[129] Still, Söderberg emphasized that it was propertied peasants who controlled this democracy—it was in fact a true class society.[130] The last remark, that the democratic peasant republic was not for everyone, has often been made.[131] But even so, the emphasis remains: Gotland was *democratic* and *independent*.

Gotland between East and West

A central element in the discourse of a democratic, farmer-controlled, peaceful, and equal Gotland as a trade centre was the island's extensive contacts across the Baltic Sea.[132] In the nineteenth century, it was stressed

---

[123] Erlandsson 1900, 12 ('De gutar, som upprättade dessa äldsta handelsförbindelser, voro bosatta på *landsbygden*').

[124] G. Jonsson 1940, 182 ('folklig författning', 'oberoende av herremäns skrankor och påbud').

[125] Nylander 1945, 8 ('handelsböndernas imponerande släkte … praktiskt taget behärskade Östersjöns och Rysslands handel').

[126] See also Roosval 1926, 7 ('fri republik'); Nerman 1942, 246; Nylander 1945, 8; Schück 1945, 179 ('denna gotländska folkrepublik').

[127] B. Söderberg 1948, 108 ff.; B. Söderberg 1949, 42–3; see also Schück 1940, 89.

[128] B. Söderberg 1949, quotes at 40–1, 41, 42 ('en praktiskt taget autonom stat, ett slags bonderepublik', 'en fri bondebefolkning som givit sig själv samhällsform och lagar', 'en demokrati utan maktkoncentration i någon enskild hand'). He also used the term 'peasant state' ('bondestaten'): *Gotland – ett bildverk* (1959), 143.

[129] Linderborg 2001, 299–315.

[130] B. Söderberg 1948, 110–1; B. Söderberg 1949, 42.

[131] For example, Wessén 1945b, 169 ('det gutniska samhället var en demokratisk bonderepublik, men endast bönderna hade full medborgarrätt'); Jakobson 1966, 16 ff.

[132] See, for example, G. Jonsson 1940, 201.

that the Gutes had important contacts eastwards when the island was a trade centre in the early Middle Ages. The written sources bore witness to Gotlandic trading factories in Novgorod, as well as strongholds in the cities of the Baltic's eastern shore, such as Riga in the thirteenth century.[133] Such local patriotism was very evident in Erlandsson's *Gotland, dess historia och geografi* (1900). Not only were the Gutes a dominant element in Novgorod, but he also stressed that Indian and Persian riches could come to Europe by one of two ways, through Venice or through Gotland.[134]

These narratives of Gotland's eastern contacts were shaped at a time when Scandinavian history-writing overall turned its eyes towards relations across the Baltic Sea in the Viking period. Towards the end of the nineteenth century, so-called Normannism—the idea that Scandinavians had founded the Russian Empire—gained greater currency. It was a notion that sat well with increased nationalism and, in some cases, to growing anti-Russian feeling in Swedish conservative circles.[135]

The Swedish archaeologist who devoted most energy to Viking Scandinavian influences in Russia, Ture J. Arne, organized repeated excavations in Russia during the first half of the twentieth century. He claimed Scandinavian archaeological finds at a number of sites along the river routes to the east, and saw them as evidence of a fairly large exodus of people from Sweden in the ninth and tenth centuries.[136] Arne was for his time relatively reluctant to make far-reaching ethnic and national capital out of his findings. Yet, his research was generally viewed as confirming the sizeable influence of the Swedes in the East during the Viking Age. He also gave Gotland a central role: even if the wealth was perhaps not so equally distributed across the island in the Viking Age, 'the entire island of Gotland was a large trade republic'.[137]

Arne emphasized that the Viking Age was characterized by its Eastern or Oriental cultural impact on present-day Sweden.[138] That was especially the case on Gotland, where the influence remained long afterwards: 'The Byzantine and Persian motifs, which penetrated into Sweden, survived the Middle Ages and were further enriched thanks to Gotland's relations

---

[133] Bergman 1870, 60–1; Snöbohm 1871, 109 ff.; Bergman/Rosman 1898, 89–90; Bergman (1885) 1901, 5–6.
[134] Erlandsson 1900, 11–12.
[135] Edquist 2012; see also Latvakangas 1995; Gustin 2004, 59–86.
[136] Arne 1917, 62.
[137] Arne 1931, 295 ('Hela ön Gotland var en stor handelsrepublik').
[138] See, for example, Nihlén 1928b, 42 ff.; Nerman 1942, 176, 248–9.

with its large neighbour to the east.'[139] Arne was also among the first who in the 1910s highlighted the Byzantinesque murals in a number of Gotland's medieval churches, for example in Garda and Källunge. Another was the art historian Johnny Roosval, who specialized in church art in medieval Gotland.[140]

However, in the early twentieth century, these Eastern influences were only traced in art and architecture in Gotland's churches, according to the researchers. Christianity itself did not come from the East. When the adoption of Christianity is discussed, the explanation given in *Gutasaga* to this day plays a key role in the representations of Gotland's religious transition. According to *Gutasaga*, the Gutes embraced Christianity because of the Norwegian king Olaf II Haraldsson (St Olaf), who introduced the new religion during his stay on the island in the early eleventh century. Just as in the case of the annexation to Sweden, the importance of *Gutasaga* has gone largely unchallenged, since there are virtually no other written sources about this event. Thus, both Bergman and Snöbohm followed *Gutasaga* closely.[141] In the twentieth century, scholars highlighted the similarities between church regulations on Gotland and in Norway, and thus confirmed the importance of Olaf Haraldsson, an example being Elias Wessén in *Boken om Gotland* (1945).[142]

The history-writing about relations between Sweden, Gotland, and the lands to the east of the Baltic Sea generally depicted the Scandinavian peoples as the active ones, and those in the East—Balts, Slavs, and Finno-Ugric peoples—as passive recipients. Birger Nerman had lots to say on this matter. In his nationalist history-writing about Swedish penetration in the East, Gotland played an important role. In the 1920s, Nerman claimed that, mainly on the basis of Norse literature and Rimbert, the Swedish kingdom had expanded to the eastern Baltic coast as early as the seventh century. Soon, he was able to strengthen this hypothesis with fresh archaeological finds. In the years 1929–32, he excavated various sites along the eastern Baltic and East Prussian coast. Based on grave finds near

---

[139] Arne 1917, 62–3, quote at 63 ('De bysantinska och persiska motiv, som trängde till Sverige, fortlevde under medeltiden och riktades ytterligare genom Gotlands förbindelser med det stora landet i öster'); see also Arne 1931, 296 who argues that rich finds of silver at Hemse 'indicate an unusually strong contact with the Orient' ('tyda på en ovanligt stark kontakt med Orienten').
[140] Arne 1917, 76–81; Roosval 1913; Roosval 1917.
[141] Säve & Bergman 1858, 3–4; Bergman 1870, 54 ff.; see also Snöbohm 1871, 97 ff.
[142] B. Söderberg 1949, 37–8; Wessén 1945a, 159–60.

the Latvian coastal town of Grobiņa (better known internationally by its German name Grobin), Nerman felt able to prove that a Swedish–Gutnish colony had lasted there from about 650 to 800. Swedes and Gutes had different roles, according to Nerman's interpretation of the cemeteries in Grobiņa: the Swedes stood for the military fortifications, while the peaceful Gotlanders were engaged in trade.

Nerman was convinced this proved the existence of a Swedish Baltic Empire, and he soon developed a grand theory of 'Sweden's first age of greatness' ('Sveriges första storhetstid'), which became the title of a popular history book in 1942.[143] The seventh- and eighth-century Baltic empire was followed in the ninth century by an even greater 'development of strength' in the Swedish state, which led to the founding of the Kievan Rus. During this first stage, the Russian state was nothing less than 'a sort of Swedish colony.'[144]

Nerman's claim that there were Gotlandic colonies on the eastern shore of the Baltic Sea in the seventh and eighth centuries was generally taken at face value in subsequent history-writing. It was rarely questioned.[145] However, Nerman's more far-reaching theories of a Swedish Baltic empire before the Vikings have seldom been espoused. One who did, however, was John Nihlén, who is best known as the leading representative of the Swedish local heritage movement from the 1930s to the 1960s. Between the wars he worked as an archaeologist on Gotland, where he was a driving force in the founding of Gotland's regional heritage organization in 1936.[146] He wrote essays and popular historical overviews such as *Under rutat segel: svenska äventyr i öster* from 1928. Nihlén followed in the Nerman's footsteps regarding the Swedish–Gutnish division of labour in the sixth century: the Swedes were responsible for the military and dynastic elements, while the Gotlanders were enterprising merchants.[147] Together, they went on to expand eastwards with a joint force. (It should be noted that even before the

---

[143] Nerman 1942, 14 ff., 25 ff.
[144] Nerman 1942, 72 ff., 92–114, 115 ff., 122 ff., 126 ff., 135, quotes at 115 ('kraftutveckling') and 135 ('ett slags svensk koloni'); see also Nerman 1930.
[145] Schück 1940, 80, 83; Stenberger 1945b, 95–6. From the first, Nerman's theory that there were Gotlandic colonies in Latvia came in for detailed criticism, for example Yrwing 1940, 53 ff.
[146] Nihlén 1982 (with a preface by Gunnar Svahnström and Sven-Olof Lindquist); Norrby 1986, 10.
[147] Nihlén 1928a, 20–33.

excavations at Grobiņa, Nihlén sided with Nerman over the pre-Viking Age expansion eastwards.)

According to Nihlén, then, the Swedish Baltic Empire was in fact founded long before the sixteenth and seventeenth centuries. That entity instead built on a 'Greater Sweden' that had formed during the Viking Age and earlier. Nihlén devoted a good deal of space to Gotland in his book *Under rutat segel*. The island was a centre of world trade, and above all it took Swedish influences to Novgorod.[148] Nihlén also speculated that as early as AD 500 the Gotlanders had begun to pave the way for their eastward voyages by establishing colonies across the Baltic Sea. He guessed that the 'Rus' of the Arabic sources might in fact have been Gotlanders.[149] Indeed, in a guidebook to Gotland published by STF in 1930, he wrote that it was the Gutes together with Swedes from Uppland who had probably founded Russia.[150]

Gotland's role in the expansion eastwards across the Baltic was thus that of a trade centre. Gotlanders were the peaceful ones, the 'good cops' if you will. This was well suited to the mid twentieth century, when Swedish history-writing more than ever before emphasized its non-violent aspects, especially trade.[151] Nerman claimed that the Swedish expansion towards Russia in the Viking Age was an economic endeavour, intent on tapping the vast riches of Byzantium and the Caliphate. The goal was to take the leadership in world trade.[152] According to Nerman, Sweden's political influence in the East dried up during the first half of the eleventh century, however, although when it came to trade Gotland would maintain and even advance its leading position until the fourteenth century.[153] The Gotlanders 'from time immemorial had primarily been merchants', and Nerman praised their 'outstanding entrepreneurial spirit and skill as organizers of trade'.[154] The Gotlanders in fact formed the trade

---

[148] Nihlén 1928b, 29, 32 ff., 165–6.
[149] Nihlén (1928b, 171, 173–4) also implied that Stavr, a name for heroes in Medieval Russian epic poems (*byliny*) was identical with Staver den store, a legendary Gotlandic hero.
[150] Nihlén 1930, 26.
[151] Hall 1998, 84; Hall 2000, 271; Edquist 2012, 53 ff., 76 ff., 81 ff.
[152] Nerman 1942, 163, 177 ff., 184, 196 ff.
[153] Nerman 1942, 7–8, 206 ff., ch. 7.
[154] Nerman 1942, 218 ff., quotes at 226 ('i alla tider främst varit handelsmän') and 250 ('enastående företagaranda och smidighet som organisatörer av handeln').

bridge between East and West that the Swedes had sought to accomplish in the Viking Age.[155]

This combination of nationalism and an emphasis on the role of trade and commerce in history was also to be found in the work of the contemporary historian Sture Bolin. In an often-cited article from 1939, he asserted that Sweden and its waypoints in Eastern Europe—the conquered 'stora Svitjod' ('Great Svitjod')—emerged as the centre of world trade during the Viking Age by dint of connecting Western Europe and the Caliphate. Bolin argued against the Belgian historian Henri Pirenne's thesis that trade between the Orient and Western Europe across the Mediterranean Sea had fallen to a minimum by the eighth century, for he believed that Mediterranean culture continued to flourish even after the Arab conquests—it even grew, thanks to silver flooding in from Central Asia, brought in by the Arabs. However, in the ninth century a new direct trade route opened between Scandinavia and the Arabs through Eastern Europe. It was in this context that Gotland in particular played an important role. In *Boken om Gotland* (1945), Bolin repeated his thesis, concentrating on the important part played by Gotland in this world trade system, since it was already a centre of Baltic trade.[156]

Paradoxically, Gotland was often simultaneously viewed as having a strikingly insular character in the late prehistoric epoch: Gotlanders went abroad and they organized trade, but they did not let anyone in. Nerman stressed that Gotlandic culture during the late Iron Age was unusually distinctive.[157] Roosval explained Gotland's peculiar culture by pointing to 'the insular nature of the land'.[158]

In the middle of the sea

Gotland's status as a trade centre has often been read far back into prehistory, not only into the Viking Age, which saw a very large influx of Arabic silver coins to Gotland, but also earlier into the Bronze Age. Arne argued that even before the birth of Christ, Gotland had been the centre of 'the international trade in Northern Europe'.[159] Others went further. In the mid twentieth century, Mårten Stenberger and Bengt G.

---

[155] Nerman 1942, 242.
[156] Bolin 1939; Bolin 1945, quote at 127; see also Yrwing 1940, 16 ff.
[157] Nerman 1942, 37, 42.
[158] Roosval 1926, 7 ('landets insulära natur').
[159] Arne 1931, 291 ('den internationella handeln i Nordeuropa').

Söderberg wrote in their bestselling popular works that the beginnings of Gotland's role as a trading nation could be identified several thousand years back in history.[160]

In *Boken om Gotland* (1945), Stenberger identified Visby and Västerbjärs in the parish of Gothem as 'Gotland's first trading places' in the Stone Age.[161] He, like many of his contemporaries, stressed reason and rationality as the driving forces in historical evolution. Thus, *homo economicus* was made into something natural and extra-historical.[162] Gotland's lively contacts with surrounding areas, which continued into the Bronze Age, were said to show that there 'must have been a distinctive mercantile ability as well as skills in boatbuilding and the art of navigation'.[163] Gotland was 'a centre that had learned to take advantage of its naturally allotted trade position in the Baltic'. As early as the Bronze Age, everything was in place for 'Gotland's first age of greatness'.[164] After the *second* age of greatness during the Roman Iron Age, a period of decline followed during the Migration Period. But soon after that, in the seventh century, the island's third and most important age of greatness began, reaching its height in the Viking Age and Middle Ages, when peasant-led Gotland became the Baltic region's leading trading power.[165]

In a similar way, Söderberg stressed that Gotland's position as a trading centre was thousands of years old. During the Stone Age, the so-called Gothem people became Gotland's 'first merchant farmers'. They laid the foundations for nothing less than a 'societal construction of peculiar structure, which was to endure for three thousand years, at certain periods taking the lead in Northern Europe's economic life'.[166] Thus, he had constructed a continuity in Gotland's history, and the Gutes'

---

[160] Some researchers felt it was difficult to know *anything* about the island's role as a trading centre before the twelfth century (Yrwing 1940, 21 ff., 37, 40).
[161] Stenberger 1945b, 50 ('Gotlands första handelsplatser').
[162] See also Hall 2000, 270-7.
[163] Stenberger 1945b, 68 ('måste ha funnits utpräglad merkantil förmåga liksom kunnighet i farkostbyggandets och navigeringens konst').
[164] Stenberger 1945b, 68-9, quotes at 69 ('en central, som förstått utnyttja sin av naturen anvisade handelsposition i Östersjön', 'Gotlands första storhetstid').
[165] Stenberger 1945b, 80, 96 ff.; see also Stenberger 1940, 72, 78.
[166] B. Söderberg 1948, quotes at 62 ('första handelsbönder', 'en samhällsbyggnad av egenartad struktur, som skulle äga bestånd i tre tusen år och under skilda epoker bära ledarskapet i Nordeuropas ekonomiska liv'); B. Söderberg 1949, 16 is similar; *Gotland – ett bildverk* (1959), 97.

expeditions in the Viking Age were simply an extension of 'their old routes to the East'.[167]

Stenberger too was eager to discern ancient traditions of Gotlandic expansion eastwards. In *Boken om Gotland*, he dated Gotland's Eastern influences as far back as its greatness as a trading nation: the Bronze Age. At that time, Gotlandic culture was not only open to external influences, it was also 'expansive'. Gotlanders headed for the eastern shores of the Baltic, where Stenberger identified Gotlandic stone ships—almost at the same location where the Gotlanders and Swedes settled in the seventh century, at the beginning of Gotland's third age of greatness:

> Gotlandic colonization in Latvia during the Vendel Period [c. AD 550–800] can, despite its brief existence, be claimed to have been the prelude to the vigour and mercantile expansion that characterized Gotland during the Viking Age and Middle Ages.[168]

It was, however, only in that period that Gotlanders settled in the East. Otherwise, they concentrated on 'trade hegemony in the Baltic area', according to Stenberger.[169] Bengt G. Söderberg—the leading Gotlandic popular historian of the mid-twentieth century—also emphasized this Gotlandic infiltration during the Bronze Age.[170] He too followed Nerman by pointing out that 'the Gotlanders crossed the sea, founding colonies at Grobin in Latvia'.[171] Söderberg saw a very long chain of unbroken development that led to what was of course the most important part of Gotland's history: the Middle Ages.

The city, the Germans, the decline

As we have seen, Gotlandic history-writing held that the island, even after the alliance with the Swedish kingdom—whenever that happened—was

---

[167] B. Söderberg 1949, 20 ff., 36–7, quote at 36 ('sina gamla färdvägar österut'); see also B. Söderberg 1957, 32; *Gotland – ett bildverk* (1959), 128.

[168] Stenberger 1945b, quotes at 70 ('expansiv') and 96 ('Den gotländska kolonisationen i Lettland under vendeltid kan trots dess begränsade beståndstid sägas bilda upptakten till den kraftyttring och merkantila expansion, som kännetecknade Gotland under vikingatid och medeltid.'); see also Stenberger 1940, 72.

[169] Stenberger 1945b, 105–106, quote at 106 ('handelshegemonien inom det baltiska området').

[170] Stenberger 1945b, 70–1, 95; B. Söderberg 1949, 20 ff.

[171] B. Söderberg 1949, 35 ('gotlänningarna går över havet och anlägger kolonier vid Grobin i Lettland').

more or less autonomous well into the Middle Ages. However, by the late thirteenth century that started to change. The good times were about to end.

What tourists on Gotland today see, and are supposed to see, are artefacts that largely date from the very late period of Gotland's putative age of greatness: the old town of Visby and its well-preserved city wall, and, beyond, the almost one hundred medieval stone churches dotted across the Gotlandic countryside. The old churches are almost always mentioned in the Gotland books, and there are also popular publications specifically about them.[172]

Ever since the nineteenth century, medieval Visby been a tourist magnet. It is therefore natural that there has been a great deal of history written specifically about Visby,[173] and that the general history books about Gotland as a whole tend to dwell on the city.[174] Often when it is described, the focus is on its days as a wealthy Baltic entrepôt, especially in the thirteenth century, as is evident even today in the surviving buildings, church ruins, the city wall, and other remains. Sometimes, the continuity is stressed between Gotland's central role in the Viking Age and Visby's importance afterwards.[175]

Ironically, Visby's well-preserved city wall is generally considered an effect of and a symbol of the internal divisions on the island, the embodiment of city versus country. It is often said to have been erected to protect the city from the countryside, after a conflict had arisen between the two in the late thirteenth century. A key role is often attributed to the 'outsiders'—foremost among them Visby's German-speaking burghers, who were generally said to be the ones who pushed Visby towards the Hanseatic League. In the 1280s, the Gutnish burghers of Visby followed suit and chose to join the Hanseatic League, distancing themselves from the rest of Gotland. In 1288, a civil war broke out, with

---

[172] Lagerlöf, Hallgren & Svahnström 1971; B. Söderberg 1978; see also *Visby stift i ord och bild* (1951); Roosval 1952.
[173] Guidebooks that emphasize the old town are Bergman (1885) 1901; Wåhlin 1924; B. Söderberg 1972 (similar format to B. Söderberg 1971). Books dominated by pictures, with a similar focus on the medieval remnants are Romin & Bergman 1891; Österlund & af Ugglas 1914; Lundberg et al. 1939. Personal accounts and essays, still mostly relating to medieval history and/or the city inside the wall are Eckhoff 1925; Ludin 1966. Some history books treated the Middle Ages and later periods roughly equally, for example, V. Johansson 1950; while a work that mostly deals with Visby in the nineteenth and twentieth centuries is Bohman et al. 1964.
[174] Typically, some books name both Gotland and Visby in the title, for example, Öhrman 1973.
[175] Fritzell 1972, 14 ff., 21–2.

Visby pitted against the rest of the island. Soon after, Visby's importance diminished, and Lübeck took over the leading role in the Baltic trade.

It might be expected that Gotlandic history-writing would play down the level of internal Gotlandic division. In fact, nothing could be further from the truth. Instead, the civil war of 1288 is usually described as a struggle between the townspeople (both the German and the Gutnish burghers, who chose to make common cause against the rest of Gotland) and the countryside, with the Swedish king as the winning party.[176] It has even been claimed, as in Folke Ludin's collected essays on Visby from 1966, that there is still to this day a rivalry between Visby's inhabitants and other Gotlanders—but it was worse in the Middle Ages.[177]

Theodor Erlandsson, with his emphasis on Gotland's agrarian culture, gave his full attention to the divisions between country and city in his history-writing. Anti-German tendencies were also evident in his *Gotland, dess historia och geografi* (1900), which all but argues it was the German interest in controlling trade that led to the establishment of Visby, the power of the Hanseatic League, and the civil war of 1288. As Visby grew rich, the countryside grew poorer, and it was only very recently that the hostility between them finally evaporated.[178] However, Erlandsson wanted to have his cake and eat it, so he included the city wall of Visby as an example of the high level of spiritual and artistic achievement of medieval Gotland.[179]

The disaster of 1361

The fourteenth century is generally described as the period when Gotland's and Visby's ascendancy crumbled and was exchanged for decline. Trade routes were redrawn, leaving the island in a backwater, and there were disasters such as the Black Death in 1350, which according to legend turned whole parishes into wasteland.[180]

The most notorious series of events, one has become the symbol of Gotland's bad fortune in the late Middle Ages, came in 1361.[181] In this

---

[176] Wåhlin 1924, 13 ff.
[177] Ludin 1966, 51–2.
[178] Erlandsson 1900, 12, 14 ff.
[179] Erlandsson 1900, 14.
[180] Erlandsson 1900, 17.
[181] B. Söderberg 1948, 115 ff., 172 ff.; B. Söderberg 1957, 35; *Gotland – ett bildverk* (1959), 44. Carl Johan Bergman had argued as early as 1858 against the normal dating of Visby's decline to 1361—it was rather later developments when trade routes

year, the Danish king Valdemar landed on Gotland with an army and defeated a Gotlandic peasant army in a couple of battles in the countryside, and then finally outside the walls of Visby. Then the Danes entered the city, plundered it according to some, and placed Gotland under the Danish crown. These events gave rise to a number of legends, many of which were compiled and printed in the nineteenth century, adding to the modern remembrance of those events.

Many of the events during the summer of 1361 have become cornerstones in the standard accounts of Gotland's history. In a national Swedish context, as is especially the case with the supposed plunder of Visby, this was chiefly thanks to the artist Carl Gustaf Hellqvist (1851–90) and his historicist, National Romantic painting *Valdemar Atterdag brandskattar Visby 1361* ('Valdemar Atterdag holding Visby to ransom, 1361') which was completed in 1882. It is still one of Sweden's best-known paintings, an iconic image not only of Gotland's medieval history, but also of the Middle Ages as a whole. The painting shows the Danish king, Valdemar, sitting on his throne in a square in Visby, watching as his soldiers oversee the collecting of goods from the population. In the foreground, a sad-looking Visby woman with her little baby symbolize the innocent victim. In the late nineteenth and early twentieth centuries, at roughly the time when history was also reproduced in books about Gotland and Visby, 1361 was labelled an 'unforgettable year of misfortune'.[182]

From a Gotlandic perspective, the Battle of Visby, fought before the city walls at Korsbetningen on 27 July 1361, is today perhaps the most iconic event. Gotland's peasant army was massacred. Soon after the battle, a stone cross was erected at the scene, with an inscription in Latin: 'In Anno Domini 1361, on the third day of Jacob's Day [27 July], the Gutes fell at the hands of the Danes in front of Visby's walls; pray for them'. According to legend, 1,800 Gotlanders fell in battle. In the early twentieth century, some of the mass graves were excavated, revealing the direct evidence of hundreds of the slain: the corpses of badly equipped soldiers, jumbled together, seemingly confirming the legends about the event and

---

disappeared that mattered (Säve & Bergman 1858, 4); see also Lindström 1892, 107–108; Erlandsson 1900, 17; Fritzell 1972, 52–3.
[182] For example, Bergman 1870, 64 ff. (quote at 66, 'ett oförgätligt olycks-år'); Bergman (1885) 1901, 67–8.

its magnitude. It was soon revealed that many of the victims were the very young and the very old.[183]

The events are often described at length in Gotlandic histories, which tend to stress the tragedy of the occasion, with ordinary Gutes putting up brave resistance with no chance of defeating the professional Danish knights, who slaughtered them en masse. In *Boken om Gotland* (1945), an entire chapter was given over to the battle, including the grim details of the mass graves. Its author, Bengt Thordeman, who had been part of the research team that investigated the mass graves at Korsbetningen and had written a book about the Danish invasion, claimed that the battle was a drama of freedom, still living in memory after six centuries: 'The battle was lost—the men fell—the land was ravaged—a flourishing culture was destroyed. But the people saved its soul.' It is a cult of the heroic defeat, just as the loss at Kosovo Polje is a central element in Serbian nationalist history-writing: 'After 600 years, we are proud that the defeat on 27 July 1361 is a page in the annals of Sweden.'[184]

According to legend, the burgheresses of Visby stood on the city walls, looking on as the Danes slaughtered the Gutnish peasants. This has been seized on in the history-writing, even though it is not certain that it happened exactly that way—it was the ordinary country people who had to make the sacrifices, while the well-fed townspeople were left sitting pretty. It certainly fits the typical dualism between country and city, in this case between the honest and brave Gotlandic yeomen versus the foreign-influenced, sophisticated, and overly civilized urban population.[185]

Pirates, Danes, and stagnation

Mathias Klintberg pointed out in 1909 that by the sixteenth century, Gotland had been reduced to being an 'insignificant part of larger units'. The days were long gone when 'the Gutes single-handedly concluded

---

[183] Clason 1925; Thordeman 1928; Thordeman 1944. The Latin inscription runs 'Anno domini MCCCLXI feria tertia post Jacobi ante portas Wisby in manibus danorum aeiderunt gutenses hic sepulti, orate pro eis'.

[184] Thordeman 1945, 254 ('Striden förlorades – männen stupade – landet härjades— en blomstrande kultur förintades. Men folket räddade sin själ', 'Vi äro efter 600 år stolta över att nederlaget den 27 juli 1361 är ett blad i Sveriges hävder'); see also Thordeman 1928, 4; Schück 1945, 197; Thordeman 1944.

[185] B. Söderberg 1975, 24 ff. There, as in many other places, it is said that the dramatic events were naturally the stuff of legend and immediately became traditions that have survived into the modern age. For the age-old literary and ideological dichotomy of country and city, see Williams 1973.

treaties with other peoples, princes, and mighty cities'.[186] The period from 1361 to 1645 is generally described as a period of decline. There were no more churches built in the countryside, and Visby experienced a series of disasters, culminating in 1525 when the city was sacked.[187] The period is generally divided in two; before 1525, with a mess of different rulers, and after 1525, when Gotland was more firmly under direct Danish rule.

Concerning the tumultuous late medieval period, Gotlandic history-writing has had a tendency to stress the fact that pirates were harboured on Gotland, using it as a base to plunder ships in the Baltic. In Erlandsson, the period 1361–1525 was boldly characterized as 'Sjöröfvaretiden'—the Pirate Age.[188] Söderberg characterized the epoch in an even more colourful way: it had 'the character of a thrilling pirate novel, not without its picaresque elements'. The reign of the Victual Brothers on Gotland in 1394–8 was responsible for turning Gotland's history into a 'pirate novel', continuing later with ex-king Eric of Pomerania, who ruled the island in 1439–49.[189] Adolf Schück emphasized that the Victual Brothers' leader, the former Swedish king Albert (Albrecht von Mecklenburg), was a 'hated German usurper' and that his followers on Gotland were 'pirates'.[190]

There were points of light, though. Among the large number of pirates and noblemen passing in review in Gotland's history during this epoch, generally described as selfish and eager to line their own pockets, there are some exceptions. The Teutonic Knights, who liberated the island from the Victual Brothers in 1398 and ruled until 1408, have generally been praised in Gotlandic history-writing as good and popular rulers.[191] At the end of this period there was the Danish nobleman Søren Norby, who is often described at length. He was sent to Gotland in the late 1510s to be Denmark's representative on the island, but in the bitter conflicts between Denmark and Sweden in the early 1520s, Norby above all is said to have

---

[186] Klintberg 1909, 161 ('obetydlig del i större enheter', 'då gutarne på egen hand ingingo fördrag med andra folk, furstar och mäktiga städer').
[187] For example, Bergman 1870, 66 ff.; Wåhlin 1924, 18 ff.; Fritzell 1972, 52–5.
[188] Erlandsson 1900, 20.
[189] B. Söderberg 1949, 74 ('karaktären av en spännande sjörövarroman som inte saknar pikareska inslag'), 80 ff.; see also B. Söderberg 1948, 183 ff.; B. Söderberg 1975, 32 ff. (on the Axelson family).
[190] Schück 1945, 199 ('den hatade tyske usurpatorn', 'sjörövare').
[191] Bergman 1870, 67 ff.; Erlandsson 1900, 22; B. Söderberg 1949, 82 ('after them, Gotland became a "pirate island" again'); Fritzell 1972, 53 ('ten peaceful and happy years for the city and the peasant republic', 'tio för staden och bonderepubliken fredliga och lyckliga år').

acted independently, as a sort of *Gotlandic* ruler. He has also generally been seen as a colourful person, and benevolent towards the Gutes.[192]

The Danish era—a term which is mainly used for the period 1525–1645—has been perhaps the most overlooked in Gotlandic history-writing. As mentioned earlier, the nineteenth-century books on Gotland's history by Snöbohm and Bergman included fairly detailed accounts of various events and figures in the period. But in the twentieth-century history-writing, the epoch has been ignored. In general histories, it often summarily noted that Gotland, like the rest of Denmark, turned to Lutheranism, that the taxes rose, and that there was general stagnation, even if there were attempts to develop the sandstone industry.[193] There were exceptions, though. When the schoolteacher Rudolf Björkegren (1869–1964) devoted the larger part of his book *Gotländskt: några bilder från Gotlands medeltid och danska tid* (1951) to 'Gotland during the Danish period', it was considered to be 'the first comprehensive account of the Danes' domination on Gotland'.[194]

Cession to Sweden

In 1645, Gotland was ceded to Sweden by the Treaty of Brömsebro. In older history-writing, this event was regularly described as a restoration of a normal state of affairs, a reunion, when Gotland's natural belonging to Sweden was finally recognized. In nineteenth-century historiography, it was considered totally natural that Gotland was destined to be a Swedish province. In Octavia Carlén's *Gotland och dess fornminnen* (1862), it was said that by about AD 1000, Gotland *had* to seek the protection of the Swedish king. The Swedish king thereafter justly intervened in the conflict in 1288, when Hanseatic Visby tried to impoverish Gotland's peasants, who, however, were not without guilt in the conflict. The non-Swedish period after 1361, the 'year of misfortune', was racked with oppression,

---

[192] Jakobson 1966, 21–2; B. Söderberg 1975, 42 ff.; Öhrman 1994, 134–7 ('Sören Norby – sjöhjälte, kapare, politiker').
[193] For example, Bergman 1870, 72 ff.; Erlandsson 1900, 26–7; B. Söderberg 1949, 86; Jakobson 1966, 23–4.
[194] Björkegren 1951, 79–240 ('Gotland under danska tiden'), back cover ('den första utförliga berättelsen om danskarnas herravälde på Gotland'). He had previously written shorter books on the Danish period and the years under Søren Norby (Björkegren 1928–31; Björkegren 1949).

problems, corruption, until the island at last in 1645 was reunited with its *motherland*.[195] Bengt Thordeman wrote in 1944 that Gotland would soon have become an integral part of the Swedish kingdom earlier, had it not been for the events of 1361 and on. Its final integration into Sweden was therefore simply delayed.[196]

There was a much less enthusiastic account of events in Theodor Erlandsson, who argued that the Gotlanders did not welcome the return to Sweden; even less so because their new masters did not for long mean a fresh start for the island. Nevertheless, the change of ruler meant unification with their *natural motherland*:

> At last, Gotland had been firmly united with the country to which it principally belongs by nature. In the beginning, however, this unification caused a harmful interruption of people's development. Gotlandic civilization had never ever been Swedish, but had been independent from the start. Therefore, there was also long a general dissatisfaction with the new order.[197]

In *Boken om Gotland*, the events of 1645 were again described in two different ways. Adolf Schück was triumphant in the final words of his essay on Gotland's political history up to 1645. He said that after Gotland's inhabitants had sworn allegiance to the new country, they were 'adopted as fully responsible citizens of the motherland, which for nearly three centuries had felt the loss of the legendary island of the Gutes as a stinging pain'.[198] In another essay, however, Richard Steffen gave a bald account of the actual events, noting that the population, which felt itself to be neither Swedish nor Danish, were indifferent to the change.[199] Thus, the annexation of Gotland in 1645 to Sweden was hardly a triumph, but rather it stopped things getting any worse.

---

[195] Carlén 1862, 12–3, 154–5, 168 ('olycksåret'); see also Bergman 1870, 75.
[196] Thordeman 1944, 17.
[197] Erlandsson 1900, 30 ('Ändtligen hade Gotland blifvit fast förenadt med det rike, hvartill det af naturen närmast hör. I början åstadkom dock denna förening ett skadligt afbrott i folkets utveckling. Den gotländska civilisationen hade aldrig någonsin varit svensk utan från början självständig. Därför rådde också länge allmänt missnöje med den nya ordningen').
[198] Schück 1945, 225 ('upptagas som fullmyndiga medborgare i det moderland, som i snart tre sekler känt den sägenomspunna gutaöns förlust som en stingande smärta').
[199] Steffen 1945c, 10 ff.

How then did writers describe events after 1645 up to their own time? Many of them—especially the Gotlandic ones—claimed that for a long time after 1645, the new Swedish masters cared little for Gotland.[200] Erlandsson was harsh: during the eighteenth century, Gotland was in terrible shape, devastated by plague, crop failure, poverty, and the generally misled governments of Sweden for much of the century. Söderberg also wrote that for a time after 1645 Gotland was treated as a colony, and in the 1670s Visby was in a state of deepest misery.[201] There are clear echoes of the Gotlandic inferiority complex towards the Swedish mainland and Stockholm, and the anxiety that mainland Sweden looked down on Gotland and the Gutes. That sentiment was clearly visible in the works by Per Arvid Säve, for example.[202]

For some short periods, Gotland's belonging to Sweden was threatened. Danes occupied the island in 1676–9, while in 1808 there was a brief Russian occupation, the latter with practically no violence involved. Especially in the oldest history-writing, these events were described at reasonable length, but for Söderberg in the mid twentieth century, they were less important—the 1808 events almost comical. Both Erlandsson and Söderberg claimed that Gotland's population welcomed the Danish invaders in the 1670s. The island was also affected in later wars: during the Crimean War, British warships used Fårösund as a naval base, even though Sweden was formally neutral, and during the two world wars, the island was somewhat isolated.[203]

In many histories, especially those written in the 'medieval tradition', the period after 1645 is dealt with quite rapidly. But even here there is a dominant narrative, with some recurrent themes. The introduction of the lime industry, the industrious and enterprising governors of the eighteenth century, and the late eighteenth- and early nineteenth-century local merchant capitalist families of Donner and Dubbe are stereotypically and briefly mentioned.[204]

There are also people who have gained the status of heroes in the more recent past. Per Arvid Säve described the state governor in 1766–88, Carl Otto von Segebaden (1718–95), as *the* hero of Gotland's history. He

[200] Säve & Bergman 1858, 4 (only after *c.*1800).
[201] Erlandsson 1900, 30, 33–4; B. Söderberg 1949, 89; see also V. Johansson 1950, 69 ff.
[202] Palmenfelt 1993, 61 ff.
[203] Bergman 1870, 78–9, 80 ff.; Erlandsson 1900, 31, 35 ff.; B. Söderberg 1949, 90. 93.
[204] B. Söderberg 1949, 90 ff. For Jacob Dubbe, see also B. Söderberg 1975, 73 ff. Pelle Sollerman wrote about Dubbe in three novels in the 1940s.

introduced the modern age to backward Gotlandic society: reason, science, and development. Säve's descriptions of Segebaden in *Åkerns sagor* and other publications have all the ingredients that the later accounts contain. The man came to Gotland, introduced agrarian reforms and a new crop—potatoes—and, not least, oversaw the construction of a modern road system almost from scratch, where earlier it had been very difficult even to go on horseback between the parts of the islands.[205] Säve did not spare his words when describing Segebaden:

> the most fortunate man that the government so far had sent for the care and progress of Gotland ... It was he who was capable of breaking the old habits and first spurred on agriculture and water management in the area, and that in all respects: one can say that here he ended the past age and introduced a new era.[206]

Segebaden led the backward population as a patriarch, but sometimes he had to use force; however, Säve stressed that it was necessary for the Gotlanders' own good:

> For he, a great and fortunate man, far ahead of his time, in many cases saw the approaching social perils, and clearly understood the needs of the place and knew his strengths, which he used as a man for the perpetual benefit of the place, ... he knew how to use his wisdom and patience to enlighten the simpleminded, encourage the timorous, and frequently succeeded in frightening away ignorance by sheer force of will.[207]

Segebaden's 'seed corn' and the 'patriotic endeavours' of Gotland's Rural Economy and Agricultural Society (Gotlands läns hushållningssällskap) hit home with the population.[208] Säve also stressed that not all Gotlanders

---

[205] Säve 1979a (1873), 120–37, 161, 251–7; Säve 1980 (1876), 120–37, 161.
[206] Säve 1980 (1876), 120–1 ('den mest välsignade man och i stort verksamme hövding, som styrelsen dittills sänt att vårda och förkovra Gotland ... Det var han som mäktade bryta de gamla vanorna och först gav lyftning åt åkerbruket och hushållningen inom orten och det i alla riktningar: man kan säga, att han här avslutade de gamla åldrarna och införde ett nytt tidevarv').
[207] Säve 1980 (1876), 122 ('Ty han, en stor och välsignad man och långt framom sin tid, förutsåg i flera fall stundande samhällsvådor samt fattade klart ortens behov och kände sina krafter, dem han brukade som en karl till ortens evärdeliga gagn, ... han förstod att med klokhet och tålamod upplysa de enfaldiga, uppmuntra de rädda och mäktade oftast med sin kraftiga vilja skrämma fåkunnigheten').
[208] Säve 1980 (1876), 161 ('utsäde', 'fosterländska bemödanden').

were backward-minded; there were also some Gotlandic farmers who were in the forefront of turning from 'simple-mindedness' to 'reason'.[209] Bergman also wrote about Segebaden that he was 'probably the most excellent and active of all the island chiefs';[210] that he was a benevolent guide for his people; even that he was the island's equivalent to Sweden's sixteenth-century king Gustav I Vasa, generally described as the country's founding father. As in Säve, Segebaden embodied the beginning of a new and better time for Gotland. With him, the dark period that had begun in the fourteenth century was finally over:

> When Segebaden left Gotland in 1788, he had managed to waken in its enfeebled people a greater thirst for activity and understanding of their own power, for which reason he saw the dawning of a new and better time for our island. ... Long was the night that fell over Gotland after the bright, industrious days of our Middle Ages. With governor Segebaden came the dawn of a new day for the Gotlandic people.[211]

Segebaden's reforms in the eighteenth century are a continuing element in the history-writing, its main message being the importance of enlightened leaders being able to pursue reforms and efforts leading to growth, even if at the time it was against the will of the majority of Gotlanders. Segebaden is a symbol of the future, and is never seen as an 'outsider' trying to curb the Gotlandic spirit. On the contrary, his efforts were for the benefit of the island.[212]

Jakobson, who emphasized the independent spirit of the Gotlandic peasants in his *Gotland – landet annorlunda* (1966), also used Segebaden

---

[209] Säve 1980 (1876), 151 ('enfalden', 'förstånd').

[210] Bergman 1870, 83-4, quote at 83 ('troligen den ypperste och verksammaste af alla öns höfdingar'). In Snöbohm (1871, 300), however, Segebaden is described only very briefly, but still as an excellent governor.

[211] Erlandsson 1900, 34-5, 37, quotes at 35, 37 ('Då Segebaden år 1788 lämnade Gotland, hade han lyckats väcka det förslappade folket till större verksamhetslust och insikt om egen kraft, hvarför med honom gryningen till en ny bättre tid för vår ö inträdde. ... Lång var den natt, som efter vår medeltids ljusa, verksamhetsrika dag föll öfver Gotland. Med landshöfding Segebaden inbröt gryningen till en ny dag för det gotländska folket'). John Nihlén also used the Gustav I Vasa metaphor, and claimed that Segebaden was Gotland's 'father of the nation' (*landsfader*) (Nihlén 1929, 178-9, quotes at 178, 189).

[212] See also Uhr 1957, 8 who stresses Segebaden's efforts in building the Gotland's roads; for similar, see B. Söderberg 1948, 210-11; B. Söderberg 1949, 91; B. Söderberg 1975, 191-2.

in order to point out that the local patriotism of the Gutes must not get too strong. The good minority, who did not resist Segebaden's reforms but instead accepted them, consisted in those who had not been shaped and influenced by the sea robbery and general disorder during the Danish period.[213] Thereby, he also managed to explain the excessive local patriotism with external, non-Gotlandic factors.

The cult of Segebaden was the rule, but there were exceptions. Not that he was described as insignificant or in a negative light, but that he was relegated to being just one among many important persons. In *Boken om Gotland* (1945), the description of Segebaden by the historian Leif Dannert is markedly reserved. Segebaden is named as one of the three most important people for the development of the island in the eighteenth century, all of them governors, but he is mentioned only briefly.[214]

Still, modern Gotland has been relatively downplayed in the more 'official' Gotlandic history-writing. Some aspects of eighteenth- and nineteenth-century Gotland have entered the 'hall of fame' of Gotlandic history and heritage, most notably the stone houses in the countryside built in the eighteenth century, and the limekilns from the same period and later. A large part of the guidebooks, especially those for tourists and other outsiders, stressed iconic Gotland: the Middle Ages in Visby and the countryside churches, the stone houses, the limekilns, the fishing villages, all the prehistoric monuments.[215] But there was still little said about the island's most recent history. In 1959, a 'book film' about Gotland's nineteenth century was published, covering different aspects of the island's history between 1801 and 1915. In the foreword, Bengt G. Söderberg—rightfully—claimed that Gotland's thirteenth century is generally much better known than the nineteenth century. Therefore, that 'void in Gotland's cultural history' had to be filled.[216]

---

[213] Jakobson 1966, 24–5 (who also emphasized that Segebaden was his century's great man on the island).
[214] Dannert 1945, 51–2.
[215] In tourist guides such as Hamberg 1970; or personal essayistic guides such as Lundqvist & Lundqvist 1972.
[216] *Från fars och farfars tid* (1959), 7 ('tomrum i gotländsk kulturhistoria'). It was followed by *Från fars och min tid* (1972), covering the period 1915–70.

The folklore narrative, c.1850–1975

Owe Ronström claims that there are two main representations of Gotlandic history nowadays. Medieval Gotland means *Gesellschaft*: it is inclusive, individualist, urban, and somewhat elitist. Outsiders have claimed that they can say 'we' about Gotlanders going east in the Viking Age, but not concerning the eighteenth-century peasants. Then there is the other main narrative, about the old Gotlandic peasant society, mostly concerning the seventeenth to early twentieth centuries. That narrative is mostly local and symbolizes *Gemeinschaft*: it is exclusive, a version of the past more specifically suited for people who are 'genuinely' Gotlandic.[217] The latter narrative has its equivalents in several other regional and national narratives, but the contrast with the *Gesellschaft* mythology of the Middle Ages is more peculiar for Gotland.

This division seems to have been consolidated at the turn of the twentieth century. Visby was then branded a centre of commerce, an urban symbol, while the Gotlandic countryside was fixed in a folkloric and National Romanticist manner typical of that age. Before that, the difference does not seem to have been so big. Per Arvid Säve concentrated on contemporary history, for example the changes in farming and the draining of the bogs.[218] Carl Johan Bergman gave a fair deal of attention to the periods following 1361 in his textbook in 1870, even making the time between 1361 and 1645 into two different chapters, while the period before was only one chapter, as was the period 1645–1870.[219] Much of his collection of historical essays, *Gotländska skildringar och minnen*, consisted of the more recent folkloric history, about folk games, peasant weddings, but also other events and artefacts from periods after the medieval golden age, such as the death of Søren Norby, more recent buildings in Visby, and so on.[220]

But as we saw above, at the beginning of the twentieth century, the important institution of Gotlands Fornsal turned its focus more specifically towards the pre-historic and medieval periods. And there was a

---

[217] Ronström 2008, 238–49. Lotten Gustafsson (2002a, 71–2) also argues that there were two somewhat conflicting legacies.
[218] In *Åkerns sagor* and *Skogens sagor*; see Palmenfelt 1993, 77–85.
[219] Bergman 1870.
[220] Bergman 1882.

growth in the number of academic researchers studying Gotland, a majority of whom were experts on the earlier parts of the island's history. That helped the agrarian and folklore narrative develop into a more independent and internal affair.

Perhaps the single most important person responsible for producing and reproducing that aspect of Gotland's past was Theodor Erlandsson, the schoolteacher mostly known for founding the open-air museum in Bunge in 1907 (Bungemuseet). He claimed that the old Gotlandic peasant culture was a 'dying culture'. Indeed this was the subtitle of a series of books from 1923 to 1946, covering mostly folklore, manners, old dialects, and other aspects of cultural history up to the nineteenth century.[221] Erlandsson claimed that Gotland had had a more egalitarian social structure than mainland Sweden. Even though there were both peasants and labourers on the farms, they worked together and acted as equals. However, in modern society that had changed. Workers and employers no longer greeted one another, and this was obviously against the Gotlandic soul. Therefore, the Social Democrats had nothing to do on Gotland, he claimed in 1935.[222]

That explicitly conservative aspect of the folklore narrative was not the rule. As most folklore projects with the aim of strengthening the identity of a people, be it in a national, ethnic or regional context, the general tendency was to present it as something above politics, something that everyone could feel at home in. As we shall see, agents belonging to the political Left have also reproduced the folkloric aspects of Gotland.

Folkloric Gotland has been nurtured not least by the local heritage movement, gathering artefacts from the past in local open-air museums and the like. Another part of the narrative is peculiar of Gotland, namely the interest in regional folk games such as *varpa*, *stångstötning*, and *pärk*. Historian Leif Yttergren has observed that the folk games of Gotland are rarely mentioned in the dominant Gotlandic historiography, which predominantly deals with the Middle Ages. At the same time, they have a strong position in the regional identity, often being a field of conflict between the island and the mainland.[223]

---

[221] Erlandsson 1923; Erlandsson 1935; Erlandsson 1946. The Bunge museum was soon hailed as an important part of the island's culture (see, for example, Linnman 1924, 258–72).
[222] Erlandsson 1935, 194–200.
[223] Yttergren 2002, esp. 29.

Some people have tried to bridge that gap between the external medieval paradigm and the internal folklore paradigm. Henning Jakobson wanted to show that other side of Gotland for the mainland Swedes in his book *Gotland – landet annorlunda* (1966). His focus was Gotland beyond Visby, coastal Gotland. Jakobson pointed out that Gotland was first and foremost a peasant country, and described much of it in a traditionally nationalist and Romantic way, for example by stressing the Germanic spirit of the Gutnish peasants.[224]

The content is often the same in the folklore tradition as in the medieval tradition. In the folklore tradition, though, there is a bigger emphasis on the legends and myths themselves, rather than the actual events. The Danish invasion in 1361 is the most obvious example of where the folklore tradition deals with different legends. However, the different aspects—myths and historical truth—were not contradictory, instead they complemented one another.

Folkloric Gotland, with its sagas and legends gathered by people such as Säve, Bergman, and Erlandsson, has made it possible to present Gotland as an 'island of sagas', both including the prehistoric and medieval legends and folklore of more recent times. A genre that we might call the 'saga' books, where the main topics are legends, myths with or without historical truth, is to a large part focused on the period after the Middle Ages. The above-mentioned books by Säve and Bergman fall into that category, which could also be said of Nihlén's *Sagornas ö. Sägner och sagor från Gotland* (1928). However, the latter deals to a large extent with earlier history, leaning on myths from prehistoric and medieval times—the tales of *Gutasaga*, and the pre-Christian religious myths that are to be seen on the Iron Age picture stones.[225]

Shipping and fishing

For islands, contact with the surrounding sea are naturally obvious. However, compared to some other Baltic Sea islands, such as Åland, marine activities such as shipping and fishing have played a relatively minor role in the history-writing of Gotland. If you Google 'gotländsk sjöfart' (Gotlandic shipping) you get 54 results, whereas 'åländsk sjöfart' (Ålandic shipping) gets 6,350 results.[226]

---

[224] Jakobson 1966, 28–37, esp. 29.
[225] Nihlén 1928a; see also below for B. Söderberg 1975 and Wennerdahl 1985.
[226] Date of analysis 6 August 2011.

The fact that fishing, with the exception of a period in the last century, has never been a main livelihood for the Gotlanders is an important factor. There are a lot of fishing villages on Gotland; however, the fishermen in the past relied on farming as their primary livelihood. Even so, in the modern age, the old Gotlandic fishing villages are almost fully part of the historical Gotlandic 'canon'—they are remarkable physical remnants of the past, hard not to miss.[227]

Gotlandic shipping is indirectly covered in the dominant narrative of prehistoric and medieval greatness, highlighting the merchant farmers who sailed the Baltic Sea. There is a specific word for these trading farmers—the *farmän* (lit. 'travelling men'). Still, the main focus has remained on Gotland itself; the travelling Gotlanders in question were after all peasants, rooted on their native island. In the yearbook about Gotland from the Swedish Tourist Association (1940), Erlandsson stressed that Gotland had always been a *peasant country*. The well-known glory days of Visby only lasted a couple of centuries, and the Gutes who made the island a centre of trade were peasants—not merchants as we know them.[228]

Säve dealt with these aspects in two of his 'sagas', *Havets och fiskarens sagor* on the Gotlandic fishing, and *Strandens sagor* mainly about the more bleak and violent aspects of contacts with others across the sea or on the island's own beaches,[229] with sea robbery exemplified, for instance, by the story how the people of Fårö killed their competitors from Roslagen in mainland Sweden when fighting for the control of Gotska Sandön.[230]

Otherwise, the narratives have been more positive, trying to capture the heritage values of these elements of Gotland's history. In the schoolbook *Gotland* (1924), the fishing culture is covered at the start of the narrative, right after a traditional opening about Gotland's oldest elements: the rocks and the sea. The fact that Gotlandic fishing villages unlike the ones in mainland Sweden, lack year-round residential homes is made into another characteristic of Gotland—something to be proud

---

[227] See, for example, guide books such as *Se Gotland* (2006), where numerous fishing villages are included.
[228] Erlandsson 1940, 221; see also the fictional work Erlandsson 1949.
[229] Säve 1979b (1873); Säve 1979c (1880).
[230] Säve 1979b (1873), 176–7; see also, for example, Bergman 1882, 277–8; Linnman 1924, 142–4. Even if it has been said that Säve played down the negative aspects of wrecking, it is still a rather dark description (Palmenfelt 1993, 70 ff.).

of. A similar thing can only be found on the 'sister island' of Öland. However, the Ölandic fishing villages were 'never as neat and orderly as the Gotlandic ones'.[231]

In *Det gotländska vikingaarvet* from 1928, Erlandsson claimed that most books about Gotland said very little about the Gotlandic *people*, especially not those many who had left the island for a life abroad or at sea. He set out to remedy that by presenting examples of Gutes travelling to North America and other far-flung places.[232]

As we have seen, an entire period in Gotland's history—the tumultuous epoch from 1361 to 1525—has been associated with pirates. In Erlandsson's history, the period was even called *Sjöröfvaretiden*—the Age of Pirates. However, that also meant that Gotlandic piracy was generally seen as something that came from outside. The pirates were 'the others'. By connecting them to the turbulences of the late Middle Ages, they—the Victual Brothers, Erik of Pomerania, and others—came to symbolize the island's general decline after 1361.[233] The works by Säve can be seen as something of an exception; a bleaker view of the Gotlanders' past, where the islands' inhabitants were not that much better than the outsiders.

Some Gotlanders have also gained semi-heroic status thanks to perceived criminal acts connected to the sea. The Gotska Sandön tenant Petter Gottberg (1762–1831) has become legendary thanks to history-writing, being sort of a piquant curiosity. His story was told by Per Arvid Säve and then by many others: Gottberg was supposed to have lured ships into running aground where he killed the crew and looted the wrecks.[234] For example, the novelist Helmer Linderholm wrote two novels about this alleged robber and pirate, *Vrakplundraren* (1970) and *Vrakplundrarens dotter* (1972).[235]

---

[231] Linnman 1924, 31 ('systerön ... dock aldrig så prydliga och välordnade som de gotländska').
[232] Erlandsson 1928, preface; see also Nihlén 1929, 123–77; Hägg & Hägg 1945.
[233] For a more careful account, see Gardell 1987, 98–110.
[234] Fries 1964, 230; see also B. Söderberg 1975, 115–16; Wennerdahl 1985, 275, which broadly continues the legend. There were also stories about other Gotlandic 'pirates' or robbers working from Gotland (see, for example, Enström 1921, 32–5 for an example from seventeenth-century Fårö).
[235] Elvers 1997, 155–6; Siltberg 1997, 103–104.

Nature and history united

The quest for origins is not only a matter of ethnicity and socio-political unities. In historiography, there has also been a constant concern with giving Gotland the earliest possible origin—in nature itself. It is most evident in the more popular and overtly identity-generating texts. For example, a schoolbook from 1924 starts with the chapter 'Sea and beach: How Nature formed Gotland'.[236] Popular books on history typically begin with sections on geography and nature; for example, *Boken om Gotland* (1945) emphasized that the Gotland rocks were formed 300 million years ago. Thus, history is united with nature itself.[237]

So, there is a connection between Gotland as a natural phenomenon and Gotland as a socio-historical entity—at least in books that try to capture the essence of the island. The various depictions of Gotland put the emphasis on different aspects: some concentrate on nature and landscape, some focus on cultural heritage and history, and others combine them roughly equally.

In books such as Carl Fries's *De stora öarna i Östersjön* (1964) and Siv and Key L. Nilson's *Gotland - bilder från en ö* (1976), nature is the centre of attention. They are filled with lots of images, which still are easily read as specifically Gotlandic—*rauks*, meadows (*ängen*), and remnants of bogs (*myrar*) intermingled with pictures of Visby's medieval culture, where limestone combines nature with culture.[238]

Modern history-writing, c.1975 onwards

Previous analysts have noted that the Gotlandic regional identity seems to have been strengthened in the late twentieth and early twenty-first

---

[236] Linnman 1924, 7 ('Hav och strand. Hur naturen danat Gotland'); see also Klintberg 1909, where the chapter 'Gotlands tillkomst och daning' ('Gotland's origin and moulding', 1–62) is followed by chapters on the Stone, Bronze, and Iron ages (63–77, 78–84, 85–112), and finally the historical time after AD 1050, with a watershed in the 1520s (113–59, 160–75).
[237] Pettersson 1945, 13, 16; see also Uhr 1957, 5–6. This tendency in history-writing has also been noted in Häggström 2000, 72 ff.; Wallette 2004, 313; and Edquist 2009, 140–1.
[238] See also, for example, S. Jonsson et al. 1994, 115–33 on meadows, flowers, etc. There are also books entirely on its nature, for example, Ohlsson 1944, who calls for the preservation of nature, not least the bogs (*myrar*) (see ibid. 35–54 for Lina myr).

centuries. The revitalization of the folklore elements such as *Gotlandsdricka* and local games is one example.[239] This awakening of regional identity is, however, a worldwide phenomenon, and it is difficult to say whether the growth of identity production on Gotland has been either greater or less significant than in other places.

Overall, the production of history in the last three or four decades is more heterogeneous and 'democratized' than before, which also is a general phenomenon. Academic history is more marginalized, and more diverse. 'Ordinary' people write history far more than before, through study organizations or by themselves.[240] Heterogeneity and democratization are important elements in what is sometimes labelled a contemporary postmodernist or late capitalist history culture. Another important trait is the seemingly constantly growing economic influence in historical culture and identity-making, where history is sold to tourists and used for marketing and branding. In short, the identity-making and entertaining values of history are heralded more than ever. The ideological effect of this postmodernist history—being the 'cultural logic of late capitalism'[241]—is obvious: non-controversial narratives of history are naturally promoted when the purpose is to entertain or to sell a 'historical trademark' to tourists.[242] As we shall see, historical culture on Gotland is more diverse in our own time, and at the same time traditional narratives are reproduced in very stereotypical ways.

Medieval dominance

In recent decades, the Middle Ages remain at the centre of the 'official' history-writing and other uses of history on Gotland. At least that is the case when the island has been presented to tourists and people generally interested in history from the mainland and abroad. Visby's city wall and church ruins, the monastery ruins at Roma, and the almost one hundred medieval stone churches remind us of what is usually described as Gotland's golden age. It is therefore no coincidence that Visby and Gotland since 1984 have hosted a well-visited Medieval Week, which attracts considerable attention.

---

[239] Salomonsson 1979; Yttergren 2002, 24. The old Gotlandic games are sometimes discussed at length in the histories, for example, S. Jonsson et al. 1994, 166 ff.
[240] See Edquist 2009.
[241] Jameson 1991.
[242] For example, Walsh 1992; Samuel 1996; Samuel 2000; Lowenthal 1998.

The dominance of the Middle Ages is clearly visible in many contemporary works on Gotlandic history, for example those written for a national Swedish audience by the tourist or popular education agencies. Two of the three books issued by the Workers' Educational Association's (ABF) publishing company Brevskolan (later Bilda) are good examples. There, prehistoric times and Middle Ages are dealt with in great detail, while the centuries afterwards are very briefly described. Of course, these books have long thematic chapters that deal with contemporary Gotland, but more recent events are still treated as something else than *history*.[243]

There are also a great many books about Visby from the late twentieth and early twenty-first centuries, many of which have a tendency to stress the medieval period. However, there are some exceptions.[244]

The majority of researchers on Gotland have specialized in the prehistoric and medieval periods. Many archaeologists have continued to work on Gotland, engaging in debates on for example the meaning of the sheer number of silver hoards from the Viking Age, mainly filled with Arab coins.[245] In 2008 much of the Swedish National Heritage Board (Riksantikvarieämbetet) was moved from Stockholm to Gotland, a manoeuvre

---

[243] Bergqvist & Wennerdahl 1987, 42–3; Wennerdahl 2001, 72–83. Bergqvist & Wennerdahl 1987, 45; and Wennerdahl 2001, 79–80 have about only one page on the nineteenth century. Only in the latter work is there a specific chapter on the twentieth century (ibid. 80–83). The third book, Werkelin 1981, gives more space to later centuries, but, equally, the description of some events of the prehistoric and medieval periods are among the most traditional in modern Gotlandic history-writing. See also Bohman 1990, 187 who stressed that most general histories of Gotland had not covered the modern social and political history of the island—his own works did, however. He also noted that *Boken om Gotland* (1945) covered modern social and political history fairly well.

[244] Longer textbooks: Svahnström 1984; Yrwing 1986 (only the Middle Ages). Guidebooks that emphasize the old town: Falck 1991; Svensson 1998; see also Forsberg 1983 (based on a newspaper competition, with small details from around the old town—including from the twentieth century—for readers to explore and find). Coffee-table books: Mogren 1992 (amateur, mostly contemporary pictures); M. Jonsson 2000 (official). Mostly covering Visby of the nineteenth and twentieth centuries: Söderberg N. 1985; Falck 1988; Sjöstrand & Hallroth 1998. Confident 'amateur enthusiasts' (see below), often giving traditional accounts of the past: T. Gannholm 1994d; Wase 2005 (see ibid. 5 for his claims to be the leading expert on medieval Gotland following the death of Hugo Yrwing). Specifically on the city wall: Ludin 1980 (amateur guidebook); Erikson & Falck 1991; Falck 1994 (the two last the products of a campaign to ensure the preservation of the wall). For schools on Gotland: Bohman 1983. There are also more official, antiquarian accounts of Visby, with shorter sections that tell its history chronologically: *Visby: staden inom murarna* (1973); Engeström, Falck & Yrwing 1988.

[245] The interpretations are different. Frands Herschend (1979), for example, claimed that Gotland's silver hordes should not be interpreted as signs of war and unrest, but

for regional politics, but also because of Gotland's traditionally central role in the antiquarian discourse and praxis.

Of course, there are historians who have specialized in later periods of Gotland's history, and some of them have also written general Gotlandic history. Even so, the book *Gotlands historia i fickformat* (1987) by the historian Carl Johan Gardell, who wrote his doctoral dissertation about Gotland's seventeenth century, leans toward the medieval paradigm, at least in the chronological sense. Gardell's narrative is in all aspects modern and lacks all traces of historical romanticism, but the time frame is still concentrated on prehistoric and medieval times.

The origins of Gotland?

Towards the end of the twentieth century, the discourse about the Gutes, and other Scandinavians being Germanic peoples and/or Indo-Europeans who had migrated some time in the distant past has more or less vanished. An exception can be found in the first of ABF's three province books about Gotland, from 1981. It is the most striking example among latter-day popular province overviews that carry the older style of historiography into our days. The book mostly deals with present-day Gotland, with focus on politics, economics, and societal issues; however, in the middle section of the book there is a history chapter in which it is claimed that Goths immigrated to Gotland in the Migration Period (375–500). The reasoning is partly based on history-writing from the late nineteenth century:

> In the Germanic Migration Period, 375 to the sixth century AD, Goths 'for real' populated Gotland. From the Black Sea mainly Germanic peoples and Goths went north. The Germanic peoples halted at what is now Germany, while the Goths continued north to what is now Denmark, Sweden, and Norway (Gothenburg—the Goths' castle, Västergötland—the land of the West Goths, Östergötland—the land of the East Goths, Norway—the land of the North Goths). When the Germanic peoples turned away into Germany, a group of Goths headed out to an island in the Baltic Sea, which they made their own, the land of the Goths (Gotland).

rather that they had been means of exchange between Gotlanders, which could be a sign of a certain prosperity.

That the Gutes are a branch of the great Gothic tribe is shown among other things by the language of the Gutes, that is to say Old Gutnish, and their ancient habits, customs, and laws. Like the rest of the ancient Indo-Germanic tribe, the Goths who emigrated to Gotland worshipped fire and a number of Gutes who have been associated with fire. Even well into the nineteenth century, the belief existed that fire protects against witchcraft.[246]

You can trace the division between 'Goths' and 'Germanic peoples' in Snöbohm's *Gotlands land och folk* (1871), as well as the words about 'Indo-Germans' and their cult of fire. Werkelin also claimed that the Gutes immigrated from the south a couple of centuries BC. Perhaps that was an influence from Bergman's *Gotlands geografi och historia i lättfattligt sammandrag* (1870), where the Gutes are said to have come together with the Goths from the Black Sea—however, without dating the event. The argument also seems to have been inspired by the early twentieth-century academic discussions about various 'returns' of Germanic tribes to Scandinavia from the south during the Migration Period.[247]

Apart from this, the outright *ethnic* discourse of origin has vanished, but a more 'non-ethnic' discourse is prospering. Up to the present day, history-writers have tended almost unthinkingly to describe the population of Gotland in prehistoric times as 'Gotlandic', even if they have not entered into any speculation about their language or ethnic belongings. Throughout the twentieth century, it was considered perfectly normal and natural in this way to make 'Gotlanders' into something eternal, something that has existed for many thousands of years. From the very beginning of Gotland's history as a country inhabited by humans, there

---

[246] Werkelin 1981, 41 ('Under den germanska folkvandringstiden 375–500-talet e Kr befolkades Gotland "på allvar" av goter. Från Svarta Havet gick framför allt germaner och goter norrut. Germanerna stannade vid det som idag är Tyskland, medan goterna fortsatte norrut till det som idag är Danmark, Sverige och Norge (Göteborg - goternas borg, Västergötland - västergöternas land, Östergötland - östergöternas land, Norge - nordgöternas land). När germanerna avvek mot Tyskland begav sig en grupp goter ut till en ö i Östersjön som de gjorde till sin, till goternas land (Gotland). ... Att gutarna utgör en gren av den stora gotiska stammen visar bl a gutarnas språk, dvs forngutniskan, och deras urgamla bruk, sedvänjor och lagar. De till Gotland utvandrade goterna har, liksom den övriga indo-germanska urstammen, dyrkat elden och en rad gutar som har haft samband med elden. Ännu långt in på 1800-talet har tron funnits att eld skyddar för trolldom.')

[247] See, for example, Arne 1917, 35; Lindqvist 1922.

were also Gotlanders.[248] There are exceptions though—such as Gardell's *Gotlands historia i fickformat*, where Stone Age people are referred to as 'Gotlanders' in quote marks.[249]

The non-ethnic discourse about the origins of Gotland's inhabitants is flourishes just as much as the other origin discourse, about Gotland as a natural entity. It is regularly claimed that the island was formed when the rock solidified, for example that the fossils and *rauks* of Gotland are more than 400 million years old. Then, Gotland was reborn when the ice melted and the first rocks—'the highest parts of Lojsta'—stretched up above the water 11,500 years ago. It seems as if this discourse of natural geographies has become more common recently. Where it has become a bit controversial to talk about ancient ethnic or national continuity, it is still fully acceptable to highlight the continuity in nature itself. The function is the same: to create the notion of eternity for a specific territorial division, stressing its great age.[250]

The romance of Old Gotland

Academic research in history, archaeology, and the humanities has undergone a quite radical change in the last couple of decades. There has been a general shift towards using theories, often taken from the social sciences. There is a growing willingness to question and deconstruct the ways that research and academic historiography has nurtured ethnic and national identity projects. Many accepted truths have been attacked and deemed ideological anachronisms. That is also evident in the case of Gotland, especially when it comes to its much vaunted golden age in the prehistoric era and Middle Ages.

The traditional image of medieval Gotland as an egalitarian peasant republic still exists in the research community, but now rather as a minority position. The discourse that the Gotlanders were a 'free and independent' people with no royal power above them, and with relative equality, is to be found even among researchers in the late twentieth and

---

[248] For example, Stenberger 1945b, 47; Werkelin 1981, 41; Wennerdahl 2001, 24 ('gotlänningarna').
[249] Gardell 1987, 15 ('gotlänningar').
[250] Öhrman 1973, 4; Gardell 1987, 13 ff.; Öhrman 1994, 8 ff.; Arb 1981, 9 ff.; Bergqvist & Wennerdahl 1987, 10; Wennerdahl 2001, 9–15, 23–4, quote at 15 ('Lojstas högsta delar'). For the general tendency, see Edquist 2009.

early twenty-first centuries.[251] One can also discern it in other contexts, for example in the assumption that the Christianization of Gotland—as in Iceland—was accomplished through a 'common and democratic decision at the thing'.[252]

However, many professional historians and archaeologists have in recent decades directed devastating criticism against the old standpoints. When the professional archaeological review *Meta* devoted a special issue in 1990 to Gotland's Viking Age and the period immediately following, Anders Broberg pointed out that there were still large areas that were poorly studied, even though so much research had been produced about Gotland during those epochs. First and foremost, researchers had studied artefacts, monuments, and chronological problems, but had done little to analyse the character of society, the structure of settlements, and the conditions of production.[253] He claimed—tellingly—that the main question of debate, was now whether Gotland had been 'an egalitarian peasant republic' or 'a strongly socially differentiated society'.[254]

Anders Carlsson claimed that some researchers, for example his fellow archaeologist Gun Westholm, still seemed to presuppose that Gotland during the Viking Age had been a wealthy, peaceful, and independent peasant republic, with no magnates and little social antagonism. Westholm defended herself and struck back. She criticized Carlsson's view that there was a small elite of magnates ('*stormän*') on Gotland in the Viking Age, and branded his suggestions as 'mainland-based theses' that ignored local circumstances. There was no nobility, but instead a class of wealthier farmers who made collective decisions.[255]

The debate on the egalitarianism of old Gotland has also been visible among historians. The doctoral dissertations of Carl Johan Gardell and Jens Lerbom, who studied sixteenth- and seventeenth-century Gotland, were both attacked by historian and archivist Tryggve Siltberg. The latter

---

[251] Yrwing 1978, 89; Nylén 1979, 12; Östergren 1983, 37 ('fritt och självständigt'); Westholm 2007, 50 ff.
[252] Trotzig 1983, 393 ('gemensamt och demokratiskt tingsbeslut'). The similarites with Iceland had earlier been stressed in Schück 1940, 80.
[253] Broberg 1990, 2; see also Carlsson 1988, 7.
[254] Broberg 1990, 3 ('en egalitär bonderepublik', 'ett starkt socialt differentierat samhälle').
[255] Carlsson 1990, 5; Westholm 1990, 33–4, quote at 33 ('fastlandsbaserade teser'); see also, for more 'iconoclastic' arguments, Rönnby 1990, 40–1; Staecker 1996, 79–80 (but compare Nylén 1979, 12). See also Nylén 1992 who, like Westholm 1990, attacks overly mainland-based research, in this case Kyhlberg 1991.

defended the idea that the old Gotlandic peasant society had been relatively egalitarian, and that Gardell and Lerbom had been too radical in revising the picture. Gardell and Lerbom more or less openly identified Siltberg as a proponent of the traditional view. The former claimed that the meagreness of source material for Gotland's history before the seventeenth century had helped nourish the notion of the peasant republic.[256]

If we turn our eyes to the non-academic history-writing, the picture is a little different. Roger Öhrman stressed in *Vägen till Gotlands historia* (1994) that it was 'perhaps ... not entirely correct' to call Gotland a peasant republic, but still it mirrored society quite well. At the same time, he emphasized that medieval Gotland had large social differences between the classes.[257] In the schoolbook *Gotland förr och nu* (1996), Öhrman used the term 'peasant republic' as a name of the period—1050–1525.[258] The vision of a peasant republic is, thus, tenacious and recurs constantly in contemporary popular surveys, albeit with a standard reservation that Gotland nevertheless was a class society.[259]

One of the most traditional accounts can be found in the artist and writer Erik Olsson's *Gotland vår hembygd* (1985). He starts by claiming that 'our homestead and our history is our pride', and that the Gutes have been a free people, thanks to the sea that surrounds 'us'. *We* sent out Avair Strabain in the ninth century 'in democratic order' to get protection from Sweden, but we kept our independence, Olsson claims.[260]

Another standpoint that has been attacked by researchers is the one about Gotland and Visby as important centres of trade. No one claims that the island was unimportant, but the excesses are criticized. Hugo Yrwing in his book on Visby's medieval period from 1986 harshly critical towards those who said that Visby had been an international centre of trade—that was to exaggerate. He was especially critical of Gunnar

[256] Gardell 1986; Lerbom 2003; Siltberg 1989; Gardell 1989, esp. 387–8; Siltberg 1990; Siltberg 2006; Lerbom 2006; see also Siltberg 1993.
[257] Öhrman 1994, 72–3, quote at 72 ('kanske ... inte helt korrekt').
[258] Olsson & Öhrman 1996, 66–7 ('bonderepubliken'); see also Öhrman 1973, 15, where it is emphasized that Gotland continued to be a 'free and independent peasant republic' ('fri och självständig bonderepublik') after the treaty with the Swedes, ruled by the self-owning peasants with no interference from any king. In a similar vein, Funck et al. 1984, 14 write that the Gutes would not give up their 'ancient freedom and independence' ('urgamla frihet och självständighet').
[259] Wennerdahl 1985, 165; Bergqvist & Wennerdahl 1987, 39; Wennerdahl 2001, 7; S. Jonsson et al. 1994, 26 ff.; see also Arb 1981, 71.
[260] Erik Olsson 1985, 8 ff., quotes at 8 ('vår hembygd och historia är vår stolthet', 'oss', 'i demokratisk ordning').

Svahnström's recent book on Visby's history, whose medieval part he deemed was of almost no value.[261]

Recent popular history is not as explicit as before about Gotland's historical greatness as an international trade centre. However, there are clear reflections of the previous historiography. In Brevskolan's history books, it is said that the Gotlanders had extensive contacts in the Middle Ages, centring on trade. It is also stressed that the Gotlanders were a peaceful people during the Viking Age and the Middle Ages.[262] The dichotomy between peaceful Gutes and warlike Swedes has survived well into our time. Archaeologist Ingmar Jansson, for example, stressed the Gotlanders as peaceful on the basis that swords are not found in the graves after c.900.[263]

There were still tendencies to extend Gotland's position as a centre of trade far beyond the Viking Age. For example, it was argued that by the Middle Ages, the Gotlanders had already for more than a thousand years been engaged in transit trade.[264] Another history book, *Gotland – navet i havet* from 1994, boldly stated that the Gutes have been a 'travelling people' for *seven* thousand years. And during the Middle Ages—Gotland's golden age—the island was 'the hub of the sea'.[265]

More recent popular history-writing also tends to follow *Gutasaga* in its story about Gotland's voluntary treaty with the Swedish realm—even if the actual time of the event is placed differently.[266] Otherwise, the popular historiography of the late twentieth century is rather sceptical towards *Gutasaga* as a historical source. However, it is generally regarded as an important text that at least has the function of giving colour to the historiography.[267] Academic surveys such as Carl Johan Gardell's

---

[261] Fritzell 1972 is also mentioned as an example of that exaggeration; Yrwing (1986, 338–350, particularly 339, 350) also says that Svahnström leans toward Strelow.
[262] Bergqvist & Wennerdahl 1987, 28 ff., 32.
[263] Jansson 1983b, 242–3.
[264] Bergqvist & Wennerdahl 1987, 37.
[265] S. Jonsson et al. 1994, 14, 22–3, quotes at 14 ('resande folk') and 23 ('navet i havet'); see also Funck et al. 1984, 13 who stressed that Gotland was at 'the centre of world trade' ('i världshandelns centrum') a couple of centuries after the discovery of silver in Central Asia in c.700.
[266] Even same author can give more than one date for the treaty, from the eighth to the eleventh centuries. Hence Wennerdahl 1985, 29–30, 205; Bergqvist & Wennerdahl 1987, 31, 39; Wennerdahl 2001, 43–4 (see also Wennerdahl 1985, 124–5). See also Öhrman 1973, 15; Arb 1981, 68.
[267] See, for example, Wennerdahl 1985, 29–30, 153, 159, 165, 231–2; Wennerdahl 2001, 6; M. Jonsson 2000, 23. The status of *Gutasaga* is also obvious in newer schoolbooks,

Gotlands historia i fickformat start with *Gutasaga*. However, it is explained as a typical medieval origin story, and he describes how *Gutasaga* was used in the conflicts between Sweden and Denmark in the seventeenth century.[268]

Among academic researchers, it might be possible to discern a tendency in recent decades towards a growing recognition of—or wish to stress— Eastern influences in prehistoric and medieval Gotland.[269] While it was the rule before to stress how Swedes and Gotlanders more or less had colonized the East, it is now more a question of accentuating different forms of interaction and cultural blending. Common features between for example Gotland, Finland, and the present-day Baltic states are identified.[270]

Johan Callmer has stressed that the late Iron Age ethnic groups around the Baltic Sea were small but numerous—for example, there were a lot of them within the borders of what was to become Sweden. He has emphasized the Ålanders as a link between the Finnish and Scandinavian areas, in a network of connections that also included Gotland and the present-day Baltic republics.[271] Callmer claims that the contacts between Gotland and the eastern Baltic area had the paradoxical effect of rendering Gotlandic culture in part very strict and unwilling to be influenced by other cultures.[272]

Gotland often stands in the centre of the discussions about cultural contacts across the Baltic Sea. Ingmar Jansson has emphasized that Gotland at the same time had a very marked individuality, and very lively contacts with others, out of necessity. Even if Gotland shared most common traits with Scandinavia, the similarities between Gotland and the eastern Baltic areas were greater than those between Scandinavia and the

---

which are named after Þieluar (L. Olsson 2003a, 3, *passim*), or otherwise is constantly cited (Funck et al. 1984).

[268] B. Söderberg 1975, 8 ff.; Gardell 1987, 11–2.

[269] For Bulverket, see, for example, Bendegard 1983; Manneke 1983, 72.

[270] Thunmark-Nylén 1983a, for example, 182; Lehtosalo-Hylander 1983; Callmer 1992; Gustin 2004, 83–4; see also Bożena Wyszomirska in her review of Inger Österholm's dissertation *Bosättningsmönstret på Gotland under stenåldern* (1989) in *Fornvännen* 86 (1991), 129 where she calls for a greater emphasis on Gotland's Stone Age contacts in *all* directions, pointing out that, thanks to its position, Gotland had been open to cultural impulses in all eras. Gotlandic folk sagas, she notes, had many Danish, German, Baltic, and Russian equivalents, with no equivalents on the Swedish mainland.

[271] Callmer 1992; Callmer 1994; Callmer 2000; see also Gustin 2004, 62 ff.

[272] Callmer 1992, 104; Callmer 1994, 60.

eastern Baltic areas. That was the likely reason for Gotland to develop an extensive transit trade, probably long before the Viking Age.[273]

Few researchers in recent decades uphold Nerman's view that there was a proper Swedish and Gotlandic colonization of the eastern Baltic coast before the Viking Age.[274] Jansson is quite cautious: at most, there was some Gotlandic emigration to the east, for example to Grobiņa.[275] Others have been more critical. In the 1980s, Anders Carlsson claimed that until further notice one had to give up the idea of Gotlandic colonies at Grobiņa and Elbląg. Objects that looked Gotlandic, could instead be interpreted as the native population had bought or in other ways obtaining objects with a Gotlandic provenance or just a Gotlandic style.[276] Another alternative has been to stress the mixture itself at Grobiņa and similar places between 'Baltic, mainland Swedish, and Gotlandic'.[277]

More recent works of popular history are generally silent on the alleged Gotlandic migration to the eastern Baltic coast during the seventh and eighth centuries, although it is usually mentioned more in passing as a historical fact, that Gotlandic merchants made their homes there.[278]

In the recent decades, it is only in popular historical overviews that we can find the remaining traces of Birger Nerman's theories of migration in the Migration Period, leaning on *Gutasaga*. An example is Stig Jonsson's *Gotland – navet i havet*, with the story of the Swedish-speaking inhabitants of the Ukrainian village Gammalsvenskby, who had come from Dagö in the late eighteenth century, but who were given the chance to move to Sweden in 1929. The majority of them settled on Gotland, and Jonsson interpreted this as their return to Gotland; the 'ring was closed', since the Dagö Swedes originally were supposed to have emigrated from Gotland in the Iron Age.[279]

---

[273] Jansson 1983b, 207–208, 227 ff.
[274] Edquist 2012, 95–6.
[275] Jansson 1983b, 216 ff. Jansson (1992b, 62, 74 ff) wrote of a probable Scandinavian population around Grobiņa, while at the same time being critical of Nerman; see also Jansson 1992a, 74; Thunmark-Nylén 1983b.
[276] Carlsson 1983b, 194; see also Gustin 2004, 60; Carlsson 1983a. Stalsberg 1979, 157–8 also pointed out that very few Gotlanders seem to have travelled east.
[277] Gustin 2004, 83–4, quote at 83 ('baltiskt, fastlandssvenskt och gotländskt').
[278] Arb 1981, 69; Bergqvist & Wennerdahl 1987, 28; Wennerdahl 2001, 41–2; see also Wase 2005, 7.
[279] S. Jonsson et al. 1994, 14–15, 89 ff., quote at 91 ('slöts ringen'); see also Fries 1964, 193 ff. who, without mentioning Nerman, agrees with his hypothesis of emigration via Torsburgen.

In the second half of the twentieth century, some researchers have gone further than the previously mentioned discourse on Eastern cultural influences in the question of the medieval Gotlandic churches. They have also raised the question of whether present-day Sweden—and especially Gotland—was Christianized from the east. Late in his career Ture J. Arne was one of them, and in our time for example the art historian Erland Lagerlöf (b. 1928) has emphasized the eastern–Orthodox hypothesis. However, many researchers tend to stress that we know nothing for certain about any Eastern church missions to Sweden and Gotland. Especially in the case of Gotland, the religious transition seems very obscure, and some researchers claim that the process might have lasted almost into the thirteenth century.[280]

However, there is a striking absence of these newer theories in the popular press, in which the explanation mainly refers to the story of Olaf Haraldsson in *Gutasaga*—no matter whether it is taken to be true or not.[281] However, sometimes it is stressed that the Gutnish Vikings must have met Christianity during their trade expeditions 'in the South-East'—obviously meaning the Byzantine Empire, or later Russia.[282]

It is in popular history-writing that we still find the traditional tragic dramaturgy of Gotland's fall from glory to decline and turmoil in the late Middle Ages.[283] The internal conflict of 1288 is generally blamed on the city of Visby, but especially on foreign influences: the Germans and the Hanseatic League. They had increased their influence in the city, thanks to 'good organizational skills and German thoroughness', and then tried to diminish the power of the Gotlandic countryside. For example, in *Gotland—navet i havet* (1994), the Germans' influence in Visby was labelled a cuckoo in the nest. The main winner was the Swedish king.[284]

The events of 1288 were the first 'outburst of unrest and war', beginning an age of 'disasters and decline', Maj Wennerdahl claims. It signalled

---

[280] Lagerlöf 1999, 16–21, 26–37; see also Janson 2005. For criticism of the Eastern theories, see, for example, Trotzig 1983, 386, 388; see also Yrwing 1978, 150. For other discussions on Gotland's Christianization, see, for example, Thunmark-Nylén 1989a; Thunmark-Nylén 1989b; Carlsson 1990; Wase 1995. See also Edquist 2012, 112 ff.
[281] Bergqvist & Wennerdahl 1987, 34 ff.; S. Jonsson et al. 1994, 30 ff. See also Arb 1981, 68; Werkelin 1981, 85.
[282] Öhrman 1973, 14–15, quote at 15 ('i sydost').
[283] Arb 1981, 72–8.
[284] S. Jonsson et al. 1994, 45, 49, 54–5, quote at 49 ('god organisationsförmåga och tysk grundlighet'). Nylén 1979, 12 describes Visby as 'cuckoo in the Gotlandic nest' ('gökunge i det gotländska boet').

the 'final divorce between city and countryside', even though 'the peasant republic' still would have 80 years left of 'peaceful activities', still visible in the most glorious epoch of church constructions.[285] Öhrman stressed that the civil war in 1288 was an unhappy event that left seared the 'Gotlandic people's soul' for centuries to come.[286] It was also the beginning of more sinister times. The plague came in 1350, being one of two disasters, the other happening in 1361.[287]

The events of 1361 were, according to Stig Arb (1981), 'touching evidence of the willingness of the peasant state to defend itself'.[288] Öhrman tells the story at length, first the legends,[289] then the historical sources, concluding that we 'probably' can count the following as a historical truth: 'Visby's shameful capitulation'.[290] Erik Olsson boldly complains that the ransom of Visby has attracted more attention than the Gutes' loss of life.[291] Other accounts—though less condemning in words—still give a lot of space to events, describing the brutality in detail.[292] That can be contrasted to Hugo Yrwing's major book from 1986 on Visby's Middle Ages. In that dry and academic account, the events of 1361 were depicted as only a few among a vast number of links in the historical chain.[293]

1361 more than ever lives on as the symbol of Gotland's Middle Ages, and it is no coincidence that the Medieval Week in Visby has that year as the focal point. Archaeologist and Gotlands fornsal employee Gun

---

[285] Bergqvist & Wennerdahl 1999, 39; Wennerdahl 2001, 66 ('utbrottet av oro och krig', 'katastrofer och tillbakagång', 'slutgiltiga skilsmässan mellan stad och land på Gotland', 'bonderepubliken', 'fredlig verksamhet'); similarly, Bergqvist & Wennerdahl 1987, 39–40.

[286] Öhrman 1994, 114 ff., quote at 115 ('den gotländska folksjälen'); see also L. Olsson 2003a, 262–3.

[287] Öhrman 1973, 19; Öhrman 1994, 116.

[288] Arb 1981, 77 ('gripande bevis för bondestatens försvarsvilja').

[289] Öhrman 1994, 120 ff.

[290] Öhrman 1994, 122 ff., quote at 123 ('nog', 'Visbys gentemot landsbygden skamliga kapitulation'); see also Öhrman 1973, 19 where Visby's citizens 'are said to have' ('lär ... ha') stood on the city walls, doing nothing, and 'The city–country rivalry was still strongly felt!' ('Rivaliteten stad–land kändes ännu stark!'); similarly Funck et al. 1984, 20; Olsson & Öhrman 1996, 75; see also Nylén 1979, 12.

[291] Erik Olsson 1985, 20–1.

[292] For example, Svensson 1998, 153 ff.

[293] Yrwing 1986, 157. Still, he called the Victual Brothers *pirates* ('sjörövare', 177), and concerning the split between Visby and the rest of Gotland, he claimed that the Visby Germans had got what they wanted (115). His book was marketed as covering the previously overlooked history of Visby after 1361 until the 1530s (Yrwing 1986, back blurb).

Westholm wrote a book about the events in 1361, also describing the aftermath with Gotland declining into poverty.²⁹⁴

The latter is also a continuing theme in the history-writing: in the fourteenth century, a pretty miserable period began; the economy went downhill, and the island occasionally functioned as a pirate nest for more than a hundred years after the disasters of the fourteenth century.²⁹⁵ The complexity of the time after 1361 is generally emphasized, not least that there were a lot of pirates. The chapter in Roger Öhrman's *Vägen till Gotlands historia* (1994) is typically called 'privateers and pirate castles', with accounts of the tumultuous period of the Victual Brothers, the reign of Erik of Pomerania, and so on. He, like previous history writers, pointed out the good exceptions, not least the reign of the Teutonic Knights, over whose departure in 1408 the Gotlanders were said to have felt sorry.²⁹⁶

Modern histories of modern Gotland

In newer popular history-writing, the period following 1645 is usually described in roughly the same ways as before. It is claimed that the Gotlanders themselves did not care for their new masters—they had grown used to being part of Denmark.²⁹⁷ It is also stressed that Swedish officials were not very interested in Gotland; for example it is sometimes mentioned that no Swedish king visited the island before 1854.²⁹⁸

In Roger Öhrman's *Vägen till Gotlands historia* (1994), there is much more space for the latest centuries—even for the period after 1945, with topics such as the development in schools, local politics, demographics, and administrative divisions.²⁹⁹ However, even there many of the elements are roughly the same 'as usual': popular topics such as sandstone mining³⁰⁰ and the lime industry³⁰¹ are covered in detail. There is also a short description of the Russian occupation in 1808, told as something hilarious rather than dangerous.³⁰²

---

[294] Westholm 2007.
[295] Dahlberg 1992, 82–3.
[296] Öhrman 1994, 128, 130–1, quote at 128 ('Kapare och sjörövarborgar'); see also S. Jonsson et al. 1994, 66; Wennerdahl 2001, 68–9.
[297] S. Jonsson et al. 1994, 66–7; Öhrman 1994, 150. See, for example, Wennerdahl 1985, 177 for a typical account of Jacob Dubbe.
[298] S. Jonsson et al. 1994, 86–7.
[299] Öhrman 1994, 254–63.
[300] Öhrman 1994, 143–5.
[301] Öhrman 1994, 155–60.
[302] Öhrman 1994, 185–87.

Modern history books regularly deal with transportation between Gotland and the Swedish mainland—first with the risky mail boats long into the nineteenth century, and the introduction of the regular steamboat traffic in the 1850s and 1860s.[303] Still today, the ferry transportation is a much-discussed topic, being a constant source of discontent.[304]

The big hero of earlier Gotlandic historiography, the late eighteenth-century governor Segebaden, is nowadays seldom viewed in the same way as before. But when he is mentioned, remnants of earlier discourses are visible. He often rates a brief mention as someone industrious who wanted to develop the island.[305] It is also said that the Gotlandic farmers only afterwards 'realized the value of all these proposals'.[306]

However, the main bulk of history-writing on the modern period in Gotland is not presented in general Gotland books, but mostly in specialized works about various aspects of its history, specific places, parishes, people, or industries, as we shall see in the section 'The third narrative'. The history of Gotland's popular movements, for example, is regularly downplayed in the general books.[307]

Amateur enthusiasts, enthusiastic amateurs

A category of its own might be called the amateur enthusiasts: amateur historians with often far-reaching interpretations of history. In the late twentieth century they have been more visible, thanks to the general diversification of history culture and the quantitative growth of history production overall. What I mean by this category are not the 'ordinary' local historians, but the kind of history writers who display a sharp antagonism against 'established' history-writing. Their aim is to finally present the hidden, suppressed account of the past that the dominant historiography

---

[303] From 1858, there was regular boat traffic even in winter, while the still dominant shipping company Gotlandsbolaget was founded in 1865 (Gerentz 1945, 418–19; Gardell 1987, 132; Öhrman 1994, 209–210).

[304] S. Jonsson et al. 1994, 96–101 (with a distinct pro-Gotlandic flavour, pointing to uncompetitive pricing and poor timetables).

[305] Bergqvist & Wennerdahl 1987, 43; S. Jonsson et al. 1994, 45; Wennerdahl 2001, 74.

[306] Öhrman 1994, 171 ('insåg värdet av alla dessa förslag'), in a short section (169–71) on 'powerful governors' ('kraftfulla landshövdingar'), but much like Dennert he seemed to downplay Segebaden. (In Öhrman 1973, 23 ff., an account of Gotland after 1645, Segebaden is not mentioned at all.)

[307] See, however, Öhrman 1994, 218–22; and earlier, in a book about Visby published by a mainland publisher, V. Johansson 1950, 100–107.

has tried to conceal. They are often driven by a strong regionalist sentiment, and the enemy is centralist, Swedish historiography.

Sometimes the antagonism is subtle, as with the Visby physician Folke Ludin, who has written a couple of guidebooks. One of them is about the city wall of Visby; he stresses that he, like ordinary townspeople, chooses to call it a *ringmur* (lit. 'ring wall') unlike the *experts* who call it a *stadsmur* ('city wall').[308]

Contrary to the common form of amateur history, which mostly deals with local history and particular objects, normally in fairly contemporary history, these historiographers take on old and classic topics in history. In Sweden, this kind of history-writing is best known in the province of Västergötland, where a group of amateur historians have claimed that the origins of the Swedish nation in fact were situated there, not in the Mälaren valley in the vicinity of Stockholm and Uppsala.[309]

But there are also examples on Gotland. The most outspoken of the Gotlandic amateur enthusiasts today is Tore Gannholm (b. 1940), who is noted for his radically regional patriotic historiography, emphasizing the independence and glory of Gotland through the ages—especially in older times. His father Karl Erland Gannholm had similar interests and engaged himself in the debate on so-called grooves (*slipskåror* or *sliprännor*).[310] In that debate, some amateur historians have adopted a harsh tone towards the academic experts, who are described as too learned to have any common sense.[311]

Tore Gannholm has cast his net wider than his father, and has dealt with almost every aspect of Gotland's early history. He has studied the prehistoric political frictions between Gotlanders and Swedes, written in a spirit reminiscent of the nationalist archaeologists such as Birger Nerman during the first half of the twentieth century. Gannholm's magnum opus is a general Gotlandic history, which was first published in 1990 with the title 'History of the Gutes', and in an enlarged version in 1994 named 'Gotland – The Pearl of the Baltic Sea'. For Gannholm,

---

[308] Ludin 1980, 11.
[309] Janson 1999.
[310] K. Gannholm 1974; K. Gannholm 1987; see also T. Gannholm 1994d, 30 who presents as fact that the grooves were 'astronomical calendars' ('de astronomiska kalendrarna'), the oldest dating back to 3200 BC.
[311] Larsson et al. 1986.

Gotland's history really ended when the island was finally 'annexed' by Sweden in 1679.[312]

Gannholm states that since he is a 'consultant in problem solving', he knows how to 'distinguish what is related and essential' in a historical material, and he emphasizes that he is an 'old Gute with my roots deep down in the story told'.[313] In 1992, he published the Old English epic *Beowulf*, with the subtitle 'the national epic of the Gutes'.[314] The *geatas* of Beowulf have generally been interpreted as either Jutes (*jutar* from Jutland in Denmark) or Geats (*götar* from southern Scandinavia), but Gannholm was certain that they in fact were—Gutes. He also claimed that Avair Strabain probably was identical with the epic's hero, Beowulf. Thus, the treaty with the Swedes had taken place in the sixth century.[315] Gannholm has characterized the entire period from 1000 BC to AD 1300 in the following way: 'The Gutes dominate trade in the Baltic Sea and seems at times to have a monopoly on this. Gotland is the centre of the Baltic culture.'[316]

In shorter pamphlets, he has also covered the history of Visby, the origins of the Swedes (originally Heruls, who immigrated to Scandinavia in the sixth century), and the Baltic trade and the Hanseatic League in the fourteenth century.[317] As for Visby, Gannholm emphasized—following Strelow—that the city was founded in 897, and is thus the oldest city in the Baltic area. It was also an important centre long before the Germans arrived in the twelfth century and took over. He also claims that Visby merchants formed the nucleus when Stockholm was founded in 1252.[318]

Gannholm's history-writing is well known on Gotland, but it has been somewhat marginal, as a kind of curiosity. It has not influenced the dominant history-writing on the island, for example the one displayed in other authors' works or in the activities of Gotlands fornsal.

---

[312] T. Gannholm 1990, 170; T. Gannholm 1994a, 217, back cover ('annekterade').
[313] T. Gannholm 1994a, 11 ('konsult i problemlösning', 'urskilja vad som är relaterat och väsentligt', 'urgute med mina rötter djupt ner i den historia som berättas').
[314] T. Gannholm 1992.
[315] T. Gannholm 1994a, 74-88, 92 ff.; T. Gannholm 1994d, 30.
[316] T. Gannholm 1994d, 30 ('Gutarna dominerar handeln i Östersjön och tycks tidvis ha monopol på denna. Gotland centrum för Östersjökulturen'). Just like Mårten Stenberger, Gannholm claimed that there were three different ages of greatness in Gotland's history: 1000–500 BC, 100 BC–AD 500, and AD 600–AD 1300 (T. Gannholm 1990, back cover).
[317] T. Gannholm 1994d; T. Gannholm 1991 (enlarged version T. Gannholm 1994c); T. Gannholm 1994b.
[318] T. Gannholm 1994d, 1, 3, 5, 9, 12 ff.

The two dominant narratives

At the turn of the millennium, there were still two dominant narratives on Gotland: the medieval one and the folklore one. The relationship between them is not easily summarized; sometimes they are entangled, in other instances, contradict one another.

An example of the former is the handbook and history guide *Vägen till kulturen på Gotland* (1987 and several further editions), issued by Gotlands fornsal. It tries to address a wide range of historical phenomena, from prehistoric remains to modern villages developed around railway stations. In the book, emphasis is laid on peasant society in history, such as remnants of old farms. The emphasis, however, is limited to the Iron Age and the Middle Ages. It is stressed that Gotland has a particularly well-preserved cultural landscape for favourable historical reasons in relation to the rest of Sweden. These reasons, though, are of a socioeconomic nature: sparse population and large urban continuity, lower population growth, the opportunity to cultivate the bogs instead of meadows, and so on. The explanation does not link Gotland's peculiarities to 'ethnic' reasons, such as a specific historical consciousness or the piety of the Gotlandic people. There is no historical romanticism of the traditional kind, but instead a mainstream, modern heritage ideology: it is considered important to preserve the island's historic remains, and it is stated that currently many good efforts are being made in this direction.[319]

The tourist guidebooks are regularly filled with a similar sort of condensed version of the island's past, containing both the medieval and folklore narratives. A mainstream history is transmitted, with all the standard topics: the city walls of Visby, the large number of medieval churches, fishing villages, limekilns, medieval *and* eighteenth-century stone houses, Iron Age sites, and so on.[320] A similar mix is reproduced in schoolbooks, where old games and the old dialect *Gutamål* is presented for children, along with essays on Gotlandic nature, limestone, and industry, Visby as a UNESCO World Heritage Site, and the like.[321] The same can be said about Roger Öhrman's voluminous history of Gotland from 1994. Even if the Middle Ages took up relatively few pages compared to many other Gotland books, he still gave a lot of space to classic themes

---

[319] Jonsson & Lindquist (1987) 2002.
[320] *Se Gotland* (2006).
[321] L. Olsson 2003a.

such as medieval Visby and the rural churches. Thus, the two narratives were intertwined somewhat.

This is also the case in the later versions of 'saga' books, such as Söderberg's *Gotlands sällsamheter* and Wennerdahl's *Sällsamheter på Gotland*. There is no chronological disposition; instead there is a geographical one. The reader is taken on a journey through the parishes of Gotland, and presented with legends and histories from all ages—from the Stone Age to the twentieth century. However, the bulk of the stories are from later centuries, about villains, robbers, ghosts, and legendary personalities. We are also told about Segebaden, Søren Norby, and the Gotska Sandön robber Gottberg.[322] There is also a predilection for disasters, such as the catastrophe of the Danish–Lübeckian navy in 1566, or the details of an infamous mailboat crossing in the winter of 1830.[323]

Wennerdahl's *Sällsamheter på Gotland* (1985) was released by the same publisher as Söderberg's decade old *Gotlands sällsamheter*. However, it was even more modern, with a greater focus on for example twentieth-century writers, such as the poet Gustaf Larsson.[324] She also dwelt on the history of Gotland's popular movements, popular education, railways, and suchlike.[325]

Another typical example of the mixture of medieval and folklorist narratives is *Gotland vår hembygd* (1985) by the artist and writer Erik Olsson. The paintings and texts in the book deal with the fishing villages and life at sea, along with pictures of peasant culture from the past centuries. The beginning of the book deals with medieval Gotland, Avair Strabain, the battles in 1361, and the old churches in a starkly regionally patriotic way. However, there is no trace of the real, modern Gotland, not a word about industrialization or contemporary life.[326]

Carina Johansson notes that the stereotypical images seem to have been strengthened in the representations of Gotland. For example, in the mid twentieth century, windmills were often depicted as typical for the

---

[322] B. Söderberg 1975, 42 ff., 115–16, 191–2, 200 ff., the last a thieves' on Stora Karlsö, earlier described in Säve 1979b (1873), 177–8.
[323] B. Söderberg 1975, 51 ff., 204–205.
[324] Wennerdahl 1985, 22–3, 31 ff., 127 ff., 139 ff. The twentieth-century authors are frequently treated at length as regional heroes of sorts (Bergqvist & Wennerdahl 1987, 109 ff.; Wennerdahl 2001, 131 ff).
[325] Wennerdahl 1985, 28–9, 33 ff., 180 ff.
[326] Erik Olsson 1985; see also Erik Olsson 1990, a cheerfully burlesque collection of modern legends and tall tales of interesting people and events.

Gotland countryside; now, however, windmills are limited to Öland, and are seldom seen in Gotland narratives.[327]

There are many signs that medieval Gotland and Visby have been further strengthened as symbols of Gotland's past in recent decades, with the rise of cultural tourism that is profiting by the stereotypes—the history that is already well known. So, in a society where the historiography is democratized and made more heterogeneous, there is a simultaneous opposite trend: using history to brand and exploit traditional identity projects.[328] In Visby, the Middle Ages have gained grounds in the last decades. In 1984, the Medieval Week (*Medeltidsveckan*) was launched in Visby which eventually extended to the whole island.[329] A decade later, there was rapid and successful application to make the historical centre of Visby a UNESCO World Heritage Site. A small group in the heritage bureaucracy at the municipal and county level managed to obtain official protection for a variety of medieval buildings in Visby. Owe Ronström states that this has resulted in a sort of theme town, one of many different but still streamlined heritage sites that follow a fixed template. In 'medieval' Visby, diversity and dissonance are vanishing.[330]

As is often the case nowadays, official heritage and history policies are openly pursued as cooperative projects between state and municipal agents, museums, corporate interests, and local heritage associations, with the common denominator being the ambition to attract even more tourists and investors to the island.[331] Gotland is no exception to the prevailing ideals, according to which heritage and cultural identity are important for a region's economic prosperity.[332] In a document listing the 'strategies' for 'Gotlandic Heritage' for the period 2004–2008, issued by a project group appointed by the municipality, county, Gotlands fornsal, and Gotlands hembygdsförbund (Gotland Heritage Association), it was emphasized that contemporary heritage work (*kulturarvsarbete*) should focus on areas, not objects, and that heritage should be a development resource. Heritage was claimed to be a positive factor for the well-being of the residents, as well as

---

[327] C. Johansson 2006, 53.
[328] Edquist 2009, 310–1.
[329] Gustafsson 2002a; Sandström 2005.
[330] Ronström 2008; see also Gustafsson 2002b; C. Johansson 2009.
[331] Oscarsson 2006. A number of recent heritage projects, mostly in the countryside, have been covered in Johansson et al. 2000
[332] Syssner 2006, 111–20; L. Larsson 2002, 25, ch. 5; Edquist 2009, 318–27.

attracting new islanders and investors.[333] The document mentioned various examples of Gotlandic heritage worthwhile using in this work—a good example of the amalgamation of the two dominant narratives: the medieval churches, the Gutamål dialect, the folk games, collections of people's memories, photographs, and objects, animal breeds and plants specific to the island, the World Heritage Site of Visby, and the cultural landscape with old farms, fishing villages, and prehistoric relics.

Branding is also important in these matters. Gotland in 2008 was officially branded 'the magical island' in a document drawn up by a group made up of representatives from the municipality, enterprise, cultural associations, and Gotland University. It was considered important to widen the image of the island—no longer should Gotland be an island only symbolizing summer and holidays. But what about Gotland's past— was there any ambition to use that in any other way than before? Hardly. The extremely vague document—typical for branding strategies—only notes that 'heritage' and 'world heritage' are among Gotland's positive assets. There is no mentioning of a wider conception of what Gotland in fact means when it comes to history.[334]

But there are also conflicts today between the medieval and folklore narratives. In contemporary heritage matters, some observers have noted a conflict between the city (Visby) and the Gotlandic countryside.[335] Carina Johansson cites complaints that the island's medieval heritage, centred in Visby, is being strengthened at the expense of its folkloric heritage. Staff at the open-air museum at Bunge claim that fewer tourists visit their museum. As of 1980s it is no longer the case every Gotlandic schoolchild gets to visit the museum. They feel that the concentration on Visby, utilizing its new status as a World Heritage Site, has put the countryside in the shadow.[336]

There are also many voices from the countryside, or claiming to be speaking for the countryside, that criticize the Medieval Week in similar words. They say that it is primarily something for educated people in Visby, many of whom are also mainlanders in origin. The artist Erik Olsson has been outspoken about the fact that the tragedy of 1361 was

---

[333] *Det Gotländska Kulturarvet, strategier 2004–2008* (2004), 2, 6.
[334] *Vision och varumärkesplattform för Gotland – den magiska ön* (2008).
[335] Kriström 2000, 83.
[336] C. Johansson 2000b, 38, 40.

celebrated—he wondered if that would have happened in the case of Pearl Harbor.[337]

The events of 1361 are still vivid to the Gotlandic population, Lotten Gustafsson notes—perhaps because of the very stark reminders in Gotlands fornsal of fallen peasant soldiers, and thanks to the popular legends. It is therefore not surprising that 1361 was chosen to be the year reenacted in Medieval Week, since it is possible to use different angles and perspective in the story, with different actors in focus, and different endings.[338] In comparison with the painting of Carl Gustaf Hellqvist, nowadays the open nationalism and blind faith in the past is missing.[339]

However, Medieval Week as an event means that the greatness of medieval Gotland and Visby is pronounced. Gustafsson connects that with a generally growing appreciation of the Middle Ages. That period is no longer the Dark Age, but instead an epoch of light, culture, and international trade. The cult of the Middle Ages is sometimes associated with the dominant EU ideology of regionalism and supranationalism. There, the Middle Ages are seen as an epoch, before the nation-states came into existence, when trade connected different regions rather than states.[340]

The Germans and the Hanseatic League have traditionally been seen as 'the bad guys' of Gotland, even if the spectacular riches of Visby were a result. Due to late twentieth-century European integration efforts, there have been projects to revive the idea of the Hanseatic League and similar aspects of medieval history. That could also be used as a new trademark for Visby and Gotland. Those ideas are also prominent in ideas such as those behind the (new) Hanse, a network founded in Zwolle in 1980, with 176 member cities and towns.[341] It has revived the idea of 'Hanseatic days', with one held in Visby in 1998. A little earlier, Visby took the slogan the 'Hanseatic town of Visby' (Hansestaden Visby). Another Hanseatic Day is already scheduled for Visby for 2025.[342]

---

[337] Gustafsson 2002a, 119 ff.
[338] Gustafsson 1998; Gustafsson 2002a, 99–129.
[339] Gustafsson 2002a, 106.
[340] This kind of rhetoric is also seen among participants in Medieval Week; C. Johansson 2000c, 96.
[341] Gustafsson 2002b, 39 ff.; <www.hanse.org>.
[342] <http://www.hanse.org/en>, s.v. '2025'.

The Baltic Sea perspective

In the 1990s, there was also greater interest in the Baltic connections, for example leading to various kinds of cooperation between Gotland and the Baltic republics. Gotland was at this time often referred to as 'the hub of the sea' (*navet i havet*)—a slogan repeated in the book by Stig Jonsson, published in 1994.[343]

That development was of course a result of the fall of the Berlin Wall. After that, the Baltic Sea region could now be seen as an integral whole, which united more than it separated. The B7 Baltic Islands Network was founded in 1989 as an organization for cooperation between the seven largest islands in the Baltic Sea: Åland, Saaremaa, Hiiumaa, Gotland, Öland, Bornholm, and Rügen. The organization has mainly dealt with issues of political and economic issues, striving for common strategies across the political divisions.[344]

That ambition was also visible in the history writing, and the number of books with a truly Baltic perspective has increased. Before, there were only occasional initiatives. During the inter-war period, the local amateur historian Per Josef Enström wrote *Östersjön: strövtåg och drömmar i hansestäder och andra gamla städer* (1929), with essays about places around the Baltic Sea—Gotland, Germany, and the Baltic republics. There has also been a more Swedish Baltic Sea perspective, when Öland and Gotland are mentioned in the same breath, as is evident in books such as Carl Fries's *De stora öarna i Östersjön* (1964).[345]

Then at the end of the 1980s, the Nordic Institute on Åland—a cultural institution subject to the Nordic Council of Ministers—took the initiative by commissioning a common history for the Baltic Sea islands, just at the time when the islands were seeking closer cooperation in trade and tourism. The Danish teacher, novelist, and schoolbook author Søren Sørensen (b. 1937) was recruited to write the general history book *Öarna i Östersjön – förr och nu* about six Baltic Sea islands—Åland, Saaremaa, Hiiumaa, Gotland, Öland, and Bornholm (not Rügen, though). The book had a cross-Baltic editorial committee, with Gotland being represented by the head of Gotlands fornsal, Sven-Olof Lindquist.[346]

---

[343] Gustafsson 2002a, 127 ff.; S. Jonsson et al. 1994.
[344] <www.b7.org>.
[345] Enström 1929; Enström 1967; Fries 1964.
[346] Sørensen 1992, 4.

Öarna i Östersjön – förr och nu deals with the islands' history from the beginning to the present age. The main difference from regular history books is that the islands are discussed as a group, albeit 'one by one' when necessary. The similarities between the islands are underlined, for example concerning nature itself and how it has affected human society in the Baltic region.[347] Naturally, though, since the book relies on existing books and research, traditional topics in historiography reoccur. For example, where Gotland is concerned, Mårten Stenberger is quoted as claiming that Gotland had a 'second age of greatness' around the birth of Christ, when 'the Gutes founded colonies in East Prussia and Courland'.[348] In the early 1990s there was also a schoolbook issued in Sweden with a focus on the history of the Baltic Sea, which was quite unique.[349] Still, these efforts from the leading political and heritage institutions on the major Baltic Sea islands in the early 1990s were really an elite project. It found few counterparts in the more popular history-writing, which mainly takes a local perspective, and, where not, it looks towards the Swedish mainland.[350] From Gotland's horizon, when you look across the sea you generally look towards mainland Sweden, the place with which Gotlanders have so many more contacts and relations than with other countries. Contacts with other parts of the Baltic area are limited. At the time of writing, there is for example no regular ferry service between Gotland and other countries.

Which mainland?

Thus, a dominant trait in Gotland's history-writing is that Gotland is primarily viewed relative to the rest of Sweden. When one talks about 'the mainland' (*fastlandet*), it goes without saying that it is the rest of Sweden that is intended—never, for example Latvia, 150 km away and closer than Stockholm. Of course it is natural enough for the epochs when Gotland actually did belong to Sweden, but more questionable when writing about pre-Christian times, let alone the period 1361–1645.

---

[347] For example, Sørensen 1992, 9–30 for brief discussions of the limestone industry and stone as building material for houses.
[348] Sørensen 1992, 36, 40 ('andra storhetstid', 'gutarna grundar kolonier i Ostpreussen och Kurland').
[349] Dahlberg 1992.
[350] See, for example, Erik Olsson 1983, a book on Gotland's ships and harbours from the Viking Age to the present, which stresses Gotland's position in the middle of the Baltic Sea. That said, the focus is wholly on Gotland—the Baltic Sea is only something that happens to surround the island.

A similar recurring tendency in the descriptions of Gotland is to emphasize its peculiar character, making it unique in a Swedish setting. That is also evident when the island is viewed from a mainland perspective. Stig Arb's *Gotland* (1981) is one of many books written by mainlanders who regularly visit Gotland, he being a typical 'summer Gotlander'. Arb begins his book by stressing 'the un-Swedishness of the landscape' that clearly emerges as 'we spot the Visby Coast from the ferry'.[351] In a similar manner, Carl Fries's *De stora öarna i Östersjön* begins by considering the contrasts between the coastlines of the mainland and of Gotland: low-lying rocks versus steep limestone cliffs.[352]

We have seen that history-writing has tended to emphasize that Gotland was more or less independent during the Middle Ages. That independence was especially viewed in relation to mainland Sweden. However, after Gotland's 'dark' period from 1361 to 1645, the island returned to Sweden, a point at which, few history writers stress Gotland's independence in matters that really count—only the cultural peculiarities are allowed to prosper. The story of Segebaden, the late eighteenth-century governor who introduced a great many modern habits and technologies, stands out: Gotland was a weak province that could not do well on its own. The Gotlandic independence was after all a thing of the past.

For pioneers such as Säve, the Swedish connection was not at all a problem. And in the more recent histories of Gotland, modernity was in fact introduced from the mainland. Säve quoted Segebaden—*the* modern hero of Gotland's history, who had hoped that it would turn into a rich and prosperous province of great importance *for the entire Swedish fatherland*.[353] For Erlandsson too, Segebaden was the person who finally remade Gotland as a developing province, and even if the first part of the Swedish rule after 1645 had been quite bad, in the present Gotland was firmly attached to Sweden, 'our new but still original fatherland'.[354]

There is almost a kind of colonial discourse that can be paralleled with classical Western descriptions of the 'Orient'. It had its golden age in the Middle Ages, when it was equal to or even superior to the West. However, afterwards the East went into decline, and for later periods the roles were switched. Then, the West could be the benevolent teacher of the East. In

---

[351] Arb 1981, 9 ('det osvenska i landskapet', 'vi från färjan siktar Visbykusten').
[352] Fries 1964, 11 ff.
[353] Säve 1980 (1876), 214.
[354] Erlandsson 1900, 40 ('vårt nya och dock ursprungliga fädernesland').

the same manner, development and civilization in the eighteenth and nineteenth centuries had to come from the 'West' in the case of Gotland, from enlightened mainland government officials.

Metahistory, or the history of Gotland's history

Finally, there is growing interest in Gotland's history-writing as a form of cultural history itself. Texts such as *Gutasaga* and figures such as Strelow, Säve, Snöbohm, and Bergman have become important parts of the Gotland canon, which is one of the elements that today shapes perceptions of Gotland's heritage.

The first history writers have often been cited and reused in later historiography, not least in the 'saga book' genre. There the connection between the earliest and more recent Gotlandic history-writing seems particularly obvious and direct. It was not only a matter of quotations and re-usages of topics and examples—there was also a frequent reuse of whole stories. Söderberg's *Gotlands sällsamheter*, for example, directly lifts stories straight from Bergman.[355]

Another important instance of the interest in older Gotlandic historiography is the tendency to republish older historical works; hence the edition of Haquin Spegel's *Rudera Gothlandica* (1683) in 1901. *Gutalagen* and *Gutasaga* have been published on a number of occasions, and the same goes for Carl Linnaeus' description of his journey to Gotland (and Öland) in 1741, which has been reprinted in more than 10 times from the late nineteenth century up to after 2000. A local publisher, Barry Press, republished Strelow's *Cronica Guthilandorum* (1633) in 1978.

The works of the 'classical' history writers of the late nineteenth and early twentieth centuries have also been reprinted. The collected works of Per Arvid Säve were republished a couple of times (1937–1941 and 1978–1983), including some texts that had never been printed. From the 1970s onwards, a number of classic Gotlandic history works were reissued: Säve and Bergman's *Gotland och Wisby i taflor* in 1975, Bergman's *Gotländska skildringar och minnen* in 1976, Snöbohm's *Gotlands land och folk* in 1975, Gustaf Lindström's *Anteckningar om Gotlands medeltid* in 1978, and Theodor Erlandsson's *En döende kultur* in 1975 and 1981.[356]

---

[355] B. Söderberg 1975, 48 about a horde found in a church ruin in the sixteenth century.
[356] Other examples are Hans Hildebrand's *Från forna tiders Gotland* (1909/1910) in 1993; J. N. Cramér's *En gotländsk postfärd och En natt på havet* (1872) in 1982; and Albert Engström's *Gotska Sandön* (1926) in, for example, 1941 and 1992. Essays by

There are various institutions with an interest in Gotland publications. The regional public archives of Gotland—Landsarkivet i Visby—have issued a number of reprints and books about earlier historians. They have regarded it an important matter to raise awareness of earlier historical works that were not accessible enough. Therefore, they translated the works of the sixteenth-century pioneer Nicolaus Petreius (Niels Pedersen) and issued a volume about Alfred Theodor Snöbohm.[357]

A related phenomenon is the printing of older forms of archival material, maps, and the like, for the benefit of future history-writing. Gotlands fornsal has in the series *Acta eruditorum Gotlandica* (1984–) printed older source material, laws, and regulations.[358] Others have issued for example the three-volume *Revisionsbok för Gotland 1653* and *Sören Norbys räkenskapsbok för Gotland 1523–24*, useful not least for local historians.[359]

The third narrative

Books such as *Vägen till kulturen på Gotland* are a form of amalgamation of the two narratives (medieval and folklore) that have dominated in Gotland's history-writing. The real 'other' is the history-writing that is different from *both* of those two. That historiography might be called the third narrative.

Owe Ronström has highlighted the deep division between an established image of Gotland, with a focus on its medieval greatness or folkloric peasant culture, and a more truly 'internal' memory culture, where more recent and non-official aspects of history are emphasized, often with a stress on everyday life. For example, modern Visby outside the city wall is a typical arena for this memory culture. He calls this extramural district

---

Per Josef Enström were reprinted in 1970 (*Romantikens ö: Gotlandsvandringar och drömmar*) and 2004 (*Gotländska vandringar: bland ödekyrkor och gamla gårdar*).
[357] Körner 1984 (see esp. 11); Körner & Pedersen 2008. Other publications, largely of previously unpublished texts, include C. G. G. Hilfelings *gotländska resor* in 1994–5; Carl Säve's *Alskogsstenarna* in 1993; Mathias Klintberg's *Fångst och fiske* in 1983; and John Nihlén's *Utgrävningarna på Stora torget i Visby 1924–1926* in 1982. Anders R. Johansson has published some work by the local historian Carl Franzén (1881–1972) (Franzén & Johansson 1999a; Franzén & Johansson 1999b; Johansson A. 2000).
[358] For example, *Ivar Axelsson Totts räkenskapsbok för Gotland 1485–1487* (1991).
[359] See also Georg Westphal's *Utkast till ekonomisk beskrivning över Gotland* (1779) in 1982.

'a country in-between' that is absent from most representations of Visby and Gotland.[360]

However, that kind of history is to be found—at least partially—in the more 'internal' mediation of history on Gotland. The popular education and local heritage movements can be said to represent an at least partially alternative sphere in historical culture, where other aspects of Gotland's past are highlighted to a greater extent. There are no strict boundaries between this sphere and the dominant narratives. On the contrary, there are strong similarities and overlapping areas of interest between them. The history-writing of the popular education and local heritage movements—especially in the landscape descriptions produced by these movements or their publishers—nowadays takes part in the reproduction of the traditional image of Gotland's past, and we have already seen examples where for example the discourse on medieval greatness is reproduced.

In the periodical *Från Gutabygd*, published by Gotlands hembygdsförbund (the Gotland Heritage Association) from 1979 onwards, a fairly modern historical content dominates. It is a different story of Gotland compared to the one presented to tourists, and it is far more varied. On the one hand the movement has firm foundations in the early twentieth-century Romanticism of agrarian and premodern culture in the countryside, and on the other hand there has been a growing interest in the 'everyday' history of the recent past, of industries, shops, schools, transportation, and the like. Thus, there is an old 'Erlandsson paradigm' which has to a certain part been modernized and extended to the more modern aspects of life.

Från Gutabygd mainly consists of traditional cultural history, with a preponderance of articles on agrarian culture from the seventeenth century onwards. Other popular themes are the popular movements and the history of schools, as well as elderly people's memories of their childhood. There are articles on the use and subsequent drainage of Gotland's bogs, and about the limestone and sandstone industries. Attention is also paid to the history and efforts of the organizations themselves: there are many articles about prominent local historians and local history museums. A similar tendency (although I have not had the possibility to further investigate it) characterizes the large number of local

---

[360] Ronström 2008, 60–1, 64–5, quote at 64 ('mellanlanden', a concept taken from Dag Østerberg). Ronström uses the examples of the humorous recording artists Smaklösa ('The Tasteless') and histories of Sixties' Visby (Ingelse 1997).

history books, which normally deal with a specific parish and have been written by one or many amateur historians, often connected to a local heritage association.

The popular education associations also entertain a particular version of Gotland's history. They have largely dealt with more recent history, where for example study circles have done research on the match industry, brewery, fishing, and shipping—sometimes also publishing their results in book form.[361]

Furthermore, there are many individuals writing about Gotland's history from this more 'internal' aspect. Journalist Arvid Ohlsson, for example, wrote the history of Gotland's lime industry from the seventeenth to the twentieth centuries in a book a published in 1964.[362] Schoolteacher Lennart Bohman (1921–2005) has written a number of books and articles on the social and political history of modern Gotland, not least the history of political institutions and various organizations. In a similar vein, he has written about the nineteenth-century Visby.[363]

A more recent example is Anders R. Johansson (b. 1948), who since 1984 has edited the journal *Haimdagar* with articles about various aspects of Gotlandic history. He has also published a number of books on various aspects of Gotlandic history, mostly about the last 400 years, from the local history of the parish of Hellvi, to the history of the workers' movement on the island.[364]

Among an even younger generation, we find Martin Ragnar (b. 1972), born in Visby but now working on the mainland, who has written a number of local history books about Gotland.[365] For example, he has studied the Lummelunda paper works, and the gasworks in Visby that existed until 1954. He writes from a pure and simple fascination with the subject, but also from a conviction that modern welfare is grounded on industrial production, not 'Internet consultants' build webpages for one another.[366] He has also published extensively on the railways on Gotland,

---

[361] See also the ABF-sponsored Britse 1999, although this was a private project.
[362] Ohlsson 1964.
[363] Bohman 1962; Bohman et al. 1964; Bohman 1981; Bohman 1990.
[364] Until 1997, *Haimdagar* was a supplement to *Sockenmagasinet Hellvi-nytt*, the magazine of the local heritage association in Hellvi. Haimdagar is now also a publishing company, publishing local and regional history books, but also other genres. In 2006, Johansson was awarded the Rudolf Meidner-priset by the Labour Movement Archives and Library in Stockholm.
[365] <http://www.gotland.net/bo-leva/arkiv/unikt-gotlandicabibliotek-doneras-tilllandsarkivet>.
[366] Ragnar 2007, 7 ('internetkonsulter'); Ragnar 2008.

presenting his results with lots of details, accounts, and photographs from archival sources.[367]

It is also in these environments we mostly find history-writing about Gotland's contacts with the sea—shipping and fishing.[368] There is also a shipping guild in Visby with a long history: *Skepparegillet i Visby* was founded in 1682, which today functions as an association for those interested in shipping history.[369]

All these authors have mainly written various kinds of fairly 'regular' history, based on archival studies and the results of previous researchers, with the main purpose being to present the facts about a specific subject. A slightly different genre that has grown more common is a more explicitly personal version of the past. These books often deal with history seen in terms of the authors' own life stories, or their older relatives.[370]

All these examples constitute what I have previously called a *people's history*, which has slightly different distribution channels to the better-known official histories.[371] This is not at all a specific to Gotland—it is much the same in the rest of Sweden and in other countries as well.[372] We are dealing with a kind of division of labour, where different aspects of history are distributed through different channels. One should not simplify—it is not the case that people who are active in the popular education and local heritage movements are unilaterally interested only in Gotland's recent and/or everyday history, while scientists and tourists are passionate about ancient and medieval times, old stone churches, and the independent peasant republic. It is rather a question of differences in emphasis. As we have seen above, quite a few contemporary books issued by the popular education movement have also reproduced a traditionalist history-writing. That indicates that the 'alternative' people's history has not changed the overall picture presented in the tourist guides and reference works. That Gotland would have had prehistoric and medieval grandeur and independence can of course be claimed to be based on

---

[367] For example, Ragnar & Hardings 2002.
[368] Olsson Elof 1983; *Fårös båtsmän* (1996).
[369] Its history is covered by Rosman 1932. As of 1951, it has published a members' periodical.
[370] See, for example, Elof Olsson 1983 (mainly on the life in fishing and shipping); Sjöstrand & Hallroth 1998 (an essay on life in early twentieth-century Visby); Gahnström 2007; Emilsson 2007.
[371] Edquist 2009.
[372] Eriksen et al. 2002.

wishful thinking and anachronisms, but the attraction of that kind of history-writing can hardly be overestimated.

The implications of the dominant medieval narrative

During the nineteenth and twentieth centuries Gotland has been graced with a history-writing that stresses its glorious past, including the golden age when the island was at its peak. On Gotland, this is dated to the Middle Ages, an era whose remnants today attract tourists from far and wide. The island's role as an international trading centre has always been accentuated, as has the notion that Gotland, at least until the thirteenth century, was a democratic agrarian society where common decisions were made at the *things*. This last discourse is a version of the myth of the ancient Germanic peoples that ultimately goes back to Tacitus.

There has also been much made of the idea that the Gotlanders were a peaceful people in their age of greatness, contrasted to the more warlike Swedes. Gotland was given an important role in the description of Scandinavian adventures in the East during the Viking Age—even if they dealt in trade rather than war and the foundation of nation-states. Until recently one has, generally speaking, emphasized that the Gotlanders, like other Scandinavians, were *active* in relations across the Baltic Sea. They were the expanding part. Eastern cultural influences on Gotland—if they have been discussed at all—have been explained as a result from trade relations that Gotlanders themselves had instigated. The traces of Eastern Christianity on the island in the Middle Ages, as was already being noted in research in the early twentieth century, have only in recent years been more emphasized.[373]

Contemporary research on Gotland during the Viking and Middle Ages is mostly cautious when it comes to ethnicity. Therefore it is difficult to find more open reminiscences from earlier, more grandiose modes of history-writing about Gotland being the centre of world trade or an independent peasant democracy. When the research was popularized, it more often alluded to ideals such as 'strong women' or multiculturalism, or it stressed Viking cuisine with lots of tips.[374] Nevertheless, the narrative of the democratic peasant republic is still being repeated, mainly in

---

[373] Janson 2005; see also Edquist 2012.
[374] *Gotland – vikingaön* (2004), 7, 78 ff.

popular works, although usually with the qualification that the island was also a class society.

Those who today write the history of Gotland cannot be expected—if they are not themselves researchers—to be fully up to date with the current research. That kind of historiography uses the old and cumulative knowledge as a memory bank to draw on, and hence nineteenth-century history-writing can in some cases live on in our time, with theories that have long been out of fashion in the academic community more likely to be replicated in other contexts.[375]

The Middle Ages have in many ways been useful for creating and reproducing collective identities. It is a borderland between history and myth: to some extent, we know what happened during the Middle Ages, but at the same time the standard picture is full of myths and fictional images. In most European countries, the Middle Ages are the principal period considered in the search for the origins of contemporary national identities.[376] In many cases, for example Gotland, that is also the case for the regional collective identities.

On the whole, local and regional identities seem today to be regarded as less dangerous and controversial than national identities. It is therefore easier to pass on late nineteenth- and early twentieth-century myths of origin when they are centred on provinces and local communities, while the same rhetoric linked to the nation is readily associated with all the evils that nationalism has brought.[377] But, if we move from the level of rhetoric, it is not at all certain that regional identities are really becoming stronger at the expense of nationalism. All the same, the Gotlandic regional identity in most cases serves as a complement to Swedish national identity. And just as Swedish nationalism generally is a *banal nationalism* in the words of Michael Billig—a national ideology reproduced every day in seemingly harmless forms such as flying the flag, singing the national anthem, and in all forms of everyday practices reproducing the difference between Swedish and non-Swedish—

---

[375] The same can be said of *Gutasaga*, which in itself is an example of the tenacity in historiography all the way from medieval times to the present. Since there are not so many other sources to use for such central themes as the Christianization of Gotland and the island's connection to the Swedish kingdom, it is understandable that the saga continues to be a sort of mythic framework in the understanding of the island's earliest history.
[376] Geary 2002.
[377] Edquist 2008, 29–30.

Gotlandic regionalism is mostly is a *banal regionalism*.[378] It is seldom aggressive or overtly xenophobic, but nevertheless it is a doctrine about *us* being something different from all the others.

References

Gotland's history-writing

Arb, Stig (1981), *Gotland* (Stockholm: AWE/Geber).
Arne, Ture J. (1917), *Det stora Svitjod. Essayer om gångna tiders svensk-ryska kulturförbindelser* (Stockholm: Hugo Gebers).
— (1931), 'Gotländska silverfynd från vikingatiden. En inventering', *Fornvännen*, 26.
Bendegard, Christina (1983), 'Bulverket i Tingstäde träsk', in Jansson 1983a.
Berg, Gösta (1945), 'Gotländskt bondeliv', in Stenberger 1945a.
Bergman, Carl Johan (1870), *Gotlands geografi och historia i lättfattligt sammandrag* ['Gotland's geography and history in a simple form'] (Visby: n.pub.).
— (1882), *Gotländska skildringar och minnen* ['Gotlandic stories and memories'] (Visby: Gotlands Allehandas tryckeri).
— (1898), *Gotlands geografi och historia*, rev. Holger Rosman (4th edn., Stockholm: Norstedt) (first pub. Bergman/Rosman 1898)
— (1901), *Visby. Korta anteckningar om stadens topografi, historia, statistik, fornlemningar och nejder* (4th edn. [1885], Visby: Gotlands Allehandas tryckeri).
Bergqvist, Ulf & Wennerdahl, Maj (1987), *Gotland: den förhäxade ön* ['Gotland: the enchanted island'] (Stockholm: Brevskolan).
— (1999), *Gotland: den förhäxade ön* ['Gotland: the enchanted island'] (4th revised edn., Stockholm: Brevskolan).
Björkegren, Rudolf (1928-31), *När Gotland var danskt lydland. Några bilder* (5 vols., Visby: Ridelius/Sylve Norrbys bokhandel).
— (1949), *Sören Norby och hans bravader på Gotland. En 1500-talsbild* (Visby: J. Ridelius).
— (1951), Gotländskt. *Några bilder från Gotlands medeltid och danska tid* (Stockholm: Wahlström & Widstrand).
Bohman, Lennart (1962), *Gotlands läns landsting: 1863-1962* (Visby: Gotlands läns landsting).
— Fritzell, Gunnar & Falck, Valdemar (1964), *1800-talets Visby. En bildbok utgiven med anledning av Sällskapet D.B.V.:s 150-åriga tillvaro* (Visby: Sällskapet DBW).

---

[378] Billig 1995.

— (1981), När tiden ömsar skinn (Karlstad: Press).
— (1983), Turist i egen stad (Visby: Säveskolans gymnasieskola).
Bolin, Sture (1939), 'Muhammed, Karl den store och Rurik', Scandia, 12.
— (1945), 'Gotlands vikingatidsskatter och världshandeln', in Stenberger 1945a.
Borger-Bendegard, Lisbeth (1993), Kära Gotland! En personlig kärleks–förklaring ['Dear Gotland! A personal declaration of love'] (Stockholm: Svenska Dagbladet).
Britse, Gunilla (1999), Tändstickor och malt. Wisby tändsticksfabrik och Gotlands maltfabrik. En dokumentation (Klintehamn: G. Britse).
Broberg, Anders (1990), 'En inledande kommentar', Meta: Medeltidsarkeologisk Tidskrift, 3: 2–3.
Callmer, Johan (1992), 'Interaction between Ethnical Groups in the Baltic Region in the Late Iron Age', in Birgitta Hårdh & Bożena Wyszomirska-Werbart (eds.), Contacts across the Baltic Sea during the Late Iron Age (5th–12th centuries). Baltic Sea Conference, Lund October 25-27, 1991 (Lund: Arkeologiska institutionen, Lunds universitet).
— (1994), 'Interaktion mellan etniska grupper i Östersjöområdet i yngre järnåldern', in Lars-Erik Edlund (ed.), Kulturgränser – myt eller verklighet? En artikelsamling (Umeå: Institutionen för nordiska språk, Umeå universitet), 51–78.
— (2000), 'The archaeology of the early Rus' c. AD 500–900', Mediaeval Scandinavia, 13: 7–63.
Carlén, Octavia (1862), Gotland och dess fornminnen. Anteckningar rörande öns historia, folksägner, språk, seder och bruk samt minnesmärken (Stockholm: S. Flodin).
Carlsson, Anders (1983a), Djurhuvudformiga spännen och gotländsk vikingatid. Text och katalog (Stockholm: Stockholms universitet).
— (1983b), 'Djurhuvudformiga spännen – produktion och konsumtion', in Jansson 1983a.
— (1988), Vikingatida ringspännen från Gotland. Text och katalog (Stockholm: Stockholms universitet).
Carlsson, Anders (1990), 'Gotland och Visby mellan vikingatid och medeltid – ett debattinlägg', Meta: Medeltidsarkeologisk Tidskrift, 3.
Dahlberg, Hans (1992), Östersjön – Vallgrav och förbindelselänk (Stockholm: Almqvist & Wicksell).
Dannert, Leif (1945), 'Huvuddragen av Gotlands politiska historia. Förvaltningen och rättsväsendet', in Steffen 1945b.
Det Gotländska Kulturarvet. strategier 2004–2008 (Visby: Gotlands kommun), available at <http://www.gotland.se/imcms/13499>.
Eckhoff, Märta (1925), Stenarna tala: Visby-skisser (Visby: Norrbys bokhandel).
Elvers, Erik (1997), 'Gotska Sandön i litteraturen', in Mari-Sofi Lorantz (ed.), Gotska Sandön. En tvärfacklig beskrivning (3rd rev. edn., Stockholm: Föreningen Natur och samhälle).

Emilsson, Anders (2007), *Från oljeställ till sjöjacka. En återblick på ett arbetsliv* (n.p.).
Engeström, Ragnar, Falck, Waldemar & Yrwing, Hugo (1988), *Visby. Historisk bakgrund, arkeologiska dokumentationer* (Stockholm: Riks–antikvarieämbetet).
Enström, Per Josef (1921), *Bland ödekyrkor och gamla gårdar. Gotländska vandringar och drömmar* (Visby: Gotlands Allehandas).
— (1929), *Östersjön: strövtåg och drömmar i hansestäder och andra gamla städer* (Stockholm: Seelig).
— (1967), *Om Gotland och Östersjön* (Visby: Wessman & Pettersson).
Erikson, Olof & Falck, Valdemar (1991), *En vandring runt Visby ringmur* (Stockholm: Riksantikvarieämbetet).
Erlandsson, Theodor (1900), *Gotland, dess historia och geografi i lättfattligt sammandrag för fosteröns barn och ungdom* ['Gotland, its history and geography, in a readily understood summary for the mother-island's children and youth'] (Visby: n. pub.).
— (1920), *Gotland, dess historia och geografi i lättfattligt sammandrag för fosteröns barn och ungdom* ['Gotland, its history and geography, in a readily understood summary for the mother-island's children and youth'] (3rd edn., Visby: Sylve Norrbys bokhandel).
— (1923), *En döende kultur. Bilder ur gammalt gotländskt allmogeliv* ['A dying culture: images from old Gotlandic peasant life'], i (Visby: Ridelius).
— (1928), *Det gotländska vikingaarvet* (Stockholm: Seelig).
— (1935), *En döende kultur. Bilder ur gammalt gotländskt allmogeliv*, ii (Visby: Ridelius).
— (1940), 'Bondeåret. Gammaldags gotländskt arbetsliv', in Gösta Lundquist (ed.), *Svenska Turistföreningens årsskrift* (Stockholm: Svenska Turistföreningens förlag).
— (1946), *En döende kultur. Bilder ur gammalt gotländskt allmogeliv*, iii: *Gotländskt i sägn och sed* (Visby: Ridelius).
— (1949), *Farmannasagor*, illus. David Ahlqvist (Visby: Wessman & Petterssons bokhandel).
Falck, Waldemar (1988), *Visby förr i tiden. En kulturhistorisk sammanställning i ord och bild* (Visby: Hanseproduktion).
— (1991), *Bli din egen guide i Visby: läs, lyssna, läs* (Visby: J.-E. Christiansson).
— (1994), *Visbys stadsmur: en kulturhistorisk vandring* (Stockholm: Riksantikvarieämbetet).
Fårös båtsmän (1996) (Visby: Studieförbundet Vuxenskolan).
Floderus, Erik (1934), 'Västergarn', *Fornvännen*, 29.
'Föreningen Gotlands Fornvänners fastigheter' (1998), *Gotländskt Arkiv*, 70: 183–216.
Forsberg, Bo (1983), *Visby bakom knuten. En bok att upptäcka Visby med* (Visby: Ord & bild).

Franzén, Carl & Johansson, Anders R. (1999a), *Jordbruket före traktorn. Arbetsgång, åkerberedning, skörd och bisysslor samt fiske, båtar och annat i äldre jordbruk: andra samlingen* (Lärbro: Haimdagars).

— (1999b), *Kalk, ugnar, arbete, lön och boende kring förra sekelskiftet. Arbetssånger, bondeskeppare m.fl. uppteckningar och berättelser* (Lärbro: Haimdagars).

Från fars och farfars tid. En bokfilm om gutarnas ö (1959), ['In father's and grandfather's day: a picture book about the island of the Gutes'], ed. Carl-Eric Ohlén, Dag W. Scharp & Mats Rehnberg (Stockholm: Sv. bokfilm).

Från fars och min tid. En bokfilm om Gotland 1915–1970 (1972) ['In father's day and mine: a picture book about Gotland, 1915–1970'], ed. Bengt G. Söderberg & Leif Funck (Visby: Gotlandskonst).

Fries, Carl (1964), *De stora öarna i Östersjön* (Stockholm: Wahlström & Widstrand).

Fritzell, Gunnar (1972), *Visby i världshandelns centrum. Om stadens tillblivelse och utveckling till forna dagars handelscentrum* (Stockholm: Sveriges radio).

Funck, Leif, Nordahl, Tommy, Svensson, Sven-Olof & Öhrman, Roger (1984), *Gotland: ett faktahäfte för högstadiet* (3rd edn., Visby: Gotlands läromedelscentral) (first pub. 1974).

Gahnström, Kjell (2007), *En sjöman älskar havets våg* (Visby: Nomen).

Gannholm, K. Erland (1974), *Slipskårestenarnas gåta. Gotlands och Nordens slipskåror i ny belysning* (Stånga: K. E. Gannholm).

— (1987), *Arkeoastronomiska fornlämningar på Gotland* (Stånga: K. E. Gannholm).

Gannholm, Tore (1990), *Gutarnas historia. Från förhistorisk tid till slutliga svenska annekteringen 1679* (Burs: Tore Gannholm).

— (1991), *Svearnas härkomst* (Burs: Tore Gannholm).

— (1992) (ed.), *Beowulf: gutarnas nationalepos. Samt Gutasagan* (Burs: Tore Gannholm).

— (1994a), *Gotland. Östersjöns pärla. Centrum för handel och kultur i Östersjöområdet under (2000 år* (Ganne Burs: Tore Gannholm).

— (1994b), *Gotland och den tyska Hansan. 1300-talets Europamarknad* (Ganne Burs: Tore Gannholm).

— (1994c), *Svearnas härkomst samt invandringen till Skandinavien* (Ganne Burs: Tore Gannholm).

— (1994d), *Visby. Regina maris (Havets drottning). 1100 år, 897–1997* (Ganne Burs: Tore Gannholm).

Gardell, Carl Johan (1986), *Handelskompani och bondearistokrati. En studie i den sociala strukturen på Gotland omkring 1620* (Uppsala: Uppsala universitet).

— (1987), *Gotlands historia i fickformat. Forntid, medeltid, nutid* ['A pocket history of Gotland: prehistoric times, the Middle Ages, the present'] (Visby: Immenco).

— (1989), 'Genmäle', *Historisk Tidskrift* 109: 387–94.

Gerentz, Sven (1945), 'Handel och sjöfart från 1645', in Steffen 1945b.
Gotland – Vikingaön (2004), ed. Gun Westholm (Gotländskt arkiv, 76; Visby: Länsmuseet på Gotland).
Gotland – ett bildverk (1959) ['Gotland – in pictures'], text by Bengt G. Söderberg (Malmö: Allhem).
Gustavson, Herbert & Nyman, Åsa (1959–60) (eds.), *Svenska sagor och sägner*, xii/i: *Gotländska sägner upptecknade av P. A. Säve* (Uppsala: Lundequistska bokhandeln).
— (1961) (eds.), *Svenska sagor och sägner*, xii/ii: *Gotländska sägner upptecknade av P. A. Säve* (Uppsala: Lundequistska bokhandeln).
Hägg, Jacob & Hägg, Erik (1945), *Bilder från Gotland* (Stockholm: Aktiebolaget Svensk Litteratur).
Hamberg, Ingegerd (1970), *Gotland – en landskapsguide* (Stockholm: Aldus/ Bonnier).
Herschend, Frands (1979), 'Om vad silvermynt från Gotlands vikingatid kan vara uttryck för – en idéartikel', *Fornvännen*, 74.
Hildebrand, Hans (1866), *Svenska folket under hednatiden. Ethnografisk afhandling* ['The Swedish people in heathen times: An ethnographical dissertation'] (Stockholm: n. pub.).
— (1872), *Svenska folket under hednatiden* (2nd rev. edn., Stockholm: Seligmann).
Ingelse, Robert Tom (1997), *Höken & haren* (Täby: Lind).
Ivar Axelsson Totts räkenskapsbok för Gotland 1485–1487 (1991), ed. Evert Melefors & Dick Wase (Acta eruditorum Gotlandica, 7; Visby: Gotlands fornsal).
Jakobson, Henning (1966), *Gotland – landet annorlunda* (Visby: Gotlandskonst).
Janson, Henrik (1999), *Till frågan om Svearikets vagga* (Vara: Västergötlands Hembygdsförbund).
— (2005) (ed.), *Från Bysans till Norden. Östliga kyrkoinfluenser under vikingatid och tidig medeltid* (Skellefteå: Artos & Norma).
Jansson, Ingmar (1983a) (ed.), *Gutar och vikingar* ['Gutes and Vikings'] (Stockholm: Statens historiska museum).
— (1983b), 'Gotland och omvärlden under vikingatid – en översikt', in Jansson 1983a.
— (1992a), 'Österled', with Evgenij N. Nosov, in Else Roesdahl (ed.), *Viking og Hvidekrist. Norden og Europa 800–1200* (Copenhagen: Nordisk Ministerråd), 74–83.
— (1992b), 'Scandinavian Oval Brooches found in Latvia', in Aleksander Loit, Ēvalds Mugurēvičs & Andris Caune (eds.), *Die Kontakte zwischen Ostbaltikum und Skandinavien im frühen Mittelalter. Internationale Konferenz 23.–25. Oktober 1990, Riga* (Studia Baltica Stockholmiensia, 9; Stockholm: Centrum för baltiska studier, Stockholms universitet).
Johansson, Anders R. (2000), *Hellvitrakten. Platser och historik A–Ö, från Abburrstainen till Östra Djupvik. Platsnamn i och runt Hellvi med förklaringar*

och kommentarer samt kortfattad historik över Hellvi, Hammarslandet, Vägumevik, holmarna, fiskeställen, Rutestranden, Fardumeträsk (Lärbro: Haimdagars).
Johansson, Valton (1950), Visby (Stockholm: Wahlström & Widstrand).
Jonsson, Gunnar (1940), 'Gotland. Sagaland—farmannaland—bondeland', in Gösta Lundquist (ed.), Svenska Turistföreningens årsskrift (Stockholm: Svenska Turistföreningens förlag).
Jonsson, Marita (2000), Visby världsarv (Stockholm: Byggförlaget).
— & Lindquist, Sven-Olof (2002), Vägen till kulturen på Gotland (7th edn., Visby: Gotlands fornsal) (first pub. 1987).
Jonsson, Stig et al. (1994), Gotland – navet i havet ['Gotland—sea hub'] (Visby: Guteböcker).
Klintberg, Mathias (1909), Några anteckningar om Gotland i verkligheten och Gotland i skrift (Stockholm: Fritze).
— (1914), Spridda drag ur den gotländska allmogens liv ['Some notes on the Gotland peasant's life'] (Stockholm: Cederquists).
— & Hedin, Svante (1983), Fångst och fiske (Visby: Visum).
Körner, Sten (1984), Folkskollärare Snöbohms okända Gotland (Visby: Hanseproduktion).
— (1991), 'Vilka medeltida källor om Visby och Gotland fanns bevarade, då Strelow skrev sin krönika på 1600-talet?', Gotländskt Arkiv, 63: 143–54.
— & Pedersen, Niels (2008), Slottsprästen Petreius berättar: Gotlands äldsta historiekrönika i gotländskt och europeiskt perspektiv (Visby: Landsarkivet).
Kyhlberg, Ola (1991), Gotland mellan arkeologi och historia. Om det tidiga Gotland (Stockholm: Stockholms universitet).
Laago, Thordbjörn & Sjöstrand, Eva (1995), Gotland. En förtrollad ö (Visby: Labyrint).
Lagerlöf, Erland, Hallgren, Sören & Svahnström, Gunnar (1971), Gotlands kyrkor: en vägledning. (2nd edn., Stockholm: Rabén & Sjögren) (first pub. 1966).
— (1999), Gotland och Bysans: bysantinskt inflytande på den gotländska kyrkokonsten under medeltiden (Visby: Ödins Förlag AB).
— (2005), 'Gotland och Bysans. Östligt inflytande under vikingatid och tidig medeltid', in Janson 2005.
Lamm, Jan Peder (1980), 'De första fynden från Paviken', Fornvännen, 75.
Larsson, Axel O., Johansson, K. J., Engquist, Ingrid & Engquist, Sture (1986), Svärdslipningsrännor och slipytestenar. Ett vetenskapligt standardverk (Hemse: E. Larsson).
Lehtosalo-Hylander, Pirkko-Liisa (1983), 'Gutarnas förbindelser med Finland', in Jansson 1983a.
Lerbom, Jens (2003), Mellan två riken. Integration, politisk kultur och förnationella identiteter på Gotland 1500–1700 (Lund: Nordic Academic Press).

— (2006), 'Genmäle till Tryggve Siltberg', *Historisk Tidskrift*, 126: 291–7.
Lindkvist, Thomas (1983), 'Gotland och sveariket', in Jansson 1983a.
Lindqvist, Sune (1922), 'Till vår folkvandringstids historia', *Fornvännen*, 17.
Lindström, Gustaf (1892–5), *Anteckningar om Gotlands medeltid*, 2 vols. (Stockholm: n. pub.).
Linnman, Johannes (1924), *Gotland. Läsebok för skola och hem* ['Gotland: a reader for home and school'] (Uppsala: Lindblad).
Ludin, Folke (1966), *Visby. Tankar och teckningar från ett litet hus i en liten stad* (Stockholm: Vepe).
— (1980), *Visby ringmur: ett bildverk* (Karlstad: Press).
Lundberg, Erik, Andersson, Ingvar & Nihlén, John (1939), *Visbybilder från forntid och hansevälde*, illus. Ferdinand Boberg (Stockholm: Nordisk rotogravyr).
Lundqvist, Margit & Lundqvist, Rolf (1972), *Strövtåg på Gotland* ['Rambles through Gotland's history'] (Halmstad: Spektra).
Manneke, Peter (1983), 'Gotlands fornborgar', in Jansson 1983a.
Mogren, Folke (1992), *Visbyminnen* (Munkedal: Munk-reklam).
Nerman, Birger (1923), *En utvandring från Gotland och öns införlivande med Sveaväldet* (Kungl. Vitterhets-, historie- och antikvitetsakademiens handlingar, 34/4; Uppsala: Almqvist & Wiksell).
— (1930), 'Smärre meddelanden. Fynden från Grobin i Lettland', *Fornvännen*, 25.
— (1934), 'Det forntida Västergarn', *Fornvännen*, 29.
— (1942), *Sveriges första storhetstid* (Stockholm: Skoglunds).
— (1963), 'Den gotländska utvandringen och sveaväldets expansion', in Sjöberg 1963.
Nihlén, John (1928a), *Sagornas ö. Sägner och sagor från Gotland* ['Fabled island: legends and tales from Gotland'] (Stockholm: Natur & Kultur).
— (1928b), *Under rutat segel. Svenska äventyr i öster* [Under the Square Sails: Swedish Adventures in the East] (Stockholm: Natur & Kultur).
— (1929), *Från det okända Gotland* (Stockholm: Wahlström & Widstrand).
— (1930), *Gotland* (Svenska turistföreningens resehandböcker; 4th edn., Stockholm: Wahlström & Widstrand).
— (1982), *Utgrävningarna på Stora torget i Visby, 1924–1926. En berättelse om ett arkeologiskt äventyr*, ed. Gunnar Svahnström (Visby: Hanseproduktion).
Nylander, Erik (1945), 'Fosterön', in Stenberger 1945a.
Nylén, Erik (1979), 'Introduktion', in Waldemar Falck et al. (eds.), *Arkeologi på Gotland* (Visby: Barry Press).
— (1992), 'Professionell fastländsk mot "amatörmässig" gotländsk lokalpatriotism', *Fornvännen*, 87.
Ohlsson, Arvid (1944), *Från gotländska marker* (Uppsala: Lindblad).
— (1964), *Gotlands kalkpatroner. En berättelse om Gotlands kalkbruksindustri* (Visby: Arvid Ohlsson).

Öhrman, Roger (1973), *Visby – jämte en kortare översikt av Gotlands och Visbys historia* (Visby: Gotlandskonst).
— (1994), *Vägen till Gotlands historia* ['The road to Gotland's history] (Visby: Gotlands fornsal).
Olsson, Elof (1983), *Havet, stranden och bygden. Toftaminnen* (Visby: Hanseproduktion).
Olsson, Erik (1983), *Gotland – mitt i Östersjön. En bilderbok om sjöfart* (Klintehamn: Taurus).
— (1985), *Gotland vår hembygd* (Visby: Hanseproduktion).
— (1990), *Mänskar u pasjasar pa Gotland* (Visby: Hanseproduktion).
Olsson, Lars & Öhrman, Roger (1996), *Gotland förr och nu* ['Gotland, then and now'] (2nd edn., Visby: Gotlands läromedelscentral) (first pub. 1993).
— (2003a), *Efter Tjelvar: Gotland kors och tvärs* ['After Tjelvar: Criss-crossing Gotland'] (Visby: LC Förlag).
— (2003b), *Efter Tjelvar*, i: *Södra Gotland* ['After Tjelvar: Southern Gotland'] (Visby: LC Förlag).
— (2003c), *Efter Tjelvar*, ii: *Mellersta Gotland* ['After Tjelvar: Central Gotland'] (Visby: LC Förlag).
— (2003d), *Efter Tjelvar*, iii: *Norra Gotland* ['After Tjelvar: Northern Gotland'] (Visby: LC Förlag).
— (2003e), *Efter Tjelvar*, iv: *Visby* ['After Tjelvar: Visby'] (Visby: LC Förlag).
Östergren, Majvor (1983), 'Silverskatternas fyndplatser – farmännens gårdar', in Jansson 1983a.
Österlund, John & af Ugglas, Carl R. (1914), *Visby. En bok om en gammal stad* (Stockholm: Norstedt).
Pettersson, Bengt (1945), 'Natur och kultur i det gotländska landskapet', in Stenberger 1945a.
Ragnar, Martin & Hardings, Eje (2002), *Järnvägen till Ronehamn. Spekulationer från början till slut* (Stockholm: Svenska järnvägsklubben).
— (2007), *Berlinerblått i blåklinten. En berättelse om Visby gasverk* (Visby: Gotlands hembygdsförbunds förlag).
— (2008), *Lumppapper från Lummelunda. En rätt igenom fastländsk historia om Gotlands enda pappersbruk* (Handen: Gäddsax).
Romin, Karl & Bergman, Carl Johan (1891), *Wisby* (Stockholm: Bonnier).
Roosval, Johnny (1913), 'Medeltida stenhuggarkonst', in Axel L. Romdahl & Johnny Roosval (eds.), *Svensk konsthistoria* (Stockholm: Ljus).
— (1917), 'Sveriges och Danmarks östliga konstförbindelser under medeltiden', *Konsthistoriska sällskapets publikation*.
— (1926), *Den gotländske ciceronen. Vägvisare genom den gotländska konsthistorien med huvudvikten lagd på medeltida kyrkokonst. Till den resandes tjänst* (Visby: Gotlands turistförening).
— (1952), *Gotlands kyrkokonst* (Stockholm: Generalstabens litografiska anstalt).

Rosman, Holger (1932), *Skepparegillet i Visby under 250 år* (Stockholm: Skepparegillet).

Rönnby, Johan (1990), 'Bulverket – varumagasin, motståndsfäste eller platsen för Gotlands tidigmedeltida femtekolonnare?', *Meta: Medeltidsarkeologisk Tidskrift*, 3: 35–41.

Säve, Per Arvid & Bergman, Carl Johan (1858), *Gotland och Wisby i taflor* (Stockholm: A. Bonnier).

— (1979a), 'Samfärdseln på Gotland i gamla tider', in Per Arvid Säve, *Gotländska skrifter II* (Visby: Hanseproduktion), 213–72 (first pub. 1873).

— (1979b), 'Strandens sagor – en vikingaruna från Gutarnas ö', in Per Arvid Säve, *Gotländska skrifter II* (Visby: Hanseproduktion), 159–212 (first pub. 1873).

— (1979c), 'Havets och fiskarens sagor' ['Sea-tales and fishermen's tales'], in Per Arvid Säve, *Gotländska skrifter II* (Visby: Hanseproduktion), 5–158 (first pub. 1880).

— (1980), 'Åkerns sagor', in Per Arvid Säve, *Gotländska skrifter III* (Visby: Hanseproduktion), 5–214 (first pub. 1876).

— (1983), 'Jaktens sagor samt Djurlivet på Gotland, spridda drag ur Öns forntid och folklivet därstädes' (1872/1882), in Per Arvid Säve, *Gotländska skrifter V* (Visby: Hanseproduktion), 9–135 (first pub. 1940).

Schück, Adolf (1940), 'Gotland och Sveriges krona', in Gösta Lundquist (ed.), *Svenska Turistföreningens årsskrift* (Stockholm: Svenska Turistföreningens förlag).

— (1945), 'Gotlands politiska historia intill Brömsebrofreden', in Stenberger 1945a.

Se Gotland. Natur och kultur från Fårö till Hoburgen (2006), ed. Anki Dahlin et al. (Visby: Länsmuseet på Gotland).

Siltberg, Tryggve (1989), 'Tingsdomarna på Gotland – aristokrati eller storbönder?', *Historisk Tidskrift*, 109: 375–87.

— (1990), 'Teori och källor om Gotlands sociala struktur under 1600-talet', *Historisk tidskrift*, 110: 84–7.

— (1993), 'Bondestatistik och bonderepublik på Gotland. En replik till Janken Myrdal', *Gotländskt arkiv*, 65: 131–6.

— (1997), 'Gotska Sandöns historia. En översikt', in Mari-Sofi Lorantz (ed.), *Gotska Sandön. En tvärfacklig beskrivning* (3rd rev. edn., Stockholm: Föreningen Natur och samhälle).

— (2006), 'När staten invaderade Gotland. Några synpunkter på Jens Lerboms doktorsavhandling', *Historisk tidskrift*, 126 (2006): 279–90.

Sjöberg, Åke G. (1963) (ed.), *Historia kring Gotland* ['History of Gotland'] (Stockholm: Wahlström & Widstrand).

Sjöstrand, Eva & Hallroth, Henry (1998), *Örat mot stenen* (Fårösund: Malmgren).

Snöbohm, Alfred Theodor (1871), *Gotlands land och folk. Hufvuddragen till en teckning af Gotland och dess öden från äldre till nuvarande tider* ['Gotland's land and people: Towards a sketch of Gotland and its destinies from ancient to current times'] (Örebro: A. Bohlin), available at <http://runeberg.org/gotlands>.

Söderberg, Bengt G. (1948), *Gotland* (Stockholm: Wahlström & Widstrand).

— (1949), *Gotland i historien* (Stockholm: Radiotjänst/Gotlands turistförening).

— (1957), *Vad skall jag se på Gotland* (Stockholm: Svenska Turistföreningen).

— (1971), *Strövtåg i Gotlands historia* (Visby: Gotlandskonst).

— (1972), *Visby – en vandring genom sekler* (Visby: Gotlandskonst).

— (1975), *Gotlands sällsamheter – sagor och sannsagor från gutarnas ö* ['Gotland's peculiarities—tales and true stories from the island of the Gutes'] (Stockholm: Rabén & Sjögren/Svenska turistföreningen).

— (1978), *Kyrkorna på Gotland/The churches of Gotland* (Visby: Gotlandskonst).

Söderberg, Nils Vilhelm (1985), *Det var en gång. Kulturbilder från Visby* (Visby: Hanseproduktion).

Sørensen, Søren (1992), *Öarna i Östersjön – förr och nu* (Visby: Gotlands fornsal-/Nordens institut på Åland).

Staecker, Jörn (1996), 'Searching for the Unknown. Gotland's churchyards from a Gender and Missionary Perspective', *Lund Archaeological Review*, 2.

Stalsberg, Anne (1979), 'Skandinaviske vikingetidsfunn fra det gammelrussiske riket', *Fornvännen*, 74.

Steffen, Richard (1943), *Gotlands administrativa, rättsliga och kyrkliga organisation från äldsta tider till år 1645* (Lund: H. Ohlsson).

— (1945a), 'Gotlands indelning och organisation', in Stenberger 1945a.

— (1945b) (ed.), *Boken om Gotland. Minnesskrift med anledning av Gotlands återförening med Sverige genom freden i Brömsebro den 13 augusti 1645*, ii: *Gotlands historia från och med år 1645* ['The Book about Gotland: To mark the occasion of Gotland's reunion with Sweden under the Treaty of Brömsebro on 13 August 1645: Gotland's history from 1645'] (Visby: Sylve Norrbys bokhandel).

— (1945c), 'Återgången 1645', in Steffen 1945b.

Stenberger, Mårten (1940), 'Människan i Gotlands forntid', in Gösta Lundquist (ed.), *Svenska Turistföreningens årsskrift* (Stockholm: Svenska Turistföreningens förlag).

— (1945a) (ed.), *Boken om Gotland. Minnesskrift med anledning av Gotlands återförening med Sverige genom freden i Brömsebro den 13 augusti 1645*, i: *Gotlands historia fram till år 1645* ['The Book about Gotland: To mark the occasion of Gotland's reunion with Sweden under the Treaty of Brömsebro on 13 August 1645: Gotland's history until 1645'] (Visby: Sylve Norrbys bokhandel).

— (1945b), 'Det forntida Gotland', in Stenberger 1945a.

Svahnström, Gunnar (1945), 'Bondens gård och bostad', in Stenberger 1945a.

— (1984), *Visby under tusen år* (Stockholm: AWE/Geber).

Svensson, Britt (1998), *Visbyguiden* (Visby: Gotlands fornsal).

Thordeman, Bengt (1928), *Korsbetningsfynden från Valdemarsslaget den 27 juli 1361* (Stockholm: Statens historiska museum).
— (1944), *Invasion på Gotland 1361. Dikt och verklighet* (Stockholm: Hugo Gebers).
— (1945), 'Den 27 juli 1361', in Stenberger 1945a.
Thunmark-Nylén, Lena (1983a), 'Dräkt och dräktsmycken på Gotland under vikingatiden', in Jansson 1983a.
— (1983b), 'Gotland och Ostbaltikum', in Jansson 1983a.
— (1989a), 'Samfund och tro på religionsskiftets Gotland', in Anders Andrén (ed.), *Medeltidens födelse* (Nyhamnsläge: Gyllenstiernska Krapperupstiftelsen).
— (1989b), 'Skattfynd, gravfynd och religionsskifte på Gotland', in Lars Larsson & Bożena Wyszomirska (eds.), *Arkeologi och religion. Rapport från arkeologidagarna 16–18 januari 1989* (Lund: Arkeologiska institutionen, Lunds universitet).
Tiberg, Nils (1944), 'Utvandringsberättelsen i Gutasagan', *Gotländskt Arkiv*, 16–47.
Trotzig, Gustaf (1983), 'Den gamla och den nya religionen', in Jansson 1983a.
Uhr, Sven (1957), *Gotland. Minnenas ö* (Klassbibliotekets landskapsböcker, 2; Stockholm: Carlson).
Visby stift i ord och bild (1951), ed. Ernst Hejneman (Stockholm: Idun).
Visby: staden inom murarna. En bok om Visby innerstad, dess historia, stadsbild och verksamheter med ett handlingsprogram för innerstadens bevarande (1973) (Visby: Gotlands kommun, Kommittén för planering av Visby innerstad).
Vision och varumärkesplattform för Gotland – den magiska ön (2008) (Visby: Gotlands kommun), available at <http://www.gotland.se/imcms/37732>.
Wåhlin, Hans (1924), *Visby* (Stockholm: Norstedt).
Wase, Dick (1995), 'De Strelowska kyrkoårtalen', *Fornvännen*, 90.
— (2005), *Människornas Visby. En ciceron till Visbys medeltid* (Stockholm: Oeisspeis).
Weibull, Lauritz (1943), 'En forntida utvandring från Gotland', *Scandia*.
Wennerdahl, Maj (1985), *Sällsamheter på Gotland* ['Peculiarities of Gotland'] (Stockholm: Rabén & Sjögren/Svenska turistföreningen).
— (2001), *Gotland* (Stockholm: Bilda).
Werkelin, Janne (1981), *Gotland* (Stockholm: Brevskolan).
Wessén, Elias (1943), 'Förklaringar till Gutasagan', in Elias Wessén & Åke Holmbäck (eds.), *Svenska landskapslagar*, iv: *Skånelagen och Gutalagen* (Stockholm: Geber).
— (1945a), 'Gutasagan och Gotlands kristnande', in Stenberger 1945a.
— (1945b), 'Gutalagen', in Stenberger 1945a.
Westholm, Gun (1990), 'Visby – bönders hamn och handelsplats. En efterskrift', *Meta: Medeltidsarkeologisk Tidskrift*, 3: 16–34.

— (2007), *Visby 1361: invasionen* (Stockholm: Prisma).
Yrwing, Hugo (1940), *Gotland under äldre medeltid. Studier i baltisk-hanseatisk historia* (Lund: Gleerup).
— (1978), *Gotlands medeltid* (Visby: Gotlandskonst).
— (1986), *Visby – hansestad på Gotland* (Stockholm: Gidlund).

Other works cited

[*] = can also be considered part of Gotland's history-writing
Anderson, Benedict (1991), *Imagined communities: reflections on the origin and spread of nationalism* (rev. edn., London: Verso).
Arcadius, Kerstin (1997), *Museum på svenska. Länsmuseerna och kulturhistorien* (Stockholm: Nordiska museet).
Aronsson, Peter (2004), *Historiebruk – att använda det förflutna* (Lund: Studentlitteratur).
Baldacchino, Godfrey (2007) (ed.), *A world of islands: an island studies reader* (Charlottetown: Institute of Island Studies).
— (2008), 'Studying Islands: On Whose Terms? Some Epistemological and Methodological Challenges to the Pursuit of Island Studies', *Island Studies Journal*, 3 (1).
Bergh, Lennart, Engeström, Ingvar & Rydberg, Birgitta (1991), *Vägen till litteraturen om Gotland. Ett kommenterat urval inom olika ämnesområden* (Visby: Föreningen Gotlands Fornvänner).
Berman, Marshall (1982), *All that is solid melts into air: the experience of modernity* (New York: Simon & Schuster).
Billig, Michael (1995), *Banal Nationalism* (London: SAGE).
Bohman, Lennart (1985), 'Ett Badhus i Wisby', *Gotländskt arkiv*, 57, available at <http://www.utflykten.se/badhus.htm>.
— (1990), *Gotländsk självstyrelse. Från landstinget till enkommunen* (Visby: Hanseproduktion).
— (1992), 'Per Arvid Säve som folkbildare – det naturliga sambandet skola–fältarbete–museum–press', in Lindquist et al. 1992.
Clason, E. (1925), *Om i korsbetningsgraven vid Visby funna skelett* (Kungl. Vitterhets Historie och Antikvitets Akademiens handlingar 28/3, n.s. 8/3; Stockholm: Akademiska Förlag).
Edquist, Samuel (2004), 'Den lokalpatriotiska nationalismen. Identitetsskapande i uppländska bruk av historien', in S. Edquist et al. (eds.), *En helt annan historia. Tolv historiografiska uppsatser* (Uppsala: Uppsala universitet).
— (2008), 'En folklig svenskhet? Nationalismen och folkrörelserna i vår tid', in Urban Lundberg & Mattias Tydén (eds.), *Sverigebilder. Det nationellas betydelser i politik och vardag* (Stockholm: Institutet för framtidsstudier).
— (2009), *En folklig historia. Historieskrivningen i studieförbund och hembygds-rörelse* (Umeå: Boréa).

— (2012), *I Ruriks fotspår. Om forntida svenska österledsfärder i modern historieskrivning* (Södertörn Academic Studies, 47; Huddinge: Södertörns högskola).
Eriksen, Anne, Garnert, Jan & Selberg, Torunn (2002) (eds.), *Historien in på livet. Diskussioner om kulturarv och minnespolitik* (Lund: Nordic Academic Press).
Eriksen, Thomas Hylland (1993), *Ethnicity and nationalism: anthropological perspectives* (London: Pluto Press).
Fewster, Derek (2006), *Visions of past glory. Nationalism and the construction of early Finnish history* (Helsinki: Finnish Literature Society).
Fletcher, Lisa (2008), 'Reading the News: Pitcairn Island at the Beginning of the 21st Century', *Island Studies Journal*, 3 (1).
Geary, Patrick J. (2002), *The myth of nations. The medieval origins of Europe* (Princeton: PUP).
Gerentz, Sven (1989), 'Richard som Gotlandsforskare', *Saga och Sed*, 39–50.
Gislestam, Torsten (1975), *Gotländska hävdatecknare* (Visby: Barry Press). [*]
— (1992), 'Per Arvid Säves bakgrund och ursprung – Om släkten Säve och deras insatser i gotländskt kulturliv', in Lindquist et al. 1992.
— (1996), 'Th. Erlandsson – Gotlands Hazelius', *Från Gutabygd*, 9–25. [*]
Gotlands turistförening 75 år (1971) (Visby: Gotlands Turistförening).
Grandien, Bo (1974), *Drömmen om medeltiden: Carl Georg Brunius som byggmästare och idéförmedlare* (Stockholm: Nordiska museet).
Gustafsson, Lotten (1998), ' "Idag ska vi ändra historien!" Sex sätt att berätta om Valdemar Atterdags härjningar på Gotland', *Rig*, 81 (2): 65–75.
— (2002a), *Den förtrollade zonen. Lekar med tid, rum och identitet under medeltidsveckan på Gotland* (Nora: Nya Doxa).
— (2002b), 'Medeltidskartor och minnespolitik', in Anne Eriksen et al. 2002.
Gustin, Ingrid (2004), *Mellan gåva och marknad. Handel, tillit och materiell kultur under vikingatid* (Stockholm: Almqvist & Wiksell International).
Häggström, Anders (2000), *Levda rum och beskrivna platser. Former för landskapsidentitet* (Stockholm: Carlsson).
Hall, Patrik (1998), *The Social Construction of Nationalism. Sweden as an Example* (Lund: LUP).
— (2000), *Den svenskaste historien. Nationalism i Sverige under sex sekler* (Stockholm: Carlsson).
Hay, Pete (2006), 'A Phenomenology of Islands', *Island Studies Journal*, 1 (1).
Hobsbawm, Eric J. (1992), *Nations and nationalism since 1780: programme, myth, reality* (2nd edn., Cambridge: CUP).
Jameson, Fredric (1991), *Postmodernism, or, the Cultural Logic of Late Capitalism* (Durham: Duke University Press).
Johansson, Carina, Kriström, Örjan & Leijonhufvud, Christina (2000a) (eds.), *Kulturarvets betydelse: människors tankegångar kring åtta kulturarvsprojekt på Gotland och ett i Bohuslän* (Visby: Högskolan på Gotland).
— (2000b), 'Bungemuseet. Två kulturarv i ett', in C. Johansson et al. 2000a.

— (2000c), 'Om medeltidsveckan på Gotland', in C. Johansson et al. 2000a.
— (2006), ' "Beautiful girls and antiquities". Visuella och narrativa representationer av Visby och Gotland', *Kulturella Perspektiv. Svensk Etnologisk Tidskrift*, 15 (3): 49–59.
— (2009), *Visby visuellt. Föreställningar om en plats med utgångspunkt i bilder och kulturarv* (Linköping: Linköpings universitet).
Jönses, Lars (1999), 'Ett Sverige i smått eller ett Tyskland över allt? Nation och territorium genom upptäckt och försvar under 1800- och 1900-tal', in Lars Petterson (ed.), *I nationens intresse. Ett och annat om territorier, romaner, röda stugor och statistik* (Uppsala: Uppsala universitet).
Kriström, Örjan (2000), 'Roma Kungsgård och Romateatern', in C. Johansson et al. 2000a: 63–91.
Kronborg Christensen, John & Smitterberg, Bertil (2007) (eds.), *Kulturhistoriska museet i Bunge 1907–2007: 100 år i ord och bild. Ett museum, socknen, byggnaderna och människorna. Jubileumsskrift* (Fårösund: Kulturhistoriska museet i Bunge).
Källgård, Anders (2005), *Sveriges öar* (Stockholm: Carlssons).
Larsson, Lars (2002), *När EU kom till byn. Leader II – ett sätt att styra landsbygdens utveckling* (Uppsala: Uppsala universitet).
Latvakangas, Arto (1995), *Riksgrundarna. Varjagproblemet i Sverige från runinskrifter till enhetlig historisk tolkning* (Turku: Turun yliopisto).
Linderborg, Åsa (2001), *Socialdemokraterna skriver historia. Historieskrivning som ideologisk maktresurs 1892–2000* (Stockholm: Atlas).
Lindquist, Sven-Olof, Gislestam, Torsten & Palmenfelt, Ulf (1992) (eds.), *Per Arvid Säve och hans samtida. Rapport från Visbysymposiet 1987* (Visby: Gotlands fornsal).
Lowenthal, David (1998), *The Heritage Crusade and the Spoils of History* (Cambridge: CUP).
Myrberg, Nanouschka (2008), 'Ingen människa är en ö – om orsak och verkan i skapandet av en lokal identitet', in Bodil Petersson & Peter Skoglund (eds.), *Arkeologi och identitet* (Lund: Lunds universitet).
Nerman, Birger (1945), *Den gotländska fornforskningens historia. En översikt* (Stockholm: Wahlström & Widstrand). [*]
Nordin, Svante (1989), *Från tradition till apokalyps* (Stockholm/Stehag: Symposion).
Norrby, Paul (1986), 'Gotlands hembygdsförbund 50 år', *Från Gutabygd*, 8: 9–15.
Nyman, Åsa (1992), 'Per Arvid Säve som sagoforskare', in Lindquist et al. 1992.
Oscarsson, Tony (2006), 'Berättelsen Vamlingbo prästgård. Kulturarvsproduktion och fantiserade händelser', *Kulturella Perspektiv. Svensk Etnologisk Tidskrift*, 15 (3): 60–66.
Palmenfelt, Ulf (1992a), 'Säves sägner som uttryck för en gotländsk världsbild', in Lindquist et al. 1992.
— (1992b), 'Per Arvid Säves tryckta skrifter', in Lindquist et al. 1992.

— (1993), *Per Arvid Säves möten med människor och sägner. Folkloristiska aspekter på ett gotländskt arkivmaterial* (Stockholm: Carlssons).
Persson, Fredrik (2008), *Skåne, den farliga halvön. Historia, identitet och ideologi 1865–2000* (Lund: Sekel).
Persson, Mats (2007), 'Nietzsche och revolten mot historien', *Lychnos*, 95–128.
Ronström, Owe (2008), *Kulturarvspolitik: Visby. Från sliten småstad till medeltidsikon* (Stockholm: Carlsson).
— (2009), 'Island Words, Island Worlds: The Origins and Meanings of Words for 'islands' in North-west Europe', *Island Studies Journal*, 4 (2).
Rosander, Göran (1993), 'Hur Dalarna blev svenskt ideal', *Saga och Sed* (1993).
Rossipal, Maria (1994), 'I turismens barndom. En studie av den turistiska infrastrukturens framväxt på Gotland 1850–1900' (BA diss., Uppsala: Historiska institutionen, Uppsala universitet).
— (1996), 'Drömmar på bruk. Att sälja och köpa gotländska produkter utifrån folks föreställningar och förväntningar kring Gotland och det gotländska' (BA diss., Uppsala: Etnologiska institutionen, Uppsala universitet).
Salomonsson, Anders (1979), *Gotlandsdricka. Traditionell kultur som regional identitetssymbol* (Karlstad: Press).
— (1992), 'Om museibyggarnas ideologi', in Lindquist et al. 1992.
Samuel, Raphael (1994), *Theatres of Memory*, i: *Past and Present in Contemporary Culture* (London: Verso).
— (1998), *Theatres of memory*, ii: *Island Stories, Unravelling Britain* (London: Verso).
Sandström, Erika (2005), *På den tiden, i dessa dagar. Föreställningar om och bruk av historia vid Medeltidsveckan på Gotland och Jamtli historieland* (Östersund: Jamtli förlag/Jämtlands läns museum).
Syssner, Josefina (2006), *What Kind of Regionalism? Regionalism and Region Building in Northern European Peripheries* (Frankfurt am Main: Peter Lang).
Wallette, Anna (2004), *Sagans svenskar. Synen på vikingatiden och de isländska sagorna under 300 år* (Malmö: Sekel).
Walsh, Kevin (1992), *The Representation of the Past. Museums and heritage in the post-modern world* (London: Routledge).
Wickström, Johan (2008), *Våra förfäder var hedningar. Nordisk forntid som myt i den svenska folkskolans pedagogiska texter fram till år 1919* (Uppsala: Uppsala universitet).
Williams, Raymond (1973), *The Country and the City* (London: Chatto & Windus).
Yttergren, Leif (2002), *Ti kast' varpe: Varpan, fastlandet och den gotländska identiteten under 1900-talet* (Stockholm: HLS).

Appendix 1: The disposition of fifteen typical Gotland books[1]

Works in order of publication	Number of pages					
	Stone and Bronze Ages	Iron Age (includes Viking Age)[2]	The Medieval 'age of glory', c.1050–1361[3]	Danish period, 1361–1645	Sweden, 1645–
Bergman, *Gotlands geografi och historia* (1870)	1	4	8	9	11
Snöbohm, *Gotlands land och folk* (1871)	6	26	49	132	23
Erlandsson, *Gotland, dess historia och geografi i lättfattligt sammandrag* (1900)	1	5	9	10	11
Boken om Gotland (1945)[4]	29	91	183	94	612
Söderberg, *Gotland* (1948)	38	22	75	12	44
Söderberg, *Gotland i historien* (1949)	18	14	40	6	8

[1] Books that have no chronological element have been omitted, for example Linnman 1924.
[2] Including picture stones, rune stones, and Christianization.
[3] Including the events of the summer of 1361.
[4] The page divisions are SA–BA, 44–72; IA–eleventh century, 73–150, 153–60, 179–81, 226–7; eleventh century to 1361, 151–2, 161–78, 182–97, 228–9, 233–7, 254–313, 316–34, 336–51, 355–69, 402–421, 424–9, 433–6; 1361–1645, 198–225, 230–2, 238–53, 314–15, 335, 352–4, 370–401, 422–3, 430–2, 437–40.

Jakobson, Gotland – landet annorlunda (1966)	2	5	1	5	4
Öhrman, Visby (1973)	2	4	6	2	4
Arb, Gotland (1981)	0	4	7	8	7
Werkelin, Gotland (1981)	0	1	3	3	6
Gardell, Gotlands historia i fickformat (1987)	13	23	55	15	26
Wennerdahl/Bergqvist, Gotland – den förhäxade ön (1987)	6	13	7	1	3
Jonsson et al., Gotland – navet i havet (1994)	5	13	33	2	49
Öhrman, Vägen till Gotlands historia (1994)	21	39	61	19	116
Wennerdahl, Gotland (2001)	8	23	13	4	12

Åland
Navigating between possible identities, 1852–2012

Janne Holmén

Equipped with its own parliament and government, Åland is the only of the Baltic islands which at present enjoys regional autonomy. It is of great interest to investigate how its autonomy has contributed to the direction taken by Ålandic history-writing. The fact that Ålandic regional identity has been described as a form of micro-nationalism also sets it apart from the other Baltic islands. Åland's geographic location between two mainlands, Sweden and Finland, is also unique among the islands in this study. Its demilitarized and neutralized status is another factor that might have affected its history-writing and the formation of a regional identity. The aim of this study is to investigate how history-writing has been used to construct an Ålandic identity, and how this construction of identity has changed through the political developments on Åland from the mid nineteenth century until today.

The section 'Methods, sources and earlier research', summarizes the findings and conclusions other researchers have made about the Ålandic view of history and Ålandic identity. The following section 'Authors and funders', gives a chronological overview of the bodies that have written and financed publications on Ålandic history. The subsequent four sections contain empirical analyses of how different themes in Åland's history have been portrayed in regional history-writing, and how they have been used in the construction of a regional identity. Finally, the main results are summarized, and it is discussed how the conclusions of this study contribute to our understanding of the development of Ålandic identity.

Methods, sources and earlier research

It is methodologically easier to research regional history-writing on Åland than is the case with the other islands in this study. Åland's provincial government has since its establishment in the 1920s initiated or funded most publications about Åland's history, making the task of delimitating what constitutes regional history-writing during this period unusually straightforward. The comprehensive Alandica database of publications about Åland has further facilitated the identification of the books that constitute the source material of this study.

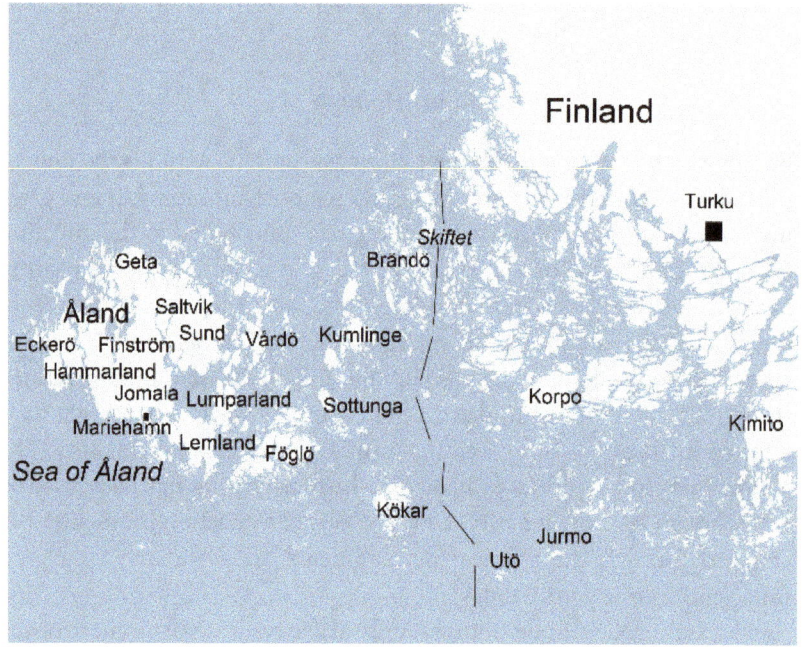

Map of Åland. Source: base map from Wikimedia Commons, edited by Janne Holmén

Quite a few shorter works have been written about Ålandic historiography as well as about regional identity on Åland. In an article in *Finsk Tidskrift* in 1984 Nils Erik Villstrand commented on some recently published Ålandic history books, including two school textbooks. He identified some central myths in Ålandic history-writing, primarily the idea that the Ålanders had longed for reunification with Sweden throughout the nineteenth century, and that an ancient autonomous Åland was the predecessor to the province's twentieth-century autonomy. He also concluded that the emergence of a second newspaper on Åland in 1981 had exposed conflicting views regarding the island's past which existed in Ålandic society. This was exemplified by the debate over Kurt Lindh's school textbook published in 1984, which was supported by *Nya Åland* but heavily criticized by *Åland*, the newspaper that defended the traditional Ålandic interpretation of history.[1]

In 1996 Per Olof Sjöstrand published a book about Finland's integration into the Swedish realm in the Middle Ages, in which he treated Matts Dreijer's view of Åland's Viking Age and early medieval history. Sjöstrand was of the opinion that history here was completely subordinate to political demands, and he compared Dreijer's attempts to locate important historical places and events on the islands to so-called biblical archaeology. Sjöstrand linked Dreijer's discovery of what he believed was Birka on Åland in 1950 to the thorough revision of Åland's autonomy which was taking place at the time. Dreijer's grandiose visions of Åland's past, according to Sjöstrand, can also be seen as a desperate reaction to the theory that Åland had been depopulated in the twelfth century, first presented in 1948 by the archaeologist Helger Salmo.[2]

Dan Nordman has studied how Swedish and Finnish historians used historical arguments to strengthen their countries' claims on the islands when the Åland question was most acute 1917–1921. Nordman claimed in 1986 that for most of the twentieth century, regional Ålandic history-writing was an echo of the Swedish historians' argumentation from these years.[3]

Pertti Hakala, who has studied how the peasant uprising against Russian troops in 1808 has been depicted in Ålandic history-writing, concludes that authors used the uprising as proof that the Ålanders wanted to belong to Sweden—hence the Swedish historians at the time of the Åland question. He notes that there has been a shift of paradigm from the rhetoric of the Åland movement since the mid 1980s: the uprising is no longer seen as a fight to remain Swedish. However, one old trait that still remains is the tendency to consider the local elite who have roots in mainland Finland as traitors.[4]

---

[1] Villstrand 1984, 328–43.
[2] Sjöstrand 1996, 91 ff.
[3] Nordman 1986, 139–58.
[4] Hakala 2006, 51 ff.

Martin Hårdstedt has studied the Ålanders' sense of loyalty during the Crimean War. He concludes that the source material is insufficient to tell us what the Ålanders really felt, but that despite this, Ålandic history writers—primarily Matts Dreijer—have supposed that they were in favour of joining Sweden or gaining independence. Hårdstedt considers Dreijer's works part of an Ålandic nation-building process.[5]

In a book about minorities around the Baltic Sea, the Swedish historian Harald Runblom mentions how the Ålanders, particularly Matts Dreijer, have tried to stretch the past, placing important events on the islands. He compares Dreijer's campaign to place Birka on Åland to the seventeenth-century professor Olof Rudbeck's attempt to make Sweden the cradle of mankind. Runblom finds it true that ethnic groups and minorities commonly misunderstand their history, but he points out that there is also a strong counter-tendency, particularly in Western Europe, where representatives of minorities through academic schooling put their local history in a wider perspective.[6]

While these historians have attempted to deconstruct how Ålanders have used history for nation-building purposes, the ethnologist Yvonne De Geer-Hancock has instead tried to depict events from an Ålandic perspective. She has investigated how Ålanders, from being fervent Swedish patriots in 1921, by 1986 had evolved into supporters of an autonomy that they want to defend and develop. According to her, it was during the 1940s, when the island's relations to Sweden and Finland were frozen, that the Ålanders came to describe themselves more frequently as a separate people. A process of national schooling began in the 1940s, when it was directed at schoolchildren with the help of Matts Dreijer's textbook *Åland och ålänningarna* (1943). During the 1950s monuments were erected on Åland that were intended to make Ålanders conscious of the fact that they were a separate people with a common history with deep roots. The subsequent phase in the national schooling was initiated by the provincial authorities in 1964. De Geer-Hancock describes this as a marketing campaign of Åland's autonomy directed at Ålanders, tourists, and the Finnish mainland. The campaign included the use of national terminology, labelling the *landsting* a parliament and the *landskapsstyrelse* a government. According to De Geer-Hancock it was in a brochure written by Thorvald Eriksson, speaker of the provincial parliament, that Swedish patriotism was officially

---

[5] Hårdstedt 2004, 172, 181.
[6] Runblom 1995, 116.

declared dead, since Eriksson said that the Ålanders old desire for reunion with Sweden had been replaced by their firmly rooted will to govern themselves.[7]

In the second half of the 1990s Ålandic identity was a source of much debate, in part in Ålandic papers and journals, but also among mainly Finno-Swedish ethnologists, sociologists, political scientists, and historians. Not only did they analyse what Ålandic identity was, but they also gave recommendations about what it should be. The Swedish historian Harald Runblom suggested in 1995 that Åland could be described as 'The Island of Bliss' because of its successful protection of minority rights. Runblom noticed that Åland, like many other European autonomies, is a border region which has been at the intersection of strong international interests, and that the Ålanders are one of many minorities that live on islands or in mountain regions, partly protected by natural barriers. He believed that Ålanders avoided pushing for full independence because of a feeling of loyalty towards Finland. For example, they supported Finland in sports in contrast to the Hungarians in Romania say, who support Hungary.[8] However, the following year the question of political independence for Åland was raised by Professor Dag Anckar, a specialist on islands and micro states.[9] In 1999 the sociologist Susan Sundback used a survey from the early 1990s to support her claim that many Ålanders identified with the Finno-Swedes, and that this group would not appreciate independence. She also argued that a break between the Ålanders and the Finno-Swedes could weaken the Finno-Swedes, and might put the Ålandic identity under threat of assimilation by the Swedes.[10]

In 1999 the society Åland's framtid (the Future of Åland) which was in favour of an independent Åland was formed, led by Thorvald Eriksson. The society commissioned a study by professor Dag Anckar that amounted to a framework for an independent Åland, drawing on the experiences of other micro states. Anckar claimed that despite lack of academic studies into the subject it was quite obvious that many Ålanders were interested in independence. True, there were many who were against independence too, but that was not a major concern since experiences from the Caribbean islands showed that once independence was achieved

---

[7] De Geer-Hancock 1986, 10–11, 118–25.
[8] Runblom 1995, 114–15, 120.
[9] Anckar 1996, 417 ff.
[10] Sundback 1999, 38–9.

it rapidly became popular.[11] Åland's framtid was transformed into a political party that gained 6.5% of the votes in the elections to the regional parliament in 2003. The support has grown to 9.7 % in 2011.

The late 1990s also saw local initiatives to gather data about Ålandic identity. In 1997 *Åländsk odling* published interviews with 50 Ålanders representing different occupations and sub-populations. There was no synthesis or analysis of the answers, but the editorial committee expressed the hope that they could be used in future research projects.[12] In 1999 the magazine *Radar* conducted an extensive survey on identity with 427 respondents. 'Ålander' was the far most common identity. 'Nordbo' followed a distant second, followed by 'Finlander'[13] and 'Finno-Swede'. The survey also showed that the Swedish language was the most important factor for Ålandic identity, while church activity was the least important. The respondents considered better knowledge of Åland's history and culture the most important factor for the further development of the Ålandic identity.[14] When relevant, the answer from the interviews and the survey will be used in the present study in order to clarify how the expressions of identity revealed in regional history-writing correspond with the views of these relatively broad groups of Ålanders.

In 2008 Barbro Allardt Ljunggren published a doctoral dissertation on linguistic attitudes among adolescents on Åland. Her theory was that Ålanders constituted a secure minority in Finland with a high ethnic profile, safeguarding their rights, and an insecure majority on Åland with a high ethnic profile, anxious about the intrusion of Finnish into society. The results from her survey showed that the respondents held Åland in very high regard, no matter if their first language was Finnish or Swedish. The adolescents who spoke Finnish at home were more positive towards Finland and Finns, however. Her assumption that the Ålanders' high ethnic profile would prevent them from regarding English positively was however not borne out; on the contrary, English was perceived very positively. She concluded that the majority probably favoured the assimilation of Finnish speaker, although some results hinted that they preferred to exclude Finns. Adolescents from homes where Finnish is

---

[11] Anckar & Bartmann 2000, 10–1.
[12] Åländsk odling 1997, 7.
[13] In the survey a distinction was made between 'finländare' and 'finnar', the latter signifying Finnish-speaking Finns.
[14] Häggblom et al. 1999, 15, 21, 24–5.

spoken instead favoured integration, with a preservation of their language. She regards this divergence as potentially problematic but not as a cause of conflict, as long as the majority does not go down the road of exclusion.[15]

Authors and funders

Regional Ålandic history-writing did not arise until the second half of the nineteenth century. In this respect Åland began later than Gotland, Bornholm, and Saaremaa, but earlier than Hiiumaa. The first publications on Åland's history appeared in the mid nineteenth century, when conurbations started to form on the island—first the short-lived Skarpans, which was destroyed in 1854, then Mariehamn which was founded in 1861. The beginning of Ålandic history-writing was initially closely linked to the rise of Finnish nationalism, and the persons of Ålandic decent who wrote the island's history also pioneered Finnish historical research. The national archives—important in the creation of a Finnish national identity—were 'actually for many years in Ålandic hands'.[16]

The first Ålander to write the island's history was Karl August Bomansson (1827–1906). Bomansson, who went to Helsinki University in 1847, wrote Finland's first dissertation on archaeology, *Om Ålands fornminnen*, in 1859. An employee at the archive of the Finnish Senate, he helped transform it into a modern National Archive, and he became its first director in 1880–1883. He also standardized Finland's coat of arms in its present form.

Before his doctoral dissertation, Bomansson had already written two works on Åland's history. In 1853 he published *Skildring af folkrörelsen på Åland* about the popular uprising against the Russian troops in 1808. Together with K. A. Reinholm he published a work in 1856 on Kastelholm Castle on Åland, supposed to be the first in a series on Finland's castles. The subtitles of Bomansson's writings integrate Åland's history with Finland's: *En scen ur Suomis sista strid* ('A Scene from Finland's last Battle') and *Finlands fornborgar* ('Finland's ancient castles').

Bomansson also wrote a dissertation on Johan Vasa, duke of Finland in the sixteenth century. Many nineteenth-century Finnish historians searched for historical predecessors to the grand duchy of Finland, which

---

[15] Allardt Ljunggren 2008, 224 ff.
[16] Hausen 2000, 7, foreword by Kjell Ekström ('i själva verket i många år i åländska händer').

had been formed as a part of the Russian Empire in 1809 when Finland was seized from Sweden. During the Swedish period, Finland had been a mere geographic concept with vague borders, but during duke Johan's rule large parts of modern Finland had been governed as an autonomous unit. Thus Bomansson's choice of topic was typical for nineteenth-century national Finnish history-writing. Bomansson was indeed one of the first proponents of Finnish national history-writing. His 1854 book on the 1808 uprising was published between the first (1848) and second (1860) volumes of *Fänrik Ståhls sägner*, the pioneering national epic about the 1808–1809 war. His writings predate the language battle that would later divide the Finnish national movement. Finnish nationalism first surfaced among the primarily Swedish-speaking educated classes in the mid nineteenth century. The issue of national language became divisive, and two conflicting versions of Finnish nationalism developed in the 1870s and 1880s. While the Fennomans wanted to replace Swedish with Finnish in administration, culture, and at home, the Svecomans tried to defend the position of the Swedish language. Part of the Svecoman programme was to create a sense of unity between the Swedish elite and the Swedophone peasant population in Finland, mainly by spreading Swedish education, culture, and the Svecoman version of Finnish patriotism in the countryside.

On Åland this process started relatively late, in part because the Fennoman movement did not reach Åland until the early 1890s. As a reaction to this, the association Ålands vänner (Friends of Åland) was founded in 1895 to preserve Swedishness on Åland. After a brief foray into politics in order to stop the Fennomans from entering Mariehamn city council, the association focused on culture. It founded a museum in 1905, and from 1910 it published historical writings in the series *Åland*.[17]

One of the most prolific writers in the publications of Ålands vänner was Reinhold Hausen (1850–1942). He was Bomansson's successor as director of the National Archives, and like him had been born on Åland. Hausen's Ålandic mother had married a doctor of Baltic German descent who worked in Skarpans until Reinhold was four years old. Skarpans, the first conurbation on Åland, was situated at Bomarsund fortress until 1854, when British and French troops demolished them both. The rest of his life Hausen lived in mainland Finland, but he wrote articles about

---

[17] Sjöblom 1945, 11, 17, 26.

Åland, and spent his summers there for much of his life. His mother's and Bomansson's families were neighbours on Åland, and Bomansson involved Hausen in excavations when he was a schoolboy. When Bomansson had to retire because of failing eyesight in 1883, Hausen became his successor.[18]

On a national level, Hausen's most important contribution was his extensive publication of historical documents regarding Finland's history. His writings about Åland were mainly concerned with cultural history, describing the island's few manors and noble families.[19] No other writer of local Ålandic history has shared Hausen's focus on the island's elite; most have instead emphasized the egalitarianism of Åland's peasant society and the absence of a native upper class. Representatives of the higher estates—the nobility, government officials, and priests—have often been seen as foreigners representing the Finno-Swedish elite from mainland Finland. Hausen fitted into this category, as did Lars Wilhelm Fagerlund (1852–1939), the other main author of Ålands vänner's publications. Fagerlund was professor of pathology in Helsinki and worked as provincial doctor on Åland, and the main part of his writings concerned medical history. In 1922 he became Åland's *landshövding*, the Finnish state's highest representative on the island.

According to the 50-year history of 'Ålands vänner', the association's early leaders were intellectual aristocrats. They made the tactical error of not involving Åland's peasantry, who considered 'Ålands vänner' to be a bunch of genteel enthusiasts preoccupied with irrelevancies. However, the new chairman elected in 1942 came from 'an old Ålandic and ancient Swedish peasant family', and tried to reach out to people in the countryside.[20]

The early writers of Åland's history, Bomansson, Hausen, and Fagerlund, all belonged to the Finnish establishment, and they treated Åland's history as part of Finland's. However, Kari Tarkkiainen—director of the Finnish National Archives at the turn of the millennium—believes that Bomansson and Hausen primarily espoused an Ålandic identity, and that they 'in language and mindset were one degree more Swedish than the mainland Svecomans'.[21] Before 1917 there was no conflict between their

---

[18] Hausen 2000, 11, 15–16, 21.
[19] For example, Hausen 1920.
[20] Sjöblom 1945, 37 ff. ('en gammal åländsk och ursvensk bondesläkt').
[21] Tarkiainen 2000, 14 ('till språk och sinne klart en grad mera svensk än fastlandets svekomaner').

view of history and the one championed by Åland's political leaders, who until that time also supported the Svecoman version of Finnish nationalism. In fact, Julius Sundblom, who as a politician and editor of the paper *Åland* was the leading voice in the province, had been the driving force behind the foundation of Ålands vänner. However, the new political aspirations of the Åland movement brought a different strand of regional historiography.

The Åland movement, or history as a weapon

The unrest caused by the Russian Revolution in 1917 gave rise to a strong movement on Åland to join the Swedish kingdom. The Swedish government supported this attempt, but the government of newly independent Finland opposed it. The question was settled in Finland's favour in 1921, but as compensation Åland gained autonomy. The Swedish and Finnish governments were aided by historians who provided historical arguments to support their country's claim to the islands.

Dan Nordman, who has studied this battle of the historians, concludes that only one of Sweden's two camps of historians took part: the followers of Harald Hjärne, professor at Uppsala University. In their ideology, historians should serve the national interest, which meant it was natural for them to support the Swedish cause. Hjärne, however, considered this unwise. The Weibullites, based at Lund University, on the other hand criticized the use of history for political ends, and therefore did not participate in the debate.[22]

Finland's historians were more unanimous than Sweden's. Leading historians and lawyers signed the declaration *Ålandsfrågan och Finlands rätt* ('The Åland question and Finland's right'), which claimed that Finland had an undisputed right to the islands. Reinhold Hausen signed the document, and so did many of his Fennoman rivals from before. Nordman notes that both Finno-Swedes and Finnish nationalists supported Finland's right to Åland, but with varying intensity and different arguments. The Finno-swedes threw themselves wholeheartedly into the battle for Åland, whereas the Finnish nationalists prioritized the contemporaneous border conflict with Russia in Karelia, their ideological heartland. In Helsinki some young Ålanders took the initiative by setting up an informal Ålandskommittén, which strived to keep Åland within

[22] Nordman 1986, 143–4.

Finland. The committee, which came to be important for Finland's policies towards Åland, was almost entirely constituted by people closely associated with Ålands vänner.[23]

A loss of Åland would have reduced the already small number of Swedish speakers in Finland, directly affecting the number of seats for the Swedish Peoples Party in the Finnish Parliament. The Finno-Swedish historians may also have feared loosing some of their historical legitimacy in Finland, since Åland was the oldest Swedish-speaking area in the country. Much of the early Finno-Swedish archaeological and historical interest had been directed towards Åland, just as Finnish ethnologists and linguists had turned their eyes towards Karelia.

Åland's earliest history became important in the conflict, since both parties claimed to have been the first to settle the islands. Since there were no written sources older than the fourteenth century, the Swedes used archaeological remains to support their right, while the Finns mainly resorted to place names of supposedly Finnish origin, such as Jomala and Finnström. The Finno-Swede Karsten claimed that in the Stone Age Swedish speakers had migrated to their present homes in Sweden and Finland via different routes from a common ancestral home; Åland had then been populated by Swedish speakers from the east. Karsten's theory contradicted all the archaeological and historical evidence, but it had strong political advantages: it provided Finno-Swedes with a long history in Finland, useful in the language battle with the Fennomans, and it separated Finno-Swedes and Ålanders from Sweden, useful in the battle for Åland. However, other Finno-Swedish scholars rejected the theory, since such a far-fetched and easily disproven idea could weaken their cause.[24]

There was also a debate about Åland's position during the Swedish period in Finland's history (from the twelfth century to 1809)—was Åland already a part of Finland even then? Historians from Finland stressed Åland's administrative ties eastwards, while Swedish historians emphasized that Finland had not been a unified province, that Åland had been quite autonomous, and that the islands were culturally Swedish.[25]

The war of 1808–1809 was also used in the conflict. To strengthen the idea of Åland's special relationship with Sweden, Swedish historians pointed to forward the Ålanders' uprising against the Russians, Sweden's

---

[23] Nordman 1986, 144; Köhler 1996, 23–4.
[24] Nordman 1986, 146.
[25] Nordman 1986, 152.

attempts to keep Åland even after it lost Finland, and the fact that Åland had a representative at the 1809 Diet in Stockholm. Historians from Finland claimed that uprisings were not unique to Åland, that Sweden wanted to keep Åland purely for strategic reasons, and that Åland's true representative in 1809 was present at the Diet in Borgå, where the Finns swore allegiance to Tsar Alexander I.[26]

The few historians who opposed their country's official line were heavily criticized. The most prominent was Harald Hjärne, who on purely political grounds supported Finland's claim. He considered the whole question of whether Åland had historically been more closely tied to Sweden or Finland as skewed: Finland prior to 1809 was a mere geographic concept within Sweden, like Svealand or Norrland—the idea of Finland as a separate unite before 1808 was a Fennoman construction. He also criticized the Swedish interpretation of the 1808 uprising, which to his mind lacked all traces of nationalism and language politics. With time, most historians have come to agree with Hjärne's view on the shortcomings of the heavily politicized academic debate.[27]

The Åland movement had multiplied the writings about Åland's history, however. This provided inspiration for the regional history-writing on Åland that appeared in the following decades. Nordman claimed in 1986 that Åland's history-writing still was like 'a Swedish pamphlet from 1919'.[28] Yet while Åland's leading regional historian, Matts Dreijer, initially shared the Hjärne disciples' view of history, he came to revise it an a creative way, well adapted to the changing needs of Åland's society. The turbulent years 1917–1922 had not only given Åland a great deal of Swedish national history-writing, but also autonomy—an autonomy that eventually gave rise to demands for a new view of history.

Matts Dreijer, identity builder

The historian who has had the greatest influence on Åland's regional history-writing is Matts Dreijer (1901–1998). He was born on the Estonian island of Ruhnu, but moved to Mariehamn at the age of six. In his autobiography he lamented the fact that he did not have a single drop of Ålandic blood, but he still considered himself an Ålander. He claimed that, with roots in Västerbotten, Österbotten, Nyland (Uuismaa), and

---

[26] Nordman 1986, 152–3.
[27] Nordman 1986, 155.
[28] Nordman 1986, 158.

Ruhnu, only thick Swedish peasant blood flowed in his veins.[29] Since he came to dominate regional history-writing for such a long time, to an extent that has no parallel on the other Baltic islands, there is reason to focus on his background and the development of his theories.

Dreijer studied economics in Helsinki, and upon his return to Åland he worked as director of the producer cooperative Ålands Centralandelslag. In 1933 he applied for and was appointed to the position of *landskapsarkeolog* (county archaeologist) on Åland. According to his autobiography, the local politician Carl Björkman realized that Ålanders needed to investigate their own history, since a strong identity was vital for the defence of Åland's autonomy. The local authorities had earlier tried to acquire an archaeologist by financing a young Ålander's studies in Helsinki, but the attempt failed because of the student's exam nerves.[30]

Initially, Dreijer attempted to raise awareness about the ancient remains on Åland, since many locals valued ancient cairns as a source of building materials rather than as part of their cultural heritage. Preservation was one of the main purposes of the booklet *Ålands forntid och forntida minnesmärken* (1937), intended for schools and tourists. In it Dreijer claimed that Åland had been part of the old Sveonian kingdom since pagan times.[31] In his 1943 textbook for the primary schools, Dreijer claimed that the purpose of the book was to instil a love of the '*hembygd*'[32] by spreading knowledge about Åland.[33] The description of Åland's older history was dominated by fictional stories.

Until this point, Dreijer's view of history had been heavily influenced by the Swedish nationalist school of historians from Uppsala. These historians had been very active during the struggle for Åland, and Dreijer used their arguments for Åland's old historical and cultural ties to Sweden. Dreijer claimed in his memoirs that he started to re-evaluate his views in 1949, when he discovered a limestone lion's head in Jomala Church that led his thoughts to Lund Cathedral.[34]

---

[29] Dreijer 1984, 16.
[30] Dreijer 1984, 131–2.
[31] Dreijer 1937, 3, 11, 49 ff.
[32] *Hembygd* is a Swedish word without a direct English equivalent, but comparable to the German *Heimat*, as it refers to the local community from which a person stems, feels connected to, and identifies with.
[33] Dreijer 1943, 7.
[34] Dreijer 1984, 249–50.

In his later writings Dreijer started to unpick Åland's ties to Sweden, creating a more autonomous role for Åland in history. This was in line with a contemporary political re-orientation on Åland. In 1945 leading politicians from Åland had approached the Swedish foreign ministry in a final attempt to cede to Sweden. The Swedish authorities were completely alien to the idea. Subsequently, Åland's leaders abandoned the idea of joining Sweden, focusing their efforts on developing autonomy instead. The Finnish parliament approved a new law in 1952 that deepened Åland's autonomy. Dreijer helped prepare the new legislation, in both official and unofficial roles.[35] Political developments thus paved the way for a new more self-assertive Ålandic history-writing.

During the 1950s, Dreijer published a number of articles where he outlined his new ideas, mainly in *Åländsk odling*. In 1960 he summarized his views in *Kaufleute und Missionare im Norden vor tausend Jahren*, published with the help of Ålands kulturstiftelse and Ålands landskapsstyrelse.[36] The book treated the history of Northern Europe in the Viking Age and early medieval period, giving Åland a central position in the description.

Dreijer's interest in ancient history was such that when a local insurance company asked him to write a company history to mark its centenery in 1966 he offered, by way of background, to describe the history of the Ålandic people, and thereby the society in which the company had functioned. The background, *Glimtar ur Ålands historia*, was published together with the company history in 1966, and separately the following year. It began with the arrival of the first inhabitants to Åland 5,000 years ago, and had nothing at all to do with insurance. The actual company history started with the laws about fire under King Magnus Eriksson in the mid fourteenth century.[37]

Gradually Åland's history became increasingly important—and ancient—in Dreijer's writings. Already in the 1950s Dreijer claimed that the Viking Age trading place Birka was situated on Åland, and although in *Glimtar ur Ålands historia* from 1966 he still held with the conventional wisdom that Kastelholm Castle was built in the 1380s. In 1976 he estimated it to have been built in the twelfth century.[38]

---

[35] Dreijer 1984, 230 ff.
[36] Dreijer 1960, 3.
[37] Dreijer 1966, 5, 7.
[38] Dreijer 1967, 19; Dreijer 1976, 25.

In the 1970s there was still no comprehensive work on Åland's history, and Dreijer therefore set up the series *Det åländska folkets historia* ('The history of the Ålandic people'). According to his autobiography, the purpose of the series was to instil the old feeling of belonging to a separate Ålandic people in the younger generation. Because of their history, their struggle for freedom, and their autonomy, Ålanders deserved to be described as a people, despite their Swedish nationality.[39] The identity-building aspirations of the project could not have been more clearly articulated.

Det åländska folkets historia is a gigantic work funded by *Åland's kulturstiftelse*. The foundation was originally founded in 1949, when the Ålandic bookseller and former Olympic middle distance runner Frej Liewendahl convinced the organization of Swedish magazines, Vectu, to donate their earnings on Åland to this purpose. The Swedish publishers were hindered to bring their profits out of Finland because of currency restrictions in the years after the Second World War.[40]

New interpretations of history

By the early 1980s Matts Dreijer had dominated history-writing on Åland for half a century. Politically Åland was unified. It was not until the late 1960s that party politics started to take form, and in the mid 1970s the modern party system was fully established. The newspaper *Tidningen Åland* had dominated the media landscape, and it was a reliable defender of the ruling political line, as it had been since the days of Julius Sundblom, who was both editor in chief and Åland's leading politician until his death in 1945. In the late 1970s a new editor-in-chief, Hasse Svensson, brought a more critical journalism that annoyed local politicians. Svensson was fired in 1981, but most journalists followed him to the new paper *Nya Åland*.

Thus the society on Åland started to become less monolithic in the 1980s, and this was reflected in the history-writing. In 1986, the department of history at Åbo Akademi University published a report on Åland, *Väster om skiftet*. It contained articles by two students from Åland, Dan Nordman, and Gyrid Högman, who critically examined the Åland movement. The report also contained an article by Åsa Ringbom about

---

[39] Dreijer 1984, 323.
[40] Tudeer 1993, 151.

the 'Wenni cross' in Sund—used by Dreijer to identify Åland with Birka—where she pointed out that Dreijer's drawing of the grave in *Det åländska folkets historia* from 1979 bore little resemblance to his original sketches and reports from the excavation in 1951. Ringbom's research was in the 1990s dispersed through Ålandic school's, since it convinced the teacher and textbook author Kurt Lindh that the cross could not mark the grave of Wenni—Unni, bishop of Hamburg, buried in Birka.[41]

New volumes in the series *Det åländska folkets historia* were published at a slow pace. Part two, published in 1988, was a meticulous investigation of dealings in Åland society in the sixteenth and seventeenth centuries, closely retelling information from the available sources. There were no attempts at making Åland's history seem more grandiose, Swedish, or autonomous than the sources suggested, as had been the case with Dreijer's and Nyman's volumes in the series. Perhaps the fact that the author Carl Ramsdahl died before the book was finished contributed to its lack of analysis and conclusions. Because of these weaknesses, the Swedish historian Jan Samuelsson has been contracted to write a new volume in the series about Åland's sixteenth and seventeenth centuries.

Part five, published in 1993, dealt with the period 1920–1990. The author Erik Tudeer was a former banker, and he put a strong emphasis on economic history. The following part in the series, part three about the eighteenth century, was not published until 2006. The author, Stig Dreijer, son of Matts Dreijer, and author of a doctoral thesis about Åland during the Great Northern War, brought a new academic rigour to the series. Stressing Åland's connections with Sweden and the islanders' appreciation of autonomy, the book can be considered a modernized and toned-down version of Ålandic national history-writing. Part four, published in 2008, on the other hand represented a radical break with earlier history-writing. This time Ålands kulturstiftelse had appointed professional historians from Sweden (Martin Hårdstedt) and Finland (Christer Kuvaja and Pertti Hakala), who confronted several myths in Ålandic history-writing, such as the uprising of 1808 and the sentiments on Åland during the Crimean War, and concluded that earlier writers had been involved in an identity-building project. The last volume, about the Åland movement, has yet to be published.

[41] Ringbom 1986, 20, 31; Lindh 1998, 336.

Since the publication rate of *Det åländska folkets historia* was so slow and the format became so voluminous, Ålands landskapsstyrelse took the initiative to publish a briefer overview of Åland's history. In 2000, Benita Mattsson-Eklund's *Tidernas Åland* was published, in many ways a break with the older view of history. She distanced herself from Dreijer's theories, and was of the opinion that the Åland movement's racial rhetoric was completely reprehensible.[42] Her critique of the darker chapters in Åland's history can be seen as part of the 'moral turn' in Nordic historiography in the 1990s.

Maritime history

Maritime history stands out as a separate part of Ålandic history-writing. While almost all other history-writing has been financed by the provincial government, maritime history has primarily been funded by the shipping industry. In 1935, roughly at the same time as Åland's politicians decided to employ an archaeologist, a number of captains and shipowners founded 'Ålands Nautical Club'.[43] Gustav Eriksson, the last ship owner in the world with a fleet of tall sailing ships, became the largest donor. The Club financed Åland's Maritime Museum, which was built in 1949 and opened in 1954.[44] It also financed the bulk of the publications on Åland's maritime history, including the yearbook *Sjöhistorisk årsskrift för Åland*.

The most voluminous work of Ålandic maritime history-writing is *Den ålandska segelsjöfartens historia*, first published in 1940 by the teacher and author Georg Kåhre. In 1988 a second edition was published by Karl Kåhre, which brought the narrative forward to the end of the last sailing ships in the early 1950s.

The period covered by maritime histories also differs from the rest. Although maritime history sometimes mentions older periods as background, its main focus is on the period from the mid nineteenth century to the mid twentieth century, the era of the great sailing ships. Nostalgia for the era of sails has led to an international interest in Åland's maritime history. For example, Georg Kåhre's *Under Gustaf Eriksons flagga* (1948)

---

[42] Mattsson-Eklund 2000, 341.
[43] Note the Swenglish name of the club. English loanwords were common on Åland and in other maritime societies before they became a truly global phenomenon at the end of the twentieth century.
[44] Åland's maritime museum, <http://www.sjofartsmuseum.ax/sjomuseum/historik.pbs>, accessed 12 December 2011.

was published in English in 1977, edited by Basil Greenhill, director of the National Maritime Museum in Greenwich.[45]

The character of Åland

Regional history-writing portrays the Ålanders as local patriots who hold their home islands and Swedish language in high regard at the same time as they have good international connections, especially to the English-speaking world. Peace-loving but staunch in their defence of their freedom, they are thrifty capitalists with an egalitarian outlook and simple manners.

Åland's borders

Islands are often imagined to have sharp borders. Of the island regions in this study, Åland is the one with the blurriest geographical borders, since the border with Finland passes through an island-rich archipelago. The international agreements about Åland's demilitarization, neutralization, and autonomy, however, made a strict definition of its borders important. Åland's autonomy has also made the border with Finland ideologically significant.

Åland's border with Sweden in the Sea of Åland is quite well defined, although it is partially a land border on the island of Märket. This became a national border when Sweden lost Finland and Åland to Russia in 1809. According to the written border description of 1810, the border should divide the island in two equal halves, one Swedish and one Russian; however, the map drawn by the border commission the line misplaced by a few millimetres to the west, an error equivalent to several nautical miles. Misled by the map, the Finnish-Russian authorities built a lighthouse on the Swedish side of the island in 1885. The error was not corrected until 1985, when Finland and Sweden agreed on a new border. According to the Åland Convention of 1921, the border was to pass through the central point of the island of Märket. The new, at first glance strangely drawn, border manage to pass through this point, divide the island in two halves of equal size, and place the lighthouse on the Finnish side.[46]

---

[45] Kåhre & Kåhre 1988, 10.
[46] Ekman 2000, 13–21.

The first map where Åland's borders are defined was published in 1789. The borders were however hand-painted on the map, somewhat differently on different copies. In 1855, after the destruction of Bomarsund fortress but before the Treaty of Paris, the Tsar transferred the inhabited Utö and Jurmo islands from Åland to Korpo. The fact that Åland's fate was uncertain at the time probably contributed to the decision.[47] As a consequence of this, Utö and Jurmo did not become demilitarized the following year, and Utö has housed military installations throughout most of the twentieth century.

Since Åland's borders are defined differently in different international treaties, there is in some places a discrepancy of 2 km between the border of the autonomous province of Åland and the demilitarized zone of Åland, which has caused some confusion. Some small, demilitarized islands in the border regions have been included in Finnish military areas.[48]

All these confusions are found in the southern part of the archipelago. In the northern part, Åland's border with Finland follows the Skiftet strait. Skiftet is often said to clearly separate Åland from Finland, although this is actually only accurate in the northern part of the archipelago. In spite of— or perhaps in part because of—the fact that Åland's border with Finland is anything but sharp in geographical and legal terms, great efforts have been made to describe it as a sharp cultural border.

On many questions Matts Dreijer revised his opinion completely during his long career, but on one point he did not waver: there was a sharp and clear historical border between Åland and Finland. In *Åland och ålänningarna* from 1943 he stressed that in ancient days the burial customs and the people were completely different on the other side of Skiftet. Ålanders should look upon the tumuli that dot the landscape with veneration, since they were proof that their ancestors had lived there in heathen times. According to Dreijer, they also proved that Åland had been the easternmost outpost of the Scandinavian peoples in the Viking Age.[49] Dreijer focused his argument on one period, the Iron Age, and one aspect, graves, which fitted his purpose of drawing a sharp border between Åland and Finland. A history writer with the opposite aim could have chosen another period, for example that of the Comb Ceramic culture, to illustrate Åland's prehistoric links to the East.

---

[47] Ekman 2000, 13–16.
[48] Ekman 2000, 36–43.
[49] Dreijer 1943, 69–70.

In *Det Åländska folkets historia*, Skiftet is described as one of the world's sharpest place name borders. Dreijer refused suggestions that some place names on Åland could be of Finnish origin, with the sole exception of Koskenpää in Brändö, and possibly also Jurmo in the same parish, not to be confused with the island with the same name, further south, which was connected to Åland until 1855. In contrast, Dreijer claimed, the areas east of Skiftet showed a pattern of old Finnish place names mixed with younger Swedish ones, of which some such as Ulfsby (today Pori/Björneborg) bore witness to Ålandic settlement.[50] Neither Dreijer nor any other Ålandic history writer has lamented the fact that Åland lost Utö and Jurmo in 1855. Although unknown to most Ålanders, this was certainly known to Dreijer. Since Jurmo is a Finnish place name, the alteration helped sharpen the place name border that was so essential to his claims.

Swedishness

In 1943, Matts Dreijer summarized Åland's history by claiming that the islanders' Swedish ethnicity was the only thing which had remained constant down the centuries:

> The social structure, the way of life, ideas and religion might change or perish. Even the ground under our feet can be taken from us... But two things have been preserved and should be preserved, the blood and the language, which are our people's most precious heritage.[51]

The Ålanders who tried to achieve reunification with Sweden in 1917 legitimated their attempt in part by claiming that the Swedish language needed to be safeguarded against Fennification.[52] The autonomy within Finland that the League of Nations in 1921 outlined for Åland was intended to 'guarantee to the population of the Aaland Islands the preservation of their language, of their culture, and of their local Swedish traditions'.[53] Successive extensions of Åland's autonomy in the twentieth

[50] Dreijer 1983, 153 ff., 433.
[51] Dreijer 1943, 105 ff. ('Samhällsform, levnadssätt, föreställningar och religion kunna förändras och gå under. Ja, till och med den jord vi trampa, kan tagas ifrån oss... Men två ting hava bevarats och böra bevaras, det är blodet och språket, som äro vårt folks dyraste arvedel').
[52] Högman 1986, 119.
[53] *League of Nations Official Journal*, September 1921, 701, <http://www.kulturstiftelsen.ax/images/internationellaavtal/engelskaavtal.pdf>, accessed 26 March 2012.

century have all been made with the protection of the Swedish language in mind, and with the Åland Convention of 1921 as a blueprint. Against that background, it is no surprise that Ålandic history-writing is preoccupied with the Swedish language and the threat of Fennification.

The number of Finnish speakers on Åland was low throughout the nineteenth century. The language battle between Fennomans and Svecomans on the Finnish mainland reached Åland late; in 1891, the paper *Åland* could claim that the battle did not concern the island. Increasing Fennoman agitation combined with considerable Ålandic emigration to America, which forced industrialists to employ Finnish workers from the mainland, finally awoke fears of Fennification later in the 1890s.[54]

The author and publicist Johannes Salminen and the historian Christer Kuvaja believe that the conflict was mainly based on differences in lifestyles between Swedish-speaking farm owners and Finnish-speaking workers. The Finns' propensity to drink, their bad temper, and their high criminality contributed to the Ålanders' growing resolve to keep Åland Swedish. This description of the Finns is very common in Ålandic history-writing.[55]

The drunken, violent, criminal Finnish speaker is a stereotypical male Finn. However, the majority of Finnish immigrants to Åland during the nineteenth and twentieth centuries were women.[56]

In the early twentieth century, some Ålanders went on to formulate their resistance to Fennification in racial terms, which is acknowledged in Ålandic history-writing from the late twentieth century. This is a parallel to the interest in Sweden for the darker sides of its twentieth-century history that surfaced in the late twentieth century. The writers of Ålandic history have been directly inspired by the Swedish discourse on racism and racial hygiene, as is evident from their references.[57]

The issue that divides writers of Ålandic history is not if Åland's monolingual Swedish status should be preserved, but how much awareness and resistance to Fennification they consider necessary; to what degree is Åland's monolingual Swedish status under threat?

Some authors display great confidence. In an essay 'The Ålander is not a threatened species', Erik Tudeer explains that although historically there

---

[54] Kuvaja et al. 2008, 98 ff., 111; Salminen 1979, 34–5.
[55] Kuvaja et al. 2008, 102; Salminen 1979, 36; Tudeer 1993, 26, 67.
[56] Högman 1990, 193–4; Tudeer 1993, 273.
[57] Tudeer 1993, 55–6; Mattsson-Eklund 2000, 331; Kuvaja et al. 2006, 102.

have been threats such as high mortality, emigration, and low birth rates, these threats are now reduced. He believes it is typical for islanders to consider all immigration a threat, but that on Åland this has mainly been directed towards non-Swedish speakers, in essence Finns. Tudeer himself considers immigration to be a fortunate compensation for emigration.[58]

Except for the stereotypical description of male Finnish workers, which usually refers to the first half of the twentieth century, it is in fact very difficult to find negative attitudes towards immigrants among any writers of Åland's history, which to an extent contradicts Tudeer's claim about the xenophobic nature of the islanders. Writers for whom the defence of Swedishness is their first priority resist the Fennification emanating from the government and Parliament in Helsinki, not Finnish immigrants. The most noteworthy example is Thorvald Eriksson. He has a background as a regional politician who has firmly opposed all intrusions of the Finnish language into Ålandic society, and he is one of the founders of the political party Ålands framtid, which since the late 1990s has worked for an independent Åland. Eriksson's writings consist of political memoirs and short pamphlets with an outspokenly political use of history. He believes that Ålanders will always need a defensive attitude, since Åland is so small and Finns constitute such a large majority of Finland's population. In the 1970s he seemed more optimistic about Finland's willingness to live up to its obligations. In 1996 he admitted that he once believed that the Finnish president, Kekkonen, could improve Finnish attitudes towards Åland, something he now considered a bit naïve.[59]

Eriksson's writings deal extensively with the 1960s, when he as chairman of the Ålandic Parliament fought several battles to defend Åland's autonomy and language. One of them was caused by the introduction of television: Finnish national television was predominantly in Finnish, and the Finnish authorities made it difficult for Åland to get access to Swedish television. Sweden 'reached out to help an ancient Swedish province' by building a transmitter on Väddö directed at Åland.[60]

A close reading of Eriksson's writing reveals that he sees resistance to the Finnish language as instrumental; the only way to mobilize international opinion in support of Åland's autonomy is to act as a small

---

[58] Tudeer 1993, 272.
[59] Eriksson 1976, 44–5; Eriksson 1996, 162.
[60] Eriksson 1976, 40–1; Eriksson 1996, 59–65 ('räckte … ett ursvenskt landskap en hjälpande hand').

minority in need of protection from engulfment by an overwhelming majority population. Factors such as Åland's status as a neutral zone, its history, and its insular location can in Eriksson's view only be used as supportive arguments. If the Finnish language became common on Åland, the argument that monolingual Swedish Åland needs its special status within Finland would collapse.[61] Thus the defence of Swedishness is used to uphold and develop autonomy, rather than the other way around as originally intended.

The Åland Convention of 1921 was the foundation of Åland's autonomy, and it forces Ålandic politicians who want to defend and develop autonomy—and that is all of them—to stress the importance of the islands' monolingual Swedish status. The leading Ålanders who fought for the islands' reunification with Sweden had their roots in the Svecoman camp in the Finnish language battle, and drew their arguments from that discourse. The Åland Convention made the language argument permanent, institutionalizing it to such an extent that the new Ålandic autonomy had to continue building its identity around it. Some writers and politicians have attempted to build an alternative, or at least complementary, Ålandic identity around an older international agreement, however: the Convention of 1856 on Åland's demilitarization.

The islands of peace

The Åland Islands have been demilitarized since the Crimean War, although this agreement was violated during the First and the Second World Wars. After each war the islands have been demilitarized anew, and in 1921 Åland also became a neutral zone. There is general agreement among Ålandic writers that the demilitarization has been a sufficient protection for Åland, and that the fortifications have been superfluous.[62] When Sweden and Finland in the 1930s proposed a plan to fortify Åland, most Ålanders were negative, although some like Carl Björkman were of a different opinion. Julius Sundblom claimed that fortifications attracted war; if none were built on the islands there was no reason to attack them.[63] The idea that demilitarization and neutralization offers better protection than military measures has become common on Åland, and it almost amounts to a tenet of security policy—although security policy is officially

---

[61] Eriksson 1996, 132 ff.
[62] Salminen 1979, 174, 182; Eriksson et al. 2006, 112.
[63] Salminen 1979, 183–4.

an area which belongs to the Finnish government in Helsinki, not to the local government in Mariehamn. It is possible that the idea was inspired by the fate of Bomarsund fortress during the Crimean War. Yet it could be noted that the allied fleet mainly attacked Finland's unfortified coast and the unfinished Bomarsund fortress, while they did not dare to attack the stronger fortresses in Sveaborg and Kronstadt.

However, military thinking is not the main reason behind the Ålandic opposition to fortifications. There is no doubt that during the period of autonomy, Ålanders have opposed fortifications primarily out of fear that garrisons would mean the Fennification of the islands.[64]

Since the 1980s, hoever, there is ample evidence that peace has become part of Ålandic identity in its own right. Already in 1979 Johannes Salminen was of the opinion that instinctive pacifism has become a second nature to Ålanders.[65] Inspired by the international peace movement, a peace association was founded in 1981 and a peace institute in 1992. According to Barbro Sundback, local government was sceptical of the outburst of international peace activity that suddenly took place on the islands.[66] Sundback is herself a leading figure in Åland's Social Democrat Party. It could be argued that the concept of Åland as 'the islands of peace'[67] has been used by the political left as a means to reshape Ålandic identity away from the old language of nationalism, which in a way was monopolized by the political right.

No political fraction on Åland claims that the Swedish language is not important. The difference is rather that Sundback stresses that the Åland model has been successful in maintaining the Swedish language on Åland, while those on the other flank claims that the Swedish language is continuously under threat. This is vividly illustrated by the fact that Sundback calls her chapter in *Fredens öar* 'A success story', while Thorvald Eriksson, one of the stoutest defenders of the Swedish language, named his book 'Åland in a headwind'.[68]

---

[64] See, for example,Wernlund 1953, 97; Eriksson & Virgin 1961, 83.
[65] Salminen 1979, 181.
[66] Eriksson et al. 2006, 108–109.
[67] The term 'the islands of peace' was first heard on Åland in 1984, but was supposedly coined by Ålandic politicians at a peace conference in GDR a few years earlier (e-mail from Kenneth Gustavsson, 8 january 2013.). The related term 'the sea of peace', referring to the Baltic, was used in Soviet rhetoric from 1957 onwards.
[68] Eriksson et al. 2006, 77–81 ('En succéhistoria'); Eriksson 1996 (*Åland i motvind*).

The claim that Åland's model of autonomy is a success is strongly linked to Åland's role as a peace ambassador. Sundback describes Åland's autonomy within Finland as 'an intelligent and forward-looking way [of] solving ethnical conflicts without violence or bloodshed'.[69] If Åland's autonomy were instead described as a failure it would be impossible to use it as a positive example in foreign conflicts.

The concept of Åland as the island of peace has not been directly questioned in Ålandic history. However, although the author claims that he has consciously refrained from attempting a grand analysis, the picture given by Kenneth Gustavsson's meticulous investigation of Åland's military history in 1919–39 is at odds with pacifist history-writing. Beside the obvious irony of the fact that it is possible to write a 431-page military history of the island of peace *between* the world wars, many of the details counteract the picture of a consistent Ålandic pacifism, as well as of demilitarization and neutralization as a successful solution, satisfactory to all parties. Instead, Gustavsson gives several examples of how Ålanders have been willing to contribute to the military defence of the islands, and how Åland has caused more or less constant security concerns to Finland and Sweden, from the 1920s into the cold war.[70]

In a series of newspaper articles and interviews from 2006, Gustavsson more directly criticized the idea of Åland as the islands of peace. He claimed that the demilitarization and neutralization never had protected Åland in wartime, and that Ålanders had forgotten the latest and perhaps most important agreement about the demilitarization: the bilateral agreement between Soviet and Finland in 1940, renewed in 1992, which was drafted while the Soviet Union was making military plans to conquer Åland in the first week of a war. Gustavsson stressed that the agreements of 1856, 1921, and 1940 all were military political documents intended to benefit the stronger party, not to protect the Ålanders. He also claimed that because of Åland's strategic location neither Sweden, Finland, nor Russia would ever accept Ålandic independence.[71]

---

[69] Eriksson et al. 2006, 78 ('ett intelligent och famsynt sätt [att] lösa etniska tvister utan våld och blodsspillan').
[70] Gustavsson 2012, 11, 246–7, 325, 410.
[71] *Tidningen Åland*, 7 March 2006, 18.

Åland and the Anglo-Saxons

Among writers of Ålandic history, it is a common assumption that Åland has been oriented towards the Anglo-Saxon world. For example, it is used to explain why most Ålanders were negative to the Continuation War (1941–44), when Finland's opponent the Soviet Union was allied with the UK and the US. 'A war of aggression in alliance with Nazi Germany did not attract the Anglo-Saxon-oriented Ålanders', according to a popular and richly illustrated book intended for Åland's youth.[72]

Martin Isaksson, an Ålandic politician who after retirement wrote a number of books on Åland's history, claims that the contact with British troops during the Crimean War laid the foundation for Åland's relationship with the English-speaking world. Some links seems to have existed earlier: Isaksson mentions that the British naval officer Sullivan, who did a reconnaissance mission in Åland's archipelago prior to the British attack, encountered a man in Degerby on Föglö island who spoke English; he also found a colour print of Queen Victoria and Prince Albert in a cabin.[73]

The most common explanation is that it was Åland's shipping industry that brought the islanders in contact with Britain. Tsar Alexander II's economic liberalization gave Ålandic ships access to the North Sea trade from 1856.[74] In Britain there was great demand for Baltic wood products, and in following decades Ålandic ships also started to take part in the transoceanic trade. There was also a huge emigration from Åland in the late nineteenth and early twentieth centuries, primarily to the US.

In *Åländskhet* ('Ålandic-ness'), Yvonne de Geer Hancock quotes an observer who in 1902 claimed that shipping and travels to America had made it unusual to find an Ålander who did not speak English.[75] Although this was probably a great exaggeration, the English language seems to have had a huge influence on Åland, especially in maritime circles. For example, *Den åländska segelsjöfartens historia* cites an 1878 log from an Ålandic ship which needed maintenance in St. Petersburg: 'Hadde stimbåt och flyttade fartyget in uti Man-of-War dockan'.[76] The name of

---

[72] Skogsjö & Wilén 1997, 29 ('Ett angreppskrig i förbund med Nazityskland lockade inte de anglosaxiskt orienterade ålänningarna'); Salminen 1979, 247–8; Mattsson-Eklund 2000, 341.
[73] Isaksson 1981, 131, 136, 211.
[74] Kåhre & Kåhre 1988, 78.
[75] De Geer-Hancock 1986, 14.
[76] Kåhre & Kåhre 1988, 119.

the 'Ålands Nautical Club', publisher of many books on maritime history, is another example of English influence on the language.

This mixing of languages was common also in maritime communities elsewhere, but in a small town with a huge shipping sector like Mariehamn—in 1880 home to fewer than 500 citizens—the impact was greater. Matts Dreijer, who grew up in Mariehamn in the early twentieth century, still used Anglicisms such as 'steambåt', 'girlfriend', and 'ålandsminded' in his 1984 autobiography.[77] The expression 'ålandsminded' is particularly interesting, since it describes a person willing to defend Åland and the Swedish language—against the Finnish language, that is.

The former local politician and banker Thorvald Eriksson, founder of the independence party Ålands framtid (Åland's Future), in 1996 described his identity as lacking emotional ties to any nation-state. Åland came first, then Scandinavia, then something universally Western influenced by Åland's maritime traditions. He is more attracted by the US than by the EU, because he shares the American dream: 'The dream about the strong individual who can take care of himself, about the small local community that manages most public matters … and the great community where moral intent carries weight'.[78] The book was partially written in Florida.

The strong position of the English-speaking world and the English language on Åland further illustrates the fact that the Ålandic defence of Swedishness is an entirely different phenomenon from the defence of national languages, or even minority languages, elsewhere. It is not the language in itself that is considered valuable, but autonomy, which could be threatened if the Finnish language became so common that the Åland Convention of 1921 became redundant. The incursion of English and other foreign languages is completely irrelevant in this respect, and is therefore not perceived a threat.

National character

Many writers of regional history on Åland describe the islanders' character. The early descriptions are the most detailed, but all the descriptions old and new, share some common traits. K. A. Bomansson claimed that

---

[77] Dreijer 1984.
[78] Eriksson 1996, 177–8 ('Drömmen om den starka individen som klarar sig själv, om det lilla lokala samhället som klarar det mesta av det gemensamma … och om den stora gemenskapen där moraliska uppsåt väger tungt').

ignorant observers had spread prejudices about the Ålanders, when actually they were a happy, lively, polite, and educated people. They had a tremendous sense of honour and therefore could not stand any kind of oppression or assaults. They were sober,[79] tidy, and had a sense of order. Furthermore, they were fast learners, skilled craftsmen, and born sailors. Many of them took to the waves in the summers, like the ancient Vikings leaving their homes in the care of their wives and servants. They did not lack courage when their duty to monarch and fatherland required it. Unfortunately they had a taste for luxury and levity, and a tendency to imitate the customs of the gentlefolk ('herrskapet'). The inhabitants of the skerries lagged behind the main Ålanders in education, but surpassed them in simplicity of dress and customs. The Ålanders' exaggerated propensity to engage in legal processes ('process-sjuka') had diminished of late, as so had their superstition.[80]

'Process-sjukan' had been mentioned in the eighteenth century by two Swedes who had written descriptions of Åland, Radloff and Ehrenmalm. Radloff even then concluded that superstition was almost unknown on Åland.[81] Part of Bomansson's description of the Ålanders, their love of freedom and courage in defence of the fatherland, was probably intended to help explain the uprising in 1808, which was the point of his book. On the other hand, Bomansson might have chosen that topic because he considered love of freedom and patriotism to be important values. Bomansson's description also reveals that he considers the Ålander to be a relatively wealthy married male farmer; he has a wife and servants, but he was not one of the gentlefolk.

Johannes Eriksson, one of the Åland movement's leaders, claimed that national character contributed to the Ålanders' yearning westwards:

> the Swedish people's temperament, their hospitality and their high culture, which have been allowed to develop freely on the foundation of the well-tried Nordic freedom, [have] exercised a strong attraction on us, a small remnant of a nation which loves freedom and wants to ... nurture it.[82]

---

[79] Coffee had supplanted alcohol, Bomansson claimed.
[80] Bomansson 1852, 28–9.
[81] Dreijer 2006, 319.
[82] Eriksson & Virgin 1961, 16 ('det svenska folkets kynne, dess gemyt och dess höga kultur, som fritt fått utvecklas på den beprövade nordiska frihetens grundvalar, utövat stark dragningskraft på oss, en liten folkspillra som älskar frihet och vill ... vårda denna'), 21.

Although the Russian troops on Åland raised flags red as blood as a symbol of freedom and fraternity, Eriksson doubted that the vast Russian masses could feel the responsibility that was the true foundation of freedom.

In his biography of Julius Sundblom, Johannes Salminen writes that 'the Ålanders are not a breed that accepts being put under guardians'.[83] The idea that Åland is a free, egalitarian society where people rule themselves and do not bow to authority is one of the most central parts of Ålandic identity.

In the volume about the eighteenth century of *Det åländska folkets historia* (2006), Stig Dreijer claims that the Ålanders were known to be extrovert and good at handling people. The happy and talkative Ålanders who carried passengers along the mail road made an impression on travellers with their insights into politics and social issues.[84] According to Justus Harberg, who has written the history of Åland's motorized shipping, Åland's insular position forced its inhabitants into maritime trades, which made them entrepreneurial and individualistic, important characteristics for successful seafarers.[85] These examples illustrate how Åland's geographic location, close to the sea and important routes of communication, is seen as the foundation of the islanders' character.

You can also find regional stereotypes within Åland. Bomansson was of the opinion that the inhabitants of Kumlinge parish in Åland's eastern archipelago were similar to their Finnish neighbours, since they stuck to their decisions through thick and thin.[86] Unlike twentieth-century Ålandic history writers, Bomansson did not stress the difference between Ålanders and Finns.

An egalitarian island

Åland is often depicted as an egalitarian peasant society without an aristocracy or a proletariat. There were very few manors on Åland. Mariehamn was founded in 1861, but effectively remained a village until the early twentieth century, with a tiny bourgeoisie.

---

[83] Salminen 1979, 147 ('Ålänningarna är inte ett släkte som låter sig ställas under förmyndare').
[84] Dreijer 2006, 419.
[85] Harberg 1995, 10.
[86] Bomansson 1852, 112.

Ålandic history-writing has been negative towards the role of the local elite during the 1808 uprising and the Crimean War. Yvonne De Geer-Hancock claims that there is a widespread historically founded suspicion of priests from mainland Finland. According to her, many priests were Fennomans during the language struggle in Finland, and those from Nyland had a 'manor mentality' that clashed with Åland's democratic and egalitarian traditions. She mentions several instances of priests who were appalled by the Ålanders unwillingness to bow or tip their caps.[87]

Kuvaja also recognizes that a large number of Finnish-speaking priests were active on Åland in the late nineteenth and early twentieth centuries, and that many of them sympathized with the Fennomans. Fennoman priests were particularly common in Brändö, the parish closest to the Finnish mainland. However, he claims that since the Ålandic parishes were so small and poor, they only attracted priests at an early stage in their careers or who could not find work elsewhere.[88]

Bomansson had noted the smallness of Åland's parishes. He concluded that this factor compromised the wealth of the peasants since they had to support 'numerous clergy'. According to the book *Bomarsund* (2006), Bomansson was impressed by the casual relations between French officers and soldiers during the Bomarsund campaign, and compared this to the regional elite's inability to get along with ordinary people.[89]

In his 1998 textbook, Lindh mentions discussions on Åland in the 1960s and 1970s about greater independence for the Church on Åland, with the intention of maintaining the small parishes. Lindh's picture of Åland's priests is relatively positive, with the exception of one Bondestam in Jomala, who in 1924 wanted to plough up the Stone Age remains at Jettböle. The hero of that story is the cottager Karl Johan Karlsson, who discovered the site in 1905 and in 1924 tried to stop the priest from destroying it.[90]

It must also be mentioned that some priests from the mainland gained widespread popularity on Åland. The most notable example was Valdemar Nyman, who wrote the art historical appendix to Matts Dreijer's first volume of *Det åländska folkets historia*.

---

[87] De Geer-Hancock 1986, 113–14.
[88] Kuvaja et al. 2006, 85–6.
[89] Bomansson 1854, 39 ('ett vidlyftigt kleresi'); Robins et al. 2004, 92.
[90] Lindh 1998, 15 ff., 388.

Egalitarianism and suspicion of the authorities can also be traced in Åland's maritime history-writing. A dichotomy is made between Ålandic peasant captains and city captains from the mainland. According to *Den åländska segelsjöfartens historia* by Georg and Karl Kåhre, the self-taught Ålandic captains differed from their educated counterparts from Finland's coastal cities: 'The peasantry had an established mistrust of the city captains' personal characteristics, their propensity to spend and live extravagantly, and not least to their bullying'. In order to prevent new legislation that made education a requirement for captains, Ålanders in 1873 petitioned the Senate in Helsinki with statistics that proved that Ålandic captains had fewer and less costly accidents than their educated mainland colleagues. A city captain replied in *Helsingfors Dagblad* that this was due to the fact that Ålandic captains stayed at home with their wives during the dangerous winter, and that they mainly freighted wood which kept their ships afloat after shipwreck. According to Kåhre, the Ålanders' aversion to educated captains was in part founded on their unwillingness to submit to strict discipline: they wanted to maintain the equality they were used to at home.[91]

With time the Ålandic captains got education, and as the voyages got longer the captains' authority was strengthened. 'The equality of the Stockholm voyages proved to be unsustainable in critical situations on foreign seas and in foreign harbours'. Farmhands learned that the equality they were accustomed to was blown clean away at sea. However, the difference between Ålandic and city captains did not disappear. According to Kåhre, the Ålandic captain remained an Ålandic farmer, courteous in a rustic way, moderate, thoughtful, and a bit of a miser. The captains from Finland's cities were ashamed of him in his simple clothes, but the Ålander just smiled at their fine manners and waited for the moment when they would ask him for a loan.[92]

This ideal of simplicity and equality seems to have endured at least within parts of the Ålandic shipping industry. The legendary ship owner Algot Johansson, elected Ålander of the twentieth century, was also known for his simple manners. The CEO of Viking Line, Gunnar Eklund,

---

[91] Kåhre & Kåhre 1988, 134–5 ('Allmogen hyste en ingrodd misstro till stadskaptenernas personliga egenskaper, deras lust att spendera och leva högt och inte minst till deras översittarfasoner').

[92] Kåhre & Kåhre 1988, 146 ff ('Stockholmsseglatsernas jämlikhet visade sig ohållbar i kritiska situationer på främmande hav och i främmande hamnar').

claimed in 1997 that it was part of the Ålandic shipping philosophy not to indulge in exclusive habits that isolate you from the people you are dependent on, and he saw pluralism and non-elitism as the most important characteristics of Ålandic culture.[93]

According to a survey from the early 1990s, 41.5% of Ålanders claimed they did not belong to any class, compared to 28% among mainland Finno-Swedes. Only 4.6% of Ålanders considered themselves upper middle class or higher, compared to 14.8% of Finno-Swedes.[94] The survey was conducted by researchers from Åbo Akademi University. In the survey about identity that was initiated and carried out regionally on Åland in 1999 no questions were asked about class. Thus the questions asked in these surveys might tell us as much about identity as the answers given.

Education

According to Ålandic history-writing, it was not only maritime education that met with resistance on Åland. Farmers also opposed the introduction of agricultural education, and attempts to establish primary schools were opposed by Åland's municipalities. The association Svenska folkskolans vänner, which wanted to improve the situation for primary schools in the Swedish-speaking parts of Finland, toured Åland in 1884 in order to speed up the process. At one of their meetings, on Kökar in the archipelago, one local claimed that they could found a school—if Finnish, Russian, and the classical languages were on the curriculum.[95]

This was beyond the purpose of the primary schools, where basic skills in arithmetic and the mother tongue (Swedish) were taught. The primary schools also played an important role in promoting Finnish patriotism, Swedish cultural heritage, and affection for the local community ('hembygdskänsla').[96]

Sottunga and Kökar in the archipelago were among the last municipalities in Finland to get primary schools. Of course, geographic and economic factors contributed to the late start for primary schools in the archipelago, but even in main Åland's richest parishes primary schools faced stiff opposition. In Jomala some of the wealthier inhabitants were in favour of a municipal primary school, but the majority of farmers were

---

[93] Åländsk odling 1997, 61.
[94] Sundback 1999, 33.
[95] Kuvaja et al. 2006, 280 ff., 451 ff.
[96] Kuvaja et al. 2006, 477.

against it. In 1887 a private primary school was established, with the future leader of the Åland movement, Julius Sundblom, as the teacher, followed two years later by another. Only because the number of votes in the municipal elections was dependent on income—and many no-votes were declared invalid— did the wealthy minority manage to rally a majority of votes behind making the schools municipal in 1893. Their opponents managed to delay the take-over until 1895 by appealing to the Senate in Helsinki.[97]

Kuvaja also mentions that there were two Finnish-language primary schools on Åland in the late nineteenth century; they were only active for a few years, however.[98]

In 1904 and 1914 the newspaper *Åland*—where Sundblom was editor-in-chief—complained that Ålanders from the countryside were reluctant to send their children to the grammar school in Mariehamn. In Österbotten and Nyland, two Finnish mainland provinces with Swedish-speaking populations, the situation was much better. Kuvaja is of the opinion that the grammar school in Mariehamn contributed to the formation of an Ålandic intelligentsia. As late as the 1910s the bulk of civil servants appointed to offices on Åland were from the mainland.[99]

In the volume about the twentieth century in *Det åländska folkets historia*, Erik Tudeer claims that Ålanders had a low propensity to enter secondary education throughout the twentieth century, in the 1960s and 1970s still the lowest in Finland. He believes that the economic structure of Åland did not demand education, and that the few who did educate themselves had problems finding work.[100]

Matts Dreijer also mentioned the difficult start for Mariehamn's city library: from its late beginning in 1922 until 1939 it was crammed into a single room. He recalled how a member the city council during a debate about the library's budget exclaimed that he could not understand why anyone would read books, since such people were not considered quite right in the head. According to Tudeer, lending at the library was still lower than the Finnish average in the late twentieth century.[101]

---

[97] Kuvaja et al. 2006, 455–6.
[98] Kuvaja et al. 2006, 458.
[99] Kuvaja et al. 2006, 490.
[100] Tudeer 1993, 68, 73, 234.
[101] Dreijer 1984, 171; Tudeer 1993, 242.

Although education has been held in relatively low regard on Åland, regional writers of history—since they have bothered to put pen to paper—might be expected to have a more positive view, yet even some of them display less than favourable attitudes towards culture and learning. Matts Dreijer claimed that he was never interested in literature, and that his home environment during his school years did not encourage such interests. At university he passed the literature courses by approaching even more important works with a special, time-saving method: he only read the very beginning, the middle, and the very end. Torvald Eriksson stated that he lacked stylistic ability and had never intended to write a book in the first place; he also claimed to dislike politicians who posed as intelligent and educated by using such abstract, academic language that common people could not understand what they were saying.[102] Eriksson's writings all have outspoken political aims, and as an experienced local politician he probably concluded that appearing overly educated was not a political asset in the Ålandic environment.

The artist Tage Wilén, painter of motifs from Åland's history that can be seen in the parliament building in Mariehamn, says that his Ålandicness made him paint 'popular and understandable' pictures, but that he lately he has become less popular and less understood.[103]

In his school textbook, the teacher and headmaster Kurt Lindh concluded that the Ålanders have not been a literary people, compared to, say, the Icelanders or Faroese. He found it surprising that the seafaring Ålanders were not inspired by their contacts with foreign lands. As an explanation he cited Salminen's view that the harsh conditions on Åland have made the inhabitants stick to what is practical and useful; the extravagances of poetry, religion, or fantasy have not been able to have an impact on the Ålander's world of down-to-earth realities. 'Harsh conditions have taught him to ... hold on to what he has, and that means a quite severely curtailed horizon—no matter how wide the sea swells around his skerries'.[104] Lindh and Salminen are thus of the opinion that different aspects of an island's geographical conditions affect the mentality of the islanders in different ways. The waterway connections widen

---

[102] Dreijer 1984, 117–18, 171.
[103] Åländsk odling 1997, 233.
[104] Lindh 1998, 342 ('Sträva villkor har lärt honom att ... hålla fast vid det lilla han har, och det betyder en ganska hårt beskuren horisont—hur vida havet än svallar kring hans kobbar').

the intellectual horizons, while the scarce resources encourage a narrower, practical focus on economic realities—and on Åland the latter has become dominant.

Money

Although Ålanders have had low levels of education compared to surrounding areas, they have for several decades had higher incomes than both Swedes and Finns.[105] Money and the economy are important elements in Ålandic history-writing. The maritime history-writing is of course in essence economic history, and it was also funded by donations from shipowners. Business is also well represented among the writers of Ålandic history. Erik Tudeer, writer of the volume on Åland's twentieth century in *Det åländska folkets historia*, was active in the banking sector in Turku and Helsinki before returning to Åland in the late 1980s. Torvald Eriksson was, beside his political career, CEO of the island's leading bank, Ålandsbanken. Matts Dreijer, the most important figure in Ålandic history-writing, was director of Åland's producer cooperative before he—according to himself because of the higher salary—turned to archaeology. He devoted a chapter of his autobiography to his wartime business enterprises; most notably he made money on the export of Swedish iron ore to Germany, aided by an unsecured loan from his friend Torsten Rothberg at Ålandsbanken. He also made some less fortunate speculations. Dreijer claimed that society needed more people who could put money to good use, and lamented the fact that he lacked such entrepreneurial skills himself.[106]

Ship-owners are among the most respected figures in Ålandic history, as was confirmed in a poll to pick the most important Ålander of the century run by Åland's Radio in 1998. The winner was shipowner Algot Johansson, and three others were among the top ten. Julius Sundblom, founder of the newspaper *Åland*, the island's leading politician for the first half of the century and regarded as the man behind Åland's autonomy, came only second.[107] Perhaps Sundblom's failure as a businessman cost him the top position. He tried to make it as a shipbuilder and ship owner in the 1920s, using his position as editor-in-chief to agitate for the state's forests to be used to supply Åland's ships with timber at a low cost

---

[105] Tuder 1993, 270.
[106] Dreijer 1984, 180–1.
[107] *Nya Åland*, 31 December 1998, 'Algot är århundadets ålänning', <http://www.nyan.ax/nyheter/arkiv.pbs?news_id=5758>, 26 May 2014.

or free. Poorly judged speculation contributed to his fall, but Tudeer also describes him as an incompetent amateur. He also criticizes Sundblom's use of his position in Åland's society and in Ålandsbanken to further his family's economic interests. Sundblom's debts amounted to millions and almost bankrupted the bank, a fact that was kept hidden to the public at the time.[108]

Since Algot Johansson was elected Ålander of the century, a closer look at the description of him might reveal something about Ålandic identity. A biography of Algot was published in 1998, which might have helped him win the poll the same year. The initiative for the book was taken by his sons and family, who wanted to describe how the 'crofter boy in half a lifetime built the Sally company ... into Finland's ... largest shipping company ... [which] affected a large proportion of Ålanders'.[109]

According to his biographer Hasse Svensson, the Ålanders' interest in Algot stems from the fact that he employed so many of them: at the peak around 2,000 persons, or ten per cent of Åland's population at the time. His simple manners contributed to his popularity: he loved physical work and at an old age could still be seen cleaning up construction sites together with his wife.[110]

Algot made his first money working in the forest and by selling hay to the Russian troops on Åland during the First World War. He had a brief career as a sailor before he tried his hand at coffee smuggling. (According to Tudeer, smuggling has not been seen as a serious crime on Åland.[111] There is also a museum of smuggling in Degerby, Föglö.) When Algot was caught the third time he escaped to New York to avoid prison. There he worked as a construction worker building skyscrapers and bridges; in the evenings he privately built houses on Long Island. He married Agda, another Ålander working in the US, and just before the Great Depression they returned to Åland. He invested his money in property and various businesses, mainly in ships. In the 1950s and 1960s he owned Finland's largest tanker company. He also helped finance the start of the passenger traffic between Sweden and Finland. To improve housing for his employees he constructed apartment buildings in Mariehamn, where his wife could be

---

[108] Tudeer 1993, 34, 37–8.
[109] Svensson 1998, 6, preface by Sven-Erik Johansson ('torparpojken som på en halv livstid byggde upp Sally-bolaget ... till Finlands ... största rederi ... [som] berörde en stor del av ålänningarna').
[110] Svensson 1998, 15–16.
[111] Tudeer 1993, 66.

seen sweeping the stairs at night.[112] Algot, at least as he is portrayed in the biography, seems to embody the Ålandic virtues of a simple, inexpensive life, his money wisely invested rather than squandered on luxury. Probably the regional economic elite had to maintain simple lifestyles to avoid the animosity that Ålanders had traditionally shown towards pretentious priests and administrators from the mainland.

In the book *Bomarsund* from 2004 it is claimed that Ålanders have a passion for business. A Russian major-general is quoted as saying that the Ålanders' leanings are more directed at making money than at abstract speculations. The authors conclude that this business-mindedness was a consequence of the fact that Åland was not self-sufficient in grain; the inhabitants depended on trade for their subsistence.[113]

It is a common perception that Ålanders, rich or poor, are good at handling money and that they want to support themselves. For example, Tudeer explains the low costs of poor relief in 1920 compared to the rest of Finland in part by national character: Ålanders back then wanted to manage without help as long as possible, as they still do today. The main reason behind the low number of poor was however according to Tudeer Åland's economic structure.[114]

Åland in the twentieth century is portrayed as a predominantly right-wing society, an image which is confirmed in regional elections. In such a climate, the Ålanders' propensity to keep and multiply their money is seen as something positive. From a socialist viewpoint this thrift can of course be described more negatively. In Åland's most renowned piece of fiction, *Katrina* (1936), the author Sally Salminen described some greedy ship-owners in Vårdö, based on a recognizable family. According to Dreijer, Salminen had quite advanced socialist ideas, which in his opinion was not uncommon 'even on Åland' at the time. Algot Johansson chose to name his shipping company 'Sally' in her honour, since he saw her as a successful businesswoman—and on top of that the name did not cost him anything.[115]

According to Matts Dreijer, there was also a widespread resistance to trade unions on Åland. Dreijer was working for Åland's chamber of commerce, and wanted to establish a functioning labour market on Åland

---

[112] Svensson 1998, 30–42, 70, 87, 92 ff.
[113] Robins et al. 2004, 15.
[114] Tudeer 1993, 26, 70.
[115] Dreijer 1984, 218–19; Svensson 1998, 49.

in order to avoid damaging conflicts. When in 1969 he visited a construction site in Mariehamn together with the head of the Organization of Labour Unions in Finland, Niilo Hämäläinen, one worker claimed that he would never join a union since only Finns and communists were members. It has been common on Åland to equate Finns with communists and socialists.[116]

Interestingly, the view of history closely associated with socialism, materialism, has been mentioned in connection to Ålandic history-writing. Tudeer writes that Matts Dreijer's 'ability as an economist and businessman to apply the materialist view of history to Åland's past has attracted attention', and Bjarne Lindström claims that Dreijer and Marx agree upon the cultural sphere's dependency on economic factors. Based upon the same materialistic reasoning, Lindström argues that Åland's cultural autonomy is doomed to fail if it is not matched by economic autonomy.[117] The Ålandic version of materialism seems to be limited to the idea that the economic base determines the cultural superstructure. This corresponds with the often expressed idea that Ålanders give priority to practical, economic matters over culture and abstract speculations. The similarity to the Marxist version of historical materialism is however weak, since the idea of class struggle as the driving force in history is nowhere to been seen. This is hardly surprising considering the fact that Åland is portrayed as an egalitarian, classless society.

Differences on Åland

In recent decades, writers of Ålandic history have started to acknowledge the stratification that did exist within traditional Ålandic peasant society. In his volume about the eighteenth century in *Det åländska folkets historia*, Stig Dreijer mentioned that an elite formed among Åland's peasants, from which lay judges (*nämndemän*) of the regional court (*häradsrätten*) were elected. In the volume about the nineteenth century, Christer Kuvaja asks whether Åland was a homogenous society with small social and cultural differences, and answers that no, there was not only one but several Ålands.[118]

---

[116] Dreijer 1984, 191–2; Tudeer 1993, 56.
[117] Tudeer 1993, 150 ('förmåga att så som ekonom och affärsman tillämpa den materialistiska historieuppfattningen på Ålands förgångna har väckt intresse'); Lindström 1996, 401–402.
[118] Dreijer 2006, 364; Kuvaja et al. 2006, 70–1.

On main Åland, Jomala, Finström, and Sund constituted the core, Geta and Lumparland were the most peripheral, while Lemland, Hammarland, and Saltvik had a position in between. Among the archipelagic municipalities, Eckerö and Föglö had a special position because of their closeness to main Åland and their importance for communications. Vårdö had a position in the middle, while Kumlinge, Brändö, Sottunga, and especially Kökar were peripheral with problematic communications. For the inhabitants on Brändö, Turku was closer than Mariehamn. Economically there were three Ålands: in Jomala, Finström, Sund, Saltvik, and Hammarland agriculture was most important; in Eckerö, Föglö, Geta, Lemland, Lumparland, and Vårdö shipping and fishing were most important; while fishing dominated on Kumlinge, Brändö, Sottunga, and Kökar. According to Kuvaja, Eckerö in the west was strongly oriented westwards and Brändö in the east eastwards, which affected the islanders' view of Sweden and Finland. However, he concludes that there were no doubts that in both cases the Ålanders' first affinity was to the inhabitants of main Åland.[119]

Statistics and Research Åland today divide the island region into Mariehamn, the rural districts, and the archipelago. Eckerö is no longer considered part of the archipelago, since it is connected to main Åland by a bridge. Although Åland's total population is growing, all the municipalities in the archipelago have a shrinking population, with the exception of Vårdö which has a very short ferry connection to main Åland. In contrast, all of main Åland's municipalities are growing, with the exception of Geta in the north where the population is stagnant.[120] Åland of today is thus divided along the same lines as in the late nineteenth century. Kuvaja's observations about the attitudes towards Finland in the eastern archipelago are reflected in modern material. A 1999 survey showed that persons born in the archipelago identified themselves as Finns to a slightly greater extent than persons born in the rural districts. Their primary identity was Ålander, although not to the same extent as for main Ålanders. Interestingly, out of the eight respondents in the survey who chose to add a freely formulated identity, identification with Brändö and the archipelago surfaced. In the interviews about Ålandic identity conducted in 1997, a respondent from Brändö answered that he did not feel very special just because he was an

---

[119] Kuvaja et al. 2006, 70–1.
[120] Statistics and research Åland 2011, 3, <http://www.asub.ax/files/alsiff11en.pdf>.

Ålander; the inhabitants of Brändö live close to the Finnish mainland and know a lot of people there.[121]

Since expressions of identity in the archipelago differ from the pattern on main Åland, it is not surprising that it is in the archipelago that we can find most examples of local, municipality-level history-writing. In fact it is the small, easternmost municipalities, Kökar and Brändö, which have been most prominent in this field. Brändö is the only municipality on Åland which has published an official municipal history. Kökar has seen a number of works devoted to its history, most notably by Ulla-Lena Lundberg.[122] In contrast, the municipalities on main Åland, much larger in terms of population, have not had their histories written. Probably the need for a local, municipal history is low on main Åland, since the inhabitants there can to a large extent identify with the regional Ålandic history, where main Åland has centre stage. The production of municipal history-writing in the archipelago is probably influenced by a strong sense of local identity, influence by the municipalities' insularity and distance from main Åland, as well as by differences in traditional economy and culture.

Prehistory and the early Middle Ages

Until the late twentieth century, Åland's prehistory and Middle Ages were the dominating theme in regional history-writing. Since written records are absent or scarce, the interpretations have mainly been based on archaeological remains and place names.

The first Ålander

The first writer of Åland's history, K. A. Bomansson, believed that Åland had originally been populated by Sami, who had later been replaced by Finns. They were in turn replaced by Swedes who were the ancestors of the modern Ålanders. He based his assumptions entirely on place names.[123]

In the early twentieth century, a Stone Age settlement was found at Jettböle in Jomala parish, and the Germanic appearance of the skeletons caused celebrations among the Svecoman-minded elite in Mariehamn,

---

[121] Häggblom et al. 1999, 14, 17; *Åländsk odling* 1997, 217.
[122] Nordman 2006; Lundberg 1976.
[123] Bomansson 1852, 25–6.

who saw it as proof of the Swedish language's provenance. However, in the inter-war years it was discovered that the oldest human remains on Åland belonged to the eastern Comb Ceramic culture. According to Matts Dreijer this was a shock to orthodox Ålanders. When he spoke about the new findings, one of his listeners told him to bury the potsherds and shut up. Considering these attitudes, it is not surprising that Dreijer did not elaborate on where the first Ålanders came from in his 1943 school textbook—he just mentioned that they probably arrived in small open boats.[124]

In his later writings, Dreijer expressed the opinion that ceramics and tools indicate that the first Ålanders came from the vicinity of Turku. He does stress, however, that Stone Age cultures cannot be equated with modern nations, and that many languages were probably spoken within the vast Comb Ceramic area, not only Finnish. A critique of older tendencies to identify Stone Age cultures with modern peoples is common in Ålandic history-writing. Benita Mattsson-Eklund also mentions that although on Åland the eastern Comb Ceramic culture was followed by the western Pitted Ware culture, many scholars question the difference between the cultures, and claim they were only regional variations.[125]

The textbook *Åland* from 1982 called the eastern Comb Ceramic peoples 'Ålanders' in scare quotes. From the Bronze Age onwards, the inhabitants of Åland are called Ålanders without scare quotes.[126] The marks were probably intended to indicate that the easterners were not real Ålanders.

The debate about Åland's prehistoric settlement has for a long time mainly concerned how large the eastern and western influences were. However, in 1997 the archaeologist Kenneth Gustavsson, born on Kökar and employed at Åland's museum, wrote a doctoral dissertation which, based on analyses of grain and pottery, concluded that the Bronze Age settlement in Otterböte, Kökar, was probably a seasonal camp for seal hunters from the Lusatian Culture on the southern coast of the Baltic Sea, mainly in present-day Poland. This finding found its way into the Ålandic school textbook that was published the following year.[127]

---

[124] Dreijer 1984, 134–5; Dreijer 1943, 52.
[125] Dreijer 1983, 21 ff., 46 ff.; Mattsson-Eklund 2000, 57.
[126] Gustafsson 1982, 24 ff., 1991, 24 ff.
[127] Gustavsson 1997, 132.

The Ålandic perception of the islands' earliest inhabitants has thus undergone several stages: first they were believed to be western, which was equated with being Swedish; then they were admitted to be eastern—which was not equated with being Finnish. During recent decades the east–west dichotomy has finally become less relevant.

However, in Åland's maritime history-writing, the ethnicity and origin of the first Ålanders has always been quite irrelevant. In *Den åländska segelsjöfartens historia*, the question of where the first Ålander's came from is not touched upon; what matters is that they came by sail. The possibility that they might have come over the ice is initially mentioned, but quickly forgotten. The first Ålander, who according to the book might have arrived a beautiful summer's day on a vessel with a sail of elk skin, was courageous and without fear of the sea horizon. The author's main point is obviously that Ålanders have always been great sailors. He criticizes the Roman historian Tacitus claim from AD 98 that the Sveonians in the Baltic did not have sails, but only oars; this was based on hearsay, and probably only referred to the local intra-archipelagic traffic.[128] The identification of Sveonians with Ålanders hints that the author believed they were ethnically western. However, their ethnicity was secondary compared to the overarching question of their skill as sailors.

Dreijer's view of the Middle Ages

In the first volume of *Det åländska folkets historia* (1979) Dreijer described Åland's history from the Stone Age to the sixteenth century. His theories were now fully developed, although he later made some minor additions and alterations. His main line of thought is that Åland was Christianized before the adjacent Swedish mainland (Svealand), and that Finland was Christianized through a series of Ålandic–Danish crusades in Åland's heyday in the twelfth century. Dreijer's argumentation rests on three main pillars, which he repeatedly returns to in his writings:[129]

- ❖ Lauritz Weibull's method of source criticism.
- ❖ Erik Aarup's thesis that initiative to economic contacts always reached from more developed peoples to barbarian peoples.

---

[128] Kåhre & Kåhre 1988, 15 ff., 21.
[129] Dreijer 1987, 3.

❖ The conviction that it was impossible to navigate the open sea before the Hanseatic cogs were developed in the early thirteenth century.

A consequence of Dreijer's view of history is that the historical importance of the Vikings was reduced. Since it was impossible for the Vikings to cross the open Atlantic Ocean, he did not believe in their westward travels to the Faroe Islands, Iceland, Greenland, and America; when mentioned in early sources those names referred to places in the Baltic Sea. Eastward travel to Russia and the Byzantine Empire was the preserve of Frisian and Jewish merchants and slave traders, not Swedish Vikings.[130]

The discovery of the trade route to southern Russia and the Near Orient in the early ninth century brought the Nordic area under continental, mainly Frankish influence, Dreijer argued. The appalling seaworthiness of early ships made it necessary for tradesmen to use the protected route through Åland's archipelago. Taxation of this trade was the foundation of Åland's period of greatness. According to Dreijer, Åland's position on the trade route was the main reason why bishop Ansgar visited Birka/Åland in about 830: his aim was to safeguard the commercial and political interests of the Frankish superpower. Björkö in Lake Mälaren, traditionally considered the location of Birka, was a short-lived slave trade colony, and not a product of the primitive culture in the surrounding valley. Borrowing the words of Lauritz Weibull, Dreijer describes Björkö as a 'robbers nest'.[131]

Denmark was the first of the Nordic countries to become civilized, and according to Dreijer Åland experienced a period of greatness as Denmark's strategic outpost in the east in the eleventh and twelfth centuries. Finland was Christianized in a series of Danish crusades from Åland, which was ruled by crusader jarls. In the twelfth century Kastelholm Castle was built with the help of the Order of St John. Six large stone churches were erected in the early to mid twelfth century, and towards the end of the century they were equipped with large defensive towers for protection against pirate attacks by heathen Finns and Balts. Dreijer argued that the conventional dating of the churches to the thirteenth

---

[130] Dreijer 1983, 170–7, 182.
[131] Dreijer 1983, 90–1, 113, 203–204, 182 ('rövarnäste').

century was based on the misconception that Åland was Christianized after the coast of Uppland in Sweden.[132]

Dreijer developed his theories of Åland's medieval greatness during the cold war, a period when especially in it Finland was believed that small states had very little room for manoeuvre, and that history was decided by struggles between great powers. In line with this, Dreijer saw the Frankish and Danish–English 'superpowers' as the most important actors in the early Middle Ages. Åland's importance came from its location on the superpowers' eastward trade route.

In Dreijer's vision, Åland's Golden Age ended with the construction of high-boarded cogs, which could cross the open waters of the Baltic and did not need to follow the route through Åland's archipelago. In the early thirteenth century the Danish power collapsed, and Åland came to be dominated by Sweden. Following Weibull, Dreijer claimed that the legends about early Swedish crusades in Finland were biased accounts that were later used to claim sovereignty over Finland.[133] Dreijer used Weibullian criticism of the Swedish national history-writing he had previously supported himself. Much of this criticism, for example the scepticism towards the early Swedish crusades, is today embraced by most scholars. However, the deconstruction of Swedish national myths made room for Dreijer's new construction of Ålandic myths.

Since the earliest reliable sources for Åland's history are from the fourteenth century, Dreijer's interpretations of early history are to a large extent based on architecture and archaeological remains. Of those, the so-called Wenni cross has a central position. The cross stood at Sund Church, and in the 1950s some rune inscriptions were discovered on top of it. Dreijer interpreted the cross as the grave of bishop Wenni (aka Unni), who is supposed to have been buried in Birka. In his mind, this proved that Birka had been situated on Åland.[134]

Dreijer also constructed Åland's period of greatness by borrowing pieces of history that traditionally had been part of other areas' historical edifices. According to Bomansson, the word Åland stemmed from the ancient 'aa', meaning water. Dreijer rejected the theory that the Å in Åland referred to water; he was strongly convinced that it stemmed from the ancient Germanic word 'ahwi-o', island. He was of the opinion that the Finnish

---

[132] Dreijer 1983, 9, 255–6, 268 ff., 325, 350–1, 349 ff.
[133] Dreijer 1983, 240–1, 291, 293.
[134] Dreijer 1983, 196 ff.

name for Åland, Ahvenanmaa, had preserved the oldest form of Åland's name, Ahviland. (Bomansson had been of the opinion that the Finnish name Ahvenanmaa—literally meaning 'Perchland'—was a product of a jocular mind). It was central to Dreijer to interpret the name Åland as 'Island', since it enabled him to suppose that all mentions in medieval sources of place names that meant island in any language actually referred to Åland. Islandan, Island, Hislandia, Islanorum, 'the islands of the Baltic Sea', Värend, Guarandia, Varidland, Olandia, Holm, Saari, Sjaland, Gulandia, Oningus, Oltlandia are all names in medieval sources which Dreijer equated with Åland. He was also of the opinion that the medieval Hälsingland Law had originally been the lawcode of Åland.[135]

During the Åland movement, Finnish scholars had suggested that the island of Saari ('Island') in the Finnish national epic Kalevala was identical to Åland. Their objective was to strengthen Finland's historical claims to the island.[136] After he abandoned Swedish nationalism for a more independent Ålandic view of history, Dreijer used his former opponents' idea to strengthen ancient Åland's importance.

Dreijer's interpretation of Åland's etymology did not gain widespread acceptance on the island; all other local history writers believe that 'Åland' stems from water, except the 1982 school textbook *Åland* that presents both theories.[137]

The view of Sweden's and Åland's early medieval history that Dreijer presented in *Det åländska folkets historia* was in part based on Lauritz Weibull's school of thought: it was pro-Danish, regionalist, and most importantly used selective source criticism to attack the nationalist school of historians from Uppsala, the disciples of Harald Hjärne. Dreijer's view of Åland's later Middle Ages was however in line with the Swedish nationalist history-writing of Hjärne's circle. He interpreted the power struggles within the Union of Kalmar as a fight between the Danish and Swedish peoples, and he considered Ålanders who took part in the struggle against the Danes as heroes. One of them was Peter Fredag, 'one of those ruthlessly bold partisans, who always tend to step forward at decisive moments, when a true people fight for their freedom'.[138]

---

[135] Bomansson 1852, 14; Dreijer 1983, 90, 207 ff., 217 ff., 250–1, 260, 265, 283, 293, 485.
[136] Nordman 1986, 146.
[137] Mattsson-Eklund 2000, 57; Westergren & Nygren 2008, 63; Kåhre & Kåhre 1988, 21; Dreijer 1943, 46; Gustafsson 1982, 23.
[138] Dreijer 1983, 497, 511 ('tillhörde dessa hänsynslösa partigängare, som alltid plägar träda fram i avgörande stunder, då ett livsdugligt fol kämpar för sin frihet').

Nyman and Bertell in Dreijer's footsteps

A later part of *Det åländska folkets historia* treated Åland's medieval church art. It was authored by Valdemar Nyman (1904–1998), a priest who had moved to Åland in 1935, and was an art historical appendix to Dreijer's first volume in the series. In the preface, Nyman opposed nationalist thinking (for example, that Åland's art should be treated together with Finnish art), and considered it surprising that Åland was not always included in treatises on Scandinavian medieval art.[139]

Nyman adhered to Dreijer's idea that Åland's oldest churches had been erected in the twelfth century, at a time when Åland was governed by crusader jarls. Nyman opposed earlier interpretations of Åland's medieval church art whenever they suggested that artefacts had been manufactured in Finland or were copies of Finnish originals. He stressed that Åland's church art from early on had a 'self-evident, independent orientation to the south and west, [without] any room for emanations from the east whatsoever'.[140]

One example is the wooden baptismal font in Eckerö Church, suggested by one scholar to have been made in Finland in the seventeenth century. Nyman considered this to be romantic Ensign Stål adulation. (*The Tales of Ensign Stål* is an epic poem about the 1808–1809 war, one of the first examples Finnish National Romanticism.) Nyman rhetorically asked what could have driven Ålanders, 'ship's carpenters since heathen times, to the interior of Finland to get a wooden bowl crafted?' Given some understanding of Ålandic church life and mentality, it was according to Nyman self-evident that the Eckerö font was a local carpenter's attempt to copy the font in the mother parish of Hammarland when Eckerö Church was rebuilt in the late thirteenth century.[141]

Although Nyman supported Dreijer's view of Åland's grand past, Dreijer described Nyman as a European and world citizen who distanced himself from old-fashioned Ålandic-ness. He was also inspired by Catholicism.[142] It is possible that Nyman's emphasis on Åland's medieval connections to the west and south can be interpreted as an attempt to link

---

[139] Nyman 1980, ix.
[140] Nyman 1980, 4, 8 ('självfallna och självständiga orientering söderut och västerut, [utan] rum för någon som helst utstrålning österifrån').
[141] Nyman 1980, 17 ('skeppstimmermän sedan hedenhös, till det innersta Finland för att få en träskål slöjdad?').
[142] Dreijer 1984, 170.

the island to the larger Western European–Catholic–cultural sphere, not merely to Scandinavia.

Another Ålander who in the 1980s and early 1990s gave Dreijer's theories support was Erik Bertell. In his books about medieval taxation on Åland, he considered the taxation unit '*bol*' to be evidence that Åland had been part of the Danish realm during the early Middle Ages. In his latest work published 1993, *Medeltida skattesystem på Åland*, he also adhered to the ideas that Åland was the Iceland of the Norse sagas, and that Birka was situated on Åland.[143] However, by this time Dreijer's theories were already questioned at home.

Controversial school textbooks

In his autobiography, Matts Dreijer described his 1943 school textbook as overly influenced by National Romanticism and completely out-dated, and said he was ashamed to have written it. However, at least his old book showed that a defence of Swedishness had earlier been held in high regard on Åland. Dreijer considered this value to have been eroded lately, illustrated by the publication in 1984 of the textbook *Det åländska samhället*, intended to teach history and social studies for years 7–9 in Åland's schools.[144]

In the mid 1980s Dreijer's theories were still much debated. The author Kurt Lindh used five pages of *Det åländska samhället* to discuss whether Birka had been situated on Åland or not, giving roughly equal weight to both sides of the argument. However, Dreijer, who was thanked in the foreword as a reviewer, source, and advisor to the author, described the textbook's content as a shock. According to Dreijer, Lindh claimed that all researchers denounced Dreijer's interpretations of sources and place names, which was not a very accurate description of the carefully balanced textbook text. Lindh does not seem to have been taken back by Dreijer's critique; on the contrary, later editions of his textbook were more outspoken against the Birka hypothesis, since he added that a study in 1986 had showed that the cross in Sund could not be the grave of bishop Wenni. Dreijer's main objection, however that Lindh did not emphasize the differences between Åland and Finland clearly enough regarding place names, public opinion during the Crimean War, and whether Åland had

---

[143] Bertell 1983, 218, 1993, 83–4, 190 ff., 223, 203 ff.
[144] Dreijer 1984, 315.

been an ancient independent kingdom. Dreijer claimed that the textbook was an attempt to give a Finno-Swedish view of Åland's history.[145] Dreijer is extreme among Ålandic history-writers in his uncompromising stress on the differences between Åland and Finland in prehistoric times. In that respect most other history writers, from Bomansson onwards, are proponents of what Dreijer describes as a Finno-Swedish view.

Åland, a textbook in *hembygdskunskap* (local geography and history) first published in 1982 for use in years 3-6, accepted more of Dreijer's theories than did Lindh's book. The Birka thesis was presented rather carefully—it was stated in a caption that some scholars believe Birka was situated on Åland—but it did not question that the Sund cross was indeed the grave of archbishop Wenni. *Åland* also accepted Dreijer's dating of the island's churches and Kastelholm Castle. It also followed Dreijer's idea that Åland had not been integrated into the Swedish kingdom until the thirteenth century, and that it had possibly been ruled by Danes before.[146]

The most interesting aspect of the textbook *Åland* is that more clearly than any other book it portrays an autonomous Åland in the Middle Ages: 'Before the Danes came, Åland was probably an independent small kingdom. In the early days of the Swedish period it had an extensive autonomy'. Åland also had a county court (*landsting*) where lords and landowning farmers met to judge or mediate according to the laws of the province. The construction of Kastelholm reduced autonomy since power was transferred to the king's bailiff. The paragraph is followed by a student assignment: 'Discuss the similarity between the Middle Ages and our time—Åland has its own county court and laws of its own'.[147] The textbook was clearly drawing parallels between the political institutions of present and ancient Åland in an attempt to give historical legitimacy an autonomy that was still very recent.

New interpretations of the Middle Ages

The first year of the new millennium saw the first comprehensive volume on Åland's history. *Alla tiders Åland – Från istid till EU-inträde* was authored by Benita Mattsson-Eklund, and the initiative to the book came

---

[145] Lindh 1984, 272 ff., 1998, 336; Dreijer 1984, 315 ff.
[146] Gustafsson 1982, 3 ff.
[147] Gustafsson 1982, 35 ff ('Diskutera likheten mellan medeltiden och våra dagar—Åland har eget landsting och egna lagar').

from the regional government *Ålands landskapsstyrelse*. This was considered necessary since the publication of *Det åländska folkets historia* took such a long time, and the series was too detailed for readers looking for a general overview.[148] The author, a culture journalist at *Tidningen Åland*, had a view of Åland's Viking Age and Middle Ages that differs dramatically from Dreijer's.

Mattsson-Eklund had more confidence in Viking Age culture and the seaworthiness of Viking Age ships. She mentioned Dreijer's theories about Birka and that Kastelholm might have been built in the twelfth century by the Order of St John, but concluded that they were incorrect. She placed Åland's oldest churches in the thirteenth century, not the eleventh. Mattson-Eklund stated plainly that 'Dreijer's sweeping theories' have caused many historians to read everything written about Åland's history with suspicion. However, she consider it positive that he had placed Åland in a Nordic context, since the island is easily omitted or placed in the periphery in Swedish as well as Finnish accounts.[149]

In the opinion of Mattsson-Eklund, the oldest stone castle in Kastelholm was built in the late fourteenth century as a link in the fortress chain of the Victual Brothers, a body of privateers supporting king Albrecht of Mecklenburg in his power struggle with Margaret I of Denmark. Mattsson-Eklund did not believe the fortress offered protection to the islanders; rather it brought pirates and war to the islands.[150] The idea that fortifications attract war is widespread in Ålandic historiography.

In the booklet *Vikingatid på Åland*, published 2005 by Åland Board of Antiquities (Ålands Museibyrå), Dreijer's theories were not even mentioned. The author concluded that Birka was of great importance to Åland's trade, but referred to Birka on Björkö in Lake Mälaren. In Piotr Palamarz's extensive work *Kastelholms slott*, Dreijer's theories were only mentioned in one sentence: 'Based on a local idea about Åland's role in the Baltic Sea during the early Middle Ages, the castle has been dated to the late 1100s'. Palamarz himself is of the opinion that the main castle was probably built in the 1380s, and not later than 1400.[151] Thus authors from the Åland Board of Antiquities, Dreijer's old workplace, today barely

---

[148] Email from Benita Mattsson-Eklund, 15 June 2009.
[149] Mattsson-Eklund 2000, 80 ('Dreijers yviga teorier'); Mattsson-Eklund 2000, 85.
[150] Mattsson-Eklund 2000, 98 ff.
[151] Tomtlund 2005, 8; Palamarz 2004, 20 ('På basis av en lokal uppfattning av Ålands roll under tidig medeltid i Östersjöområdet har man daterat slottet till slutet av 1100-talet').

mention his ideas even if only to dismiss them; they rather pass over them completely.

Neither does the school textbook *Tidernas Åland–Från stenåldern till svenska tidens slut* (2008) mention Dreijer's theories. Birka, Kastelholm Castle, and Åland's churches are placed and dated conventionally.[152]

Although Dreijer's speculations about Åland's past never gained acceptance among academics, his writings highlighted the fact that knowledge about Åland's past rested on a very little evidence. In 1990 the art historian Åsa Ringbom started a research project about Åland's churches. The still on-going project was for the first seven years funded by the Academy of Finland and thereafter by Åland's Provincial government. 'One of the main aims of the project was to finally put an end to all speculations about the age of the churches', Ringbom notes. The project has used a wide range of scientific dating methods, including an improved method for mortar dating that has been developed by the project. Ringbom's conclusion is that the six oldest churches were built in the thirteenth century. In a spin-off, the 'International Mortar Dating Project', the methods developed on Åland have been used to date ancient Portuguese and Roman mortars.[153]

Ålandic Vikings

Bomansson in the 1850s was of the opinion that the farming Swedish colonists on Åland built fortresses to protect themselves against Vikings who were hiding in the labyrinthine archipelago. Thus he did not consider the Ålanders to have been Vikings, but he believed it was possible that some Vikings had settled among them.[154]

However, on 'the Viking island, Kökar' the population lived 'a romantic Viking life in the very present'. The Kökar islanders did not engage in agriculture, they were raised on the waves and moved in the summer to distant fishing grounds. They were different from other Ålanders in their physical appearance, and they spoke an almost incomprehensible dialect. The old word "viung' (Viking, vikung)' lived on in the

---

[152] Westergren & Nygren 2008, 42, 53, 62.

[153] Ringbom 2010, 4–5, 134 ('En av projektets viktigaste målsättningar var att äntligen sätta punkt för alla spekulationer kring kyrkornas ålder'), 138–9, 152; Ålands kyrkor website, 6 December 2010; International Mortar Dating Project website, 6 December 2011.

[154] Bomansson 1858, 10 ff.

local dialect in the sense of defiant and enterprising individual.[155] In Bomansson's eyes, settled famers like the population of Åland were not Vikings, while the peripatetic maritime life of the Kökar islanders rendered them worthy of the epithet Viking even in his time.

In of Matts Dreijer's later work, the Vikings were peripheral barbarians whose navigational skills had been grossly overestimated. In the first half of the twentieth century he had been more positive. According to his autobiography, the foundation for his early interest in Vikings was laid by the priest K. G. E. Mossander, who founded the scout movement on Åland and gave speeches to the boys about 'the Vikings' bravery, nobility, and self-sacrifice, how these sons of our land roamed the seas and conquered distant countries'. Dreijer also recalled from his childhood how the discovery of a dolichocephalic, Germanic, Stone Age Ålander in 1911 prompted high society in Mariehamn to throw a party, where the customs inspector Leonard Hagman gave a speech praising the great deeds of the Vikings. (Hagman's gravestone would be decorated with rune inscriptions.)[156]

In his textbook *Åland och Ålänningarna* (1943) Dreijer still described the Vikings in traditional Swedish fashion, including the myths of Old Uppsala ('the holy place of pilgrimage for all Swedes'), Great Svitjod, and Torgny the Lawspeaker. Songs and sagas are said to have been the spiritual foundation of the Viking expeditions: 'Thus was the spirit born and hardened, which enabled [them] to overcome all hardships and destroy all resistance'. According to Dreijer, the heroic Viking Age songs and sagas were a reaction to the decay that had begun to enter from the south.[157]

Dreijer's 1943 textbook also contains a twelve-page fictional story about the Viking Holmger from Gardö, who travelled eastwards. Here it is claimed that Tjockakarl (Kökar) was the Sveonian kingdom's easternmost outpost, from which a chain of beacons stretched all the way up to Hälsingland. Holmger's Ålandic Vikings were attacked by foreign Vikings,

---

[155] Bomansson 1858, 22 ff ('vikingalandet Kökar', 'ett romantiskt vikingalif midt i nutiden').
[156] Dreijer 1984, 26, 135.
[157] Dreijer 1943, 62 ('alla svenskars heliga vallfartsort'), 66 ('Så föddes och härdades den anda av stål, som gjorde det möjligt ... att övervinna alla svårigheter och nedkämpa allt motstånd').

short men with broad faces who were easily identified as easterners.[158] Viking was thus not an ethnic term to Dreijer.

Holmger is portrayed as a cautious leader who does not carelessly enter battles, although some of his men are upset that victories and loot escape them. In the chapter about shipowner August Troberg (1855–1935) Dreijer reconnects to the fictive Holmger and the historical Petter Ålander, a wealthy fourteenth-century merchant in Stockholm, who Dreijer portrays as a hero in the struggle against German influence. Despite the fact that centuries separated them, it was obvious to Dreijer that they were 'offshoots of the same family tree, full-blooded sons of their Ålandic people. The same male energy, the same courage to take responsibility, and the same cool afterthought characterized them all'.[159] These men were no doubt intended to be role models for the primary school pupils of the 1940s.

Karl and Georg Kåhre remarked in *Den åländska segelsjöfartens historia* that no Ålanders are mentioned in connection with Viking expeditions. However, since eastward-bound Viking fleets had to pass Åland it is likely that they contributed to the crew, the authors concluded.[160]

Mattsson-Eklund quoted *Finlands historia* by professor Torsten Edgren, who claimed that the Swedish-speaking Ålanders were the only ones in Finland to take part in the eastward Viking expeditions. Mattsson-Eklund also concluded that the Vikings' language was not Swedish, at least not such that we would understand it. She also mentioned a number of Vikings named in medieval sources that might have been from Åland.[161]

One of them, Hlödver from Saltvik, who participated in the Battle of Svolder, was celebrated in 2000 by Saltvik municipality on Åland. Since that year an annual Viking market has been arranged in Saltvik; in 2008 it attracted a total of 9,600 visitors over the course of three days. The celebration caused an intense debate in the regional newspapers concerning the appropriateness of using Hlödver as a front figure for the market even though it was highly questionable whether he really was from Åland.[162]

---

[158] Dreijer 1943, 73, 79–80.
[159] Dreijer 1943, 75 ff., 187 ('skott på samma stamträd, fullblodiga söner av sitt åländska folk. Samma manliga dådkraft, samma mod att taga ansvar och samma kalla eftertänksamhet kännetecknade dem alla').
[160] Kåhre & Kåhre 1988, 21–2.
[161] Mattsson-Eklund 2000, 49, 51.
[162] Fornföreningen Fibula, 'Historien om Hlödver den långe och Fornföreningen Fibula', <http://www.aland-vikingar.com/text.con?ipage=2>, 14 July 2009.

The discovery in 2014 of what seems to be a 40-meter-long Viking Age hall in Saltvik on Åland made several regional journalists remember Dreijer's theories, and in one case even apologize for having questioned them.[163] This demonstrates that few people on Åland are familiar with Dreijer's theories in detail. They associate them with Viking Age greatness in general, despite the fact that Dreijer himself believed the Vikings were grossly overestimated.

In a booklet from Åland Board of Antiquities, Jan Erik Tomtlund described Åland as the easternmost part of a fairly homogenous Viking Age Scandinavian cultural area. During periods when there was a central seat of power it was probably located outside Åland, but there might also have been times when Åland constituted an independent province. In the chapter 'Ålandic identity', Tomtlund stated that it is difficult to point out anything specifically Ålandic in the archaeological material, but mentions certain type of fibulas from female garments, and clay paws as amulets in the graves. The fibulas can be found both in Finland and Sweden, but are particularly common on Åland. He found the paws extremely exciting since huge finds of them in Russia illustrate Viking Age Åland's extensive network of contacts.[164]

The textbook *Tidernas Åland* from 2008, like Dreijer's 1943 textbook, contains a fictional story about an Ålandic Viking travelling eastwards. Sigbjörn returns in AD 950 from a journey to the Volga, where he among other things he had come in contact with Christianity. The chapter is preceded by a picture of a clay paw, which is used to confirm Åland's contacts with the Volga region.[165]

It is clear that Ålandic history-writing from the first decade of the new millennium is more open to the possibility of cultural influence from the east than was the case in the work of Matts Dreijer and Valdemar Nyman. In another respect there is however strong continuity in Ålandic history-writing: the question whether Åland was depopulated or not in the eleventh century.

---

[163] *Nya Åland*, 15 May 2014, 'Dagen då jag bad Matts Dreijer om ursäkt', <http://www.nyan.aland.fi/ledaren/spalten.pbs?news_id=83047&news_instance=266>, 26 May 2014.
[164] Tomtlund 2005, 29, 32–3.
[165] Westergren & Nygren 2008, 42 ff.

Interpretations of the eleventh-century gap

In 1943 Matts Dreijer was of the opinion that Thor and Odin were still venerated on Åland in the eleventh century, and that Christianity had established itself a century later.[166] This was probably a consequence of the emphasis he put in the 1940s on Åland's links to the Sveonian kingdom and Old Uppsala, which was considered to be the last stronghold of heathendom.

In his later writings he claimed that the Thing in Birka (for him, in Åland) had officially changed religion in around 1000—this conclusion probably derived from his belief that Åland was the Iceland of the Norse sagas. There is however a broad consensus among Ålandic history writers that the islands were Christianized early.[167]

Early Christianization is used to explain the lack of rune stones and heathen burial mounds from the eleventh century. This absence has also been used to support the idea that Åland was depopulated during the period, a hypothesis which has not gained acceptance among Ålandic history writers. For example, the 2008 school textbook *Tidernas Åland* claimed that the population continued their lives as before in the early Middle Ages, and that the farms remained in the same locations as in the Viking Age.[168]

The depopulation theory implies that Ålanders descend from a relatively late wave of Swedish immigration in the twelfth century, and not from the island's Viking Age population, making their historical continuity on the islands shorter. Depopulation is thus connected with the hypothesis that Åland had a Finnish-speaking population in the Iron Age.

Åland's eleventh century has interested scholars from Sweden and Finland. During the Åland movement when Åland's history was highly politicized, Swedish archaeologists claimed that the artefacts showed continuous Swedish settlement, while Finnish scholars used place names to support the theory of an earlier Finnish settlement.[169] Although the Swedish–Finnish conflict had disappeared from the debate in the late twentieth century, the divide between linguists and archaeologists seemed to remain. The Swedish linguist Lars Hellberg suggested in 1980 that

---

[166] Dreijer 1943, 89.
[167] Dreijer 1983, 209 ff.; Gustafsson 1982, 33; Lindh 1984, 18; Mattsson-Eklund 2000, 77.
[168] Lindh 1984, 18; Mattsson-Eklund 2000, 77 ff.; Westergren & Nygren 2008, 50.
[169] Nordman 1986, 126.

Åland's place names showed no traces of Viking Age names, which led him to support the depopulation hypothesis.[170] According to the Finnish archaeologist and art historian Åsa Ringbom, recent archaeological excavations, pollen analysis, and the placement of churches close to Iron Age grave fields suggest continuity. Her conclusion is that depopulation seems unlikely. She finds it tempting to interpret the changes that do occur as a sign of an early Christian mission, but admits that the evidence is still insufficient.[171]

Ringbom's publications and research, which corresponds with the Ålandic view, have received funding from Ålandic institutions. Hellberg, who presented theories that conflict with the Ålandic view of history, is one of the few people writing about Åland who has not been published on the island or received funding from it. According to the preface of his book it was originally intended to be published on Åland, but it became too long.[172] The fact that his conclusions conflicted with the regional consensus probably did not help, since the influence of Matts Dreijer's theories was still very strong in the late 1970s and early 1980s.

Swedish rule, Russian rule

Although Ålandic history-writing has emphasized that Ålanders during the Russian period yearned to be Swedis, the period of unchallenged Swedish rule on Åland between the Danish attacks in the early sixteenth century and the Russian invasion in 1714 has not received much attention. During this period, Åland was situated at the centre of the Swedish kingdom, and was probably more of a normal, integrated, province than at any other time in history. In *Alla tiders Åland*, so far the only comprehensive book about Åland's history, the narration of the Swedish centuries includes rich material on general political and cultural developments in Sweden. In the account of the period after 1809 the general Swedish history disappears without being replaced by Russian or Finnish history; the perspective becomes more regional. The Swedish kings up to Gustav IV Adolf are part of Åland's history in their own right, while Russian and Finnish leaders are only mentioned when they are

---

[170] Hellberg 1980.
[171] Ringbom 2010, 9.
[172] Hellberg 1980, 3.

directly involved in questions concerning Åland. The Swedish period is not portrayed as a Golden Age, however; the focus is on how the monarchs gradually increased their control over their subjects.[173] This is consistent with the modern understanding of the period in Swedish academic circles. It is also similar to how the Baltic German writers on Saaremaa portrayed the Swedish period, although they focused more specifically on criticizing the return of aristocratic land to the Crown.

The mail route

One aspect of the Swedish state's increased control was the improved mail system, which was introduced in 1636. Farmers along the mail route were obliged to deliver mail and to transport passengers along their section of the road. The mail route connecting the western and eastern parts of the realm passed Åland, and it continued to function for a hundred years after Sweden's loss of Finland in 1809. The mail route has become a central point of the Ålandic memory of the Swedish period. The often hazardous delivery of mail across sea and treacherous ice has not only been commemorated in writing,[174] but since 1974 also in the yearly Postrodden boat race, carried out with traditional boats and equipment.[175]

All writers agree that the mail regulations of 1636 were not the beginning of Åland's position as a link between Sweden and Finland. Åland 'is situated as a bridge between Sweden and Finland', the Swedish king Charles IX told the Ålandic peasantry in an open letter in 1604. This function was especially important during winter, when ships could not navigate between Sweden and Finland. Ramsdahl believed the Swedish Crown had already made arrangements to transport men across Åland, although there is a lack of hard evidence.[176]

The county governor Lars Wilhelm Fagerlund wrote about the mail route in 1925, but it was not until the last quarter of the century that it became a central part of Ålandic history-writing and historical consciousness. It is possible that this is linked to Åland's increased economic dependence on the ferry traffic between Sweden and Finland; the mail route illustrates that Åland's position as a connecting link between Sweden and

---

[173] Mattsson-Eklund 2000, *passim*.
[174] For example Fagerlund 1925; Dreijer 2006, 218–232; Mattsson-Eklund 2000, 181 ff.; Ramsdahl 1988, 49–67.
[175] Griessner 2012, 87.
[176] Ramsdahl 1988, 49.

Finland has roots deep into history. When Thor-Alf Eliasson, former CEO of Viking Line, wrote a history of the company, he used four pages of the 'Prehistory' chapter to describe the old mail route. He also noted that his successor as CEO of Viking Line, Nils Erik Eklund, had won the Postrodden boat race several times.[177] The competing Ålandic ferry company Eckerö Line is even more strongly involved in Postrodden. Their ferries traffic the same route, Grisslehamn–Eckerö, as the old mail boats, and they transport competing boats to and from the start and finish, and allow spectators to watch the race from their ferries. Åland has issued stamps since 1984, and letters conveyed by the boats in the race are sold to philatelists. It must be stressed that Postrodden is not only an Ålandic but a regional event that also attracts individuals, clubs, and companies from nearby Swedish areas.

The great flight, 1714–21

In 1714 Åland was invaded by Russian troops, and the majority of the island's population fled to Sweden, where they remained until the peace of 1721. K. A. Bomansson described this as the most remarkable event in the history of Åland.[178] With the exception of Stig Dreijer, who has written a doctoral dissertation on the subject, the period has not been elaborated upon much by Ålandic writers, who usually cover this period in a few pages. The basics are the same: most Ålanders fled, and a few hundred were taken to Russia. The islands were so devastated that it took many years to repopulate and rebuild them; during the recovery Ålanders were exempted from tax. They also mention events from national history that took place on Åland during the flight: Åland was used as a base for the Russian galleys which terrorized the Swedish coast, and Peter the Great himself visited the islands. The exploits of the Swedish partisan hero Stefan Löwing and the unsuccessful peace congress in Lövö are also often part of the narrative. The most recent and extensive accounts mention that returning Ålanders came in conflict with hunters and fishermen who had become accustomed to using the depopulated area—Stig Dreijer mentions people from Swedish Roslagen, while Mattsson-Eklund also writes about people from Turku province.[179]

[177] Fagerlund 1925; Eliasson 2005, 7 ff., 89.
[178] Bomansson 1852, v.
[179] See, for example, Dreijer 2006, 18–25; Mattsson-Eklund 2006, 206–220; Gustafson 1982, 51.

Let us compare this Ålandic account of events with the one we can find in the recently published history of the Finno-Swedes. According to this work, Åland acquired a 'not insignificant' Fennophone population during this turbulent period, who in the 1730s duly demanded that Åland's priests speak Finnish. In Sund there were 60 Finnish parishioners, but the minority was swiftly assimilated.[180] This Fennophone population is not mentioned in any Ålandic account of the events.

The uprising of 1808

In 1852, K. A. Bomansson published a book about the uprising in 1808, when Ålandic peasants captured the Russian troops who were based on Åland. He based his narration mainly on interviews with eyewitnesses, since he believed that the Swedish naval officers who arrived in the midst of the uprising exaggerated their own role in their reports. Bomansson considered the Ålanders' 'patriotic freedom fight' as one of the many uprisings by the 'ancient brave Finnish peasantry' against the Russians during the war. Bomansson declared that he was against popular uprisings in principle, but that the events in Finland during the war were an exception, since the Russians did not yet have formal authority over the area.[181] Thus Bomansson's account is permeated by Finnish nationalism, at the same time as he made clear that he did not encourage new uprisings against the Russians, who had become the lawful rulers.

During the period from the Åland movement 1917–21 to the 1980s, Ålandic history-writing in general described the uprising as resulting from the Ålanders' wish to remain Swedish, and claimed that the hope of returning to Sweden was alive throughout the nineteenth century.[182] In recent decades, Ålandic history-writing has downplayed the rebels' Swedish patriotism; instead they have emphasized that the uprising had its roots in the local community. 'The Ålanders wanted to decide on their future themselves', according to the school textbook *Åland*.[183] There has been continuity from Bomansson up until today on one point, however: the uprising has been seen as a revolt by the Ålandic peasants, while the local elite, often with roots on the mainland, have been portrayed as

---

[180] Villstrand 2009, 12–13.
[181] Bomansson 1852, vii, 11–12.
[182] See, for example,Eriksson 1976, 4. This aspect of Ålandic history-writing is treated thoroughly in Hakala 2006.
[183] Gustafsson 1982, 52.

collaborators. The priest Hambraeus in Jomala is described as a collaborator who was incarcerated by the rebels in 1808. However, he also happens to be the person who represented Åland at the Diet in Stockholm in 1809, when the rest of Finland had already sworn allegiance to Tsar Alexander I at the Diet in Porvoo. Thus the same person has been used to illustrate both the disloyalty of the Finnish elite and the Ålanders' loyalty to Sweden. Pertti Hakala, who in 2006 studied how the 1808 uprising has been portrayed in Ålandic history-writing, claimed that in the latest works there had been a paradigm shift away from the rhetoric of the Åland movement. Hakala also wrote the chapter about the 1808 uprising in the volume about the nineteenth century in the series *Det åländska folkets historia* which was published in 2008.[184]

Hakala's description of the uprising is very similar to Bomansson's, who is his main source. The 200 Russian infantry and cavalrymen who had invaded Åland over the ice in the winter of 1808 found themselves in danger when spring arrived. The ice first melted over the open waters in the south-west, enabling ships from Sweden to reach the islands early, while the ice in the archipelago between Åland and Finland melted slowly, hindering navigation as well as safe passage on foot. Afraid that they might be attacked by the Swedish navy without possibility to escape to mainland Finland, the Russians ordered each Ålandic parish to provide them with 15 boats and clear a passage through the ice from the harbours within 24 hours. Ålanders who argued the task was impossible faced death threats and mutilation. The Russians' demands for such a large number of boats made the Ålanders fear that they intended to abduct all the men from the islands.[185]

A few young sons of peasants took the initiative on 5 May. The following day, *länsman* Erik Arén and *pastorsadjunkt* Henrik Gummerus became the leaders of the uprising. Since the rest of the local elite opposed or distanced themselves from it, Hakala describes it as purely a peasant uprising. Like earlier Ålandic history-writing, Hakala recognizes that the peasants mistrusted the elite. He does note, however, that outside the parishes of Jomala and Lemland the peasants had few complaints, and that Gabriel Poppius, who investigated the supposed collaboration, concluded that most offences were minor, and that the elite might have been overly cautious but not criminal. Poppius believed that the peasants'

[184] Hakala 2006, 40–53; Kuvaja et al. 2008, 21–32.
[185] Kuvaja et al. 2008, 21–2.

accusations were based on an old mistrust of the masters, which might have its foundations in the civil servants' thankless task of demanding taxes and obedience.[186] Compared to earlier Ålandic history-writing, Hakala downplays the rift between peasants and elite.

Hakala describes the uprising as a reaction to Russian provocations and impossible demands, not as a patriotic defence of Sweden. At other times during the war the Ålanders showed less interest in fighting the Russians. When the Swedish king in an address read in all the churches in February 1808 encouraged the peasants of Finland to take arms, not a single Ålander volunteered—although the landed peasants on Kumlinge had offered the authorities to take as many as they wanted of 'useless and in many ways detrimental persons, the parish's artisans not excluded'. In 1809, when the peasants were organized into a militia, Landstorm, the Ålanders accepted arms and munitions but were often reluctant to exercise. The Swedish commander on Åland, von Döbeln, considered Åland's Landstorm useless, and wanted it dissolved since they mutinied before the enemy was even sighted.[187] From this description of the Ålanders actions before and after the actual uprising, which has been the sole focus of earlier Ålandic history-writing, the local peasants seem less heroic and patriotic.

Hakala also describes how the Swedish military burned down all the houses on Brändö and Kumlinge, and evacuated the inhabitants from the path of the advancing Russians in 1809.[188] This incident has not received much attention in earlier Ålandic history-writing.

Ålandic identity before the Åland movement

In 1852 K. A. Bomansson claimed that Ålanders, when asked what people they belonged to, answered neither 'Finn nor Swede, but firmly and determined Ålander'. Perhaps this self-consciousness might be considered exaggerated, Bomansson argued, but lack of national consciousness deserves not to be dismissed as exaggeration.[189]

In spite of this, Bomansson himself often labelled the Ålanders as Swedes and the Åland Islands as part of Finland. He described a huge,

---

[186] Kuvaja et al. 2008, 23–32.
[187] Kuvaja et al. 2008, 12–13 ('onyttige och i många afseenden härhemma skadelige personer, socknens handtverkare icke undantagne').
[188] Kuvaja et al. 2008, 47–53.
[189] Bomansson 1852, 29 ('Finne eller Svensk, utan fast och bestämdt Ålänning').

feared Cossack who walked back and forth in his lodging, murmuring 'The Swede is coming'. Bomansson concluded that the Cossack's premonitions were correct, since he was soon overpowered by Ålandic peasants. Similarly, an Ålander who was forced to lead the Russian Major Nejhardt's horse shouted 'Swedish man' to avoid getting shot by his fellows.[190]

The subtitle of the book, *En scen ur Suomis sista strid*, placed Åland within Finland. In the introduction, the battles on Åland are described as part of the Finnish war, a war that will be remembered 'as long as a Finnish heart beats for honour and country'. However, when Bomansson describes Brändö as 'Åland's last outpost at the border of Suomi', he places the Åland Islands outside Finland.[191] These inconsistencies illustrate that to Bomansson and his contemporaries, the borders between Åland, Finland, and Sweden did not yet carry the same political and ideological importance as they would during and after the Åland movement.

Later Ålandic writers have often claimed that Ålanders longed back to Sweden during the nineteenth century. One of the key figures of the Åland movement, Johannes Eriksson, recalled childhood memories that had affected his attitudes to Sweden. During long winter nights Eriksson's grandparents had told him stories about journeys to Stockholm, Åland's finest marketplace. Interestingly, Eriksson mentioned the introduction of customs duties (in the 1830s) as the event which separated Åland from the Swedish motherland, not the political separation in 1809.[192]

According to Stig Dreijer, Stockholm was 'the City' to Ålanders in the eighteenth century. Turku came in second place, although Åland was tied administratively to Turku and Pori County, and ecclesiastically to the diocese of Turku. Åland belonged to Stockholm's inner area of trade and was important for the supply of the capital. Entire families took part in the trips, which enabled cultural influences to reach Åland.[193] This centuries-old pattern of trade was heavily affected by customs duties introduced in the 1830s.

Christer Kuvaja has written about Åland's nineteenth century in *Det åländska folkets historia* (2006). Like most Ålandic history-writing from

---

[190] Bomansson 1852, 74–5 ('Svensken kommer … Hans inre hade ej sagt en lögn'), 79 ('Svensk man').
[191] Bomansson 1852, 9–10 ('så länge ett Finskt hjerta klappar för ära och fosterland'), 107 ('Ålands yttersta förpost vid Suomis gräns').
[192] Eriksson & Virgin 1961, 15–6.
[193] Dreijer 2006, 372–3.

recent decades, this volume has distanced itself from the rhetoric of earlier decades. Kuvaja also tries to shed light on the history of the Finns on Åland. He mentions there were some Finns living on Åland throughout the nineteenth century. For a long time Åland stayed aloof of the language battle that was taking place in mainland Finland, although Kuvaja believes Ålanders sympathized with the Swedish side. In the last decade of the nineteenth century, Fennomans managed to establish a bank and a few short-lived schools on Åland. Any crimes on Åland were always blamed on the Finns. Kuvaja also mentions some outright racist ideas, as when one writer in *Tidningen Åland* in 1917 stressed the importance of keeping the Ålandic race clean from interbreeding with the lowly Finns. The writer did not consider the children of mixed marriages true Ålanders, even if they grew up on Åland. According to Kuvaja, similar ideas were prevalent also elsewhere among Finno-Swedes.[194]

There was a patriotic feeling for Finland around the turn of the century, but according to Kuvaja it was found mostly among the elite in Mariehamn, and had little support among the peasants. Even the easternmost municipalities in the archipelago considered themselves as Ålanders, which according to Kuvaja became evident during the violent protests in 1905 against the priest Mäkelä, who wanted to transfer Brändö to the deanery of Vemo in Finland, claiming that the Brändö islanders seldom called themselves Ålanders but often Finns. Interestingly, Julius Sundblom—who later became one of the Åland movement's leaders and attempted to separate Åland from Finland—in this debate claimed that all Ålanders were Finns.[195]

Kuvaja's conclusion is that most Ålanders had weak or non-existent feelings towards Finland as a fatherland. Neither was there any strong longing for reunification with Sweden. He sums up his conclusion in a sentence very similar to the one used by Bomansson 150 years earlier: 'The Ålander neither considered himself a Finn nor a Swede, but explicitly an Ålander'.[196]

Like many earlier Ålandic writers, Kuvaja bases this in part on the 1871 travelogue by the Finnish art historian Emil Nervander. However, Kuvaja stresses that Nervander did not consider the loose bonds to Finland to be

[194] Kuvaja et al. 2008, 98 ff.
[195] Kuvaja et al. 2008, 563, 582–3, 585–6.
[196] Kuvaja et al. 2008, 587 ('Ålänningen kände sig som varken finne eller svensk, utan uttryckligen som åländning').

unique to Åland; he also mentioned that the inhabitants of the Finnish islands Korpo and Nagu considered themselves to be *neighbours* of Finland and Åland. Kuvaja finds Åland's lack of affinity with Finland unsurprising; the inhabitants of Österbotten considered themselves such first and foremost, and only secondly as Finns. Kuvaja, however, does mention several sources which claim that Ålanders had started to orient themselves slightly more towards Finland in the late nineteenth century.[197]

In 1905 the need for a written history of Åland was raised in an editorial in *Tidningen Åland*. The writer concluded that Ålanders might also be inspired by the Finnish Hakkapeliitta cavalry in the Thirty Years War, but not as much as the descendants of these 'hakkapelitians'. The fact that Åland was a nation of its own was at the same time the island's weakness and its strength. Its weakness since it made the patriotic movements less fruitful than on the mainland, its strength since

> it endows us with a small separate fatherland of our own beside the big one, a country that we can more easily fathom with mind and feeling, a country, which is ours and *exclusively ours*. This patriotism of ours is no parochialism. It is fully justified because of historical as well as geographical circumstances.[198]

The writer thus encouraged Finnish patriotism, but he doubted it could engage Ålanders enough. Only regional patriotism could help Ålanders experience the blessings of deep patriotic feeling. In late 1917 Sundblom's paper *Åland* switched allegiance to Swedish patriotism. Here, the desirable thing was the patriotic feeling in itself, while the object of desire, the actual fatherland, was secondary and might vary according to conjuncture. The fact that Sweden and Finland were historically one country probably facilitated the rapid shift in patriotic feeling. The core myths and symbols in Swedish nationalism were virtually identical to the ones in Finnish nationalism. For example, in both Sweden and Finland Johan Ludvig Runeberg's *Our Country* was being considered as a possible national anthem in the early twentieth century.

---

[197] Kuvaja et al. 2008, 589.
[198] Kuvaja et al. 2006, 587–8 ('den skänker oss ett eget litet enskildt fosterland jämte det stora, ett land, som vi lättare kunna omfatta både med tanke och känsla, ett land, som är vårt och uteslutande vårt. Denna vår patriotism är ingen knutpatriotism. Den har sitt fulla berättigande på grund af både historiska och geografiska förhållanden').

The Russian military and Bomarsund

The last Swedish commander on Åland, von Döbeln, told the islanders that 'If you become Russians—you and your descendants, against Turks—Persians—Greeks—will have to fight at 200 miles' distance in eternal wars and never more return to your happy Island!'[199] This war propaganda turned out to be false: although the Russian military brought Ålanders into contact with a wide range of nationalities, it did so by bringing soldiers from foreign lands to Åland, not the reverse.

The cultural diversity on Åland during the Russian period has been emphasized in Ålandic history-writing in recent years. Martin Hårdstedt's and Benita Mattsson Eklund's accounts are both based upon an article by David Papp in *Åländsk odling 1991*. Hårdstedt describes Åland in 1809–53 as a religious and cultural melting pot. From 1809 until the early 1840s, Russian troops were billeted in houses on Åland, primarily in the parishes on Fasta Åland. Some farmers housed up to 70 soldiers in their buildings. In the early 1840s the soldiers moved to Bomarsund Fortress, where construction had begun in 1829. According to Hårdstedt, billeting affected Åland much more directly than the building of the fortress. In his view, this period of Åland's history should be described as 'the Age of the billets' rather than as 'the Age of the Fortress', as had been the case in earlier Ålandic history-writing.[200]

In the military society that developed around Bomarsund Fortress, five religions were represented, reflecting the cultural diversity of the Russian Empire. There were Lutherans from Finland and the Baltic countries, Polish Catholics, Turkish and Chechen Muslims, Orthodox Russians, and Jews from different corners of the empire. There was a great deal of interreligious marriages. Weddings between Orthodox and Lutherans followed the rituals of both religions. Illegitimate children took their mother's religion, while children of married couples where the father was Russian became Orthodox. According to Hårdstedt, there was some confusion when children were baptized incorrectly or 'the Lutheran minister baptized according to the Catholic ritual with Lutheran, Catholic, and Orthodox witnesses to the Baptism'. Hundreds of Ålandic women married Orthodox Russians. Many also married Lutheran

---

[199] Kuvaja et al. 2008, 53 ('Blifven I Ryssar—får I och efterkommander, mot Turkar—Perser—Greker—på 200 mils afstånd kjämpa i evigtvarande krig och aldrig mer återse eder lyckliga Ö!').
[200] Kuvaja et al. 2008, 153, 157, 194, 204–205 ('inkvarteringarnas tid … fästningens tid').

Estonians or Estonian Swedes, and some married Catholic Poles. No one seems to have married Jews or Muslims. That does not mean that these groups were not in close contact with the local population. The Persian priest Ramazan Mustafa Oglii was deported to Åland from Dagestan, and was housed at a farm in Godby. He is said to have taught the peasant's daughter Persian.[201] While on Saaremaa and Bornholm Asian troops were described more negatively than troops from European Russia, there are no negative descriptions of these exotic nationalities in the Ålandic histories.

Hårdstedt also mentions that economic difficulties and differences in language and religion contributed to the fact that many Russian soldiers did not acknowledge paternity of their children. For officers it was often inconceivable to marry the daughter of a peasant. When the officer Sergei Romanoff found a bride from Åland, the couple were exiled to Romanoff's manor by the Tsar, who found it unsuitable for his relative to marry below his estate.[202]

Both Mattsson-Eklund and Hårdstedt mention the many Russian words that have entered the Ålandic dialect.[203] In contrast to Finnish, nothing is mentioned in Ålandic history-writing about negative attitudes towards Russian influence on the islands' language.

The Crimean War

During the Crimean War, when the Russian Empire faced the Ottoman Empire, France, Britain, and Sardinia, Bomarsund Fortress was attacked and destroyed by French and British troops. Two aspect of this conflict have been of special interest to Ålandic historians: the Ålanders' feelings regarding the possibility that Sweden could have retaken the islands, and the fact that Åland was demilitarized as a consequence of the war.

Johannes Eriksson, one of the peasant leaders of the Åland movement, recalled what his father told him about events on Åland during the 'Oriental war'. The great powers, France and Britain had control of Åland for a while, and the joyous news that the island would be returned to Sweden circulated. However, this did not materialize since the priest Sandelin in Hammarland told the conquerors that the Ålanders did not

---

[201] Kuvaja et al. 2008, 198–203. A similar, albeit shorter, account is found in Mattsson-Eklund 2000, 273–4.
[202] Kuvaja et al. 2008, 203.
[203] Kuvaja et al. 2008, 193; Mattsson-Eklund 2000, 276.

want any change, without having asked the people for their opinion.²⁰⁴ It is highly unlikely that Swedish foreign policy would have been influenced by the views of a single priest, but the fact that such stories circulated illustrates once again the peasants' mistrust of the local elite, particularly the priests.

Matts Dreijer was of the opinion that Ålanders, in contrast to mainland Finns and Finno-Swedes, did not support Russia in the war and longed for reunification with Sweden. Martin Isaksson, a former Ålandic politician who has done extensive research on the period when Russia fortified on Åland, gives another explanation for the Ålanders' disappointment after the war: the French and British troops used Swedish interpreters who hinted at great freedoms after the war, even about an Ålandic Free State. He believes that the sense of being a region that could attract Europe's attention never died, but blossomed again at the end of the First World War.²⁰⁵ To Isaksson it was freedom for Åland, not reunion with Sweden, which sparked the imagination of the Ålanders.

According to the book *Bomarsund* (2004), the French and British had offered Åland to Sweden, but cautious king Oscar I declined the gift. Martin Hårdstedt points out that the British Navy lacked ships suitable for archipelagic warfare, which the Swedes possessed. Since the Swedes could also provide bases and supplies, the British and French tried to use Åland as bait to lure the Swedish king into the war. ²⁰⁶

Benita Mattsson-Eklund is of the opinion that there was no hatred between Russians and Ålanders, but that the elite—the nobility and the often immigrant priests and civil servants—showed more solidarity with the Russian rulers. The peasants were suspicious of how the elite were toadying to the Russians. According to Mattsson-Eklund, it is necessary to have the popular sentiment of 1809 and 1854 in mind if you want to understand developments on Åland after 1917.²⁰⁷

In Hårdstedt's view it would have been very foolish of the Russians to distribute arms and ammunition among Åland's peasants if they had any doubts about their loyalty. Benita Mattsson-Eklund, however, is of the opinion that the Ålanders fooled the Russians into giving them guns.

---

²⁰⁴ Eriksson & Virgin 1961, 17–18.
²⁰⁵ Dreijer 1967, 13–20; Isaksson 1981, 211.
²⁰⁶ Robins et al. 2004, 102; Kuvaja et al. 2008, 218–19.
²⁰⁷ Mattsson-Eklund 2000, 283.

They intended to use the weapons in the spring hunt for seabirds, not against the French and British.[208]

During the war Ålanders sailed to Sweden under the French flag. None of the authors consider the choice of the tricolour as a sign of identification with France or as a protest against Russia, however: Russian ships were under blockade, and it was easy to remodel the existing Russian flags into French ones since they displayed the same colours.[209]

Hårdstedt questions whether resistance to the authorities during the Crimean War was directed at the Russian authorities or at all authorities in general. He doubts whether a Swedish takeover would have changed the peasants' attitudes towards the priests and the local administration. In his opinion, the sources cannot shed light on the Ålanders' attitudes towards a reunion with Sweden. According to Hårdstedt, writers with strong connections to Åland have taken part in the identity-building: the Ålanders' independence in relationship to the authorities and mainland Finland is important to Ålandic identity, and so is the connection to Sweden.[210]

Hårdstedt gives a good picture of how the Crimean War has been used in the building of Ålandic identity. What might be added is a comment on how the nature of this identity has gradually changed during the twentieth century. While Johannes Eriksson expressed the patriotic Swedish stance of the Åland movement, writers from the 1980s onwards maintain a more independent, Ålandic, position.

Consequences of the Crimean War

Russia lost, which paved the way for Åland's demilitarization, another important factor in Ålandic identity-building. Bomarsund Fortress was built to withstand a naval bombardment from a distance. However, the allies approached the fortress on land, and their cannon fire at close range had a devastating effect. The Russian commander capitulated before the walls of the main fortress were breached. The British and French suggested that Sweden might like to take over the fortifications, but King Oscar I was not interested. According to Hårdstedt, he realized that Sweden would be alone with Russia when the French and British were gone, and the experiences of 1809 showed that it was impossible to defend Åland against

---

[208] Kuvaja et al. 2008, 227; Mattson-Eklund 2000, 281.
[209] Isaksson 1981, 209.
[210] Kuvaja et al. 2008, 260–1.

Russian troops advancing over the ice. The only alternative that remained for the allies was to blow up the fortress, which they duly did in late August and early September 1854.[211]

The war ended in 1856. Sweden tried to acquire Åland during the peace negotiations, but the allies saw no reasons to support its claim since Sweden had not participated in the war. Mattson-Eklund mentions that the Swedes then suggested an independent Åland under Swedish or allied protection. This idea met with Russian opposition, but the third Swedish suggestion, that Åland remain Russian but be demilitarized, was acceptable to all parties. In an amendment to the peace treaty the Russian tsar accepted 'that the Åland Islands shall not be fortified, and that no military or naval establishments whatsoever shall be maintained or created there'.[212]

There is a general agreement that the demilitarization of Åland was a great relief for the local population at the time. Since the 1980s, there has been an increased emphasis on the long-term effects of the 1856 treaty on Ålandic identity.

According to Martin Isaksson, it is impossible to understand what Ålandish-ness means without taking into account the heavy burden of billeting troops in the years of the construction of Bomarsund Fortress. The demilitarization was therefore perceived as a great relief. In Isaksson's view, it is possible to consider the amendment about Åland's demilitarization in the 1856 treaty of Paris an important part of the 'inheritance of freedom' that is mentioned in *Åländningens sång* ('The song of the Ålander', Åland's unofficial national anthem first sung publicly in 1922).[213]

According to *Bomarsund*, the decisions that made Åland part of the Grand Duchy of Finland in 1809, demilitarized in 1856, and autonomous in 1922 were all taken over the heads of the local population and contrary to their wishes—apparently the authors mean that the Ålanders' first choice in all three instances was to become part of Sweden. Given this, they find it remarkable that autonomy and demilitarization today are embraced by the great majority of Ålanders, and are even considered the cornerstones of Ålandic society.[214]

[211] Kuvaja et al. 2008, 246.
[212] Kuvaja et al. 2008, 268; Mattsson-Eklund 2000, 288, 'Convention on the Demilitarisation of the Åland Islands 1856', <http://www.kulturstiftelsen.ax/images/internationellaavtal/engelskaavtal.pdf>.
[213] Isaksson 1981, 213.
[214] Robins et al. 2004, 116.

Martin Hårdstedt is of the opinion that demilitarization has reduced the risk of war on Åland, but that the islands' strategic location has inevitably drawn them into military activities whenever war has broken out. However, he stresses that the idea of Åland as a protected zone is an important part of Ålandic identity.[215]

While the notion that Ålanders hoped for a reunification with Sweden during the Crimean War was most prominent in history-writing from the mid twentieth century, and has since faded, the emphasis on the importance of Åland's demilitarization has gradually increased.

The great sailing ships

The history of Åland's shipping industry is at the same time a regional and a global history. The conflict between Åland and Finland, which is central to Ålandic history-writing in general, is peripheral or even non-existent in maritime history. A negative view of captains from Finnish mainland cities can be found in *Den åländska segelsjöfartens historia*, but rather than echoing 1917–21, it probably dates back to the time when the burghers considered trade to be their privilege, something that was challenged by the Ålandic peasants' right to trade.[216]

The transoceanic trade is literally described as rooted in the local society; the ships were built from Ålandic timber, and the shareholders supplied the ships with food from their farms. One main export was wood from Åland's forests. According to Kåhre 'The economic connection between sea and earth laid the foundation for an intimate cultural, social and psychological interaction'. Kåhre refrained from investigating this connection in detail, since it would have made the history of Åland's seafaring into a history of Åland's agriculture as well. However, he mentioned that agricultural land on Åland was so heavily taxed that Ålanders could not sustain themselves without going to sea.[217]

With time the peasants were replaced by professional shipowners, a process that was finished during the First World War. By then, wooden ships had already been replaced by steel ships bought on the international

---

[215] Kuvaja et al. 2008, 268–9.
[216] Kuvaja et al. 2008, 328.
[217] Kåhre & Kåhre 1988, 236 ('Det ekonomiska sambandet mellan havet och jorden lade grund till en intim växelverkan i kulturellt, socialt och psykologiskt avseende'), 259.

second-hand market.[218] Still, the Ålandic crews' connection to their home islands is emphasized.

According to Kåhre, Ålandic men in the 1870s were still outside 'the rootless, cosmopolitan society of deep-sea shipping', which made escapes quite rare, although they became more common later. During the First World War, Ålandic sailors jumped ship in American harbours, and had to be replaced by new men from 'the cosmopolitan breed of sea nomads'. For example, when Germany declared unrestricted submarine warfare in 1917, the entire crew except the first mate deserted the ship *August* in Beaumont, Texas; 19 sailors were shanghaied as replacements.[219] Kåhre made a clear distinction between Ålanders and 'cosmopolitans'—the fact that Ålanders travelled widely did not make them cosmopolitans, since they were firmly rooted in the Ålandic soil. In the years after the Second World War, when the first edition of the book was published, the term cosmopolitan still retained its negative connotations, usually referring to Jews and other groups considered rootless and stateless.

In the volume about the twentieth century in *Det åländska folkets historia*, Tudeer claimed that Gustav Eriksson could make a profit from sailing ships long after it was considered feasible elsewhere, since his commanders and most of the crew were Ålanders. 'They were decent people with the sea in their blood'. The narrow profit margins made Eriksson impose strict economies on his captains. Tudeer considered this professional thrift, but he adds that others misunderstood it as penny-pinching.[220] In this way, Tudeer links thrift—a national characteristic—to the fact that Ålanders were the last to maintain a large fleet of sailing ships—a national symbol.

As a contrast, Captain Justus Harberg, who has written the history of Åland's motorized shipping, claims that lack of capital was what made the Ålanders cling to old types of ships. According to him, Åland was half a century behind Great Britain and mainland Finland in acquiring large sailing ships, and a century behind in the transition to steam. The Ålandic development was initially delayed by the lack of a city with wealthy burghers and wholesalers. Not until the 1980s did Åland catch up with cutting-edge of maritime transportation. Harberg also stresses the many

---

[218] Kåhre & Kåhre 1988, 296, 400.
[219] Kåhre & Kåhre 1988, 224, 439, 463–4.
[220] Tudeer 1993, 40.

advantages that modern ships offer crews compared to the heavy, dangerous work with sails and rigging.[221]

Autonomy

The birth and development of Åland's autonomy is a central theme in Ålandic history-writing. When in 1917 it became apparent that the Russian Empire was about to collapse, some Ålanders began to push the idea that the island should be reunified with Sweden. This sparked a sudden and unexpected chain of events which eventually gave Åland autonomy within Finland in 1922.

The Åland Movement

Although the Åland movement, which urged Åland's reunification with Sweden in 1917–21, had a lasting impact on the Ålandic society, it took some time before it became a major theme in Ålandic history-writing. The volume about the Åland movement in the series *Det åländska folkets historia* is still to be published.

Matts Dreijer, who was employed as an archaeologist by the provincial government, focused on the island's ancient and medieval history. In his school textbook *Åland och ålänningarna* from 1943, the section about history comprised 58 pages. Only 22 of them were devoted to the period after the sixteenth century, and the Åland movement was confined to approximately 1 page. In addition, one of the extraordinary Ålanders who were treated in separate chapters was the peasant Johannes Eriksson, an important figure in the Åland movement. One chapter was also devoted to Åland's autonomy.[222] The fact that the book was written during the Second World War, when the rivalry between the two Nordic countries had been replaced by a sense of unity in face of the Soviet and German threats, might have contributed to the fact that Dreijer kept his description of the Åland movement short.

One of the reasons why the Åland movement initially received relatively little attention in regional history-writing was the movement's own rhetoric: it claimed that the Ålanders' willingness to join Sweden was

---

[221] Harberg 1995, 7, 12.
[222] Dreijer 1943, 47–104 ('History'), 93–104 ('1600–'), 103–104 ('The Åland movement'), 162–167 ('Åland's autonomy'), 190–194 ('Johannes Eriksson').

nothing new and unique, but a mere consequence of the island's ancient historical ties with Sweden. For a long time Ålandic history-writing unanimously agreed that the Ålanders had dreamed of reunification with Sweden throughout the whole Russian period, and that the dream was only revived in 1917.[223]

However, the earliest account of the Åland movement was however written in 1920 by one of its most fervent opponents, the Ålander Otto Andersson who later became professor of musicology at Åbo Akademi University in Turku. He claimed that the majority of the Ålanders at the end of 1917 had not made up their minds in the Åland question. He stressed how isolated Åland had been during the First World War, and claimed that it was only a small group led by Carl Björkman, which unknown to most Ålanders, had worked for reunification.[224]

Until the 1980s, regional history-writing about the Åland movement adhered to the movement's own image of a continuous longing westwards during the nineteenth century, and Otto Andersson's views were forgotten. However, in 1986 Gyrid Högman—later the headmaster of Åland's lyceum—investigated the issue in her MA dissertation, and concluded that all sources which express a hope of reunification date from the second half of 1917 or later. Later Ålandic writers generally agree with Högman's conclusion that the Åland movement did not yet have widespread support in 1917.[225]

On 20 August 1917, representatives of Åland's municipalities gathered to discuss the future of the island. They decided to send a deputation to Sweden in order to express their wishes for a reunification. According to most accounts, this decision was fuelled by the misconduct of the Russian troops when they were based on Åland, and by the fear that the islands would become Fennified if Finland became independent. Mats Dreijer's school textbook from 1943 is an exception in the sense that it does not talk about the threat of the Finnish language, but of Russian soldiers and their strange tongue. He also concluded that the 'struggle against the East' was one of the Ålandic people's great historical missions.[226] Later writers

---

[223] Dreijer 1943, 103; Wernström 1953, 19; Eriksson & Virgin 1961, 16; Bondestam 1972, 51; Eriksson 1976, 4; Gustafsson 1991, 59.
[224] Andersson 1920, 7–8, 24 ff., 31.
[225] Högman 1986, 118; Kuvaja et al. 2008, 587; Skogsjö & Wilén 1997, 8–9, 12.
[226] Dreijer 1943, 103–104, 162; Wernlund 1953, 6; Eriksson & Virgin 1961, 22,

have generally considered the impact of the Russian language as an interesting curiosity rather than as a threat.

The book in question was written during the Continuation War between Finland and the Soviet Union, and it is possible that wartime censorship would not have approved of a more anti-Finnish description of the conflict. However, anti-Russian sentiment was welcome and flourished in Finnish school textbooks at the time. Since both Finland and Russia are situated in the east from an Ålandic viewpoint, it might be possible to interpret 'the struggle against the east' as an attempt to circumvent censorship by using an ambiguous formulation. However, the thought that Sweden—and since 1917, Finland—had a historic mission to defend the Western world against the East was also prevalent among the nationalistic Swedish historians from whom Dreijer drew most of his ideas at this time.[227]

To illustrate popular support for their aims, the leaders of the Åland movement gathered more than 7,000 signatures. The earliest writers claimed that this was 96 per cent—the Swedish military engineer Axel Wernlund even believed it was 98-9 %—of Åland's adult population, taking into account that many were absent sailors or emigrants, or were hindered from taking part by severe ice conditions in the archipelago.[228]

According to Högman 7,135 names were gathered, which was 57% of the 12,509 Ålanders who were entitled to vote, although she admits that many of them were abroad at the time and thus not able to take part. Högman was not able to find out what calculations the commonly used figures of 95–6 % were based on. The teacher Kurt Lindh's school textbook *Det åländska samhället* used 57% already in the first edition from 1984, while the more traditional textbook *Åland*, intended for younger children, in 1991 maintained that 95% had signed. However, the writers who question the high percentage also stress that the important thing was that a majority of the Ålanders were in favour of a reunification with Sweden. Even Otto Andersson, who wrote his pamphlet with the intention of keeping Åland in Finland, had admitted that the collection of names was not a result of agitation but probably correctly represented feelings on Åland at the end of 1917. In his opinion, Ålanders signed the document since they feared Russian and Red Finnish troops. He did not

---

[227] For anti-Russian sentiments and the mission of defence against the East, see Holmén 2006, 54, 124.
[228] Dreijer 1943, 103; Wernlund 1953, 6; Eriksson & Virgin 1961, 25.

agree with those who claimed the Ålanders had acted egoistically, since he believed the critics had too quickly forgotten the insecurity of December 1917. Back then the press in mainland Finland had discussed the possibility of a Swedish intervention in Finland in order to avoid 'the abysmal misery, which would afflict our society, if Russians and Reds came to power'.[229]

Thus Andersson's pamphlet left the door open for reconciliation by moving the blame from the Ålanders to the Russians and the socialist Finns who lost the Finnish Civil War. Andersson's opinion that the final text of the petition was not nearly as treacherous as had been claimed also pointed in the direction of reconciliation. His conciliatory tone might also be explained by personal experience. Johannes Eriksson, one of the persons who brought the address to the Swedish king, claimed in his memoirs that on 7 January 1918 Andersson had urged the deputation to travel as soon as possible. Eriksson found it strange that Andersson later changed his mind and opposed reunification with Sweden. Andersson had earlier the same day witnessed how Russian soldiers surrounding and storming the hotel Societetshuset, killing one Ålander and wounding another.[230] It is possible that, affected by his experience of Russian violence earlier the same day, he really encouraged the deputation to travel to Sweden. This would also explain why he later stressed the uncertainty of the period, considered support for the petition a consequence of Russian violence, and expressed understanding towards the Ålanders who had signed it.

The Finno-Swedish historian Anna Bondestam, who in 1972 published a book about the events on Åland in 1918 at the request of Matts Dreijer, claimed that the Russians actually committed few crimes. The Ålanders' fear of the Russians had been exaggerated by historians, and was not the real reason behind the Ålanders' yearning for reunification with Sweden. Instead Bondestam considered the Åland movement to be a typical nationality movement with a strong sense of their own nationality and a negative view of the Finns.[231]

---

[229] Högman 1986, 125–6; Gustavsson 1991, 61; Lindh 1984, 38; Andersson 1920, 44–5 ('bottenlösa olycka, som skulle drabba vårt kultursamhälle, därest ryssar och röda blevo de härskande').
[230] Andersson 1920, 50, 56; Eriksson & Virgin 1961, 27 does not mention the date of Eriksson's meeting with Andersson, but it can be established as 7 January since he claims it took place the night after the shootings at Societetshuset.
[231] Bondestam 1972, 34 ff., 43 ff., 49–50, 52.

In 1918 Åland became the centre of intense military activity. Around 2,000 Russian soldiers out of the maximum 7,000–8,000 were left on the islands, but in the two weeks from 10 to 24 February, around 500 fighters from each of the sides in the Civil War arrived, as well as a Swedish army battalion and several Swedish naval ships. On 5 March, 1,200 German troops also landed on the island. The reasons for the arrival of these five contingents, the relationships between them, and the events that followed are quite complicated, but it is necessary to understand them since the descriptions of them reveal a great deal about the writers' attitudes towards the participating sides.

Initially many Ålanders joined the White Finnish Nystad Corps, which arrived on 10 February after fleeing the strong Red forces in southern Finland. Andersson considered this proof that many Ålanders now wanted to change their opinion regarding the petition to Sweden, of which they had heard nothing for six weeks. Bondestam, on the other hand, considered the fact that the Ålanders abandoned the Corps on the arrival of the Swedish troops as proof that they wanted a Swedish Åland. Matts Dreijer was one of the Ålanders who joined the Nystad Corps, and he estimates that between 100 and 200 others did the same. During the Battle of Godby on 19 February, when the Whites fought Russian and Red troops, he noticed that the older and more experienced Ålanders started to desert, leaving only Dreijer and other schoolboys behind. Only later did he realize that this was caused by the arrival of Swedish troops in Eckerö. The ones who had joined the Nystad corps were on the wrong side. In his school textbook, Kurt Lindh supposes that the Ålanders hardly understood all the turns in the complicated game.[232]

Many writers portray the Swedish expedition as humanitarian, and give them the credit for the fact that the fighting ended and Åland was saved from devastation, which made the Ålanders grateful.[233]

Some give a more complicated picture of the Swedish objectives, however. Otto Andersson repeatedly called it a 'humanitarian expedition' in scare quotes, and believed it was linked to the Åland movement's attempts to join Åland to Sweden. He claimed that at least in the eastern parts of Åland the islanders were astonished and dismayed when they heard that the Swedes had disarmed the Nystad Corps and allowed the

---

[232] Andersson 1920, 61; Bondestam 1972, 110; Dreijer 1984, 46, 50; Lindh 1984, 40.
[233] Wernlund 1953, 8; Eriksson & Virgin 1961, 38; Gustavsson 1991, 58; Bondestam 1972, 14, 208–209 preface by Matts Dreijer, 101; Eriksson 1976, 16.

Russians to transport their arms and munitions to the fighting on the mainland. In the second half of the twentieth century, when Ålanders had abandoned the idea of reunification with Sweden and pursuing a line of increased autonomy, the Ålandic politician Thorvald Eriksson admitted that the Swedes might had have other motives than the purely humanitarian. According to Dreijer, the Åland movement's original plan was that Åland's fire brigades with help from Swedish volunteers should liberate their own island from the Russians, thereby paving way for a reunification with Sweden. In the event, as Johannes Eriksson described in his memoirs, the volunteers were not allowed to leave Sweden, but the Swedish government sent regular troops instead. Wilhelm Virgin, Eriksson's co-author, was one of the officers in the planned volunteer force.[234]

Högman believes that Ålandic opinion was not finally decided until 1918. Her conclusion is that Sweden became popular because the arrival of the Swedish expeditionary force brought peace, and Swedish politicians, primarily the navy minister Erik Palmstierna, treated Ålandic demands for reunification favourably. Moreover, Sweden provided free transportation between Åland and Sweden, and distributed sugar on the island which was suffering from a food shortage. Equally important, Finland made a series of mistakes which reduced its popularity. It appointed the undiplomatic colonel Hjalmar von Bonsdorff as county governor, and he rapidly managed to create an atmosphere of mistrust and confrontation. Two other decisions in the same vein were the attempts to conscript troops from Åland and the deployment of Fennophone military on the islands.[235] All other Ålandic writers mention at least some of the explanations that Högman singles out.

The Autonomy Act and the Åland Convention

In an effort to counteract the Ålandic demands for a reunification with Sweden, the Finnish Parliament passed a law which granted Åland autonomy on 30 April 1920. The Ålanders refused to apply the law. The fact that the very law which would later be the cornerstone of Ålandic society was at first vehemently rejected by the Ålanders of course makes

---

[234] Andersson 1920, 62 ff.; Eriksson & Virgin 1961, 36–7; Eriksson 1976, 16; Dreijer 1984, 50.
[235] Högman 1986, 126 ff.

the writers' descriptions of the event interesting. Quite a few accounts treat the initial rejection in just one short sentence.[236]

Subsequent developments, however, given more room. In order to persuade the Ålanders to apply the law of autonomy, Finland's Prime Minister Rafael Erich held a speech in Mariehamn on 4 June 1920, but met resistance from the Ålanders led by the Åland movement's leader Julius Sundblom. In what Matts Dreijer labels the climax of the Åland movement, Sundblom claimed that before Finland became independent the Ålanders, like other peoples in the Russian Empire, demanded to decide their own statehood. Wernlund, Salminen, and Mattson-Eklund write that after Sundblom's speech all the Ålanders marched out, while only priests and civil servants remained.[237] The statement, based on the account of the meeting that was published in Sundblom's paper *Åland*, once again illustrates that priests and civil servants were not considered real Ålanders.

As a result of the incident, Sundblom and the Åland movement's deputy leader Carl Björkman were sentenced to 18 months in jail for high treason, and Matts Dreijer became editor-in-chief of *Åland* until Sundblom was pardoned one month later.[238]

The descriptions of Sundblom's speech on 4 June 1920 highlight that the central argument of the Åland movement was the right to national self-determination. This principle was put forward by the Russian Bolshevik revolutionaries in 1917, and again by the American president Woodrow Wilson in January 1918. The school textbook *Åland* claims that the ideas of the Russian Revolution encouraged the Ålanders in their old dream of reunification with Sweden. Most writers instead connect the Åland movement to Wilson's version of the principle of self-determination.[239]

The Åland question was finally determined by the League of Nations on 24 June 1921. The fact that the Ålanders demands for reunification were not met is in regional history-writing often attributed to the dangers that such an example would have set to the states that were involved in making the decision. They all had minorities which might be encouraged

---

[236] Eriksson 1976, 19; Lindh 1984, 45; Gustavsson 1991, 61,
[237] Wernlund 1953; Eriksson 1976, 20–1; Salminen 1979, 115–16; Dreijer 1984, 81–2; Mattsson-Eklund 2000, 330.
[238] Dreijer 1984, 83–4.
[239] Gustafsson 1991, 60; Dreijer 1965, 2; Skogsjö & Wilén 1997, 13.

to exert their right to national self-determination.[240] Some writers also mention that the League of Nations questioned whether the Ålanders as a small minority really were entitled to national self-determination.[241]

Other explanations of the decision are also based on power politics: either that the League of Nations needed Finland to ward off Bolshevik Russia,[242] or that Britain did not want Sweden to single-handedly dominate the iron-ore route through the Sea of Åland.[243]

The result of the Åland movement was that Åland gained autonomy within Finland. In publications from the mid twentieth century, it is suggested that Åland might still one day become part of Sweden; Johannes Eriksson and Axel Wernlund both quoted the line 'The day will come, we are not conquered yet' ('Än kommer dag, än är ej allt förbi') from Johan Ludvig Runeberg's poem 'Fänrikens hälsning' in *The tales of Ensign Stål*.[244] Eriksson's text was published in 1961, long after his death in 1939, and although Wernlund's book was published in Mariehamn he was himself a former Swedish military man, as was Eriksson's co-author Captain Wilhelm Virgin. These sources from the 1950s and 1960s should rather be used as an indication that an interest in reunification was more alive among Åland's friends in Sweden than on the islands. The fact that both books were published on Åland, however, does indicate that the shift from an ideology of reunification to one of autonomy did not happen swiftly after the Second World War, but was a gradual process.

In the 1970s, autonomy was treated much more positively. In 1971 Matts Dreijer wrote in the preface to Anna Bondestam's *Åland vintern 1918* that autonomy had so far been satisfactory, and that nothing suggested it would not function in the future. He concluded that a bone of contention from the First World War had thereby been transformed into a fixed link between the two halves of the old Swedish realm. In 1976 the Ålandic politician Thorvald Eriksson described autonomy as indispensable, and claimed it had now replaced the old longing for reunification.[245]

Benita Mattsson-Eklund wrote in *Det åländska folkets historia* that after achieved autonomy, the Ålanders began the work of turning the worst

---

[240] Salminen 1979, 127; Skogsjö & Wilén 1997, 17.
[241] Mattsson-Eklund 2000, 332; Skogsjö & Wilén 1997, 17.
[242] Salminen 1979, 127; Skogsjö & Wilén 1997, 17; Mattsson-Eklund 2000, 332.
[243] Eriksson 1976, 23; Dreijer 1967, 39; Dreijer 1984, 96; Mattsson-Eklund 2000, 332.
[244] Dreijer 1943, 104; Wernlund 1953, 55; Eriksson & Virgin 1961, 85. The English translation is Runeberg 1952, 165.
[245] Bondestam 1972, 14; Eriksson 1976, 47.

alternative into the best. The publicist Johannes Salminen claimed that the second best alternative turned out to be good enough. He also wrote that with a knife at its throat, Finland was forced to become a pioneer in minority rights, a statement also quoted by Lind.[246] Thus Ålanders credit themselves for the fact that the islands' autonomy has been successful, and not Finland, which is portrayed as quite a reluctant pioneer.

On 20 October 1921 a conference initiated by the League of Nations renewed Åland's demilitarization in the so-called Åland Convention, which also made the island a neutral zone. This decision was welcomed on Åland and initially also in Sweden. Kenneth Gustavsson, however, has pointed out that the Swedish navy already in 1919 claimed that it was not in Sweden's interest for Åland to be demilitarized.[247]

The divisive Stockholm plan

In the late 1930s, when the threat of war became tangible, Sweden and Finland discussed the possibility of fortifying Åland. Through its strategic geographic position, a fortified Åland could act as a lock on the Gulf of Bothnia, which would ease both countries' burdens of defending their long northern shorelines. Resources could then be released to strengthen their defences elsewhere. Finland and Sweden, which had been arguing about sovereignty over Åland less than two decades earlier, now joined forces in their attempt to convince the Ålanders to accept fortifications. This question widened the rift between Åland's two political leaders, Carl Björkman and Julius Sundblom.

Björkman supported the idea that Ålanders would help in the defence of their own islands; he believed it would make it unnecessary to send Fennophone troops to Åland, and he thought Åland would have greater autonomy in exchange for its contribution. Sundblom was against all alterations to Åland's demilitarization and neutrality; he believed they were the best defence for Åland, and saw the suggestion as an attempt to undermine Åland's autonomy and its Swedish language. Sundblom used the conflict to end the political career of his rival Björkman. The Stockholm plan was never realized because of Soviet opposition.

Björkman was left in the cold until the 1980s. In 1976, the speaker of Åland's Parliament (*landsting*) Thorvald Eriksson wrote a short history of

---

[246] Salminen 1979, 133; Lindh 1998, 52; Mattsson-Eklund 2000, 334.
[247] Gustavsson 2012, 129.

Åland's history intended for visitors to the Åland exhibition the same year. In Eriksson's version of the events in 1938, the Ålanders were united against the fortifications, manifested by the march of 4,000 peasants to Mariehamn. Björkman's role is not mentioned at all. However, in 1982 Åland's provincial parliament commissioned a biography of Björkman. It motivated its decision by claiming that Björkman in 1938 acted out according to what he believed was best for Åland.[248]

All writers agree that both Björkman and Sundblom wanted to defend Åland's autonomy and monolingual Swedish status, but they differ in their evaluations of the principals' policies and personal characteristics.

In his biography of Julius Sundblom, Johannes Salminen gives full support to what he describes as Sundblom's pacifist line. In a speech in June 1938 at the inauguration of a monument to the White Finnish Nystad Corps, Björkman claimed that Ålanders were once again, as in 1808, prepared to defend their homes, if only a leader like Gummerus or Arén would step forward. Björkman used the memory of the uprising in 1808 to launch a direct attack on Sundblom's pacifism. Salminen interprets Björkman's stance as a resurfacing of ideals he had acquired during his formative years in Turku. According to Salminen, Björkman had little connection to the thinking of Ålandic villagers. In Salminen's view, Sundblom's peaceful peasant republic might lack the heroism Björkman was looking for, but it knew a lot about values and dignity. Salminen recalled that as a 13-year-old boy, he had taken part in the peasant march to Mariehamn on 31 October 1938, when 'a small island people defended their right to live their lives in peace', and wrote that he would never forget the atmosphere that day.[249]

Benita Mattsson-Eklund links Björkman's view that the Ålanders' opinions would not affect the outcome of the negotiations to his low opinion of local politicians. She describes him as an aristocratic and militaristic elitist who despised the peasants in the provincial government.[250] The tendency in Ålandic history-writing to contrast Åland's peasants to foreign elites is apparent in Salminen's and Mattsson-Eklund's descriptions of Björkman.

---

[248] Eriksson 1976, 26–7; Isaksson 1988, 3, 243.
[249] Salminen 1979, 187–8, 199 ('Ett litet öfolk ställde här upp för att värna sin rätt att i fred leva sitt eget liv').
[250] Mattsson-Eklund 2000, 341, 343–4.

Matts Dreijer, who accompanied Björkman to the negotiations with the Swedish government in 1938, was firmly supportive of Björkman in his memoirs. Dreijer was of the opinion that the local paper—where Sundblom was editor-in-chief—through a ruthless campaign incited public hatred of Björkman. Dreijer believes the participants in the peasant march acted in good faith, but did not understand that they were marching against greater autonomy. Dreijer seems to agree with Björkman's low opinion of Åland's provincial politicians. For example, he claims that Sundblom's misconception of the budget procedure in a Nordic democracy was a result of 'special circumstances within a very limited sphere of power, where the intellectual stratum is thin'.[251] While other writers portray Björkman as an elitist, Dreijer simply considers him superiorly competent.

Salminen and Dreijer have different views on how the smallness and insularity of Åland affects its political life. According to Salminen it breeds a naïve, peaceful, freedom-loving idealism, while Dreijer believed it might easily cause autocracy and corruption.

Tudeer, who puts more focus on economic factors than other writers, concludes that the introduction of conscription on Åland would only have resulted in a maximum of 200 soldiers per year, and that the conflict caused unnecessary tension between Åland and Finland. Of far greater importance for the country was the Ålanders' voluntary 'conscription' into the merchant navy.[252]

In 2012 Kenneth Gustavsson at the Åland's Museum published a book about military planning in Åland in the years 1919–1939. In it he illustrated that the well-known and much-debated joint effort by Sweden and Finland to fortify Åland in the late 1930s was the outcome of secret, separate plans for Åland which Sweden and Finland had been developing since the early 1920s. He also showed that the final Swedish–Finnish plan was mostly influenced by earlier Swedish planning, while Finland was forced to make concessions without receiving any real guarantees of help from Sweden.[253]

Gustavsson highlights the fact that the Ålandic debate in 1938 revealed that in the 1920s there were advanced plans for an Ålandic branch of the

---

[251] Dreijer 1984, 147 ('speciella förhållanden inom en mycket begränsad maktsfär, där det intellektuella skiktet är tunt'), 193, 196.
[252] Tudeer 1993, 104.
[253] Gustavsson 2012, 167–8.

Protection Corps (Skyddskår), without any protest being made by the Ålanders. On the contrary, the Ålandic provincial government had apparently discussed the need for some kind of Home Guard at its very first meeting in 1922, but it turned out to be against the Åland Convention. Gustavsson also refers to documents from the secret police in May 1939 which claimed that many young Ålanders were in fact looking forward to doing military service, and that Ålanders in general had started to calculate how they could benefit financially from them planned fortifications. The documents also illustrate that opposition to the fortifications was strongest in western Åland, which caused tensions within Ålandic society.[254] The picture of a consistent Ålandic pacifistic standpoint was thus called into question.

The Second World War

Matts Dreijer points out that after the outbreak of the Winter War, Sundblom gave a speech to Åland's newly formed Home Guard, where he claimed that nothing had made him as proud as seeing Åland's youth armed for the defence of their home (*hembygd*).[255] All writers seem to agree that during the Winter War, Ålanders supported the Finnish cause and did no longer objected to military installations on the islands; the situation had thus been completely altered by the Soviet attack on Finland.

Salminen even describes the atmosphere during the war as a brief return to the Finnish patriotism of the pre-1917 period. However, he supports Sundblom's view that the plans to fortify Åland affected Finnish-Soviet relations negatively, and in that way contributed to the war. He also believes the fact that Åland was not attacked during the war proved Sundblom right; fortifications were indeed unnecessary and Åland's best defence was its peaceful profile.[256]

During the war a Home Guard was formed on Åland. Erik Tudeer writes that Sundblom originally opposed an armed Home Guard, but when young Ålanders demanded to be armed he changed his opinion. According to Tudeer, Sundblom did not want to oppose the majority; he based his power on being the leader of public opinion.[257]

---

[254] Gustavsson 2012, 246–7, 324–5.
[255] Dreijer 1984, 199.
[256] Salminen 1979, 174, 229, 235–6.
[257] Tudeer 1993, 108, 117–18.

Salminen, who has a more positive image of Sundblom and considers Ålanders pacifists at heart, emphasizes the mainlanders' role in the formation of Åland's Home Guard; six of the leaders were former students at Svenska Normallycéum in Helsinki. He believes they hoped the Home Guard would lessen Åland's separatism.[258]

According to Tudeer, almost all men joined the Home Guard. Experienced hunters, they were good at shooting and virtually everybody owned guns. Shooting practices and manoeuvres were very popular, but drills and parades were not. A man from Saltvik's branch of the Home Guard asked his instructor whether the intention was to look good on parade or to learn to fight and handle his borrowed machine gun. The protest was accepted and the marching decreased.[259] In Tudeer's version of events, the Ålanders were not idealistic pacifists, but rather were uninterested in military discipline. This is a parallel to the description of the Ålandic militia in 1808–1809.

As a result of the war, refugees from Karelia were allotted land all over Finland. It was suggested that 500 refugees from the island of Lavansaari would be moved to Åland, but after protests from Åland the idea was abandoned. Most writers mention this incident without commenting on whether the Ålandic position was justified; Mattsson-Eklund does not mention it at all. Dreijer, however, describes the event as part of Åland's 'unarmed struggle against nationalistic tendencies', and he believes that if the local authorities had not been vigilant, Åland's Swedish character would have been seriously eroded.[260] No Ålandic writer questions whether it was right to refuse to accept Finnish refugees.

Perhaps the Finnish administrators who suggested the population transfer between the islands imagined that there was a certain 'island identity' that would have made it easier for Ålanders to welcome the inhabitants of Lavansaari, and easier for the refugees to accommodate and integrate. For the Ålandic authorities, and for the writers of Åland's history, this aspect was completely overshadowed by the language question.

All writers agree that the Ålanders were negative towards the Continuation War in 1941, when Finland attacked the Soviet Union in conjunc-

---

[258] Salminen 1979, 234–5.
[259] Tudeer 1993, 118 ff.
[260] Dreijer 1984, 207–208 ('vapenlösa kamp mot nationalistiska tendenser'); Mattsson-Eklund 2000; Salminen 1979, 239; Skogsjö & Wilén 1997, 28, Tudeer 1993, 123.

tion with the German advance during Operation Barbarossa. One explanation is that the Ålanders were Anglo-Saxon oriented and did not like to be on the wrong side in the war.[261] Another explanation is that Ålanders were not attracted by the ultranationalist ideology connected with the war. Tudeer writes that many Finns dreamed of a monolingual Greater Finland, which—like Finnish lip service to Nazi Germany—did not enthuse public opinion on Åland.[262]

Finland built strong fortifications on Åland during the war. Tudeer and Mattsson-Eklund note that Ålanders were forced to take part in the construction work under strict military discipline, while Dreijer writes they were treated almost like prisoners.[263]

Tudeer and Mattsson-Eklund claim that communication problems between Ålanders and the military were more difficult during the Continuation War than during the Winter War, since the troops this time were Fennophone. Dreijer, who served in the military on Åland during both wars, gives a more nuanced description. He claims that the Ålandic staff's financial department, where he served during the Winter War, could not communicate in Swedish. He describes the troops during the Continuation War as a Foreign Legion, consisting of Ålanders who did not understand Finnish, Finns who did not understand Swedish, Russians from the Karelian Isthmus who understood neither, and Jews from Turku.[264]

According to most writers, Ålanders were not interested in re-establishing their Home Guard during the Continuation War, although Dreijer claims that the Finnish military did not allow them to. Instead, the Finnish military founded a Protection Corps (Skyddskår) of the same model as on the mainland. They were more closely linked to the military and swore a military oath. All writers agree that Åland's politicians were against this new organization and that it gained little support. According to Tudeer, two-thirds of the old members of the Home Guard did not join the Protection Corps. Salminen is of the opinion that the 'actual peasantry' was poorly represented among those who pushed for the Protection Corps, that a large part of its members had links to the mainland, and that the percentage of 'genuine Ålanders' was not impressive. He attributes this to the old roots of Ålandic pacifism, and quoted *landshövding*

---

[261] Skogsjö & Wilén 1997, 29; Salminen 1979, 247–8; Mattsson-Eklund 2000, 341.
[262] Mattsson-Eklund 2000, 347, Tudeer 1993, 125.
[263] Tudeer 1993, 125; Mattsson-Eklund 2000, 347; Dreijer 1984, 214–15.
[264] Mattsson-Eklund 2000, 347, Tudeer 1993, 126; Dreijer 1984, 202, 211.

Österberg, who admitted that Ålanders saw exemption from military service as the main gain of autonomy. 'This was Svejk's country rather than Ensign Stål's', the novelist and publisher Salminen concludes.[265]

The Soldier Boys and Girls started on Åland was a movement seen by Julius Sundblom as an attempt to militarize Åland's society and lessen opposition to military service, and he attacked it as soon as the censors eased their grip. All Ålandic writers are strongly critical of this movement, although they have somewhat different emphasis. Dreijer quotes Sundblom's words that Åland must be kept 'neutral, democratic, and first and foremost Swedish'. Mattsson-Eklund believes many Ålanders drew the parallel to the Hitlerjugend, while in Salminen's view the Ålanders were simply against militarization.[266]

The Soldier Boys were banned in the peace treaty between the Soviet Union and Finland. After the collapse of the Soviet Union in the 1990s former Soldier Boys formed guilds, on Åland and elsewhere. In 2012 Åland's Soldier Boys published a book about the mainly Baltic refugees who passed through Åland in 1939–1945.[267]

Salminen stresses that the pacifism had nothing to do with cowardice. This was the accusation made by mainlanders during the war, but the paper *Åland* replied that the hero's grave[268] of the Ålanders was the sea. This argument is often repeated in Ålandic history-writing: Ålanders did their bit in all the ships sunk by mines or torpedoes. Justus Harberg quotes Finland's commander-in-chief, Carl Gustav Mannerheim, who thanked the merchant navy after the Winter War. According to Mannerheim, the sea had been vital for Finland's supply; mines and air attacks made the task dangerous, and he wanted to give his recognition to the crews' self-sacrifice and enthusiasm.[269] It is highly likely that Mannerheim's words, as Finland's national hero, inspired Ålandic writers to stress to role of the merchant navy during the war.

---

[265] Mattsson-Eklund 2000, 347; Dreijer 1984, 214; Tudeer 1993, 126; Salminen 1979, 243-4 ('egentliga allmogen', 'genuina ålänningarnas', 'Detta var Svejks land mer än Fänrik Ståls').
[266] Salminen 1979, 246; Mattsson-Eklund 2000, 349; Dreijer 1984, 215, Tudeer 1993, 127.
[267] Edlund 2012, 9–10.
[268] Fallen Finnish soldiers were buried in 'heroes' graves' at their local parish churches.
[269] Salminen 1979, 245-6; Tudeer 1993, 121, 132; Mattsson-Eklund 2000, 349-50; Harberg 1995, 224.

Salminen claims that the Finnish military caused surprisingly few human conflicts. The population considered the soldiers decent people who were only doing their duty, no matter if they spoke Swedish or Finnish. Matts Dreijer's memoirs from the war years are less sanguine. He recalls how one of his friends was stabbed in the kidneys by a Finnish soldier, since he could not speak Finnish. He also remembers how Ålandic youths beat up students who supported the Protection Corps. At a parade in Mariehamn in 22 May 1944 a colonel held a speech in Finnish, which the locals understood little of but believed contained criticism of Ålanders. This caused agitated scenes between local youngsters and the military, which forced the military police to intervene. Dreijer also gives several examples of how drunken Finnish men misbehaved during the war.[270]

Salminen, with his strong focus on pacifism, and Dreijer, who concentrates on the defence of the Swedish language, are two extremes in Ålandic history-writing. Dreijer also deviates from the mainstream Ålandic description of the war in several ways. He does not emphasize the difference between the Winter War and the Continuation War, and he does not speak negatively of military discipline. As one of the few Ålanders with military experience, Dreijer in some instances himself had to uphold military discipline. He was ordered to assist at the mobilization in Mariehamn in 1941, and with his Browning raised he had to calm some drunken Finnish lumberjacks who shouted 'this is the masters' war' and started fights among themselves.[271] This is in sharp contrast to Salminen's description of mainlanders as warmongers and Ålanders as pacifists. However, the bellicose mainlanders that Salminen referred to came from the Swedophone bourgeoisie in Helsinki. Like the drunken Finnish lumberjacks, Salminen's strand of Ålandic pacifism has an edge of hostility against their masters.

Ålanders and authoritarianism

Martin Isaksson claims that Carl Björkman, who lost his political post before the war, had an unconditional admiration for Adolf Hitler, and this claim is quoted by Benita Mattsson-Eklund. She also mentions that the Ålander Otto Andersson considered Hitler to be Europe's salvation from Bolshevism. Andersson was one of the Ålanders who had stood on the

---

[270] Salminen 1979, 246–7; Dreijer 1984, 205–206, 215–16.
[271] Dreijer 1984, 210, (' "tä herrojen sota", det är herrarnas krig').

Finnish side during the Åland movement, and he became professor of musicology at Åbo Akademi University in 1926. Mattson-Eklund is of the opinion that his interest in folk costumes, music, and dances was one aspect of the National Socialist passion for 'blood and earth'. She also describes the banker and politician Torsten Rothberg as an admirer of the Lapua movement, a right-wing extremist organization in Finland.[272]

Dreijer does not mention any Ålanders who were attracted by Nazism. He does describe how during the war one drunken Finnish officer attacked two 'Jewish boys' under Dreijer's command at Restaurant Miramar and ordered them to jump into the sea. He labels the incident as typical for the early war period, when German victories spread the National Socialist ideology across Europe. The officer was tried and punished, while the Jewish men were relieved from military service and returned to their gents' outfitters in Turku.[273]

In May 1941 Åland was visited by a man who wanted to recruit 15–20 Ålanders for the Finnish SS Battalion. He contacted the Ålandic banker Cederqvist, who encouraged him to speak to Matts Dreijer. Nothing came of the visit, according to the Finnish historian Mauno Jokipii probably because the battalion was full by this time.[274] Dreijer does not mention anything about this episode in his memoirs. The fact that Cederqvist encouraged the SS recruiter to contact Dreijer does not imply that Dreijer sympathized with the organization. Very few Ålanders possessed Dreijer's combination of credibility, contacts, military experience, education, and Finnish-language skills, so he was a natural choice, especially since his assistance to Björkman in 1938 might have given him an image of being defence-friendly—by Ålandic standards.

An understanding of the Ålandic political landscape during the period might help explain why the SS failed to recruit Ålanders. After Björkman's exit in 1938, Julius Sundblom completely dominated local political life, and after the brief exception of the Winter War he was firmly against any Ålandic participation in the fighting. The SS battalion would have mixed Ålanders with Finnish soldiers, exposing them to Fennification and its national ideology, Sundblom's nightmare. Although Sundblom's power as editor-in-chief was somewhat curbed by wartime censorship, anyone who opposed him risked being smeared.

---

[272] Isaksson 1988, 246; Mattsson-Eklund 2000, 341.
[273] Dreijer 1984, 213–14.
[274] Jokipii 1969, 86.

After the war the political winds changed, and Dreijer was approached by the author Aili Nordgren (sister of Sally Salminen) who suggested he take the initiative in finding an Ålandic branch of the Finland–Soviet Union Peace and Friendship Society. According to Dreijer's autobiography, he answered that nobody on Åland would dare take such a step without Sundblom's approval. Sundblom's reaction was that a separate Åland–Soviet Union Society was a better alternative, but it proved to be impossible, and Nordgren's alternative won.[275]

The example illustrates that all important political decisions on Åland were evaluated on the basis of whether they might weaken the island's autonomous status by binding it closer to Finland. The pros and cons of a possible Ålandic participation in the Finnish SS battalion were most likely analysed on the same premises.

The development of autonomy after 1945

After the war, leading Ålanders made renewed attempts to join Sweden. Several writers link this to Finland's attempt to give the Soviet Union a military base on Åland instead of in Porkkala near Helsinki; the Ålanders could not feel safe within Finland.[276]

In November 1944, Julius Sundblom approached Sweden's prime minister Per Albin Hansson, who did not give any support either to Sundblom's suggestion of reunification or to his proposal of independence for Åland. After Sundblom's death in 1945, Ålanders sent a letter to the Finnish government announcing Åland's wish to be reunified with Sweden. This caused the Swedish foreign ministry to declare that Sweden did not want a reunification, and Finland's government said that foreign policy was outside the scope of Åland's Parliament. According to Dreijer and Eriksson, the Ålanders did not expect any direct result from their letter, but wanted to demonstrate their opinion and pave the way for an improvement to Ålandic autonomy. According to Dreijer's autobiography, he belonged to the informal group of patriots who had gathered after Sundblom's death to write the letter. The meeting was held at Dreijer's workplace, the Åland Museum, with a stone axe used as a gavel.[277]

When Finland's government responded to the letter, Prime Minister Juho Kusti Paasikivi invited the Ålanders to negotiations about a new

---

[275] Dreijer 1984, 218–19.
[276] Eriksson 1976, 28; Salminen 1979, 258–9; Skogsjö & Wilén 1997, 31.
[277] Dreijer 1984, 229–30; Eriksson 1976, 28.

Autonomy Act. The most important feature of the law was regional citizenship, 'hembygdsrätt', which became a prerequisite for voting in regional elections, owning land or property or establishing a business on the island. Paasikivi, who became president the following year, is portrayed very positively in Ålandic history-writing. Eriksson and Mattsson-Eklund writes that parts of the Finnish Parliament were hostile to Åland and the new law, and that President Paasikivi pushed it through. Dreijer claims it was through Björkman's negotiations in 1938 that Paasikivi was aware of the need for a new law. Dreijer, who was secretary of the delegation from Åland that met Paasikivi in 1945, recalls that Paasikivi was of the opinion that 'Finland needs within its borders since time immemorial to have a resident Swedish population, which is not threatened with being automatically engulfed by the huge Finnish majority'. According to Dreijer, Paasikivi would have liked to give the Finno-Swedish areas in mainland Finland the same autonomy as Åland, if Finnish immigration to those areas had not already gone too far. Skogsjö and Wilén believe Paasikivi needed the Finno-Swedes and the Ålanders as a bridge westwards, that could balance the Soviet Union's alarmingly strong influence.[278] There is a clear tendency in Åland's twentieth-century historiography to see the president as Åland's friend in Helsinki.

Finland's government and Parliament is in Ålandic history-writing seen as powers that want to limit Åland's autonomy, or at least to stall its development, for example in the handling of the revised Autonomy Act in 1951 and the funding of Åland's new parliament building (Självstyrelsegården) in the 1970s. On the other hand, writers of Ålandic history have great confidence in Finland's heads of state. The presidents, especially Paasikivi and Urho Kekkonen, are portrayed as the people who have enabled Ålandic autonomy to move forward, despite the Finnish Parliament's negative attitude. Even President Paasikivi's veto of the first suggestion for a provincial flag is treated with understanding by Thorvald Eriksson.[279]

---

[278] Dreijer 1984, 231 ('Finland är i behov av att inom sina gränser ha en sedan urminnes tid bofast svensk befolkning, som inte hotas att automatiskt sugas upp av den stora finska majoriteten'); Skogsjö & Wilén 1997, 32; Eriksson 1976, 30; Mattsson-Eklund 2000, 354 ff., Tudeer 1993, 134.
[279] See, for example, Lindh 1984, 68; Mattsson-Eklund 2000, 354 ff.; Eriksson 1976, 30, 33; Dreijer 1984, 231; Skogsjö & Wilén 1997, 32, 44, Tudeer 1993, 134, 199–200.

The development of Ålandic history-writing

Åland's history-writing has undergone several distinct phases. The first Ålanders who wrote their island's history, K. A. Bomansson and Reinhold Hausen, did so as pioneers of the Finnish nation-building project during the second half of the nineteenth century. Until 1917, the political elite on Åland remained faithful to Finnish nationalism, but in the autumn that year they began to seek reunification with Sweden in the so-called Åland movement. Historians from Sweden and Finland supplied their respective governments with arguments in the diplomatic battle for Åland, and for a large part of the twentieth-century Ålandic regional history-writing was heavily influenced by the Swedish rhetoric from the days of the Åland movement.

It was probably security concerns that made leading Ålanders switch from Finnish to Swedish nationalism. They managed to get the majority of the population behind them, a shift of sentiment which was solidified in 1918 when the Swedes became popular because of their military expedition to Åland and Finland made a number of mistakes, the most important being the appointment of Hjalmar von Bonsdorff as governor. The shift in nationalism was probably aided by the fact that Finnish nationalism had never taken root among broader layers in Ålandic society. The late start of primary schools on Åland had delayed the dissipation of the national ideology among the peasants, and the bourgeoisie which was the backbone of nationalism on the mainland were very thin on the ground on Åland. The shift was facilitated by the fact that Swedish and—especially the Svecoman version of—Finnish nationalism were almost indistinguishable from each other: nationalists from both countries venerated the same historical events, myths, and symbols and sang the same songs. Although politically separated in 1809, Sweden and Finland had continued to enjoy a shared cultural life. The Ålanders were situated right on the fissure of a split country, and it was by no means self-evident where their loyalty could and should lie.

Although the Ålanders could turn from Finnish to Swedish nationalists without changing their books of national history, Åland's autonomy made necessary a rewriting of regional history. In 1933 the provincial authorities employed an archaeologist, Matts Dreijer. In his memoirs written 50 years later he claimed that his mission had been to defend autonomy by strengthening the Ålanders' identity. Initially Dreijer's version of Åland's history closely mimicked the one presented by Swedish historians during the struggle for Åland in 1917–21. He portrayed Åland as an ancient Swedish province. However, after the Second World War, when leading Ålanders gave up all hope of a reunion with Sweden, and instead focused wholeheartedly on developing Ålandic autonomy, the ancient Åland of Dreijer's writings started to become more and more autonomous and important. When his vision of the early Middle Ages was fully developed in the early 1980s, Åland was portrayed as a central player in Northern Europe, a centre for trade, and a base for the crusades against the heathens in the east.

Dreijer's history-writing, both in its early Swedish-oriented phase and in its later autonomous version, can of course be seen as an answer to Åland's demand for historical legitimacy, but it does not explain why it became so extreme in its later versions. It could be argued that a more moderately heroic past would have achieved a broader acceptance, at least in the wider world and international academic circles. However, from the prefaces of Dreijer's books it is clear that his intended audience was the Ålandic youth, in whom he wanted to instil a willingness to defend autonomy and the Swedish language.

It must also be remembered that the intellectual class on Åland for most of the twentieth century remained very small. That meant that Dreijer was long the lone voice of Ålandic history-writing; the lack of criticism probably facilitated the unhindered development of his wilder theories. Dreijer described Finnish research on Åland as distorted by nationalism, and after the Second World War the Swedish disciples of Harald Hjärne received the same verdict, in effect leaving Dreijer the only one who could write about Åland's history. Dreijer held Sweden's Weibullian school of historians in high regard, mainly because they criticized the Hjärne disciples' nationalistic history-writing, but since the Weibullians had not actually written anything about Åland they constituted no obstacle for the free development of his theories.

The frequently mentioned tendency in Ålandic society to look down on culture and education and hold the practical in high regard probably also affected Dreijer's work. As the sole representative of humanities research in a community of farmers, ship owners, and small businessmen, Dreijer needed to produce practically useful research results—and in order to make his reluctant audience listen, the message needed to be truly sensational.

wÅlandic history-writing illustrates how the Ålandic identity-building project has developed into a project of nation-building. From the Åland movement to after the Second World War, Ålandic identity can be described as ethnic nationalism, emphasizing the Swedishness of the Ålanders' language, mind, and blood. History-writing gave support to this ethnic nationalism by describing Åland as an ancient Swedish province, whose inhabitants had shown their willingness to be Swedes in 1808, 1854, and 1917. In the 1950s, when the hope of reunification with Sweden had finally disappeared, Åland's provincial government initiated a deliberate campaign which promoted awareness of autonomy. In order to defend that autonomy against Finnish encroachments, Ålanders and the surrounding world had to be made aware about the international treaties that regulated Åland's status. Thorvald Eriksson's publications were all part of this information campaign. It can be argued that the campaign has gradually transformed Ålandic nationalism from ethnic to civic and constitutional, focusing on the Ålanders' rights rather than their blood. The earlier racial interpretations of Ålandic-ness have faced harsh criticism in Ålandic history-writing from the 1990s onward. The introduction in 1951 of a regional citizenship (*hembygdsrätt*) was probably a necessary precondition for the shift towards a civic interpretation of the Ålandic identity.

Åland's status is founded on two sets of documents, the Convention on the demilitarisation of the Åland Islands of 1856, and the Åland decision and the Åland Agreement by the League of Nations in 1921, which outlined Åland's autonomy.[280] These two sets of documents are mirrored by two different strands of Ålandic identity-building. Until the 1980s Åland's autonomy and monolingual Swedish status were the undisputed core of Ålandic-ness; demilitarization had a purely auxiliary function of protecting the language and autonomy by keeping Finnish-speaking troops away and by protecting Ålandic youth from indoctrination into Finnish nationalism during military service. Ålandic nationalism based on the agreement of 1921 is at first glance difficult to distinguish from ethnic nationalism. After all, the justification that the documents give for Åland's autonomy is the protection of its language and culture. However, the fact that Ålandic-ness it not defined by heritage but by acceptance of autonomy and monolingual

---

[280] Ålands kulturstiftelse has collected and published these documents, together with later documents concerning Åland's status, <http://www.kulturstiftelsen.ax/images/internationellaavtal/engelskaavtal.pdf>.

Swedishness might have facilitated Åland's transformation into an immigration society and the rapid assimilation of Finnish speakers. It is possible that large immigration in combination with Åland's internationalized economic structure has contributed to the demise of ethnic definitions of Ålandic-ness. In fact, Åland's business-funded maritime history-writing was not concerned with ethnicity even in the 1940s; it had an international focus and showed no interest in the Swedish–Finnish dichotomy which permeated the Ålandic history-writing that was funded by the provincial government.

However, in the 1980s a new formulation of Ålandic identity based on the demilitarization started to take form. This happened at a time when Åland's politics and media had become more pluralistic, and when the most rigid extremes of monolingual Swedishness started to come under attack. The idea that peace was the core of Ålandic identity was accompanied by a campaign to use Åland's autonomy as a model for the peaceful resolution of conflicts between majority and minority populations all over the world. In this line of thought, autonomy and the protection of minority rights became instrumental to achieving peace. However, no forces on Åland claimed that the Swedish language was unimportant, but the peace camp differed from the language camp in the sense that they considered Åland's autonomy to be an example of a well-functioning protection of minority rights, while the latter stressed the continued threat from politicians and bureaucrats in Helsinki.

The writer who has been most consequent in incorporating pacifism as a trait permeating Åland's modern history is Johannes Salminen. In his view, the stipulations of Åland's demilitarization from 1854 have become second nature to the Ålanders. However, in his attempt to prove the genuine Ålanders' love of peace, he defines everyone who does not conform to these high ideals as mainlanders.

The peace discourse, however, has become a mere complement to the old language discourse. Åland's autonomy, in which defence and development is the paramount aim of all political forces on Åland, was granted as a protection of the inhabitants' Swedish language and culture, and that put limitations on how Ålandic identity can be formulated by regional history writers and politicians. This helps explain the peculiarities of the Ålandic defence of the Swedish language; it is not directed against foreign words seeping into the language, nor against the disappearance of local dialects. Neither is it opposed to immigration, even of Finnish speakers, as long as they assimilate. Rather it is a struggle against the possibility that Åland might linguistically become just another ordinary Finno-Swedish part of Finland, for example by the formation of a Finnish-speaking community, thereby undermining the claim that Ålanders are a special minority in need of the protection of their autonomy.

The development of a separate Ålandic national identity since the mid twentieth century bears many parallels to the development of the Finnish national identity since the mid nineteenth century. In both cases, political realities ensured that a continued identification with Sweden was not a realistic alternative. In a parallel to how the Russian tsars initially supported Finnish nationalism in Finland as a counterweight to the strong Swedish influence, the efforts of the Finnish presidents Kekkonen and Paasikivi were crucial in encouraging the Ålanders to embrace autonomy and abandon the idea of reunification with Sweden. Their support for the development of Åland's autonomy has seen them portrayed in a positive light in Ålandic history-writing.

Åland is described as an egalitarian society of independent, freedom-loving, practical, and enterprising individuals. Sometimes these characteristics are explained as functions of the economic necessities imposed by Åland's geographical circumstances, which has forced the islanders into trade and seafaring. Members of the upper and lower classes are often described as mainlanders, thereby strengthening the image that the genuine Ålanders are egalitarian peasants to a man and a woman. In recent decades, however, there has been an increased acknowledgement of the differences that have existed within Ålandic society.

References

Åland's history-writing

Andersson, Otto (1920), *Bidrag till kännedom om Ålandsfrågans uppkomst och stämningen på Åland, 1917–1918* (Helsinki: Schildts).
Bertell, Erik (1983), *Skattedistrikt och förvaltningsområden på Åland under tidigt 1500-tal* (Mariehamn: Ålands kulturstiftelse).
— (1993), *Medeltida skattesystem på Åland* (Mariehamn: Ålands kulturstiftelse).
Bomansson, Karl August (1852), *Skildring af folkrörelsen på Åland 1808: en scen ur Suomis sista strid: med en öfversigt af Åland i allmänhet* (Stockholm: Albert Bonnier).

— & Reinholm, H. A. (1856), *Finlands fornborgar*, i: *Kastelholm* (Helsinki: J. C. Frenckell).
— (1858), *Om Ålands fornminnen* (diss., Helsinki: n. pub.)
Bondestam, Anna (1972), *Åland vintern 1918* (Mariehamn: Ålands kulturstiftelse).
Dreijer, Matts (1937), *Ålands forntid och forntida minnesmärken* ['Åland's prehistory and ancient monuments'] (Mariehamn: Ålands museum).
— (1943), *Åland och ålänningarna* (Helsinki: Söderströms).
— (1960), *Häuptlinge, Kaufleute und Missionare im Norden vor tausend Jahren: Ein Beitrag zur Beleuchtung der Umbildung der nordischen Gesellschaft während der Übergangszeit vor Heidentum zum Christentum* (Mariehamn: Ålands kulturstiftelse).
— (1966), *Ålands ömsesidiga försäkringsbolag, 1866–1966: festskrift till 100-års jubiléet och Glimtar ur Ålands historia* (Mariehamn: Ålands ömsesidiga försäkringsbolag).
— (1967), *Glimtar ur Ålands historia* (Mariehamn: Ålands tidnings-tryckeri).
— (1976), 'Det äldsta Kastelholm', *Åländsk odling*, 37 (Mariehamn: Ålands folkminnesförbund).
— (1983), *Det åländska folkets historia*, i/i: *Från stenåldern till Gustav Vasa* (2nd rev. edn., Mariehamn: Ålands kulturstiftelse).
— (1984), *Genom livets snårskog* (Helsinki: Söderströms).
— (1987), *Nordens kristnande i ny belysning* (Mariehamn: Ålands tidningstryckeri).
Dreijer, Stig (2006), *Det åländska folkets historia*, iii: *Frihetstiden och den gustavianska tiden, 1721–1808* (Mariehamn: Ålands kulturstiftelse).
Edlund, Karl Johan (2012), *De flydde kriget. Baltiska och andra flyktingar runt Åland krigsåren, 1939–1945* (Stockholm: Leandoer & Ekholm).
Eriksson, Johannes & Virgin, Wilhelm (1961), *Ålandsfrågan 1917–1921: minnen och upplevelser* (Stockholm: Hörsta).
Eriksson, Susanne, Johansson, Lars Ingemar & Sundback, Barbro (2006), *Fredens öar: Ålands självstyrelse, demilitarisering, och neutralisering* (Mariehamn: Ålands Fredsinstitut).
Eriksson, Torvald (1976), *Så tillkom Ålands självstyrelse och så försvaras den: glimtar ur självstyrelsens historia* (Mariehamn: Ålandsutställningen).
— (1996), *Åland i motvind: Finlands moraliska Ålandskris* (Mariehamn: T. Eriksson).
Fagerlund, Lars Wilhelm (1925), *Anteckningar rörande samfärdseln emellan Sverige och Finland öfver Ålands haf och de åländska öarna* (Helsinki: Ålands vänner).
Gustafsson, Sture (1982), *Åland. Hembygdskunskap åk 3–6* (Esbo: Svenska läromedel).
— (1991), *Åland. Hembygdskunskap åk 3–6* (2nd rev. edn., Esbo: Editum).

Gustavsson, Kenneth (1997), *Otterböte: New Light on a Bronze Age Site in the Baltic* (Stockholm: Archaeological Research Laboratory, Stockholm University).

— (2012), *Ålandsöarna – en säkerhetsrisk? Spelet om den demilitariserade zonen, 1919–1939* (Mariehamn: PQR).

Harberg, Justus (1995), *Åländsk sjöfart med maskindrivna fartyg* (Mariehamn: Ålands Nautical Club).

Hausen, Reinhold, (1920), *Ur Ålands forntid: kulturhistoriska skildringar*, ii: *Bastö gård och dess ägare: mordbranden på Haga kungsgård år 1736: Kastelholms häkte: när 'mästermannen' förrättade sitt ämbete: bibliografi öfver Åland* (Helsinki: Föreningen Ålands vänner).

Högman, Gyrid (1986), 'Älänningarna och ålandsfrågan', in Jungar & Villstrand 1986: 117–37.

— (1990), *Den åländska kvinnans historia 1700–1950* (Mariehamn: Ålands kulturstiftelse).

Isaksson, Martin (1981), *Kring Bomarsund* (Helsinki: Söderströms).

— (1988), *Carl Björkman: Ålands första lantråd* (Mariehamn: Ålands kulturstiftelse).

Jungar, Sune & Villstrand, Nils Erik (1986) (eds.), *Väster om skiftet: uppsatser ur Ålands historia* (Åbo: Åbo Akademi University kopieringscentral).

Kuvaja, Christer, Hårdstedt, Martin & Hakala, Pertti (2006), *Det åländska folkets historia*, iv: *Från finska kriget till Ålandsrörelsen 1808–1920* (Mariehamn: Ålands kulturstiftelse).

Kåhre, Georg & Kåhre, Karl (1988), *Den åländska segelsjöfartens historia* ['The history of Ålandic seafaring by sail'] (Mariehamn: Ålands Nautical Club)(first pub. 1940).

Lindh, Kurt (1984), *Det åländska samhället* (Esbo: Svenska läromedel).

— (1998), *Det åländska samhället* (Saltvik: Lifam).

Mattsson-Eklund, Benita (2000), *Alla tiders Åland. Från istid till EU-inträde* ['A Land for all Times—From the Ice Age to the EU membership'] (Mariehamn: Ålands landskapsstyrelse).

Nordman, Dan (1986), 'Historiker kämpar om Åland: om de svenska och finländska historikernas argumentering i Ålandsfrågan 1917–21', in Jungar & Villstrand 1986: 139–58.

Nyman, Valdemar (1980), *Det åländska folkets historia*, i/ii: *Ålands medeltida kyrkokonst* (Mariehamn: Ålands kulturstiftelse).

Ramsdahl, Carl (1988), *Det åländska folkets historia*, ii/i: *Under Gustav Vasa och hans söner samt stormaktstiden* (Mariehamn: Ålands kulturstiftelse).

Ringbom, Åsa (2010), *Åländska kyrkor berättar: nytt ljus på medeltida konst, arkitektur och historia* (Mariehamn: Ålands museum).

Robins, Graham, Skogsjö, Håkan & Örjans, Jerker (2004), *Bomarsund: det ryska imperiets utpost i väster* (Mariehamn: Skogsjömedia).

Salminen, Johannes (1979), *Ålandskungen* (Stockholm: Rabén & Sjögren).

Skogsjö, Håkan & Wilén, Jonas (1997), *Skotten i tornvillan: berättelsen om den åländska självstyrelsens första 75 år* (Mariehamn: Ålands museum).
Tomtlund, Jan-Erik (2005), *Vikingatid* (Mariehamn: Ålands landskapsregering, Museibyrån).
Tudeer, Erik (1993), *Det åländska folkets historia*, v/i: *1920–1990* (Mariehamn: Ålands kulturstiftelse).
Wernlund, Axel (1953), *Ålands kamp för självhävdelse* (Mariehamn: Liewendals).
Westergren, Ebbe & Nygren, Tord (2008), *Tidernas Åland: från stenåldern till svenska tidens slut* (Mariehamn: Skolbyrån vid Ålands landskapsregering).

Other works cited

Åländsk odling (1997), *Åländsk identitet* (Mariehamn: Museibyrån).
Åland Maritime Museum, <http://www.sjofartsmuseum.ax/sjomuseum/historik.pbs>, 12 December 2011.
Allardt Ljunggren, Barbro (2008), *Åland som språksamhälle: språk och språkliga attityder på Åland ur ett ungdomsperspektiv* (Stockholm: Centre for Research on Bilingualism, Stockholm University).
Anckar, Dag (1996), 'Ett självständigt Åland?', *Finsk Tidskrift*, 1996, 7: 417–30.
— & Bartmann, Berry (2000), *Ett ramverk för ett självständigt Åland* (Mariehamn: Sällskapet Ålands framtid).
Convention on the Demilitarisation of the Åland Islands 1856, <http://www.kulturstiftelsen.ax/images/internationellaavtal/engelskaavtal.pdf>.
De Geer-Hancock (1986), *Åländskhet. Nationsbygget på 'fredens öar'* (Mariehamn: Ålands Tidnings-Tryckeri).
Ekman, Martin (2000), *Det självstyrda och demilitariserade Ålands gränser: historiska, geovetenskapliga och rättsliga synpunkter* (Mariehamn: Ålands högskola).
Eliasson, Thor-Alf (2005), *Viking Line i backspegeln* (Mariehamn: Viking Line).
Fornföreningen Fibula, 'Historien om Hlödver den långe och Fornföreningen Fibula', <http://www.aland-vikingar.com/text.con?iPage=2>, 14 July 2009.
Griessner, Doris (2012), 'The Åland Islands and the construction of Ålandishness', in Karin Topsø Larsen (ed.), *From one Island to another: a Celebration of Island Connections* (Nexø: Centre for Regional and Tourism Research).
Häggblom, Kenth, Kinnunen, Jouko & Lindstöm, Bjarne (1999), 'Ålänningarna och deras identitet: en enkätundersökning av ÅSUB', *Radar* 1:1999 (Mariehamn), 9–27.
Hakala, Pertti (2006), 'Trohet mot det svenska fäderneslandet – folkresningen 1808 i åländsk historieskrivning', in Sophie Holm et al. (eds.), *Åländska identiteter* (Historicus r.f:s skriftserie, 17; Helsinki: Historicus).
Hårdstedt, Martin (2004), 'Kluvna lojaliteter? Ålänningarna och den ryska överhögheten under Krimkriget 1854–56', in Ann-Katrin Hatje (ed.),

Historiens mångfald: Presentation av pågående forskning vid Institutionen för historiska studier, Umeå universitet (Umeå: Umeå universitet).
Hausen, Marika (2000), *Reinhold Hausen* (Mariehamn: Ålands museum).
Hellberg, Lars (1980), *Ortnamnen och den svenska bosättningen på Åland* (Uppsala: Seminariet för nordisk ortnamnsforskning, Uppsala universitet).
Jokipii, Mauno (1969), *Panttipataljoona: suomalaisen SS-pataljoonan historia* (Helsinki: Weilin & Göös).
Köhler, Lillemor von (1996), *Föreningen Ålands Vänner r.f: samhällsbyggare och kulturodlare 1896–1996* (Mariehamn: Ålands vänner).
League of Nations Official Journal (1921), September, 701, <http://www.kulturstiftelsen.ax/images/internationellaavtal/engelskaavtal.pdf>.
Lundberg, Ulla-Lena (1976), *Kökar* (Helsinki: Söderström).
Nordman, Dan (2006), *En boning i havet: Brändös historia till 1945* (Brändö: Brändö kommun).
Nya Åland, 31 December 1998, 'Algot är århundadets ålänning', http://www.nyan.ax/nyheter/arkiv.pbs?news_id=5758, 26 May 2014.
Nya Åland, 15 May 2014, 'Dagen då jag bad Matts Dreijer om ursäkt', <http://www.nyan.aland.fi/ledaren/spalten.pbs?news_id=83047&news_instance=266>, 26 May 2014.
Palamarz, Piotr (2004), *Kastelholms slot: Från medeltida borg till byggnadsminne* (Mariehamn: Ålands landskapsstyrelse, Museibyrån).
Runblom, Harald (1995), *Majoritet och minoritet i Östersjöområdet: ett historiskt perspektiv* (Stockholm: Natur & Kultur).
Runeberg, Johan Ludwig (1952), *The tales of Ensign Stål* (Stockholm: Lindqvists).
Sjöblom, Walter (1945), *Föreningen Ålands vänner 1895–1945* (Mariehamn: Ålands tidningstryckeri).
Sjöstrand, Per Olof (1996), *Hur Finland vanns för Sverige. En historia för nationalstater* (Opuscula historica Upsaliensia, 16; Uppsala: Historiska institutionen, Uppsala universitet).
Statistics and Research Åland (2011), *Åland i siffror,* http://www.asub.ax/files/alsiff11en.pdf.
Sundback, Susan (1999), 'Ålänningarna och finlandssvenskheten', *Radar* 1:1999 (Mariehamn), 29–40.
Svensson, Hasse (1998), *Algot: en obändig ålänning* (Mariehamn: Abacus).
Tarkiainen, Kari (2000), 'Vem var Reinhold Hausen', in Elisa Orrman (ed.), *Reinhold Hausen, 1850–1942: Kansallisen arkiston rakentaja* (Helsinki: Kansallisarkisto).
Tidningen Åland, 7 March 2006.
Villstrand, Nils Erik (1984), 'Åland – mellan Finland och Sverige', *Finsk tidskrift* (Föreningen Granskaren), (6–7).
–– (2009), *Riksdelen: stormakt och rikssprängning 1560–1812* (Helsinki: Svenska litteratursällskapet i Finland/Atlantis).

Emails to the author

E-mail from Benita Mattsson-Eklund, 15 June 2009.
E-mail from Kenneth Gustavsson, 8 January 2013.

Saaremaa and Hiiumaa
Revolutionizing identities in Baltic German, national Estonian, and Soviet histories, 1827–2012

Janne Holmén

Saaremaa and Hiiumaa have experienced several shifts of national sovereignty in the twentieth century. This provides an excellent opportunity to study the relationship between regional and national identity. The aim of this study is to investigate what the content and function of regional history-writing has been under different regimes, and how regional and national identity have been reformulated after shifts of power.

The two great Estonian Islands Saaremaa and Hiiumaa are geographically close to each other, but in spite of that at various times they have belonged to different states or Russian governments. However, the content of the regional history-writing on the islands is sufficiently similar to justify considering them in the same chapter. The main difference is that on the larger Saaremaa, regional history-writing is older and more voluminous.

Saaremaa and Hiiumaa are both situated within a few kilometres from the mainland. The population of Saaremaa constituted about 5% of the nation's total population before the Second World War, but in the period 1940–1953 the island suffered more heavily from population losses than the mainland. The population shrank from a peak of around 60,000 to 30,000. Hiiumaa is the smaller of the islands, and its population was like Saaremaa's reduced by half, from around 20,000 to 10,000, during and after the Second World War. However, still after its population loss Saaremaa constitutes a larger part of the nation to which it belongs than any other island in this research project, both in land area and population.

Saaremaa was already heavily populated during the Iron Age, while Hiiumaa is described a deserted island in sources from the early thirteenth century. In the sixteenth century, the influx of refugees from wars on the mainland saw a town grow up around Kuressaare Castle. Kärdla on Hiiumaa did not gain city rights until 1938, and not until after the Second World War did it replace Haapsalu on the mainland as the island's administrative centre.[1]

Map of Estonia showing Saaremaa and Hiiumaa. Source: Wikimedia Commons.

Saaremaa was the last Estonian province to be conquered by German crusaders, largely due to the fact that the Germans lacked a proper navy.

[1] Pao 2003, 198.

The island was finally conquered after an invasion over the ice in the winter of 1227, and as Hiiumaa it became divided between the bishopric of Ösel–Wiek and the Livonian Brothers of the Sword. Like the Baltic mainland, both Saaremaa and Hiiumaa became dominated by a German elite that maintained its power in local society until Estonia's independence in 1918, even though sovereignty shifted between Denmark, Sweden, and Russia in the intervening centuries. Estonia was a Soviet republic from 1940–1 and 1944–91, during which time a substantial amount of regional history was written by islanders in exile.

Earlier research

Very little research has been done on regional history-writing on Saaremaa. Shorter texts have been written about the early pioneers Luce and Körber, but these men were extremely versatile, and their biographers have mainly focused on other aspects of their work.[2] The earlier research does not elaborate on the contents of Luce's and Körber's historical writings, for what purposes they were written, or what views of history they represent.

A collection of documents regarding the uprising on Saaremaa in 1919 from the late Soviet age (1989) contains a historiographical overview. Some of the works mentioned in the article can be described as regional history-writing. The article, however, is limited to commenting whether the authors were right or wrong—only the explanations that the uprising was caused by proletarization and hatred of the barons were approved.[3]

In fact, as Johan Eellend has pointed out, there is a lack of Estonian historiographical research in general. He himself has set out an overview of the historical discipline's development in the country. Estonian national history-writing did not begin until the inter-war period. In the nineteenth century, history-writing in Estonia had been Baltic German. According to Eellend these publications were of high academic standards, but focused rather narrowly on the Baltic German elite, excluding the Estonian-speaking population. They saw themselves as carriers of high culture in an underdeveloped region. However, there were also Baltic

---

[2] Vinkel 1994; Rein 2007; Parbus 2007.
[3] Saaremaa ülestous 1919, 10–32.

Germans who in the spirit of Herder tried to map the Estonian language and culture.[4]

Eellend claims that when Estonia was established as an independent state after the First World War, Estonian history-writing changed focus from the German to the Estonian population. Estonian academic history became a *Volksgeschichte*, a history with a romantic approach whose focus was on writing the history of the dominant group, not a *Landesgeschichte* describing the people living in the area.[5]

According to Eellend this meant that the native Russian and Swedish populations were ignored, while the Germans found a new role as oppressors. This tendency is still visible in post-Soviet Estonia. Jüri Kivimäe, who in his article 'Re-writing Estonian history?' examines the need for a new way of approaching national history-writing, is of the opinion that a future Estonian history not only has to include all peoples, but should in the tradition of Braudel 'represent the concept of region as the first principle of historical thought and organization'.[6]

The man who in the 1920s trained the first generation of Estonian professional historians was the Finnish professor Arno Cederberg. He encouraged studies of contacts with Scandinavia and of the Swedish period in Estonia's history. This provided an alternative to the earlier Russian- or German-oriented history-writing. 'In popular works, the Swedish times were presented as "the good old times" when things were not as bad as during the Russian and Baltic German oppression.'[7]

The most radically nationalist of Cederberg's pupils was Hans Kruus, and according to Eellend his view of history became the dominant one. Since Estonia had no previous period of independence to relate to, a mythical pre-historical independence became important. This independence was interrupted by invaders and oppressors. Estonian resistance and national survival therefore became important historical themes.[8]

In 1940 Kruus underwent a political conversion and became a member of the first pro-Soviet Estonian government. Jüri Kivimäe connects this turn to an article about small-nation consciousness the in Estonian

---

[4] Eellend 2004, 71.
[5] Eellend 2004, 71.
[6] Eellend 2004, 71; Kivimäe 1999, 210–11.
[7] Eellend 2004, 72.
[8] Eellend 2004, 72–3.

national ideology that Kruus wrote in 1939.[9] In a small nation, national ideology had to be flexible in order to survive.

After the Second World War Estonian history-writing had to start anew, since most scholars had fled or were persecuted. In the new version of Estonia's history, the workers and their struggle to join the Soviet family were stressed. After Stalin's death, history-writing became more diversified and serious, but according to Eellend it took fifteen years before a new generation of historians emerged who 'could both pay attention to the official political agenda and develop their own research'. These historians in the 1960s and 1970s continued the inter-war tradition of agrarian history.[10]

With glasnost came a new important shift in Estonian history-writing. In the early 1990s there was a tremendous interest in history, with a multitude of books and historical journals. However, many of these were written by journalists and amateurs. Professional historians had compromised themselves during the Soviet era, and their fields of research did not match what was now in public demand: previously forbidden subjects such as Soviet crimes. According to Eellend, the new popular history tended to ignore the German occupation and the crimes committed then. He also claimed that studies of the recent past were financed by political groupings, and therefore have become mere mappings of Soviet crimes. Jüri Kivimäe claimed in 1999 that contemporary history-writing about the inter-war period was driven 'more by emotion and political bias than by objective and professional criteria'. Attempts at critical research were accused of being pro-Soviet by the right wing.[11]

Saaremaa identity has been addressed in a limited number of studies, some of them also touching upon historical aspects. Helen Sooväli has studied how Saaremaa's landscape has been portrayed in text and picture during the twentieth century. She claims that the 1930s were a heyday for regional studies, and that many texts were written about Saaremaa during this period. The work *Saaremaa* from 1934 is among her sources. She focused primarily on the geographic parts of the book, while the present study will investigate its sections about history. Her conclusion is that Saaremaa was described in the scholarly literature as backward compared to mainland Estonia, largely because of the late land reforms. It was also

---

[9] Kivimäe 1999, 209.
[10] Eellend 2004, 74 ff.
[11] Eellend 2004, 77 ff.; Kivimäe 1999, 206.

believed that the backwardness was aggravated by the island's isolation and the fact that agricultural work was not seen as suitable for men.[12]

Saaremaa became a popular motif for Estonian landscape painters in the early twentieth century because it represented the past, the wilderness, and the archaic lifestyle of its inhabitants, qualities which were described as backwardness and poverty in contemporary scholarly writings.[13]

Sooväli has also examined a regional committee on Saaremaa which has attempted to identify landscapes which are important for national identity. Since few locals gave any input to the project, the outcome was mainly decided by specialists. The resulting list contains landscapes with a mix of natural and historical values. Most of the historic sites are medieval, but a Soviet rocket base is also mentioned.[14]

Sooväli adds that sights such as the Kaali meteorite crater, Kuressaare Castle, and the Angla windmills have become icons of Saaremaa with the help from coffee-table books, and that they are used as 'the traditional image of Estonian national identity'.[15]

Several investigations of Saaremaa identity are linked to the plans for a bridge or tunnel to the mainland. Jana Raadik-Cottrell has analysed how the bridge plans have been received in online media and public forums. Historical arguments have been used by supporters of the bridge, who in 1996 revived the late nineteenth-century dream of a fixed link to the mainland prompted by the completion of the Saaremaa–Muhu bridge in 1896. It was also claimed that a bridge would sit well with the islanders' traditional love of freedom and rebellious mind. The project was portrayed as an old dream oppressed by the Soviet occupation. Adversaries of the bridge drew arguments from nostalgic notions of the past, claiming that it might threaten traditional life, culture, and landscape on the island.[16]

Torkel Jansson, in an article about Estonian–Swedish identification in the seventeenth to nineteenth centuries, has touched upon the Hiiumaa identity. He claims that for a long time there was a common peasant identity on the island, which encompassed both Swedes and Estonians, but that it was split by the local aristocracy in the late seventeenth century.

---

[12] Sooväli 2004, 74 ff.
[13] Sooväli 2004, 101.
[14] Sooväli 2004, 82 ff.
[15] Sooväli 2004, 104–105.
[16] Raadik-Cottrell 2010, 134 ff.

The Swedes managed to retain their privileges, and started to consider themselves better than the Estonians. Eventually the landowners also managed to split the Swedish community, since in 1685 it was decided that only the Swedes in fishing villages could retain their privileges, while the richer farming Swedes lost them.[17]

Method and sources

An investigation of regional history-writing on Saaremaa and Hiiumaa poses more methodological difficulties than is the case on Gotland, Åland, and Bornholm. Estonia's dramatic twentieth-century history has dispersed its islanders over the world. The definition of regional history-writing used here—books produced by writers from the island or commissioned by institutions from the island—also includes the historical writings by 'väliseestlased', Estonian expatriates.

The fact that part of the source material has been published in Canada, Sweden, and Germany means that it is challenging to achieve complete coverage. However, several factors have been of assistance. In 1994, Mathias F. Kuester published a bibliography of the west Estonian islands in Edmonton, Canada. Kuester's work includes a valuable thematic index, and besides books it also includes newspaper articles and other short texts about the islands. Although over 1,360 pages long, Kuester's bibliography does not include all books written about the history of Saaremaa and Hiiumaa. The archival library at Saaremaa Museum has a large collection of books and articles about Saaremaa, and its collection and thematic index has been of great help. The library's database with facts about authors from the island was of help in narrowing down which books can be considered to have been written or produced regionally.

The most complete collection of source material needed for this study is the shared online catalogue of Estonian libraries, Ester, although even that is not perfect—it lacks, for example, Mathias F. Kuester's bibliography, which was only printed in a few copies. The Tallinn University of Technology library has a separate collection of Estonian expatriate literature, which has aided the identification and study of regional history-writing produced abroad.

---

[17] Jansson 2000, 441–2.

Authors and funders

Arensburg/Kuressaare had a relatively high proportion of Baltic Germans —when Estonia achieved independence in 1918, the highest among all cities in the country[18]—and the interest in Saaremaa's history first started among the German elite. The driving force was the polymath Johann Wilhelm Ludwig von Luce, who published works in such disparate fields as agriculture, economics, medicine, education, history, and archaeology. Luce grew up in the small town of Hasselfelde in the district of Harz. He studied theology at the University of Göttingen, where the students were mainly from the nobility, and Rein believes he had a complex because of his own less lofty descent. After repeated attempts he was admitted into the Saaremaa nobility in 1795. He first came to Saaremaa as a teacher in 1781, but returned to Göttingen to study medicine. In 1792 he finished his medical studies and published his dissertation *Über die Ursachen der Degeneration der organisirten Körper*. The book spans medicine and biology as well as social and cultural studies. Like his teacher J. F. Blumenbach, Luce addressed the question of evolution (Luce's book is allegedly placed next to Charles Darwin's in the library at Göttingen). Like Blumenbach, Luce attributed the fact that parents and offspring are not identical to degeneration. He compared primitive peoples to peoples of culture, and noted for example that the higher the cultural level the more sensitive women became. For example, German women suffered more in childbirth than Estonian women, although the Estonians did heavy work during pregnancy. He considered religion one of the most important causes of degeneration in society, since it influenced almost all human actions and habits.[19]

Some of Luce's works intended for a wider audience were written in Estonian. In 1817 he founded the Arensburgische Estnische Gesellschaft, which was the first ever organization devoted to the study of Estonian language and culture. It served as an indirect example for the Gelehrte Estnische Gesellschaft founded in Tartu in 1838. Ülo Parbus claims that

---

[18] Ant 2007, 264. Luha et al. 1934, 111 claim that in 1922 there were 401 Germans out of Kuressaare's total population of 3,364. In the entire county, the Germans only numbered 509 out of 57,157 inhabitants. Saaremaa also had 290 Swedes, 255 Russians, 40 Jews, and 155 inhabitants of other origin.

[19] Rein 2007, 146, 150, 160 ff.

contrary to what has been believed, some of the Arensburg society's manuscripts were preserved and influenced later research.[20]

Luce treated Saaremaa's oldest history in the book *Wahrheit und Muthmassung: Beytrag zur ältesten Geschichte der Insel Oesel* published in 1827. It was mainly concerned with the old Estonian society on Saaremaa before the advent of the Germans. When Baron Peter Wilhelm von Buxhöwden published his *Beiträge zur Geschichte der Provinz Oesel* in 1838, he claimed it to be a continuation of Luce's work.[21] However, while Luce in the spirit of the Romanticism had focused on the Estonian peasant population, Buxhöwden's main interest was the Baltic German elite. In particular he wanted to illustrate how every new ruler had confirmed the rights and privileges of the Saaremaa nobility.

From 1865 to 1923, the Saaremaa Research Society (Verein zur Kunde Oesels) investigated the island's history and nature. The association's vice-chairman Jean-Baptiste Holzmeyer, a gymnasium teacher of classical languages with a passion for archaeology, was the driving force behind the development of the association's museum. The society published six collections of articles from 1866 to 1905, mainly within the field of archaeology. The articles published by the society were reports from different excavations or investigations of local history. Their books were thus a mosaic of local history-writing, and not regional history-writing in the sense that they attempted to write about the whole of Saaremaa as a historical unit. The members of the Saaremaa Research Society were until the end mainly male Baltic Germans; women were never accepted as members, but in 1905 a handful of its 84 members had Russian or Estonian names. However, the most prominent regional historian of Saaremaa in the nineteenth century, Martin Körber, was never a member of the society.[22]

In 1885 Martin Körber, a former pastor in Anseküla on the Sõrve peninsula, published the 332-page-long *Bausteine zu einer Geschichte Oesels*, which was the first comprehensive account of the island's history. Of Martin Körber's 36 publications, 33 were written in Estonian. Many of them were compilations of folk songs, while the majority were intended to spread religious and moral learning. His translation of Luther's catechism from 1864 is one of the most widely dispersed Estonian books

---

[20] Parbus 2007, 294–5.
[21] Buxhöwden 1838, v.
[22] Püüa 1995, 91 ff., 210.

ever, printed in at least 350,000 copies in several new editions until 1939. Körber's historical writings, however, published in German.[23]

In June 1919 the Estonian ministry of education instructed the Saaremaa Research Society to hand over its museum in Kuressaare Castle and its collections to the provincial government. In October 1919 the society was still maintaining that the museum should remain in its hands, but legislation in June 1920 that confiscated the Estonian Knighthood's property—including the castle—put an end to the matter.[24]

In the inter-war period Saaremaa's geography, economy, and history were covered in the sixth volume of the grand Estonian series *Eesti*. Although the work was published by Eesti Kirjanduse Selts in Tartu, and many of the contributors were scholars from Tartu University, the initiative for the work had been taken in 1925 by Saaremaa students and local historians. Saaremaa's provincial government contributed to the publication costs of the book.[25] The chapter about Saaremaa's history was written by the historian Evald Blumfeldt, whose speciality was the Swedish period in Estonia's history.

After the Second World War, history-writing was attempted both by regional communists and by islanders living in exile. The focal point of this wave of regional history-writing was the bloody conflicts on the island during the Second World War and the uprising in 1919. Activity was low on Saaremaa until Khrushchev's campaign of de-Stalinization began in 1956, but in 1959 the regional newspaper *Kommunismi ehitaja* published a collection of articles on regional history, *Saaremaa*. According to the preface it was intended for tourists and islanders, but also for those living overseas. The authors were mainly young members of the Kuressaare literary circle ('Kingissepa kirjandusringi').[26]

The same year, Mihkli open-air museum was inaugurated and a committee of local historians was formed, headed by the director of the Saaremaa Museum, Timoteus Linna.[27] By far the most published regional historian during this period was Vassili Riis, who in his autobiographical books *Lindpriiuse paradiisi* ('Paradise of the outlaws', 1958), *Kolmandat teed ei ole* ('There is no third road', 1960), and *Rannamännid* ('The beach

---

[23] Vinkel 1994, 55, 60, 119 ff.
[24] Pesti 1995, 98.
[25] Luha et al. 1934, vi.
[26] Hint 1959, 5–6.
[27] Allik 1985, 164.

pines', 1967) gave a description of the work within the communist movement on Saaremaa from the 1920s until the end of the Second World War. Riis was a skilled and experienced writer (he had cut his teeth doing underground propaganda work), but the main reason why he came to dominate the communist history-writing to such a great extent is the simple fact that he survived; almost all other high-level members of the communist party on Saaremaa were killed during the Second World War. In the first 10 years after Estonian independence in 1991 there was great interest in investigating the crimes committed during the Second World War and in the Soviet period. As one of the few surviving perpetrators of the crimes committed on the island during the Second World War, Vassili Riis once more found himself in the spotlight. For example, Riis was vigorously attacked in the publications of Saaremaa's Defence League (Kaitseliit).[28] Riis was tried in the 1990s because of his involvement in the mass killings on Saaremaa during the Second World War, but the case was dropped because of his old age and poor health.

During the Soviet period, works on Saaremaa's history were often published in Toronto or other Canadian and Swedish cities with large Estonian communities. The association Saarlaste ühing Torontos, founded in 1956, has published several works on Saaremaa's history.[29] Similarly, a few Baltic Germans originating from Saaremaa wrote about aspects of the island's history. Most were limited to family history, but Oscar von Buxhoeveden also wrote an article about the uprising of 1919.

It should be noted that although what could be written in Estonia about political history was very restricted during the Soviet period, studies of economic or cultural history could be pursued more freely. One example is a collection of articles from 1985, *Kingissepa rajoonis* ('In the region of Kingissep'), which numbered several employees of the Saaremaa Museum among its authors. Like *Saaremaa* from 1934, it described the island's economy, society, and nature as well as its history. Although the preface and the articles about the Second World War are permeated by Soviet patriotism, the volume also comprises unpolitical articles about the history of agriculture, fishing, railroads, and even the architecture of manors.[30] Several of the authors in *Kingissepa rajoonis* continued to write regional history after Estonia's independence.

---

[28] *Kaitseliidu* 1999, 98; *Saaremaa 1940–1941* 1996b, 16–17, 40.
[29] *Saarlane*, <http://saarlane.ca/sut.htm>, 25 April 2012.
[30] Tarmisto 1985.

Kingissepa rajoonis was published by the commission for local history at the Estonian Soviet republic's academy of science (Eesti NSV Teaduste Akadeemia kodu-uurimise komisjon). From the late 1960s until the late 1980s, this commission published a series of works about the Estonian regions such as *Viljandi rajoonis* (1968) and *Valga rajoonis* (1987).[31] The commission's descriptions can be seen as a Soviet age equivalent to the inter-war project *Eesti*.

After Estonia regained its independence in 1991 there was a great interest in writing the hitherto untold history of Soviet crimes. On Saaremaa this was in part carried out by regional branches of nationwide organizations such as the Memento Association, which represents persons who were repressed during the Soviet occupation, or the Defence League (Kaitseliit), Estonia's Home Guard.[32] The Saaremaa Museum has published works on a wider range of subjects, among them a biannual yearbook. Two large volumes on the island's history, society, and nature, *Saaremaa 1* and *Saaremaa 2* were published in 2002 and 2007, but the first initiative had been taken already in 1989 by researchers and professors in academic circles in Tallinn and Tartu who lived or came from Saaremaa.[33] Like *Saaremaa* from 1934 and *Kingissepa rajoonis* from 1985, the volumes were written and published through a combination of regional and national efforts.

The volumes from 2002 and 2007, unlike *Saaremaa* from 1934, are not parts of a great work covering the whole of Estonia. However, the layout of the books are the same as in books about other Estonian provinces, as volume one belongs to the series Maakondlikud koguteosed (Provincial Anthologies) by the publisher Eesti Entsüklopeediakirjandus.[34]

On Hiiumaa there was no Baltic German regional history-writing, and only a few booklets were published in Soviet Estonia. Although some history-writing has taken place on the local (family, village, and parish) level, the first attempts at writing a regional history of Hiiumaa as a whole were made by islanders in exile during the Soviet period.[35] The introduction to *Hiiumaast ja Hiidlasest*, published in Tallinn in 1978, contains an overview of what had been written about the island across a number of

---

[31] Maaring 1968; Tarmisto 1987.
[32] *Saaremaa 1940–1941* 1995, 1996; Vessik & Varju 1997, 2002.
[33] Küün et al. 2002, 11.
[34] Küün et al. 2002 and, for example, Vunk 2008, 2010.
[35] Vrager 1971.

academic disciplines, and it is still not more than two pages long. The overview was very inclusive and portrayed Carl Russwurm (1812–1883) as the pioneer of Hiiumaa history-writing, although his writings about the island were a small part of his huge work on the Swedish population along Estonia's coast.[36] Local history-writing on Hiiumaa is thus very limited compared to the publications about its larger neighbouring island, and it did not really take off until after the turn of the millennium, with books such as Riho Saard's overview of Hiiumaa's religious history.[37] The island lacked a centre like Arensburg/Kuressaare on Saaremaa, and instead of being seen as a separate historical unit it has often been included in the history of Läänemaa. The fact that the first time Hiiumaa appears in the historical record it is to be described as deserted might also have discouraged attempts to construct a glorious past. It is not a surprise that the small group of Hiiumaa regional historians have questioned this thirteenth-century claim.

The character of Saaremaa and Hiiumaa

Central themes in the regional history writers' description of the Saare and Hiiu peoples are their national character, their centuries of serfdom, their enthusiasm as collectors of driftwood and jetsam along the islands' shores, and their geographic location, which provided many connections to the western shores of the Baltic. However, the extent to which these themes are addressed varies between the Baltic German, Soviet Age, and national Estonian history-writing. There is also recognition of the fact that there have been huge differences on the islands.

National character

Several authors offer suggestions of what constitutes the character of the Saaremaa islanders. Baron Peter Wilhelm von Buxhöwden claimed in 1838 that they had a propensity for strife and quarrels; they were fighting before the Germans came, and no one tyrannized them more than upstarts from their own estate.[38] This less than favourable description of

---

[36] Toomsalu 1978, 5–7; Russwurm 1855, 92–116.
[37] Saard 2009.
[38] Buxhöwden 1838, 267–8.

the Saaremaa islanders' character served as a legitimization of the Baltic German nobility's dominance of the island.

According to Körber, who had a more positive view of the Saaremaa's Estonian population, the islanders of the thirteenth century were superior to the Estonian and Livonian mainlanders in intelligence, boldness, entrepreneurship, and widened horizons, and they had a defiant and unyielding love of freedom.[39]

In an article from 1931 reprinted 1962 in *Saaremaa raamat*, Saaremaa islanders were said to be taller and more powerfully built than mainland Estonian's. The women were described as having beautiful facial features and being better at agricultural work than the men, who were strangers to working the land. The people on Saaremaa are also mentally gifted. The article also claimed that the island bred good if naïve people.[40]

Robert Kreem is of the opinion that islanders on Saaremaa and Hiiumaa have a lot in common: their meditative nature, their sense of beauty, and their musicality, all qualities he connects with the beautiful beaches in the south and the waves hitting the banks in the north. He believes that the often straitened circumstances of life on 'the island home' (Saare kodu) gave them the courage to face life, along with self-awareness and a sense of community; the challenges made people tenacious and hardworking.[41] His writing was directed to young members of the Saarlaste ühing Torontos, who had grown up in Canada and needed to learn the old values of their home island.

In an essay in *Saaremaa 2* about Saaremaa islanders in exile, Mall Jõgi wrote that Saaremaa, with its barren earth, stones, junipers, and wind, is a favourable location for the development of talented and able individuals. In an effort to explain the high number of Saaremaa islanders in exile Jõgi speculated that there was not space enough for their entrepreneurial spirit and energy on their home island; it demanded a larger arena, the world.[42]

There is no clear consensus about what constitutes the islanders' national character. The authors' descriptions are closely related to their different experiences and aims, and they are not part of a common discourse. It is interesting to note, however, that several of the authors believe that the inhabitants' characters are derived from the landscape and

[39] Körber 1885, 3–4, 22, 29.
[40] Polding 1962, 10.
[41] Kreem 1984, 18; Podinget al. 1962, 8.
[42] Jõgi 2007, 1062.

nature of the island. This might be connected to the status of national symbol that the island landscape achieved in the twentieth century.[43]

Serfdom

The Estonian farmers on Saaremaa were serfs until 1819. There is great disagreement about the exact nature of this serfdom. The two nineteenth-century Baltic German writers Buxhöwden and Körber had completely different views on the matter.

Slavery is the first step from barbarianism towards civilization, claimed Buxhöwden in an attempt to defend the introduction of serfdom after the German conquest. 'Whatever the philanthropists may believe it is impossible to make the flower of freedom ... flourish in the waterlogged swaps of semi-bestial wildness'. Buxhöwden cited a 'highly cultivated' French officer who said that Algerians had to be treated with an iron fist and a sword above their heads; Arabs needed to be treated as Arabs and not as Europeans. According to Buxhöwden the same was true of the islanders on Saaremaa in the thirteenth century. They were treated better than Algerians or American Indians, since they were not pushed away into the wilderness, but voluntarily offered themselves to pay tribute to get rid of the pagan cult and be able to hear the Christian word. Additionally, in 1255 they volunteered out of gratitude to serve the knights, a promise that was confirmed by the signatures of their elders. A patriarchal relationship between master and peasant developed.[44]

Körber, on the other hand, claims that the German conquerors never introduced serfdom; in fact, it was not put in place until the Great Northern War. With the exception of Sweden and Britain, which did not experience serfdom, Livonia endured it for the shortest time in the whole of Europe. In old Livonia only the mild 'Hörigkeit' existed, which made everything the peasant acquired the property of his master, but did not, as elsewhere in Europe, give the master power of life and death. According to Körber even this mild form of serfdom would not have been introduced in Livonia without, influence of Rome and the German motherland. When Roman law with its pagan roots replaced Germanic law in Germany, it opened the doors for the introduction of serfdom. Since the

---

[43] For the importance of Saaremaa's landscape, see Sooväli 2004.
[44] Buxhöwden 1838, 267–70 ('Was auch die Philantropen sagen mögen—vergebens strengen sie sich an, die Blume der Freiheit ... im versumpften Moraste halbthierischer Wildheit aufzufinden', 'hochgebildeten').

Livonian peasants enjoyed better conditions, the German peasant uprisings of the sixteenth century did not spread into the area.[45]

A guidebook to Saaremaa's museums from the Soviet era says that the peasant's lives worsened during the Danish and Swedish periods. A photo of a pranger, according to the accompanying text, illustrates the Church's role in the enslavement of the people. The same picture had been used in the book *Saaremaa* from 1959.[46]

Buxhöwden was personally involved in the process leading up to the abandonment of serfdom on Saaremaa. Because Saaremaa had enjoyed its own constitution since the suppression of the natives it was not affected by the Livonian peasant regulations of 1804 which abolished serfdom on the mainland, Buxhöwden explained. The peasants on Saaremaa were according to Buxhöwden in reality already free, even if it was not actually spelled out, because of the moral cultivation and intelligence of the nobility. They realized that the richer the peasant, the richer the master. When Tsar Alexander I wanted to discuss the abolition of serfdom on Saaremaa, the Estonian Knighthood loyally showed up, despite the flaws in the regulations of 1804. In newspaper articles Buxhöwden had himself enthusiastically supported the granting of personal freedom to the Estonians, on condition that the laws regarding property rights had to remain untouched. He joined a deputation of the Saaremaa nobility to St Petersburg, where Alexander I declared that they were acting in the liberal spirit of the century and only had the people's welfare in mind. The 6 January 1819 there was a celebration in Arensburg honouring the freedom of the people and the sacrifice of the nobility for humanity and civilization, according to Buxhöwden.[47]

National Estonian writers from the inter-war and post-Soviet periods have significantly less to say about serfdom than the Baltic Germans, and they do not think that the abolition of serfdom improved the peasants' lot substantially. Kersti Lust writes in *Saaremaa 2* that although the farmers gained personal freedom in 1819, the land remained in the hands of the nobility. The relationship between farmers and landlords became open for free negotiations, which caused a lot of conflicts.[48]

---

[45] Körber 1885, 181–9.
[46] Allik & Hiiuväin 1969, 30–1.
[47] Buxhöwden 1838, 271, 276, 287, 291.
[48] Blumfeldt 1934, 336; Lust 2007, 217–18.

The abolition of serfdom is even more invisible in Hiiumaa history-writing. The regional historian Endel Saar writes that the era of the manors—he estimates that there were 41 of them—lasted 700 years on Hiiumaa. He adds that it has also been named the era of slavery because of the burdens of serfdom.[49] By using this periodization he indicates that he sees no difference between the last 100 years of German dominance, when the peasants were free, and the preceding 600. In fact, Saar claims that serfdom did not end on the Vilivalla estate before the land reform in of 1920–1.[50]

The relatively weak interest among national Estonian historians in serfdom thus probably stems from the fact that they considered the important break to have come a hundred years after its abolition, when Estonia's independence brought a definitive end to the Baltic German nobility's power over the Estonian peasants.

Pirates, wreckers, beachcombers

It is a common conception that the inhabitants of Saaremaa were descended from pirates. Many writers believe that the islanders' pirate heritage reveals itself in their interest in goods originating from shipwrecks. On western Saaremaa the dialect word *haakrik* describes valuable objects found on the beach.[51]

According to Körber, the pirate spirit was still noticeable in his day from the outbreak of excitement every time a ship was stranded. It also explained the psychological phenomenon that insignificant objects originating from shipwrecks attracted greater attention than something far more valuable found on land. The pirate spirit was also behind the idea that everything taken from the sea belonged to the finder.[52]

In 1939, Woldemar Miller wrote an article in the newspaper *Meie Maa* about the last Saaremaa Viking raid, which according to him had taken place in 1838. That winter many ships were wrecked along the Swedish coast. *Harmonie* off Fårö was carrying a particularly valuable cargo of iron ore. In the spring, ice was still preventing Swedish boats from reaching the wreck, but the waters between Saaremaa and Gotland were open. The Swedes could only watch while the Saaremaa islanders filled boat after boat with ore; around 100 people took part in the looting. In the end the

[49] Saar 2004, 45
[50] Saar 2004, 38.
[51] Jakovlev 2003, 169.
[52] Körber 1885, 64.

Swedes fooled the Saaremaa 'Vikings' into a trap by offering them food and wine, only to take them straight to court in Visby after the party. The cause of this new surge of Viking spirit was according to Miller the abolition of serfdom.[53]

In an article about *haakrik* in *Saaremaa museum. Kaheaastaraamat* in 2001–2002, the head of the Mihkli open-air museum Tormis Jakovlev also made a connection between the islanders' interest in jetsam and their pirate ancestry—by citing *Moominpappa at sea*.[54]

> Driftwood! Lots of it! Come and help me salvage it!' ... They threw themselves into the sea, unconscious of the cold water. Perhaps they had some pirate blood in their veins that made them plunge in like that, the spirit of some ancestor out for ill-gotten gains seemed to possess them.[55]

According to Jakovlev, maritime tradition left the finder in possession of all flotsam and jetsam, even stranded ships. There were however many instances of beach piracy where the crews were sometimes killed. Charles XII tightened the legislation and allowed only the keeping of jetsam, the objects that the crew had thrown overboard in order to reduce the draft.[56]

The golden age of jetsam was the era of sailing ships, Jakovlev claims. In bad weather there were always shipwrecks and ships run aground; you can still find valuable pieces of oak and other items from the age 'when the ships were of wood and the men of iron'. North-western Saaremaa is the closest thing Estonia has to a wreckers' coast. In the Russian period some of the local barons were paid to take care of stranded ships. The most famous of them was Theodor von Buxhoeveden (1832–1892). According to Bruno Pao this activity was very profitable for the barons and their peasants. Sometimes it was a form of disguised beach piracy. The landlords kept seaworthy ships under the command of experienced skippers ready to dash out in order to salvage valuable cargo. Ships were custom-built for this purpose, such as the 15.7-metre-long *Adler* (1859). In the 1880s, when rescue activities were taken over by the Baltic Rescue Society, Saaremaa's first divers were recruited among the crew of these small ships.[57]

---

[53] Miller 1939.
[54] Jakovlev 2003, 175.
[55] Jansson 1966, 176.
[56] Jakovlev 2003, 170.
[57] Jakovlev 2003, 171, 174; Pao 2007, 534–5.

Jakovlev also gives several examples of messages in bottles found on the shores of Saaremaa. One 8-year-old girl found a bottle with a message from a Ukrainian submariner who was trying to sell information about the location of Soviet nuclear arms to the West. The girl was awarded a medal.[58]

Soviet border patrols kept the beach under strict supervision. According to Jakovlev they became very irritated when people were found roaming the shores early in the morning in order to find jetsam. It was said that they tried to remove or destroy any stranded objects in order to keep people away. Plastic canisters punctuated by bayonets bear witness to this practice. When fishing gear and other plastic objects were washed ashore in the 1960s and 1970s they were considered very new, exciting, and modern. Boys decorated their bikes with colourful Finnish milk packaging, and plastic bags with pictures were something special. The most famous shipwreck during the Soviet era was the Greek carrier *Volare* that in 1980 hit the shores of Saaremaa. It was filled with consumer goods beyond the imaginings of the *Homo sovieticus*.[59]

What Jakovlev calls 'the *haakrik* of the century' occurred in 2000 when tens of kilometres of Saaremaa's western shoreline was covered in driftwood from shipwrecks. In no time at all around 100 people and a dredger were in place to care of the booty. Old ladies were sawing planks to get a better grip; you had to be fast in order to get a share. Jakovlev estimates that thousands of cubic metres were salvaged.[60]

Jakovlev noted that the ruling powers have often discouraged the salvage of jetsam. Now activities on the beaches are again legal, but for how long? Perhaps the government will attempt to acquire the jetsam through legislation.[61]

The salvage of jetsam is not elaborated on in the relatively few works of Hiiumaa regional history-writing which have been published so far. However, in 2009 a second edition of the novel *Hiiu lossist—Siberisse* ('From Hiiumaa Castle—to Siberia') was published with an afterword by Helgi Põllo, vice-director of the Hiiumaa Museum. The novel, with the subtitle 'A historical novel of a legendary Hiiu pirate', was first published in 1937. It is based on the life of Baron Otto Reinhold Ludwig von

---

[58] Jakovlev 2003, 179.
[59] Jakovlev 2003, 183.
[60] Jakovlev 2003, 176–7.
[61] Jakovlev 2003, 178.

Ungern-Sternberg (1744–1811), who was convicted for murder and sent to Siberia in 1804. The charges of piracy were dropped, but that is what he is still remembered for. According to Hiiu County's homepage, 'it was quite common among farmers and landlords at that time to gain "wealth" by hostile takeover'.[62]

Saaremaa and Hiiumaa history-writing about jetsam and beach piracy is reminiscent of what can be found on the other islands in this study; it includes a notion of a 'pirate spirit' and is particular to certain areas of the island region. What stands out as special is Jakovlev's description of how the beaches functioned as a window and a link to the west in the Soviet age, when the authorities tried to limit other contacts with the outside world.

Location, connections, identity

Many writers imply that the Estonian islands, due to their geographic location, have received more Western influences than was the case on the mainland. The anthropologist Leiu Heapost claims in an essay about anthropology in *Saaremaa 1* that the population of western Estonia and the islands have similar blood groups in the AB0 system as the population of eastern Gotland. In the MN system they are similar to the coastal population of the Swedish province Uppland, and even more so to the population on Åland. The author believes that this is a trace of the Bronze and Iron Age Asva culture, which spanned these areas.[63]

Although nothing is mentioned in regional history-writing about direct contacts between Åland and Saaremaa in recent times, Olavi Pesti mentions that the strategic importance of Kuressaare Fortress was diminished when Åland became part of the Russian Empire, and its cannons were moved to Bomarsund fortress, the new western outpost of the empire.[64] The islands' histories were linked through their strategic geographic locations.

The most ambitious attempt to describe how Saaremaa's geographical situation and connections have affected the island's identity can be found in the art historian Juhan Maiste's essay about the architecture of manors in *Saaremaa 2*. According to Maiste, the fact that Saaremaa's manors are more simple, puritan, and utilitarian than the mainland's is not only a

---

[62] Aitsam 2009 (1937), Hiiu county, <http://www.hiiumaa.ee/tuletorn/english.php?id=3>, accessed 23 May 2013.
[63] Heapost 2002, 590, 593.
[64] Pesti 2003, 77.

consequence of limited resources, but also of ideals that celebrated utility and disliked wastefulness. He believes they conform to a classicist ideal which emanated from Prussia in the late eighteenth century. Saaremaa has been secluded and conservative, but at the same time open for cultural traditions that have arrived by ship. The sea and naval routes have shaped Saaremaa's characteristics. According to Maiste the island is no province of the mainland; although the buildings are smaller it has more international influences from southern Scandinavia and northern Germany. Travel by sea have also brought the early models for the Muhu-style from Britain.[65]

Maiste claims that without the Great Northern War (during which Sweden lost its Baltic provinces to Russia), life and architecture on Saaremaa would have resembled that of Scandinavia even more. Russia brought with it a decline, and perhaps in the long term fatal changes of identity. For two long centuries, reactionary conditions prevailed. The Baltic countries ended up between two worlds and two identities. He concludes that Saaremaa has traits of both the metropolis and periphery simultaneously, and is at the same time open and closed.[66]

While Maiste in *Saaremaa 2* from 2007 emphasizes the peculiarities of Saaremaa's architecture, Lilian Hansar's essay about twentieth-century architecture in the same book is basically an overview of Estonian architecture with examples picked from Saaremaa. In *Kingissepa rajoonis* from 1985 Maiste did discuss the architectural differences between Saaremaa's and the mainland's manors, but he did not mention any Western influences on the island. He explained Saaremaa's peculiarities as the result of local and traditional materials and styles, such as the use of thatched roofs.[67] Maiste's case illustrates how one researcher after the fall of the Iron curtain changed his perception of contacts and cultural lending across the Baltic Sea. It is of course difficult to evaluate how much of the change was a result of self-censorship during the Soviet age.

According to Bruno Pao, despite the fact that Saaremaa and Hiiumaa are so close to each other geographically, the contacts between the islands remained weak for a long time. They belonged to different governments during the Russian period, and Saaremaa's contacts were directed south

---

[65] Maiste 2007, 826 ff.
[66] Maiste 2007, 832, 845.
[67] Hansar 2007, 867 ff.; Maiste 1985, 120.

while Hiiumaa was oriented eastwards.⁶⁸ This administrative division probably counteracted the formation of any common 'island identity' connecting the Estonian islands.

Differences on Saaremaa and Hiiumaa

Both Saaremaa and Hiiumaa have vivid local history-writing, describing the history of parishes, towns, or secondary islands. In the case of Hiiumaa this is more prominent than the regional history-writing, which only comprises a handful of works so far. As in the case of Åland, in Saare County secondary islands have the most developed local history-writing. A 663-page-long work about Muhumaa, a parallel to the two volumes about Saaremaa, was published in 2001.⁶⁹

The formerly Swedophone island of Ruhnu has seen a rich local history-writing since the second half of the twentieth century. However, this production in its entirety has taken place in exile in Sweden, since the whole remaining population of the island fled to Sweden in 1943–1944. The most prolific of the writers has been Jakob Steffensson, who has written about traditional life on Ruhnu and the islanders' escape to Sweden. A central theme in the publications about Ruhnu is that it was an ancient Nordic society, where Viking Age traits survived into the twentieth century. This view of Ruhnu—and of the Estonian-Swedes in general—as a representative of an older Swedishness was a reason for the interest Swedish scholars showed the island in the inter-war years.⁷⁰ As refugees in Sweden after the war, the Estonian-Swedes could use the earlier scholarly works about their history and culture in order to construct a common identity.

In his book *Hiiumaa—kiviajast tänapäevani* ('Hiiumaa—from the Stone Age until today') Endel Saar dedicates 24 pages, more than one-tenth of the total length, to Hiiumaa's fellowships (*seltsid*). Most of them describe people who came from the same geographic area; often they also wore distinctive clothes, used nicknames, and partied together, such as the 'vestihiidlased', who wore characteristic waistcoats. Other fellowships, such as the 'Suvehiidlased' (Summer Hiiu-islanders), were not defined by their place of origin. This term was used to describe islanders who were

---

⁶⁸ Pao 2003, 198
⁶⁹ Rullingo 2001.
⁷⁰ For example, Steffensson 1972, 1976; Klein 1924.

studying on the mainland; because of the rigid Soviet bureaucracy they could only visit the island in the summer.[71]

On Saaremaa, regional history writers mention the differences between the eastern and western parts of the island. The east, including Pöide and Muhu, is described as more problem-ridden: feudal oppression was harder, the area was underdeveloped, its population converted to the Orthodox religion to a larger extent than in the west, the uprising in 1919 had its roots there, and in the inter-war period it became a hotbed of communism.[72]

Saaremaa raamat, which was published in Toronto in 1962, contains a reprint of a text from 1931, which claims that noses and facial features differed so much between the island's parishes that it was possible to tell where people came from just by looking at them. The islanders were a mix of Nordic and East Baltic races, with elements of all other European races. The Scandinavian influence, according to the article, was most prominent in Sõrve, where it was manifested in above-average height.[73]

Just how small a community peasant society identified with prior to the First World War is illustrated by the memoirs of the ethnologist Gustav Ränk (1902–1998) who was born in Karja parish on Saaremaa. He claims that his childhood 'we' was limited to the people living in the immediate vicinity, the landscape which could be overlooked. To Gustav's question about which country they belonged to, his father answered that 'it is said' they were Russian subjects, indicating that is was of secondary importance. 'Estonia' was a concept that only could be found in books and newspapers, and mainland Estonia was called 'Ülemaa' (lit. 'Overland', or Over-the-sea-land).They did not call themselves Saare either; others called them that, just like they called others Hiiu or Muhu. As a boy Ränk never saw the sea (which was 10 km to the north), and he was never told that they were living on an island. Different dialects were spoken in each parish, and there was a great deal of prejudice against people from other parts of the island. For example, the people on the west coast were beach pirates for whom nothing was sacred. Most exotic were the inhabitants of the distant Sõrve peninsula, who were said to do things

---

[71] Saar 2004, 48–71.
[72] Püüa 2006, 83; Buxhoevden 1969, 90–1; Riis 1960, 64–5; Püüa 2006, 83.
[73] Polding 1962, 10.

like tie newly weds into a sack on their wedding night. The lack of contact meant that no one could confirm or disprove these rumours.[74]

The Baltic Germans lived geographically closer, but still in another world. Although Ränk's family lived next to a manor inhabited by a German family, he only saw them three times before his sixteenth birthday. Knowledge about the Germans was mythical: they were believed to spend their days conspiring to oppress the villagers, hunting, and partying, and it was a mystery how they could keep clean without going to the sauna. According to Ränk, the peasants did not know that Saaremaa's Germans were considered provincial by their peers on the mainland, in part because their German dialect was influenced by Estonian.[75]

These examples indicate that, among the peasant populations of Saaremaa and Hiiumaa, local identities long dominated over the regional (Saare or Hiiu) identity, which did not feature much until well into the twentieth century.

Ancient and medieval history

The history of Saaremaa from the island's settlement until it was acquired by Denmark in 1572 contains both what has been described as a pre-Christian Estonian Age of Greatness and a subsequent period of Baltic German rule. In the thirteenth century, both Hiiumaa and Saaremaa were divided between the Livonian Brothers of the Sword and the Bishopric of Ösel–Wiek, which had one of its two centres at Arensburg Castle on Saaremaa. While the Middle Ages is an important theme in Saaremaa history-writing, it is almost completely absent in history-writing from Hiiumaa.

The first inhabitants of Saaremaa and Hiiumaa

Johann Wilhelm Ludwig von Luce claimed in 1827 that Saaremaa might first have been populated by fishermen who came by boat from Prussia, which in the first centuries AD was populated by a people called the Aesti. A second possibility was that they had come from Courland (Curonia), as Luce believed that the old name of Saaremaa was Kura Saar. He did not believe that the name was derived from Kurre Saar, 'island of the cranes',

---

[74] Ränk 1979, 25 ff. ('pidavat'), 69, 122–3.
[75] Ränk 1979, 129–30.

as cranes are rare on the island. However, Luce admitted the possibility that the climate had changed or that the cranes had altered their behaviour. Immigrants had also come from Sweden; according to Luce the name Ösel was of Swedish origin and the Schworbe (Sõrve) peninsula had took its name from Sweden. Martin Körber, who served as a pastor in Sõrve in 1845–72, also stressed the Swedish origin of the peninsula's population. (Later research has indicated that only a few farms in Sõrve were populated by Swedes.)[76]

Körber quoted Luce's suggestion that Saaremaa was populated from Courland, but he believed that the island had an earlier Germanic population. That explained the islanders' Germanic skull shape and facial features, which separated them from mainland Estonians. Intermingling with slaves had according to Körber led to the loss of the islanders' distinctive physiognomy; they did not reproduce in isolation like Jews and Kalmyks. Luce claimed that the islanders' handsomer features illustrated the virtues of mixing.[77]

According to the archaeologist Aivar Kriiska's article about Saaremaa's Stone Age in *Saaremaa 2*, it is highly likely that the island was discovered during a long hunting trip at sea. The first traces of seasonal human settlement date from the Late Mesolithic (6500–4900 BC). The origin of the first settlers are not discussed outright, but the fact that Kriiska otherwise covers settlements in mainland Estonia gives the impression of a link between Saaremaa and the mainland.[78] The essay is not limited to Saaremaa, but also treats the Stone Age of Estonia's coastal areas and other islands, which was the theme of Kriiska's doctoral dissertation in 2001.[79]

Luce claimed that the first communities on Saaremaa 'naturally' were patriarchal. The family elders were called '*wannem*', a title later used by local rulers. The women worked the land while the men fished, an order which had been preserved until Luce's time on the island of Ruhnu.[80] Islands are often said to have preserved archaic traits lost on the mainland. Luce's description of Ruhnu illustrates that secondary islands can be described as even more archaic, examples of how life on the main island might have been in the past.

---

[76] Luce 1827, 1, 3 ff., 7, 9; Vinkel 1994, 45.
[77] Körber 1885, 1; Luce 1827, 30–1.
[78] Kriiska 2007, 10 ff.
[79] Kriiska 2001.
[80] Luce 1827, 27–8, 32.

Regarding the settlement of Hiiumaa, the regional historian Endel Saar refers to archaeological findings that indicate seasonal settlement as early as 5600 BC. Artefacts indicate that the settlers came from mainland Estonia. According to Saar, Hiiumaa was first mentioned in *Gutalagen*, where it is said that Tjelvar's sons moved to Dagaithi (Dagö, Hiiumaa) outside Aistlandi and built a fortress there before they moved on.[81]

Saar also remarks on the mention of Hiiumaa in a written document from 1228, when it was said to be a deserted island. Saar refers to Urmas Selirand (employed at the Hiiumaa Museum), who rejected the idea that Hiiumaa was deserted; why then was the wooden church in Pühalepa replaced by a stone-built one only 31 years later? Saar's interpretation of the chronicle is that since Hiiumaa was relatively empty it was left outside the events of the German conquest of Saaremaa.[82] There is a close parallel between how Ålandic and Hiiu history writers use the huge stone-built parish churches in order to disprove theories of depopulation.

In his book about Hiiumaa's religious history, Riho Saard claims that it is unlikely that it was uninhabited in the thirteenth century, when neighbouring Saaremaa had 27,000 inhabitants. The Soviet Age *Hiiumaa ja Hiidlased* also questioned whether the island really was completely empty, but believed that it probably saw an influx of refugees from Saaremaa as people escaped from the bloody quelling of the uprisings.[83]

Saar strongly believes that Hiiumaa was settled from Saaremaa. Based on dialectal traits he debates where on Hiiumaa migrants from different Saaremaa parishes had settled down. Elmar Vrager, a refugee who worked as a teacher in Sweden, wrote that Hiiumaa was settled in the thirteenth century by Saaremaa islanders and Swedes, probably from Gotland or Åland. According to Vrager, Swedish place names in the Estonian parts of Hiiumaa indicate that there was an older Swedish settlement. He considered it probable that there was a rift between the populations since the Swedes had christened the Estonians and considered them heathens.[84] This is the only place in regional history-writing from the Estonian islands that suggests any kind of conflict between Swedish and Estonian peasants. All authors agree that the inhabitants of Saaremaa and Hiiumaa are of mixed origin. Swedish and Estonian influences are acknowledged by

[81] Saar 2004, 10, 15.
[82] Saar 2004, 20–1.
[83] Saard 2009, 16–17; Tiik 1978, 31.
[84] Saar 2004, 22; Vrager 1971, 26.

everyone, and the German nineteenth-century writers also believed in an early German or Prussian influence. The German authors were of the opinion that the racial mixture had been beneficial for the islanders' physical appearance, and Luce saw this as an example of the virtues of racial mixing in general. Hiiumaa is geographically—and until recently administratively—the closest to its mainland of all the islands in this study, and was late in breaking away from Läänemaa and develop a regional history-writing and in that sense an island identity. Considering that, it is interesting to note that its inhabitants are claimed to have the most insular origins: according to Saar, Hiiumaa was populated entirely from other islands.

Saaremaa's pagan age of greatness

In regional German-language nineteenth-century history-writing, the Osilians of the pre-Christian era were portrayed as superior to the mainland Estonians, Latvians, and Livonians. Körber describes them as on level with the Swedes and Danes as warriors, but inferior to the Germans. Luce writes that the Osilians had learned military technology from foreign lands. This mirrors Blumfeldt's claim in 1934 that they managed to build replicas of catapults they had acquired from abroad.[85]

Later Estonian history-writing has also stressed the important role of Saaremaa in the Estonians' struggle against foreign invaders, but without claiming superiority over the mainlanders. In *Saaremaa 2* professor Enn Tarvel writes that the Osilians learned to build catapults at Varbola Fortress in mainland Estonia.[86] This contradicts Luce's and Körber's claims that the Osilians were more advanced than the mainlanders.

Evald Blumfeldt wrote in *Saaremaa* (1934) that Saaremaa was the power that might have united ancient Estonia. The process had probably already begun, but was interrupted by the crusades. The title of the chapter 'Saaremaa's ancient struggle for *independence* and *freedom*'[87]—terms that were also used in Estonia's twentieth-century history—also indicates that Blumfeldt saw ancient Saaremaa as a direct predecessor to the new Estonian republic that achieved independence in 1918.

---

[85] Körber 1885, 3–4, 22, 29; Luce 1827, 133; Luha et al. 1934, 267.
[86] Tarvel 2007, 81.
[87] Luha et al. 1934, 263, ('Saaremaa muistse *iseseisvuse* ja *vabadusvõitluse* ajal', my emphasis), 268.

The German historians described piracy and raiding as central activities in ancient Osilian society and later Estonian historians have maintained that view. In regional Saaremaa history-writing, the sack of Sigtuna in Sweden in 1188 is attributed to the Osilians, although many others have claimed the honour. A frequently cited source is the Chronicle of Henry of Livonia, which among other things describes how raiding Osilians sailed home with enslaved Swedish women. In *Saaremaa 2*, Marika Mägi gives a less brutal picture of the islanders. Based on burial patterns, she believes that women held a higher position in this society than in Scandinavia. In other respects she believes that Saaremaa was similar to Scandinavia, and especially Gotland; *Gutalagen* might also give insights into life on Saaremaa. According to Mägi, Gotlandic society was probably not as democratic as previously believed, and Saaremaa was also an aristocratic society with slaves.[88] And, true, on Åland the rich Gotlandic source material has been used to fill the gaps in the islands' historical records.

Another similarity with Åland is the lack of rune stones. Pao wrote in *Saaremaa 2* that if there ever were any, they were destroyed by the Christian conquerors. However, runes were used in calendars up until the eighteenth century. Pao considered the lack of sources about Saaremaa's participation in the Scandinavian Viking raids unfortunate, but he added that during the following period the Saaremaa islanders numbered among the eastern Vikings, which is richly confirmed in the sources.[89]

In the national Estonian *Saaremaa* from 1934 it was claimed that Gotland had good relations to Saaremaa. The Germans tried to persuade the Gotlanders to take part in the crusades, but they preferred to live in peace with Saaremaa, which probably better protected the Gotlandic traders from pirates from Saaremaa.[90] The Gotlandic self-identification as peaceful tradesmen is thus confirmed in Saaremaa history-writing.

The Soviet Age *Saaremaa* from 1959 labelled the tenth to twelfth centuries 'Early feudalism', but the content is almost the same as in other forms of regional history-writing. It mentioned Saaremaa's maritime

---

[88] Luce 1827, 30–1; Körber 1885, 5–6; Allik 1959, 31; Polding 1962, 10; Kreem 1984, 19; Mägi 2007b, 74–5.
[89] Pao 2007, 526 ff.
[90] Luha et al. 1934, 266.

strength and contacts with Gotland, but also its contacts with Russian areas.[91]

The islanders' piracy is usually compared to that of the Scandinavian Vikings, and among amateur regional historians the ancient Saare people are even described as Vikings. For example, when Robert Kreem in his autobiography remembered a boat trip to Tallinn with the Saaremaa Defence League youth organization in 1938, he added that it was not appropriate for descendants of the Vikings to take the land route. Buxhöwden drew a parallel with North African pirates, when in 1838 he used the recent French invasion of Algeria to legitimize the German crusaders' conquest of Saaremaa in the early thirteenth century.[92] Since his main aim was to safeguard the privileges of the German nobility, the island's pagan history was of little interest, and his book begins with the conquest and Christianization in 1227.

Both Baltic German and Estonian writers generally describe the pre-1227 Osilians as pagan, brutal, and heroic. The exceptions are Buxhöwden, who simply considered them brutal pagans, and Mägi, who questions whether they really were that brutal and emphasizes that graves indicate relative gender equality. The difference between the nineteenth-century Germans and the later Estonians is that the former stresses the differences between Saaremaa and the mainland, placing the islanders on a higher cultural level, while the latter instead emphasize the islanders' strong links to mainland Estonia.

The most grandiose ideas about Saaremaa's past are expressed by Edgar Saks in *Saaremaa raamat*. By analysing place names he claimed that Courland had belonged to Saaremaa.[93] Saks, who was a politician in exile, suggested on similar grounds in his works *Aesti* (1960) and *Esto-Europa* (1966) that most of Europe was once populated by Estonians. Saks is an outlier, however, and his ideas were not taken up by other writers of Saaremaa's history.

Invasions and uprisings

Regional history-writing on Saaremaa ever since Luce's day has referred to the chronicle of Henry of Livonia, which claimed that 20,000 German knights were needed to subdue the Saaremaa army of 9,000 infantry and

---

[91] Allik 1959, 31.
[92] Polding 1962, 192; Kreem 1984, 85; Buxhöwden 1838, 268.
[93] Polding 1962, 51 ff.

4,000 cavalry. In *Saaremaa 2* Tarvel questioned these numbers, although he believed that the crusader army was unusually large due to the island's reputation for having a strong defence. Behind Tarvel's calculations is the assumption that Saaremaa had 18,000 inhabitants, which would make it impossible to field an army of 13,000 men; he believes it was a maximum of 3,000. Since he calculated Muhu's population to be one-tenth of Saaremaa's—1,800—he put little faith in the chronicle's claim that 2,500 Estonians were slaughtered on Muhu alone.[94]

Tarvel is of the opinion that the Battle of Leal in 1220 was the most splendid victory of the entire Estonian struggle for freedom. There the Saaremaa islanders killed 500 Swedes including a duke and a bishop. According to Tarvel, the battle has been overshadowed by clashes where a few dozen Germans were killed because of the positive bias towards Sweden in Estonian history-writing.[95]

While Körber in 1885 described the German conqueror, bishop Albert, as the founder of the Livonian state and as a statesman of historic proportions, who realized what means were necessary to Christianize the 'barbarians of the East', a Soviet museum guide calls the conquerors 'robber knights'. The Soviet *Saaremaa* from 1959 described how German, Danish, and Swedish 'usurpers' attacked Estonia, which got help from the Russians. In 1984 Robert Kreem, exiled in Canada, wrote that the islanders had been engaged in a proud freedom fight against the Germans, and in the great post-soviet work on Saaremaa's history, *Saaremaa 2*, Tarvel describes these struggles as part of a 'pan-Estonian freedom fight'.[96]

Luce, who believed religion was the main cause of degeneration in society, was less enthusiastic than the religious Körber about Christianization; in fact, he did not even use the word when writing that the islanders' beliefs were replaced by the 'papist' religion. He also hints that bishop Albert was motivated by financial gain. According to Luce, the invasion meant that the islanders lost their freedom, and that the first *Hauptperiode* in the history of Saaremaa ended there. Later writers such as Tarvel believe that the islanders enjoyed relative freedom until the Great Uprising in 1343–5.[97]

---

[94] Körber 1885, 5; Luha et al. 1934, 276, Tarvel 2007, 82 ff.
[95] Tarvel 2007, 79–80.
[96] Körber 1885, 9 ('den östlichen Barbaren'); Allik 1959, 32–3 ('anastajate'); Allik & Hiiuväin 1969, 30 ('röövrüütlid'), Tarvel 2007, 79–80 ('üle-eestilisest vabadus-võitlusest').
[97] Luce 1827, 146–7; Polding 1962, 193, Tarvel 2007, 100.

This uprising, which was bloodily put down, was not the first time the islanders rebelled against their new masters. Körber saw the uprisings as specific to Saaremaa because of the character of its inhabitants: the islanders, in contrast to the mainlanders, had never been in a tributary relationship. Furthermore he claimed that island dwellers in general, just like mountain-dwellers such as the Swiss, the Montenegrins, and the Circassians, were animated by a bold spirit of independence. In sharp contrast to this 'insular' view, the professional Estonian historians Tarvel and Blumfeldt connected the Great Uprising on Saaremaa to an uprising in Harju province on the mainland. The Soviet Age publication *Saaremaa* described the uprising as part of the St George Night Uprising, which was in turn part of the 'Estonian peasantry's ceaseless struggle against the ... German feudal yoke'. The medieval uprisings were treated in just over two pages, while the Danish and Swedish periods in total were given one page.[98]

Peter Wilhelm von Buxhöwden's account of the Middle Ages is focused on the relationship between the German Order and the Bishop of Ösel–Wiek; the peasant uprisings are mentioned only when they caused conflict between the German rulers.[99]

The German nineteenth-century writers had divergent opinions on the conquest and the uprisings; Luce saw it as a process of downfall and loss of freedom, Körber as a rise from paganism to Christianity, and Buxhöwden as the civilization of barbarians through slavery. In the Soviet era it was interpreted as the extortion of peasants by robber barons. In Estonian history-writing, it is seen as part of the national fight for Estonian freedom.

The bishopric of Ösel–Wiek

Enn Tarvel did not include political events in the bishopric of Ösel–Wiek in his history of Saaremaa, as only half of the bishopric was situated on the island; he explained that otherwise he might as well write a history of the whole of Livonia. In contrast, Körber dealt at great length with the bishopric in his history of Saaremaa, and he did indeed end up writing what resembles a history of Livonia, which arguably was the geographical unit that he primarily identified with. He sympathized with the 'patriotic'

---

[98] Körber 1885, 54; Tarvel 2007, 96 ff.; Luha et al. 1934, 280; Allik 1959, 35 ff. ('Eesti talurahva lakkamatu võitlus ... saksa feodaalide ikke vastu'), 40.
[99] Buxhöwden 1838, 4–5.

aim of Jürgen Ungern to unite Livonia in the 1500s, but he considered him not quite up to the task.[100]

Tarvel is of the opinion that the bishopric consisted of two quite autonomous parts. Körber wrote that Ösel–Wiek on four occasions was divided when rival bishops were elected on the island. He labelled this a 'regrettable spectacle', which he believed was encouraged by the fact that the bishopric was divided by an arm of the sea.[101] Thus Körber seems to have considered Saaremaa's insularity as an important factor behind the schisms.

While Körber stressed the differences between the pre-Christian islanders and the mainlanders, he clearly identified with Baltic German Livonia and the attempts to unite the realm politically. Tarvel, on the contrary, who emphasized the links between Saaremaa and the mainland in the early Middle Ages, choose to focus solely upon the island during the subsequent period in history. The writers chose to include the mainland in their history-writing for those periods when they identified with the political entities there. A parallel can be seen in *Tidernas Åland*, where the Swedish kings are included in the narrative, but not subsequent Russian tsars and Finnish presidents.

Körber spent 18 pages attacking the last bishop of Ösel–Wiek, Johann von Münchhausen, who according to Körber pretended to be a fervent Catholic during his time as bishop, suppressing the Protestant services in the churches. Furthermore, Münchhausen pretended to protect the peasants, while he was actually interested in safeguarding the supply of grain for export. Münchhausen engaged in usury and trade, sometimes making 500% profits on commodity transactions, which in Körber's view was unsuitable for a nobleman and a bishop. He also confiscated stranded ships, wrecking being a barbaric custom that bishop Albert had tried to abandon 300 years earlier. Münchhausen appointed foreign officials, and when the local nobility protested he told them to consider their own heritage: where did the conquerors themselves come from? The bishop enjoyed parties and women; he brought his own sister with him for 'entertainment and good company'. Then, in an act of high treason, Münchhausen sold Saaremaa to Denmark, behind the back of the Estates, and promptly abandoned the sinking ship like a rat, according to Körber.

---

[100] Tarvel 2007, 100; Körber 1885, 136.
[101] Tarvel 2007, 113; Körber 1885, 146 ('beklagenswerthe Schauspiel').

Although not nearly as animated as Körber, Tarvel wrote that Münchhausen's sale of the island to Denmark was 'quite an ugly game'.[102] However, in Tarvel's account there is no trace of the aristocratic dislike for trade and profit per se that Körber had displayed 120 years earlier.

Blumfeldt acknowledged in 1934 that Münchhausen had an exceptionally wide trade network, but he writes that other bishops had also tried to monopolize trade on the island.[103] Münchhausen's conduct thus seems less unique in Blumfeldt's account than it does in Körber's.

Münchhausen challenged the local German nobility by interfering in how they treated the peasants, by exposing them to foreign competition, and by implying that they were themselves foreign conquerors. This, in combination with the question of religion was probably the root of Körber's harsh judgement of him.

The Danish, Swedish, and Russian periods

Saaremaa was ruled by Denmark from 1572 to 1645, after which it came under Swedish rule. Hiiumaa had come under Swedish rule in 1563 and did not experience any Danish period. Sweden lost both islands to Russia in 1710 during the Great Northern War, a loss confirmed in the Peace of Nystad in 1721. The Russian period in Saaremaa's and Hiiumaa's history ended when the islands were occupied by Germany in 1917.

The Danish period on Saaremaa, 1572–1645

The nineteenth-century Baltic German pastor Martin Körber clearly identified with old German Livonia and lamented its division, but he noted that its fate was sealed not by inner strife but by geographical realities; it was a small state that found itself caught between three large kingdoms. Sooner or later the battle for Livonia had to begin. According to Körber, Livonia was such a rich and well-ordered province that anyone who gained control of it was destined to become a great power.[104]

The first Danish ruler of Saaremaa, duke Magnus, wanted to unite Livonia, a project to Körber's taste. Unfortunately Magnus was frivolous,

---

[102] Körber 1885, 160–177 ('Unterhaltung und gute Gesellschaft'); Tarvel 2007, 106–107 ('päris näotu mänguga').
[103] Luha et al. 1934, 294
[104] Körber 1885, 191–2, 195.

wasteful, and sensual, and Danish ambitions were matched by the boldness of the Swedish king Eric XIV. Magnus made an alliance with Ivan the Terrible, which Körber believed he must have regretted when he saw 60,000 dead bodies damming the river at Novgorod.[105]

Peter Wilhelm von Buxhöwden focused on the fact that Magnus confirmed the nobility's old privileges, granted new ones, and bestowed more land upon the barons, among them several members of the Buxhöwden family.[106]

Körber's view of the Danish period is very positive. While Livonia was ravaged by Swedish, Russian, and Polish troops Saaremaa was spared, with the exception of a bout of burning, murdering, and kidnapping at Russian hands in 1576. According to Körber, the Poles wanted to bring Livonia under the yoke of Rome. The Danish king Frederick II wanted to reduce landholdings, but refrained since he did not want to alienate his new subjects. His reign was on the whole a happy time for Saaremaa.[107]

So were the days of Christian IV, and in 1612 the islanders refused to join Sweden after half a century of righteous, mild, and benevolent Danish rule. In Livonia, Germans and 'un-Germans' alike were suffering under the reign of the 'barbaric' Poles, whose rule according to Körber was contrary to German law and evangelical freedom. The Danes made no major changes to the administration. During Charles XI's ruthless system of robbery and Charles XII's ten years of extortions the Danish period was rightly looked upon as the golden age of Saaremaa, Körber claimed.[108] Thus he portrayed the Danish period as golden for Saaremaa both in comparison with contemporary mainland Livonia and with the following Swedish period. However, Körber's positive view of the Danes did not stem from something good they did, but from the fact that they did not do much at all, allowing the German nobility to govern the island as before.

The Estonian historian Evald Blumfeldt did mention in *Saaremaa* from 1934 that there was a Swedish-minded minority among the Saaremaa nobility during the Kalmar War of 1611–1613. Its most active

---

[105] Körber 1885, 203, 214, 219 ff.
[106] Buxhöwden 1838, 23 ff.
[107] Körber 1885, 217, 240, 255.
[108] Körber 1865, 260–1 ('undeutschen', 'barbarische'). According to Jansson 2000, 430 Estonian and Latvian peasants were labelled 'un-German', but not the Swedish peasants in Estonia and Livonia.

representatives, Otto von Buxhöwden and Heinrich von Schulmann, were executed in Copenhagen in 1613.[109]

In Soviet history-writing the Danish period is almost completely omitted. However, in *Saaremaa* from 1959 it is briefly mentioned in one paragraph, where it is stated that the manors multiplied and the burdens on the peasants became heavier.[110]

In *Saaremaa 2*, Piia Pedakmäe agrees with Körber's view that the Danes left Saaremaa untouched. According to her, the island enjoyed the same free status as Gotland; the nobility's privileges as well as the old laws remained intact. However, Pedakmäe's picture of the peasants' circumstances differs sharply from Körber's: from 1550 to 1627 the population dropped by 27%, and like Blumfeldt she writes that peasants were escaping to the mainland. The flow of refugees was so great that the nobility asked the Danish king to put pressure on Sweden to stop it.[111] Peasants fleeing from Saaremaa to Swedish-controlled areas on the mainland do not fit Körber's and Buxhöwden's view of benevolent Danish rule and Swedish oppression.

Blumfeldt too saw a conflict between the nobility on Saaremaa and on the mainland. According to him, the noblemen from the Swedish-controlled mainland—whose population had dwindled because of the wars—did not want peasants who had been abducted from Saaremaa during the Kalmar War to return to the island, since that would have left their lands fallow again.[112]

According to *Saaremaa raamat*, a book published in 1962 by islanders in Canadian exile, the peasants' legal status deteriorated during the Danish period, and their duties increased. For Kuressaare it was a time of rising fortunes, since the town gained privileges in foreign trade.[113]

The nineteenth-century German authors wrote from the viewpoint of the German nobility, and from that perspective the Danish period was positive. Estonian writers in the twentieth century have instead focused on the peasant population, and therefore reach a different verdict on the era.

---

[109] Luha et al. 1934, 297.
[110] Allik 1959, 39.
[111] Pedakmäe 2007, 152 ff.; Luha et al. 1934, 305.
[112] Luha et al. 1934, 297
[113] Polding 1962, 194.

The Swedish period on Saaremaa, 1645–1710

Saaremaa belonged to Sweden during the very period when the Crown so-called Reduction to claw back land granted to the nobility in the first half of the seventeenth century. It is therefore no surprise that nobility-friendly, Baltic German, nineteenth-century history-writing is highly critical of Swedish rule.

Körber and Buxhöwden are both of the opinion that Charles XI and the Reduction were disasters. They also agree that Saaremaa's position as one of the fiefs Queen Christina obtained after her abdication left the island more oppressed, as both the former queen and the new king put demands on it. Körber argued that the Swedish Diet did not have the right to govern Livonia since the Livonian Estates were not represented there.[114]

Körber's account of Charles XI and the Reduction was grim. When the king died the county was half destroyed, half incomplete, without credit, and with a demoralized army lacking in resources and reserves. From that starting point, how could Charles XII successfully wage war for a decade against three strong enemies? Only because he was a 'hero king' and managed to feed his troops on enemy ground, Körber answered. He also claimed that Charles XII's Polish adversary August the Strong hated the Protestant faith.[115] Körber's view of history is strongly biased towards the local nobility and against Catholicism, which explains why Charles *père* is portrayed as a villain and Charles *fils* as a hero.

The Estonian historian Elena Öpik gave a different view of the Reduction in *Saaremaa 2*; according to her, Saaremaa was exempt from the Reduction in 1680 because of its special status as Queen Christina's fiefdom. Christina wanted a reduction to improve her own financial status, but it started late, and it is unclear whether it even managed to cover its administrative costs. In the 1690s, after the queen's death, the local nobility lost one-third of its land. According to Öpik, the Reduction created the material foundations for the kingdom's centralization, homogenization, and integration, and one step in this process was the destruction of the local nobility's power in Livonia and on Saaremaa.[116]

Öpik also claims that it was during Saaremaa's days as a county under the Swede Magnus Gabriel De la Gardie that the farmers started to regard the Danish period as a golden age. She is of the opinion, however, that the

---

[114] Körber 1885, 292 ff.; Buxhöwden 1838, 86.
[115] Körber 1885, 300 ('heldenkönig'), 305.
[116] Öpik 2007, 186–7, 190 ff.

root of the problem was to be found back in the Danish period, and that the peasants' burden had come close to unbearable before De la Gardie arrived.[117]

In the Soviet Age *Saaremaa*, the Reduction is not mentioned at all. The only monarch mentioned in the chapter is Queen Christina, who is said to have extended the nobility's privileges. The conditions of the peasants are said to have worsened, especially in the time of Magnus Gabriel De la Gardie.[118] Thus the Soviet Age narrative of the Swedish period focused on its very first years, which sat best with the idea that the Swedish monarch and the nobility joined forces to exploit the peasantry. The reign of Charles XI, which was characterized by conflict between monarch and nobility, and which had been portrayed positively in inter-war Estonian history-writing, was not mentioned at all. The idea that Western rulers counteracted the power of the feudal barons was probably not something that could be discussed at this point, since the Swedish king and the nobility were seen as members of one and the same oppressive class.

Although critical of the Reduction, Körber did acknowledge that the Swedes had some positive achievements: Swedish rule was strict and they did not lack a sense of order. Mainland Livonians celebrated when Gustavus Adolphus freed them from the Polish yoke, but on Saaremaa people compared it with the Danish days. Körber drew a parallel to when the Hanoverians came under Prussian rule in 1866. He admitted that the new government earnestly tried to alleviate old problems; their new Regulations of Kuressaare showed that there had been dark sides to the Danish heyday. Körber wrote that the Swedes did much to reform the legislation, and that although this activity took a sinister turn at the end of the period it was impossible to deny that they did good things for Saaremaa.[119]

There is a broad consensus among Baltic German and national Estonian historians that the Swedish period left a positive legacy in the field of education. According to Öpik, literacy was probably twice as high on Saaremaa than on the mainland in the 1730s.[120] The exception is again Soviet Age history-writing, which does not mention anything about this.

---

[117] Öpik 2007, 176–7.
[118] Allik 1959, 39.
[119] Körber 1885, 264–5.
[120] Polding 1962, 194; Öpik 2007, 194; Körber 1885, 292; Luha et al. 1934, 206

The Swedish period on Hiiumaa, 1563–1710

Hiiumaa came under Swedish rule almost a century earlier than Saaremaa, in 1563. The most negative picture of this period is given in the Soviet Age booklet *Hiiumaast ja hiidlastest,* which claimed that the Swedish acquisition of the island ushered in a process of feudalization which made the burdens on the peasants heavier.[121]

During the Swedish period, agriculture and fishing flourished on Hiiumaa, according to Saar. There was also an emergent industry, and Jakob de la Gardie had ships built that kept a permanent connection open between Hiiumaa and Stockholm even in the early seventeenth century. Administratively Hiiumaa became a separate unit under a bailiff.[122]

Saar, however, believes that the burdens became heavier for both Swedish and Estonian farmers on Hiiumaa; they brought their complaints to the king in 1664. Maybe the Swedish period was not as happy as often claimed, Saar concludes.[123]

Saar estimates that the Livonian War (1558–1583) reduced Hiiumaa's population from 2,500 to 1,300, but that at the end of the seventeenth century it had risen to around 3,000. The Great Northern War and the plague of 1710–1712 wiped out two-thirds of Estonia's population.[124] History writers from Saaremaa stress that their island escaped the carnage on the mainland during the Livonian War, but that the neighbouring island of Hiiumaa shared the mainland's suffering. The Great Northern War affected both islands and the mainland severely.

Elmer Vrager was writing from exile in Sweden and published his book *Hiiumaa and hiidlased* in Toronto. Saar points out a few mistakes Vrager made in his description of chapels on Hiiumaa, and he attributes them to Vrager's distance from the island. Vrager gave a thorough description of how the peasants on Hiiumaa fought for their rights against the landlords. In his opinion, Swedish peasants were at an advantage compared to Estonians since they had privileges dating back to the days of the Order that gave them very few obligations towards their landlords. In 1503 the Swedes at Kärdla still had an old parchment in their possession that condemned any nobleman who acted unjustly against them. Axel Julius de la Gardie introduced export restrictions on limestone and cattle, which

---

[121] Tiik 1978, 34 ff.
[122] Saar 2004, 27–8.
[123] Saar 2004, 28.
[124] Saar 2004, 72 ff.

led to a long, three-stage conflict. In the first stage (1662–8) Swedes and Estonians worked together with the aim of reducing labour duties by half and limiting payments to the levels from the days before De la Gardie. With the help of their letters of privilege the Swedes succeeded, but the Estonians failed. During the second period (until 1668–75) the Swedes fought with confidence in order for their privileges to be respected. In the third period until 1675–85 there was a conflict regarding which villages were comprised by the privileges in the letter, since the text was not entirely clear.[125]

The Swedish period seems less happy in history-writing from Hiiumaa than is the case on Saaremaa. While on Saaremaa the central theme of the narrative is the struggle between the Crown and the nobility, on Hiiumaa it is the conflict between nobility and peasants that is the focus. The Swedish peasants are given considerable attention. It has been claimed that this group is overlooked in Estonian history-writing, but that is clearly not the case in regional history-writing from Hiiumaa. The fact that Vrager wrote his account of Hiiumaa's history when in Sweden might have contributed to his interest in the Swedish peasants. More important is probably the fact that the Swedish peasants constituted such a large proportion of the island's population that they were hard to overlook. In addition, Carl Russwurm's pioneering work from 1855 made it easy to write about them.

The Russian period on Saaremaa, 1710–1917

The writers of *Saaremaa 2* have noted that very little has been written about the Russian period in Saaremaa's history, with the exception of *Saaremaa* from 1934.[126] Another exception is Peter Wilhelm von Buxhöwden, who was very interested in the Russian period, which in his days still was roughly equated with the eighteenth century. It covers pages 112–250 in his book of 293 pages, and pages 251–293 are also related to the Russian period. The Swedish period is the second most important with 70 pages, while the periods of Denmark and the bishops get 20 pages each. Since Buxhöwden's aim was to demonstrate how the nobility's privileges had been confirmed or expanded at every shift of power, the recent period was the most important. Large sections of the book are copies of documents confirming these privileges.[127]

---

[125] Saar 2004, 33; Vrager 1971, 31 ff.
[126] Laur 2007, 202; Lust 2007, 216.
[127] Buxhöwden 1838.

Buxhöwden's account of the Russian period is very positive, and especially Peter the Great is singled out for praise. The Treaty of Nystad in 1721, where Sweden seceded its Baltic possessions including Saaremaa to Russia, was a turning point which brought uninterrupted peace, tranquillity, order, and increasing happiness. In the Swedish period the Baltic Sea had been very broad when something good was expected from Stockholm, but very narrow when riches flowed the other way. Buxhöwden considered it a great misfortune to be a distant province of a weak and impoverished state, but after the Swedish period gigantic Russia—ruled by the greatest monarch of the time—looked benevolently upon Saaremaa.[128]

One chapter in Buxhöwden's book contains a comparison of patriotism on Saaremaa in the Swedish and Russian periods. The main purpose of the chapter, indeed one of the main purposes of the whole book, is to show that the Saaremaa nobility were loyal to the Russian throne because the Russians had left them in peace and not interfered in their privileges as the Swedes had done during the Reduction.[129] Between the lines one can read that patriotism is conditional; only rulers who understand not to demand too much from the regional community and not to interfere in its internal affairs can expect loyalty.

The then Tsar Nikolas I, who had ruled Russia since 1825, is not mentioned once in Buxhöwden's book. Still, it was probably him the message is directed at. In the preface of his book, Buxhöwden expressed the hope that his presentation of how Saaremaa for six centuries had kept its own constitution would help it be left untouched in the future, aided by 'the generosity of the greatest monarch of our time'.[130] In 1831 Nikolas I had crushed a rebellion in Poland, after which a period of Russification began. It is probable that Buxhöwden perceived the police state that Nikolas I was creating as a threat to the power and independence of the Saaremaa nobility.

An interesting parenthesis is the fact that when Tsar Alexander I died in December 1925, dangerous ice conditions delayed the message that his son Nikolas had succeeded him. On Saaremaa, Alexander's brother was instead hailed as Constantine I for more than ten days. In a fictional story by Hans von Freytagh-Loringhoven, the period is extended to two months, and

---

[128] Buxhöwden 1838, 112.
[129] Buxhöwden 1838, 261.
[130] Buxhövden 1838, vii–viii ('der Grossmuth des grössten Monarchen unserer Zeit').

Peter Wilhelm von Buxhöwden is given part of the responsibility for the confusion.[131]

In *Saaremaa* from 1934, Blumfeldt gave a different picture of the Russian period. According to him it meant an end to the improvements in the peasants' conditions that the Swedish king Charles XI had achieved, and the peasants were more than ever left at the mercy of the nobility.[132]

To Soviet era history writers, the Russian period was problematic: from a Marxist standpoint the feudal system of the time had to be condemned, but on the other hand criticism of Russia could be interpreted as covert criticism of the Soviet Union, which was of course unthinkable.

According to Arnold Allik's chapter in the book *Saaremaa* from 1959, Peter the Great left all the nobility's privileges in place, and thus the exploitation of the peasants continued. On the other hand, accession to the strongest realm in Europe ended the period of war, which meant that its productive forces could be restored. The account in the museum guide *Saaremaa muuseumid* was similar: peasants continued to suffer during 'the era of the nobility and the merchants', but the population increased due to the peace that the Russian rule brought. It also made much of the Baltic German Fabian Gottlieb von Bellingshausen, born on Saaremaa, and the discoverer of Antarctica, who is described as a 'Russian seafarer born on Saaremaa'.[133] Thus the authors managed to give an anti-feudal, anti-capitalist but pro-Russian account of the period. Special emphasis was put on the benefits of being part of a strong empire.

Allik, however, recognized that conditions for the peasants worsened in the eighteenth century. Not only did he claim that their economic exploitation got worse, but he added that the landlords attempted to use their *jus primae noctis*—a custom which is traditionally dated to the Middle Ages and whose existence is disputed. Allik saw the Herrnhuter and Orthodox movements in the eighteenth and nineteenth centuries as being directed against serfdom and the plight of the peasants.[134]

The historian Kersti Lust notes in *Saaremaa 2* that administrative and cultural Russification threatened the power of the local nobility. On Saaremaa, 29.8% of the peasants converted to the Orthodox faith in 1846–

---

[131] Freytagh-Lohringhoven 1995, 131–6.
[132] Luha et al. 1934, 321–2.
[133] Allik 1959, 40; Allik & Hiiuväin 1969, 30–1 ('aadlike ja kaupmeeste', 'Saaremaal sündinud vene meresõitjat').
[134] Allik 1959, 41 ff.

8, while in Pöide parish it was 68% and on Muhu 70%. Lust believes that because of the nobility's rule and the harsh living conditions the people pinned their hopes of improvement on the tsar. Blumfeldt described it not as a religious but as a social movement, directed at improving the economic and legal status of the peasants. The conversions did not improve the peasants' lot, however, although a series of reforms in the 1860s did. Gustav Ränk's grandfather explained to him that a great number of people converted to Orthodoxy because it was the belief of the tsar, and the tsar was the opponent of the landlords; the famine also contributed, as converts were rewarded with soup.[135]

In *Saaremaa 2* Matti Laur writes that the nobility's privileges were confirmed at the Treaty of Nystad, but like the exile-Estonian *Saaremaa raamat* he notes that Saaremaa in 1719 lost its independent status and became a province in the Government of Riga. In 1731 it became the only area in Estonia to gain the status of province, probably at the request of the regional nobility. From that year the head of Saaremaa again had the Swedish name '*landshövding*' until it was Germanized to '*Landeshauptmann*' in 1739. The reasons for this were the old special status which had its roots in the Danish period, the insular geographical situation, and the large proportion of Crown land on the island.[136]

Bruno Pao considered the Swedish period to have been a great period for seafaring, since the domestic trade in grain now extended to the whole Baltic area. In the Russian period, trade was made more difficult for the peasants since a maximum size for their boats was introduced. After the Crimean War things began to improve again. Smuggling brought good profits, while popular movements and emerging capitalism enabled the accumulation of capital for large shipbuilding projects. According to Pao it was part of the people's self-image that they were seafarers of old. In 1836 peasants were allowed to build ships, but initially they needed a special passport to sail abroad, which required the permission of the landlord. Even before the Crimean War landlords and merchants owned 21 ships in Kuressaare.[137]

In the last third of the nineteenth century, shipbuilding took off due to low timber prices in combination with high custom rates on foreign ships.

---

[135] Lust 2007, 224, 255 ff.; Luha et al. 1934, 336 ff.; Ränk 1979, 133–4.
[136] Laur 2007, 203; Polding 1962, 194–5.
[137] Pao 2007, 532 ff.

The peasant seafaring also benefitted from high freight rates and possibilities for education. Incomes from seaborne trade led to the construction of town-style houses in the countryside, which were filled with prestige goods brought in by sea. Cultural exchange across the sea had begun, Pao noted. Some had their children educated and took part in the social life in cities such as Riga.[138]

While Pao stresses the importance of the sea as a route for trade and cultural exchange in his essay about seafaring in *Saaremaa 2*, in another essay Lust emphasized its isolating properties. According to her, Saaremaa's position as an isolated micro world contributed to the fact that the nobility could preserve the island as a provincial idyll until the end of the nineteenth century. The isolation slowed societal transformation, which led to poverty.[139] As a maritime historian, Pao focuses on the riches and other advantages navigation brought in the second half of the nineteenth century, while Lust instead focuses on stagnation in the agricultural sector. The contrast between vital seafaring and underdeveloped agriculture can also be seen in descriptions of Åland in the late nineteenth century.

It should be noted that there is no equivalent to the rich Ålandic maritime history-writing on Saaremaa or Hiiumaa. In *Saaremaa 2* (2007) shipping is treated in 30 pages, which is less than fishing (37), forestry (39), industry and trade (52), and agriculture (77). While the shipping industry on Åland ultimately financed publications about its sailing merchant fleet, the shipping industry on Saaremaa dwindled after the period of peasant shipping and became extinct in the Soviet period. While *Den åländska segelsjöfartens historia* is an 800-page brick funded by Åland's nautical club, *Sailing and the island of Saaremaa* is a privately published booklet.[140] It is clear that this difference in quantity is not a reflection of the relative importance of Åland's and Saaremaa's merchant fleets in the heydays of sail, but of the fate of the islands' shipping industries later in the twentieth century.

Gustav Ränk recalled in his memoirs that even before the First World War he had formed an Estonian national identity from historical novels and works of popular history. He learned who his historical enemies were,

---

[138] Pao 2007, 536–7, 540.
[139] Lust 2007, 245.
[140] Kåhre & Kåhre 1989; Juske 2006.

and sympathized with the Boers in their war of liberation against the British. Right-thinking boys and men wanted to be Boers, he claimed.[141]

The Russian period on Hiiumaa, 1710–1917

The greatest difference between Saaremaa and Hiiumaa history-writing about the Russian period is that in the latter the large-scale deportation of Swedish peasants from Hiiumaa features large. Saar writes that Hiiumaa's population rose sharply during the Russian period, in spite of a considerable emigration that was in part caused by the peasants' heavy burdens. In 1858 there were 13,955 people on the island.

In the mid eighteenth century the family de la Gardie/Stenbock got their estate back. According to Vrager, Carl Magnus Stenbock was remembered as a cruel master. The Swedish peasants on Hiiumaa continued to defend their privileges, as they had done in the seventeenth century. When Prince Potemkin heard Stenbock complain about the peasants, he tried to benefit from the situation by suggesting that they be moved to his New Russia Governorate in the south of the country, which he wanted to populate with Western Europeans. Vrager claims that the Swedes gave their consent, but Saar is of the opinion that the relocation was forced upon them, and he calls it the first deportation from Estonia to Russia, which reduced Hiiumaa's population by 1,000.[142]

The Hiiu church historian Riho Saard mentioned that some Russian prisoners of war and lumberjacks lived on Hiiumaa from the Great Northern War onwards, and that they maintained a small orthodox chapel until the early nineteenth century.[143]

During the nineteenth century many islanders from Hiiumaa moved to Siberia. According to Saar, Estonians are hardworking, and in Russia they could lead their own lives. There are still Estonian villages in Siberia and the Caucasus where you can find descendants of the Hiiumaa islanders. In the second half of the century Hiiumaa's insular seclusion was weakened, and the civilization of the outer world started to reach it shores.[144]

---

[141] Ränk 1979, 202.
[142] Saar 2004, 76–7, 79; Vrager 1971, 32–3, 35–6.
[143] Saard 2009, 142.
[144] Saar 2004, 80.

The tumultuous twentieth century

The Saaremaa uprising in 1919

Sionce the collapse of the Russian Empire in 1917, Estonia has experienced two German occupations, two periods as a Soviet republic, and two periods of independence.

The years 1917–1919 were very eventful in the history of Saaremaa. When the Russian Empire begun to collapse towards the end of the First World War, a complicated situation arose when several armed groups contested for influence: Baltic German, national Estonian, and revolutionary. Writers who sympathized with these groups have given their own disparate accounts of the armed conflicts that followed.

The island was invaded by Germany in October 1917. It is only the Soviet Age *Saaremaa* from 1959 which mentions that the German troops faced any kind of resistance: it claims that the revolutionary navy put up a brave but doomed struggle against the numerically superior German forces. All writers agree that the island was hit hard by the invasion. According to Blumfeldt the troops were allowed to plunder the island freely for three days. Kersti Lust writes in *Saaremaa 2* that the Germans restricted personal liberty and stressed the importance of German in schools. Pupils were educated to revere the ruling German class and the German army. The Estonian Knighthood on Saaremaa wanted to tie the island to Germany as fast as possible, and after the Treaty of Brest-Litovsk the Livonian nobility tried to join Germany as an independent duchy. This increased the animosity towards the nobility on Saaremaa. Lust adds that the billeting of the troops proved very difficult, and that the harvest of 1918 failed. According to Blumfeldt the attempts by the local Germans to take Saaremaa into the German Empire as an independent principality came to an end when the German troops left the Baltic after the German Revolution in November 1918.[145]

According to the history of the Saaremaa branch of the Defence League (Kaitseliit), some German minded Estonians had joined the German Landesschutzwehr. When the Estonian equivalent Kaitseliit was formed it lacked weapons since the German military refused to allow it any. However, the local landlord Odert van Poll managed to acquire 4,000

---

[145] Luha et al. 1934, 347; Prooses 1959b, 59; Lust 2007, 239–40.

confiscated Russian arms for his 'personal defence', and handed them over to the Kaitseliit. Apparently the wise German understood that in the near future they would be the only ones able to protect him, the history concludes.[146]

The communist Vassili Riis described the German Bürgerwehr as a cruel terrorist organization founded by Baltic Germans and local 'grey barons', officials, and peddlers.[147] In Estonian history-writing it is claimed that Estonian's joined the Bürgerwehr since that was the only way for them to maintain an armed organization during the German occupation. It has also been claimed that the Bürgerwehr was in fact organized by the Estonian admiral Johan Pitka, with a few prominent Germans as figureheads. At the end of the German occupation the Bürgerwehr was transformed into the Kaitseliit.[148]

After the outbreak of the German Revolution in November 1918, Germany handed over power to the Estonian provisional government, which started to mobilize troops in order to withstand the offensive by Russian Bolshevik troops. The recruits from Saaremaa were gathered on Muhu, and in February 1919 an uprising broke out among them. The event is described as 'ülestous' (revolution, uprising) in Soviet Age publications and as 'mäss' (rebellion, mutiny) in most other Estonian texts. The rebels then marched towards Kurressaare, using the local authorities to mobilize more insurgents, but were beaten by the Estonian military force that had swiftly advanced over the ice from Tallinn. The consensus is that the young Estonian government's attempts to raise taxes and conscript troops were unpopular, but apart from that the nature of the uprising is described very differently in Soviet-era history-writing, by the Baltic German Oscar von Buxhoeveden, and by regional historians with a national Estonian perspective. Riis and Buxhoeveden lived on Saaremaa as children during the uprising. Riis' father took part, and two members of the Buxhoeveden family were among the first to be killed by the rebels.[149] Riis was a leading figure in the local NKVD during the Soviet occupation in 1940-1, while Buxhoeveden lived most of his life in Germany.

---

[146] Kaitseliidu 1998, 9.
[147] Riis 1960a, 43.
[148] Uustalu 1952, 164; MacFarlane 2011.
[149] Email from Geltmar von Buxhoeveden, 20 October 2009; *Postimees* website <http://www.postimees.ee/leht/96/05/04/krimi.htm>, accessed 23 May 2013; *Saaremaa ülestoust 1919*, 210.

The disagreement over events in the revolutionary year of 1905. According to Buxhoeveden, Saaremaa was not much affected by the unrest since the patriarchal order was intact and the institutions of the Knighthood were still in place. The only incidents were a few attempts at arson. Soviet time history-writing gives a different picture. When peasants gathered to protest outside baron von Sengbusch's manor, his son shot three people dead and was subsequently almost stampeded to death by the crowd, according to Riis. Arnold Allik relates the same story, but gives the number of dead as four. He describes the revolution that was put down in 1905–1907 as an important lesson for the Saaremaa islanders' later successful fight for their social rights. The Soviet Age museum guide *Saaremaa muuseumid* highlights the strike at the leather factory, which led to shorter working days. It also describes a map at the museum which depicted manors burned in 1905. *Saaremaa* from 1959 claimed that although the uprising was quenched, the revolutionary fire in the hearts of the Saaremaa people could not be put out, and burst into flame again in 1917, 1919, and 1940.[150]

The Estonian historian Evald Blumfeldt, who emphasized in *Saaremaa* from 1934 that land was the central question in 1905, claimed that Sengbusch killed two people on the spot and that two died later of their wounds. He considered Sengbusch himself to have escaped the wrath of the peasants relatively easily.Ränk shows more sympathy for young von Sengbusch; he first tried to tell the peasants that he could not promise anything on behalf of his father, then he tried to escape, and only as a last resort he had opened fire. According to Kersti Lust's essay in *Saaremaa 2* the peasants threatened to burn the manors down if rents were not lowered, whereupon the landlords usually gave in. The peasants' demands to divide the land were not met; the nobility only conceded minor privileges such as hunting, home distillation, and the keeping of taverns.[151]

Despite small variations in details and emphasis, Soviet Age and national Estonian history-writing give similar descriptions of momentous events in 1905, in contrast to Buxhoeveden's picture of business as usual under a relatively peaceful patriarchal order.

Buxhoeveden believed that Estonian national history-writing has tried to put the blame for the 1919 uprising on the Germans by claiming that

---

[150] Buxhoeveden 1969, 91–2; Riis 1960a, 39; Prooses 1959a, 55; Allik 1985, 62 ff.; Allik & Hiiuväin 1969, 33, 40.
[151] Luha et al. 1934, 342 ff.; Ränk 1979, 195–6; Lust 2007, 226 ff.

the objective was to get rid of the barons. He believes that the uprising was a premeditated, communist attempt to create a Soviet republic.[152]

Neither Soviet Age nor post-Soviet Estonian academics support this view. Although Vassili Riis and Josef Saat (an Estonian communist politician, publicist, and academic born on Muhu) try their best to describe the rebels as good socialists, they admit that there was no organized communist party on Saaremaa at the time of the uprising in 1919. After the defeat, the party extended a helping hand towards the people of Saaremaa, Riis added. The historian Jüri Ant claims in the post-Soviet *Saaremaa 2* that there was only one known communist on Saaremaa at the end of 1918. However, the inter-war writer Evald Blumfeldt did believe outside incitement played a role: the islanders were isolated from the mainland during the war, and were therefore susceptible to deception by agitators who claimed that the mainland was still in the hands of the hated barons. The ethnologist Gustav Ränk's view is close to Blumfeldt's, as he describes how hatred of the barons in combination with political confusion on the island was a fertile ground for the ideas of the agitators. He also gives multiple examples of how completely isolated Saaremaa was during the German occupation, leaving the peasants ignorant even of what a political party was.[153]

In the Soviet Age *Saaremaa* from 1959, meanwhile, it was claimed that, despite Saaremaa's economic stagnation and isolation from the mainland, the understanding of the political situation was better on the island than in many other places in Estonia. The explanation for this was that many islanders had taken part in the war and brought home new ideas from Russian and Estonian cities, explaining to the people that only the Soviet forces could improve their lives.[154]

Although everyone agrees that the Estonian government's mobilization of troops was an important factor behind the rebellion, the interpretations vary. According to Buxhoeveden, the Knighthood had previously handled the recruitment of troops without friction for a hundred years. Vassili Riis claims that the people on Saaremaa did not want to fight their brothers in Russia. They could not defend their motherland since

---

[152] Buxhoeveden 1969, 102.
[153] Riis 1960a, 6 (foreword by Joseph Saat), 323, 332; Ant 2007, 269; Luha et al. 1934, 348; Ränk 1979, 216, 218 ff., 232 ff., 237.
[154] Linna & Allik 1959, 61.

they did not have one: Estonia was the motherland of barons and capitalists. Jüri Ant, who has written about these events in *Saaremaa 2*, believes that the sailors and soldiers who had returned from the war were unwilling to be mobilized again. They had seen great empires collapse, and had difficulties believing in the existence of Estonia.[155]

Buxhoeveden believes that many of the problems during the uprising can be explained by the way the old institutions of the nobility were rapidly replaced by new Estonian ones. The nobility and the Estonian authorities did not communicate well. Axel von Buxhoeveden, the chamberlain of the emperor, did not consider the uncultivated and uneducated 'left radical' Estonians as partners in a negotiation. The later Buxhoeveden considered it understandable that the attempts to join Saaremaa to Germany affected the Estonians' trust in the nobility.[156]

Soviet Age history-writing, however, considers the bourgeois Estonian regime the direct successor of German rule. It is most clearly expressed in *Saaremaa* from 1959, where it is said that when the Estonians took power they promised to protect the barons' interests and privileges forever.[157]

The rebellion had its strongest support on eastern Saaremaa and Muhu. Buxhoeveden writes that the western parts had a population of Swedish origin and had enjoyed good harvests, but the stagnancy in the east was a hotbed for sectarianism and mass psychosis, which was illustrated by the fact that the Herrnhuters and the Orthodox Church had gained a foothold there in the nineteenth century. According to the communist Riis, Muhu was one of the most revolutionary places on Saaremaa in those days. He explains the weak support in western Saaremaa with local officials' sabotage of the rebels' mobilization.[158]

Blumfeldt, who was writing in 1934, quite close in time to events, treated the 1919 uprising relatively briefly on one page, compared to a little over two pages for events in 1905. He did not mention how bloody the conflict was, but simply stated that the rebels' resistance was broken in a swift battle, after which the islanders fought alongside with the mainland Estonians in order to secure their country's independence.[159]

---

[155] Buxhoeveden 1969, 91–2; Riis 1960a, 69–70, 121, 138 ff.; Ant 2007, 268–9.
[156] Buxhoeveden 1969, 4 ('linksradikale'). Axel, a grandson of Peter Wilhelm Buxhöwden, was born Alexander Peter Eduard Buxhoeveden (family tree attached to email from Geltmar von Buxhoeveden, 22 September 2009).
[157] Linna & Allik 1959, 61.
[158] Riis 1960a, 64–5, 292; Buxhoeveden 1969, 90–1.
[159] Luha et al. 1934, 348–9.

The uprising against the barons in 1905 fitted into the narrative of national struggle, whereas from a national perspective the fighting between Estonians in 1919 was a parenthetic anomaly.

According to *Saaremaa* from 1959, the sacrifices during the uprising were not in vain, since the proletariat on Saaremaa learned the truth of the Marxist-Leninist thesis that the peasants' struggle against the bourgeoisie can only be successfully if it is conducted in alliance with the working class, and is led by the working class.[160]

Gustav Ränk devoted more than thirteen pages of his autobiography to the uprising. Although he was only an onlooker as he was too young to be mobilized by the rebels, he still believed it was important to give an inside view of events since most accounts had been written from outside and above. Ränk saw the uprising as an accident, without defending any of the parties involved.[161]

According to the Defence League's history-writing, the rebellion broke out when a drunken crowd from the most unstable parts of the island were influenced by agitators. They tried to make the rebellion look legitimate by claiming that it was for Estonia against the barons, against whom this premeditated uprising was directed.[162]

The latest and most detailed description of the uprising, Piret Hiie's *1919. aasta mäss Muhu- ja Saaremaal* which is based on her masters thesis, describes the lack of land reforms on Saaremaa as a main reason for the rebellion. However, she also believes that the economic problems following the German occupation and the weakness of the regional government contributed to the uprising, as did Bolshevik agitation and the island's isolation from the mainland, which deprived the Saare of correct information.[163]

The uprising of 1919 has been a highly divisive issue. Buxhoeveden and Riis were writing from the viewpoint of the Baltic Germans and the rebels. The Defence League's account from 1998 was closely tied to one of the parties in the conflict, the Estonian government side. However, in the book *Saaremaa 2* from 2007 and Hiie's work from 2010 none of the sides are portrayed as heroes or villains; rather, the whole event is described as a terrible accident brought on by extreme circumstances. This is similar

[160] Linna & Allik 1959, 68.
[161] Ränk 1979, 223–37.
[162] *Kaitseliidu* 1999, 11 ff.
[163] Hiie 2010, 49, 112 ff.

to how the event was described by Blumfeldt in 1934 and Gustav Ränk in 1979. This strand of moderate Estonian history-writing is basically supportive of the Estonian government side, however, as is illustrated by the indirect supposition that the rebellious islanders would have been good Estonian patriots if they had received correct information. National identity is thus still seen as natural, not as a constructed phenomenon.

According to *Saaremaa raamat*, when the association Saarlaste ühing Torontos was founded in 1956, Estonian newspapers announced it with ironic headlines such as 'Saare rebellion in Toronto'.[164] This illustrates that the uprising could be seen as a symbol of Saaremaa separatism. However, Saaremaa's regional history writers have never used the uprising to strengthen a separate Saaremaa identity; rather, they stress the island's ties to the mainland, and described the uprising either as an accident or, in the Soviet Age, as an act of solidarity with workers in mainland Estonia and Russia.

The communists on Saaremaa

After the uprising on Saaremaa the communist movement on the island became relatively strong, as is acknowledged in both Soviet and post-Soviet history-writing. The Soviet era museum guidebook *Saaremaa muuseumid* highlighted a display of weapons, books, and brochures that were found when the roof of a revolutionary family's house was renovated in 1961. This illustrated that the workers' struggle continued throughout the whole bourgeois period, the authors concluded. [165]

According to Vassili Riis, communism enjoyed strong support on Saaremaa. At the German attack in 1941 the Soviet authorities conscripted the inhabitants of Saaremaa into the Hävituspataljoon, (lit. 'Destruction Battalion'). Riis claimed that the ones who tried to evade conscription could be counted on the fingers of one hand, and that they were mostly members of Kaitseliit and Isamaaliit,[166] people who had already betrayed their fellow countrymen. According to him, there were patriotic scenes outside the recruiting offices, and even the women demanded guns.[167]

---

[164] Polding 1962, 146 ('Saarlaste mäss Torontos').
[165] Allik & Hiiuväin 1969, 33–4.
[166] Isamaaliit (the Pro Patria Union) was a political mass movement organized by the Estonian authoritarian leader Konstantin Päts during the period of martial law in 1935–40.
[167] Riis 1960b, 214.

According to Jüri Ant's essay in *Saaremaa 2*, the Saaremaa branch of the Estonian Communist Party had many distinctive features: it took an independent line and did not follow all the extremist decisions from Moscow and Tallinn. In the early 1930s roughly half of Estonia's 120–130 free communists were from Saaremaa. After a gunfight in which the regional communist leader Alexander Ellam was killed, the network was wound up, and in June 1940 only seven communists remained at liberty on the island.[168]

While Riis described an island where the vast majority were prepared to fight for the Soviet Union, the post-Soviet account stresses that the absolute number of communists was small, and that Saaremaa's communists were relatively independent both from Moscow and from the Estonian party.

Soviet crimes

During the first Soviet occupation of 1940–1 large numbers of people were murdered on Saaremaa. The Soviet Union occupied Estonia a second time in 1944, and large-scale deportations took place in 1949.

Vassili Riis, who as head of the NKVD on Saaremaa was presumably responsible for many of the deaths, wrote in 1960 that one of the merits of the Destruction Battalion was that it liquidated the bandits one by one before they had time to organize.[169]

The single largest Soviet atrocity took place between July and September 1941 at Kuressaare Fortress, where 90 people were shot dead.[170] When German troops entered Kuressaare they opened the fortress in order for the public to see evidence of the crime. Robert Kreem describes in his autobiography how he went straight from having seen the murdered corpses in the castle to the recruitment office of the new Home Guard organization, Omakaitse.[171] This organization replaced the Defence League (Kaitseliit) that the Germans had dissolved. The name of the new organization had historical roots since Omakaitse was the Estonian name for the Bürgerwehr organization that had existed during the German occupation in 1918.

---

[168] Ant 2007, 273–4.
[169] Riis 1960b, 216.
[170] Püüa 2006, 20.
[171] Kreem 1984, 119 ff.

The most comprehensive book covering the Soviet terror on Saaremaa is Endel Püüa's *Punane terror Saaremaal* ('Red terror on Saaremaa'), which was published by Saaremaa Museum in 2006. It includes lists of known victims (230 names) and perpetrators: members (73) and member candidates (159) of the Communist Party, members of the NKVD headed by Vassili Riis (31), members of the farmers' and workers' militia, members of the Destruction Battalion (318–324), agents and informers (113), and prison guards (16).[172] Although there might be a small overlap between the lists, those named still constitute a substantial proportion of such a small society as Saaremaa, and most islanders probably recognize family members or neighbours mentioned in the book.

According to Meelis Maripuu's essay in the post-Soviet *Saaremaa 2*, a total of 2,000 people on Saaremaa disappeared during the first Soviet repression. This is a larger proportion of the population than on the mainland, which in Maripuu's view was due to the fact that the first Soviet occupation lasted longer on the island.[173] Saaremaa's geographical position as an island surrounded by shallow waters made it difficult to conquer. History repeated itself three years later when the Germans were driven out by the Red Army; both times, the Sõrve peninsula on Saaremaa was the last piece of Estonian ground to be held by the defenders.

There is agreement that the communists' attempt to continue the partisan struggle on Saaremaa during the German occupation failed, in part because the island's open terrain was unsuitable. Riis claimed that he was against the attempts to dig foxholes in the forests; underground activity should be carried out in the midst of people. According to Püüa, the partisan struggle failed mainly because the newly discovered mass murders had blackened the communists in the eyes of the people. He writes that they chose Pöide as their hiding place since it had long been the most left-wing parish on Saaremaa. Maripuu describes the whole idea of digging foxholes for a communist partisan struggle on Saaremaa as a naïve delusion.[174]

Attitudes towards the Germans

When Robert Kreem in the 1930s attended a camp for scouts and Noorkotkad ('Young Eagles'), the youth organization of Kaitseliit, they

---

[172] Püüa 2006, 97–177.
[173] Maripuu 2007, 302.
[174] Riis 1960b, 217–18; Püüa 2006, 80, 83; Maripuu 2007, 303.

learned about their people's historical fight against the Germans and the Russians. Under the flag they swore to be and to remain Estonian.[175] Thus Germany was seen as one of the Estonian nation's historical enemies. In 1941, however, the German advance ended the Soviet occupation and mass killings on Saaremaa.

The Soviet Age *Saaremaa* blamed the Germans for the drop in Saaremaa's population from around 60,000 to 33,593 during the war. They were said to have murdered 7,000 and deported 5,189. However, the Germans did not manage to break the fighting spirit of the islanders, whose active and passive resistance contributed to the Soviet peoples' wider struggle against the fascist enemy.[176]

All non-Soviet history writers, however, agree that the German troops were at first seen as liberators who might restore Estonian independence, but that people soon realized that they were just another occupying force. Kreem, as a boy scout was especially critical of the Germans' decision to ban youth organizations. In upper secondary school Kreem was active in an anti-German group which did things like compile lists of girls who were having relationships with Germans. According to Meelis Maripuu, the Germans kept the Soviet limitations on the Estonians' freedom in place. Regional self-rule was legalized, but local representative bodies were not put in place.[177]

In post-Soviet history-writing, the arrests and executions carried out during the German occupation are described against the background of the preceding Soviet mass murders. Endel Püüa uses the term 'counter-terror' (*vastuterror*). The majority of the perpetrators of the Soviet repression were arrested by the Omakaitse, and many of them were executed the same year. The rest were sent to prison or concentration camps. According to Püüa, 334 people were killed or died in prison during the German occupation. Maripuu claims that there were 400 confirmed victims, and she also mentions the crimes of the local Omakaitse such as the execution of the communist Alexander Kuul's mother.[178] These figures should be contrasted to the above-mentioned Soviet Age figures of 7,000 killed by the Germans.

---

[175] Kreem 1984, 78–9.
[176] Tasa 1959, 96, 104.
[177] Kask 2004, 4; Kreem 1984, 127–8, 130–1; Maripuu 2007, 320.
[178] Püüa 2006, 75; Maripuu 2007, 321.

Juta Vessik and Peep Varju, the authors of the Memento association's report on crimes committed on Saaremaa, made several clear distinctions between the Soviet and the German executions. The people killed during the German period were not innocent, they had a low level of education and preferred doing other activities than work—they were called 'proletarians' by the communists. During the Soviet occupation, innocent, highly educated, industrious people were killed. The Germans also tried to establish guilt by hearing witnesses, and the ones who were found not to have taken part in communist activities were released. The executions on both sides were contrary to international law, with the exception of the German killings of civilian members of the 'bandit' Soviet Destruction battalion. These sorts of armed fighters are not included in international law, the authors conclude.[179] It is possible that Vessik and Varju, who published their booklet in 2002, were affected by the debate about 'illegal combatants' prompted by the recently ignited War on Terror.

When the German offensive on the Eastern Front started to lose momentum, Estonians were conscripted. Many, like Robert Kreem, chose to join the SS Estonian Legion. Kreem claims that he hoped the Legion would be transformed into a force fighting for the freedom of Estonia. When the conscripts left Saaremaa, they sang 'Jää terveks, kodusaar' ('Remain intact, island'). The Estonian Legion was involved in the efforts to stop the Red Army from advancing into Estonia, but when the battle was lost morale was low among the Estonians, and they did not take part in any further fighting. According to Kreem they were instead transported around Europe for the rest of the war of, among other places they stayed on what Kreem described as 'the island of Odense' in Denmark.[180]

In 1995–6 the Saaremaa branch of the Defence League (Kaitseliit) issued a triple booklet about the arrival and defeat of the Soviet troops on the island in 1940–1. In the first two booklets the Germans are described as the victorious troops of Great Germany who liberated Saaremaa. The last booklet consists of the readers' reactions to the first two parts. Many were more critical of the Germans, even describing them as 'cruel people'. The point that they actually dissolved the Kaitseliit is also made. In the summary the authors conclude that it is not possible to decide which regime was the worst, Russian Bolshevism or German Nazism. Both

[179] Vessik & Varju 2002, 7 ff.
[180] Kreem 1984, 136 ff., 180 ff., 190. Odense is in fact a city on the island of Funen.

caused irreparable damage. That was the high price of independence, and therefore independence should be nurtured and protected.[181]

Greater Finland

Finland and Estonia have many cultural and historic traits in common. Finnish and Estonian are Finno-Ugric languages which—although with difficulty—are mutually intelligible but incomprehensible to speakers of all other major European languages. The countries even share the melody for their national anthems. Both countries became independent from Russia after the First World War, but while Estonia lost its independence to the Soviet Union in 1940, Finland remained independent in the Winter War of 1939–40 although it lost some territory. When Germany attacked the Soviet Union in 1941, Finland joined the attack, but claimed to be fighting a separate war. Finnish troops regained the territory lost in the war and occupied additional land in Karelia. Since the 1920s, right-wing circles in Finland such as the academic group Akateeminen Karjala Seura (the Academic Karelia Society) had nurtured dreams of a 'Greater Finland' comprising territories outside Finland's current borders with a supposedly Finnish or Finno-Ugric population. In some versions, Greater Finland also included Estonia. With many of these territories in 1941 occupied by Finnish troops, Greater Finland suddenly seemed more realistic.

Meelis Maripuu writes in *Saaremaa 2* that the German command did not want to endanger its large naval ships in the treacherous waters around Saaremaa, and thus the majority of vessels in the attack on the island were Finnish. Jaak Sammet, vice-director of the Estonian Maritime Museum, wrote an article for the 1997–8 edition of Saaremaa Museum's biannual yearbook about the Finnish motorboat expedition that conquered Muhu in September 1941. It included hundreds of Estonians who according to Sammet had volunteered because of their recent experience of crimes committed during the Soviet occupation.[182]

According to a booklet published by the Kaitseliit, a secret society by the name of Suur-Soome Riik, (the State of Greater Finland) had been organized in Torgu back in the spring of 1941 during the first Soviet occupation. Maripuu believes that the reports of the German police might

---

[181] *Saaremaa 1940–1941* 1995, 29; *Saaremaa 1940–1941* 1996b, 6, 16–17, 25, 34.
[182] Maripuu 2007, 311; Saaremaa muuseum: Kaheaastaraamat 1997–1998, 316–17.

give a more objective view of the sentiments during the war than reminiscences coloured by later events. According to the police, 1–2% of the population supported a communist society, while 3–5% were in favour of a union with Greater Germany. In contrast to these quite meagre figures, 80% of the inhabitants of Saaremaa were judged in support joining Greater Finland. Maripuu also claims that the Finnish news broadcasts were considered the most reliable source of information during the war.[183]

There is no doubt that the Soviet Union was seen as the most lethal threat during the Second World War, but attitudes towards the Germans were also predominantly negative, partly for historical reasons but mainly because of the fact that they acted as an occupying force. Finland was like Germany fighting the Soviet Union, but was not viewed with the same suspicion; instead, the two countries were culturally and linguistically affiliated. As Estonia had recently been overrun by the great powers two times—and a third was coming—belief in the small state's chances of revival and survival was minimal. In the light of that experience, a union with Greater Finland might have seemed a more realistic way of achieving 'national' independence.[184]

It is interesting to note that the idea had surfaced earlier under similar political circumstances. Gustav Ränk recalled in his memoirs that his father heard talk about a union between Estonia and Finland during the German occupation in 1917–1918.[185]

The whirlwind of mad times

At the 2005 opening of Saaremaa Museum's exhibition covering the years 1939–49 Raul Salumäe gave a speech, later printed in the museum's yearbook. According to Salumäe, the exhibition came at the right moment, since it was only in recent years that it had become possible to discuss the period in a more objective way. Salumäe was of the opinion that the Estonian people had reached a new phase in their understanding of their history after the membership in the EU and NATO, and especially after the Lihula crisis. This was a controversy over a monument commemorating soldiers who fought against the Soviet Union in the Second World War, in the Finnish Army, the Wehrmacht or the Waffen SS. As the title of his speech, 'People in a whirlwind of mad times', suggests,

---

[183] Saaremaa 1940–1941 1996a, 5.
[184] This is illustradet by Zetterberg 1984, 519.
[185] Ränk 1979, 216.

Salumäe stresses that people on both sides were involuntarily drawn into the killings. The Second World War was not the Estonians' war; some families had members conscripted to fight on different sides in the conflict. Neither did the foreign troops come to Saaremaa of their own choice. It is not possible to condemn or glorify all individuals who during this political mess ended up on one side or the other—as victims, accomplices, or both, Salumäe concluded.[186] His view of the conflict, as a whirlwind that left individual actors little choice, offers a possibility for reconciliation through the recognition of common sufferings.

The Soviet era, 1944–1991

The Soviet era museum guide *Saaremaa muuseumid* describes the museum's exhibitions of economic progress, among them a map of the electrification of the kolkhozes in 1962–6 and model ships of modern trawlers.[187] After Estonia's second independence the focus instead shifted to Soviet crimes. In 1949 large numbers of Saaremaa's inhabitants were deported. Vessik and Varju claim that the deportations met all the criteria of genocide in the Geneva Convention.[188]

During the late 1940s and early 1950s, Estonia's forests were home to the so-called Forest Brothers. According to Garel Püüa they are usually portrayed as Estonian patriots who fought the Soviet power from armed bunkers, prepared to conquer or die. He believes that in reality most people who fled to the forest simply wanted to escape repression and stay alive. Some criminals also joined the groups.[189]

During the whole period, western Saaremaa was a military zone. According to articles in the yearbooks of the Saaremaa Museum, the relationship between the military and civilians was generally peaceful, besides a few instances of theft and murder.[190]

According to Saar and Tombak's article in *Saaremaa 2*, Soviet power was not only established by physical repression; the battle was also fought through the transformation of geography, history, and culture. Viktor Kingissepp was a revolutionary from Saaremaa who became leader of the

---

[186] Saaremaa muuseum: Kaheaastaraamat 2005–2006, 2007, 244.
[187] Allik & Hiiuväin 1969, 39.
[188] Vessik & Varju 2002, 38, 43.
[189] Püüa 2006, 247–8.
[190] Saaremaa muuseum: Kaheaastaraamat 2005–2006, 2007, 301–302; Saaremaa muuseum: Kaheaastaraamat 1997–1998, 1999, 319–20.

Estonian Communist Party and was executed in 1922. In 1952, Kuressaare changed name to Kingissepa, and with surrounding areas it formed Kingissepa rajoon. In 1959 it was united with the rest of Saaremaa, Orissaare rajoon, because the old provinces were thought to be more suitable administrative units. In 1989 Kingissepa rajoon was renamed Saare maakond. It was a far from common practice in Soviet Estonia to rename cities after revolutionaries; the Defence League's history pointed out that Saaremaa's only city was the only city in Estonia which changed name.[191]

Saar and Tombak claim that the communist regime tore down old monuments and erected new ones. They also admit that they to a large extent it also succeeded in establishing Soviet traditions and customs, which were part of the atheist education.[192]

It could be said that the first phase of post-Soviet history-writing, which was characterized by harsh and un-nuanced criticism of the Soviet Union, was replaced with more balanced interpretations around the turn of the new century. The Soviet Union's crimes are still criticized, but some of the myths which glorify the resistance are also under scrutiny, and the fact that the Soviet rule in some respects did leave a lasting impression on Estonian society is acknowledged.

Hiiumaa after 1917

In the Soviet Age booklet *Hiiuma ja Hiidlased* from 1978, almost nothing is said about the island's history after the First World War. The narrative is centred on agrarian history, and concludes briefly that the island's peasants remained poor after the land reforms of the bourgeoisie government (in other words, the government of the first independent Estonian republic).[193]

During the First World War the islanders were disturbed by the fortifications, according to Endel Saar. In 1917 a German occupation began with its thefts and violence. According to Saar, Estonians down the centuries have been agriculturalists, and the land reform after the war revitalized rural life on Hiiumaa considerably. In 1922 Hiiumaa had 16,954 inhabitants, the highest figure ever in a census, but Saar estimates that 18,000–20,000 people lived on the island before the war.[194]

---

[191] Saar & Tombak 2007, 353; Kaitseliidu Saaremaa maleva arengulugu 1999, 99.
[192] Saar & Tombak 2007, 357, 362–3.
[193] Tiik 1978, 42.
[194] Saar 2004, 81 ff.

Saar described Nazi Germany and the Soviet Union as rapacious conquerors. They entered the Molotov–Ribbentrop pact that promised the Soviet Union bases on the Estonian islands, including Hiiumaa. The island's population was hard hit by the war, islanders were mobilized on both sides, and many fled in 1944. The grim years after the war with deportations to Siberia and prison camps further reduced the population, as did the forced collectivization that made many people move to the cities. Saar gives a detailed account of how the deportations and the collectivization affected villages and individuals.[195]

According to Saar, the town of Kärdla lacked a proletariat. The Soviet authorities did not bother to keep statistics on its population, since its inhabitants were employed in service occupations and thus were considered third-rate humans. In 1948 there were 11,000 people on Hiiumaa, which Saar considers to be a surprisingly high number, given the losses during the war and the escape: it has never been higher since, and will probably never be.[196]

Saar writes that the Memento Association has calculated that between 45 and 76 people were exiled from each of the four parishes on Hiiumaa. One of those to be deported had died the year before; not even the dead were left alone, he concludes.[197]

According to Saar, the initiative to reintroduce the old counties in 1989–1990 came from the grassroots. He does not like the fact that regional authorities can only communicate with one another via the state authorities.[198] Perhaps this wish to communicate directly with other regional authorities is connected to Hiiumaa's strong links to Läänemaa, which the island was part of until the Second World War.

Conclusions

In Estonia's modern history, political power has shifted between different groups, and they have all given their views on the region's past. As a consequence, three main categories of regional history-writing can be discerned on Saaremaa: Baltic German, national Estonian, and Soviet.

---

[195] Saar 2004, 85–6, 119, 131–9, 148–202.
[196] Saar 2004, 87–8.
[197] Saar 2004, 91.
[198] Saar 2004, 146.

Hiiumaa's history has not been written from a Baltic German or Soviet[199] perspective; almost all attempts—which were few and relatively late, with the first only published in 1971—have a national Estonian viewpoint.

This division into three main categories does need to be refined in order to sufficiently describe the difference within the groups, however. It is clear that the Baltic Germans were writing history for entirely different reasons. While Luce can be described as an Estophile, who was primarily interested in describing the ancient Estonian society, Peter Wilhelm von Buxhöwden and Oscar von Buxhoeveden were instead preoccupied with defending the German nobility's privileges and position in society, extolling the patriarchal order they upheld.

Martin Körber holds an intermediary position. He showed an interest in the history of the Estonian population, and his non-historical writings all had clear Estophile aims, describing popular culture and hailing the educational standards of the Estonian peasants. However, as a history writer he identified primarily with Baltic German Livonia, and wrote in German for a German audience. He also claimed that the original inhabitants of the island had been Germans; the Estonian-speaking peasants on Saaremaa were descendants of these Germans and their slaves from the mainland.

National Estonian history-writing comprises works produced during the first period of independence, in exile during the Soviet period, and again at home during the second independence. The first independence was not a very prolific period for regional history-writing on Saaremaa. The volume about Saaremaa in the work *Eesti* is the only noteworthy example, and it was the result of joint efforts from the island and from the Estonian mainland. The work not only described Saaremaa's history, but also its topography and human geography, as well as its trades and biodiversity. The fact that Estonia was a new historical entity, based on a common language, comprising areas earlier belonging to the governments of Estonia and Livonia, might have contributed to the choice of combining history-writing with geography: one way to create a new Estonian history was to depict events that had taken place in the geographical area inhabited by Estonian speakers.

The Soviet history-writing is quite limited. No regional history-writing was published until after de-Stalinization in 1956, although by 1959

---

[199] The Soviet Age avoided all the politically sensitive topics of the twentieth century, Toomsalu 1978.

several books had been published, a committee of local historians had been formed, and an open-air museum inaugurated. The former NKGB officer Vassili Riis is the only regional author of monographs on Saaremaa's history during the Soviet period, and he focused on the twentieth century. Towards the end of the Soviet period, Saaremaa Museum published works on the island's history, and apart from the articles on twentieth-century political history it was not overtly political stuff. However, it was still affected by the Soviet *Zeitgeist*; authors then were less likely to talk about Western influences in Saaremaa's history than would be the case after the collapse of the Soviet Union.

The more openly communist view of the island's history before the twentieth century is limited to the different editions of the museum guide *Saaremaa muuseumid*. There Danish and Swedish rule is pictured as a time when the extortion of the peasants increased. The Russian period was according to the booklet characterized by oppression from the regional Baltic German nobility, but also by peace and advances brought by the Russian regime.

It could be argued that the different strands of Saaremaa regional history-writing express feelings of loyalty and affinity with different geopolitical entities. The nineteenth-century Germans wrote in an era before Estonia existed as an independent country, so it is no surprise that they showed no patriotism towards that nation. They were in fact all writing in a pre-national context. The writer who gave most space to the question of patriotism is Peter Wilhelm von Buxhöwden. He expressed loyalty towards Russia, but his comparison with the weak patriotism on Saaremaa during the Swedish period illustrates that he considered patriotism to be conditional: it only lasted as long as the central authorities did not interfere with how the regional nobility governed the island. Martin Körber, on the other hand identified strongly with old Livonia, and regarded the periods when Saaremaa had been separated from the mainland part of the Bishopric of Ösel–Wiek as regrettable. Luce seems to identify most strongly with pre-Christian Saaremaa. He describes the German conquest and Christianization as a process of downfall and degeneration, in line with his belief that degeneration was the main force behind all changes in nature and society.

The national Estonian history writers do identify with Estonia. They have emphasized the similarities between Saaremaa and the Estonian mainland, contradicting the earlier Baltic German claims that pre-

Christian Saaremaa was more advanced than the mainland and that the medieval uprisings on the island were isolated incidents. Instead, they have stressed Saaremaa's important role in the struggle for pan-Estonian freedom. Blumfeldt even suggested that ancient Saaremaa would eventually have united Estonia if not the crusades had interrupted the process.

The communist strand of history-writing did claim that workers and peasants primarily identified with their brothers in Russia. According to Vassili Riis, Estonia was the motherland of barons and capitalists, and thus the working class could not feel affinity with it.

After Estonia gained its independence in 1991, history-writing initially focused on criticizing the Soviet Union. The regional branches of the Defence League (Kaitseliit) and the Memento Association were harshest in their criticism. They tended to imply that Germany's crimes during the Second World War were not as severe as those of the Soviet Union. Later writings, such as *Punane terror* and in *Saaremaa 2* and *Saaremaa museum. Kaheaastaraamat*, offer a somewhat more distanced and conciliatory treatment of Soviet crimes, and are equally critical of German atrocities.

The results of this study of regional history-writing on Saaremaa does to a large extent correspond with the description that Johan Eellend has given of Estonian history-writing in general, but with a few interesting exceptions. The pioneers were Baltic Germans who primarily wrote the history of their own community, although some showed an interest in the Estonian peasant population. However, the pioneering national Estonian amateur historians that Eellend claims appeared in the late nineteenth century cannot be found on Saaremaa. Since the number of writers is few this might be a coincidence, but Miroslav Hroch has also claimed that the islands participated least of all the Estonian areas in the nineteenth-century national movement.[200] It is likely that their relative isolation from the mainland and the 'patriarchal idyll' that several authors claim lasted longer on Saaremaa than elsewhere contributed to a late start for Estonian nationalism among the peasant population. The international maritime contacts that other authors paradoxically claim dominated Saaremaa in the same period might also have made the national Estonian context less self-evident.

---

[200] Hroch 1985, 81.

Eellend's claim that Estonian inter-war history-writing was *Volksgeschischte*, describing the Estonian majority population, and not *Landesgeschichte*, describing all the peoples living in the geographical area, does not match the regional history-writing from Saaremaa, which in effect consists of the *Saaremaa* volume of *Eesti*. The fact that geography and history is mixed in the volume does indicate that Saaremaa's (and Estonia's) history is the history of an area—and the volume does indeed describe the history of other population groups within this area, primarily the Swedes. In Hiiumaa history-writing, which started later, the Swedes are even more prominent. In fact their struggle against the landlords receives more attention than that of the Estonian peasants, probably because it lasted longer and was more eventful. Since the Swedish peasants were concentrated in a few regions, it is logical that they are more prominent in regional history-writing than in overviews of Estonian history.

The *Eesti* publication does deserve more attention from Estonian historiographers, since it displays a different approach to the construction of Estonian identity than can be found in, for example, Hans Kruus' monographs: it was an attempt to construct a new nation using old regions as building blocks.

The positive view of the Swedish period that Eellend discerned can also be found on Saaremaa. However, the present study indicates that the Swedish orientation cannot be understood only in national terms. Estonia's independence also meant that the peasant's replaced the nobility as the dominant political class in society. What was appealing about the Swedish period to Estonian historians in the 1930s was the Reduction—the resumption of noble lands effected by Charles XI in the late seventeenth century; it might be seen as a predecessor of the land reforms on Saaremaa in the early 1920s and resonated well with the great Estonian interest in agrarian history.

Eellend's view of Estonian history-writing during the Soviet period sits well with the situation on Saaremaa. No works were published until after the death of Stalin, and the first ones—*Saaremaa* from 1959 and the writings of the former NKVD officer Vassili Riis—were strict adherents of the communist ideology. Works from the end of the Soviet period, such as the anthology *Kingissepa rajoonis*, expressed a more independent view of history, at least in areas which were not directly political. However, the mere existence of history-writing on Saaremaa during the period contradicts the claim that all research was centralized to a single institution in Tallinn.

Eellend's description of post-Soviet history-writing corresponds with developments on Saaremaa: initially it was conducted by non-professionals, focused on Soviet crimes, and had a tendency to downplay atrocities committed by the Germans. However, lately—after the publication of Eellend's article in 2004—professional historians have given a more balanced view of the period.

Because of the broad similarities between history-writing on Saaremaa and Hiiumaa and in Estonia in general, it can be claimed that regional history-writing on the Estonian islands is a variety of mainland history-writing. Despite the political revolutions of the twentieth century, there is a remarkable continuity in how Saaremaa's regional history has been presented and published: the inter-war *Saaremaa*, the Soviet Age *Kingissepa rajoonis*, and the post-Soviet *Saaremaa 1* and *Saaremaa 2* all belong to larger series of works which covers other Estonian regions as well. Their very mode of publication these makes the island's history part of Estonian history, unlike for example the series *Det åländska folkets historia*, which with its title and as an independent publication instead underlines the separateness of Åland.

This impression is strengthened by the nature of regional history-writing on Saaremaa. Although many writers recognize that the island's location has meant that history has often taken a slightly different direction than on the mainland, this has not been used to legitimize separatism. Centre–periphery conflicts with the mainland are a rare sight in Saaremaa and Hiiumaa history-writing, since the scenario 'us against the mainlanders' is completely overshadowed by the dominant theme 'us and the mainlanders against foreign invaders and oppressors'. It can be said that regional history writers on Saaremaa and Hiiumaa have attempted to bridge the straits between their islands and mainland Estonia.

References

Saaremaa's history-writing

Allik, Arnold (1959), 'Ajalooline ülevaade', in Tooms 1959: 29–46.

— (1985), '1905.–1907. aasta sündmused Saaremaal', in Vello Tarmisto (ed.), *Kingissepa rajoonis* (Tallinn: Eesti NSV Teaduste Akateemia).

— & Hiiuväin, E. (1969), *Saaremaa muuseumid* (Tallinn: Eesti NSV Kultuuriministeerium).

— & Linna, Timoteus (1959), 'Saaremaa töörahva 1919. a. ülestous', in Tooms 1959: 61–68.

Ant, Jüri (2007), 'Saaremaa poliitiline elu 1918–1940', in Jänes-Kapp et al. 2007: 264–289.

Buxhoeveden, Oscar von (1969), 'Der Kommunistenaufstand auf Oesel im Februar (1919 aus deutsch-baltischer Sicht', ed. Harro von. Hirschheydt, *Baltische Hefte*, xv (Hanover-Döhren: v. Hirschheydt).

Buxhöwden, Peter Wilhelm von (1838), *Beiträge zur Geschichte der Provinz Oesel* (Riga: Götschel).

Freytagh-Loringhoven, Hans (1995), 'Kuidas Saaremaal üks tsaar rohkem oli', in *Saaremaa muuseum kaheaastaraamat* (Kuressaare: Saaremaa museum).

Hansar, Lilian (2007), '20. sajandi arhitektuur', in Jänes-Kapp et al. 2007: 867–903.

Heapost, Leiu (2002), 'Saarlaste antropoloogiast', in Kään et al. 2002: 577–594.

Hiie, Piret (2010), *1919. Aasta mäss Muhu ja Saaremaal* (Saaremaa muuseumi toimetised, 6; Kuressaare: Saaremaa muuseum).

Hint, Aadu (1959), 'Saateks', in Tooms 1959: 5–6.

Ilus, Ants, Kasepalu, Alfred, Pank, Maret & Rauniste, Vilma (2007), 'Põllumajandus', in Jänes-Kapp et al. 2007: 459–525.

Jakovlev, Tormis (2003), 'Läänetuule toodud – muidu saadud', in *Saaremaa muuseum. Kaheastaraamat 2001–2002* (Kuressaare: Saaremaa muuseum).

Jänes-Kapp, Kärt, Randma, Enn & Soosaar, Malle (2007) (eds.), *Saaremaa*, ii: *Ajalugu, majandus, kultuur* (Tallinn: Koolibri)

Juske, Anto (2006), *Sailing and the island of Saaremaa* (Tallinn: Juske).

Jõgi, Mall (2007), 'Saarlased väljaspool Eestit', in Jänes-Kapp et al. 2007: 1028–1063.

Kaitseliidu Saaremaa maleva arengulugu (1999) (Kuressaare: Kaitseliidu Saaremaa maleva ajalootoimkond).

Kreem, Robert (1984), *Vandega seotud: Mälestusi, tähelepanikuid, otsinguid noorusaastaist 1923–1948* (London, Ontario: Kreem).

Kriiska, Aivar (2007), 'Saaremaa kiviaeg', in Jänes-Kapp et al. 2007: 9–36.

Kään, Heino, Mardiste, Heino, Nelis, Riia & Pesti, Olavi (2002) (eds.), *Saaremaa*, i: *Loodus, aeg, inimene* (Tallinn: Eesti Entsüklopeediakirjastus).

Körber, Martin (1885), *Bausteine zu einer Geschichte Oesels: fünf Jahrhunderte, von der heidnichen Vorzeit bis zum Frieden von Nystädt* (Arensburg: Typographie des Arensburgher Wochenblattes).

Laur, Matti, (2007), 'Saaremaa Vene impeeriumi koosseisus Põhjasõjast 18. sajandi lõpuni', in Jänes-Kapp et al. 2007: 202–215.

Luce, Johan Wilhelm Ludvig von (1827), *Wahrheit und Muthmassung: Beytrag zur ältesten Geschichte der Insel Oesel* (Pernau: Marquardt).
Luha, Artur, Blumfeldt, Evald & Tammekann, August (1934) (eds.), *Saaremaa: Maateaduslik, majanduslik ja ajalooline kirjeldus* (Tartu: Eesti Kirjanduse Seltsi kirjastus).
Lust, Kersti (2007), 'Saaremaa Vene impeeriumi koosseisus 18. sajandi lõpust 1918. aastani', in Jänes-Kapp et al. 2007: 216–263.
Maiste, Juhan (1985), 'Saaremaa mõisaarhitektuur: Loona ja Kõljala', in Vello Tarmisto (ed.), *Kingissepa rajoonis* (Tallinn: Eesti NSV teaduste akadeemia).
— (2007), 'Saaremaa mõisaarhitektuur', in Jänes-Kapp et al. 2007: 826–846.
Maripuu, Meelis (2007), 'II maailmasõda ja Saaremaa', in Jänes-Kapp et al. 2007: 290–304.
Miller, Woldemar (1939), 'Saarlaste viimne viikingiretk Ojamaalle', *Meie Maa*, 1–8, 2–16 January.
Mägi, Marika (2007a), 'Saaremaa muinasaeg 1500 e.Kr–600 p.Kr', in Jänes-Kapp et al. 2007: 37–54.
— (2007b), 'Saaremaa muinasaeg 600–1227', in Jänes-Kapp et al. 2007: 55–76.
Öpik, Elina (2007), 'Rootsi aeg Saaremaal', in Jänes-Kapp et al 2007: 164–201.
Pao, Bruno (2003), 'Hiidlasi Kuressaares', *Saaremaa muuseum. Kaheaastaraamat 2001–2002* (Kuressaare: Saaremaa muuseum).
— (2007), 'Merendus', in Jänes-Kapp et al. 2007: 526–55.
Pedakmäe, Piia (2007), 'Taani aeg Saaremaal', in Jänes-Kapp et al. 2007: 143–63.
Pesti, Olavi (2003), 'Kuressaare kindluse hoonestus 18.–19. sajandil', *Saaremaa muuseum. Kaheaastaraamat 2001–2002* (Kuressaare: Saaremaa muuseum).
Polding, K. (1962) (ed.), *Saaremaa raamat* (Toronto: Saarlaste Ühing Torontos).
Prooses, Endel (1959a) '1905.–1907. a. sündmused Saaremaal', in Tooms 1959.
— (1959b) 'Aastad 1917–1918', in Tooms 1959: 56–60.
Püüa, Endel (2006), *Punane terror Saaremaal 1941. aastal* (Kuressaare: Saaremaa muuseum), pub. in English as Endel Püüa, *Red Terror on Saaremaa 1941*, trans. Kristiina Paul (Woodsville, NH: Lakeshore Press, 2013).
Püüa, Garel (2003), 'Metsavendlus Saaremaal pärast II maailmasõda', in *Saaremaa muuseum. Kaheaastaraamat 2001–2002* (Kuressaare: Saaremaa muuseum).
Riis, Vassili (1960a), *Vabaduse leek: dokumentaaljutustus 1919. aasta Saaremaa ülestõusust* (Tallinn: Eesti Riiklik Kirjastus).
Riis, Vassili (1960b), *Kolmandat teed ei ole* (Tallinn: Eesti Riiklik Kirjastus).
Rullingo, Ago (2001), *Muhumaa: loodus, aeg, inimene* (Tallinn: Eesti Entsüklopeediakirjastus).
Ränk, Gustav (1979), *Sest ümmargusest maailmast* (Stockholm: Välis-Eesti & EMP).
Saar, Ilvar & Tombak, Margit (2007), 'Saaremaa teise Nõukogude okupatsiooni ajal 1944–1991', in Jänes-Kapp et al. 2007: 345–88.

Saaremaa (1940-1941), Punavõimu tulek, selle likvideerimine (1995), i (Kuressaare: Kaitseliidu Saaremaa Malev).

Saaremaa (1940-1941), Punavõimu tulek, selle likvideerimine (1996a), ii (Kuressaare: Kaitseliidu Saaremaa Malev).

Saaremaa (1940-1941), Punavõimu tulek, selle likvideerimine (1996b), iii (Kuressaare: Kaitseliidu Saaremaa Malev).

Saaremaa muuseum. Kaheaastaraamat 1997-1998 (1999) (Kuressaare: Saaremaa Muuseum).

Saaremaa muuseum. Kaheaastaraamat 2005-2006 (2007) (Kuressaare: Saaremaa Muuseum).

Salumäe, Raul (2007), 'Inimese hullumeelse aja keerises', in *Saaremaa muuseum. Kaheaastaraamat 2005-2006* (Kuressaare: Saaremaa muuseum).

Tarmisto, Vello (1985) (ed.), *Kingissepa rajoonis* (Tallinn: Eesti NSV Teaduste Akadeemia).

— (1987) (ed.), *Valga rajoonis* (Tallinn: Eesti NSV Teaduste Akadeemia).

Tarvel, Enn (2007), 'Piiskopi- ja orduaeg 1227-1572', in Jänes-Kapp et al. 2007: 77-142.

Tasa, Ants (1959), 'Saaremaa Saksa fašistliku okupatsiooni aastail 1941-1944', in Tooms 1959: 96-104.

Tooms, Evald (1959) (ed.), *Saaremaa: Kogumik materjale* (Tallinn: Kommunismi Ehitaja).

Hiiumaa's history-writing

Saar, Endel (2004), *Hiiumaa – kiviajast tänapäevani* (Kärdla: Pakett).

Saard, Riho (2009), *Hiiumaa ja hiidlased: usutuultest tormatud ja piiratud: usu ja kiriku ajalugu Hiiumaal XIII sajandist Eesti taasiseseisvumiseni: vaimulikkond, pühakojad, kogudused, usuliikumised* (Tallinn: Saard).

Tiik, L. (1978), 'Mõnda Hiiumaa ajaloost', in Toomsalu 1978.

Toomsalu, Harald (1978) (ed.), *Hiiumaast ja Hiidlastest* (Tallinn: Perioodika).

Vrager, Elmer (1971), *Hiiumaa ja hiidlased: Ülevaade saarest ja rahvast* (Toronto: Estoprint).

Other works cited

Aitsam, Mihkel (2009), *Hiiu lossist – Siberisse: ajalooline romaan legendaarseist Hiiu mereröövleist* (Tartu: Ilmamaa) (first pub. 1937, Tallinn: Tallinna Eesti Kirjastus-Ühisus).

Eellend, Johan (2004), 'A History that Needs to Be Written', in Egle Rindzeviciute, (ed.), *Contemporary Change in Estonia* (Baltic and East European Studies, 4; Huddinge: Södertörns högskola).

Hroch, Miroslav (1985), *Social preconditions of national revival in Europe* (Cambridge: CUP).

Hiiu County, <http://www.hiiumaa.ee/tuletorn/english.php?id=3>, 22 August 2012.
Jansson, Torkel (2000), 'Estlandssvenskhet före estlandssvenskheten. Kustbornas identifikation före nationalmedvetandets födelse', in Torkel Jansson & Torbjörn Eng (eds.), *Stat – kyrka – samhälle. Den stormaktstida samhällsordningen i Sverige och Östersjöprovinserna* (Stockholm: Stockholm University, Department of Baltic Studies).
Jansson, Tove (1966), *Moominpappa at Sea* (London: Ernest Benn).
Kivimäe, Jüri (1999), 'Re-writing Estonian history?', in Michael Branch (ed.), *National history and identity. Approaches to the Writing of National History in the North-East Baltic Region Nineteenth and Twentieth Centuries* (Studia Fennica Ethnologica, 6; Helsinki: Finnish Literature Society).
Klein, Ernst (1924), *Runö. Folklivet i ett gammalsvenskt samhälle* (Uppsala: Lindblad).
Kriiska, Aivar (2001), *Stone age settlement and economic processes in the Estonian coastal area and islands* (Helsinki: Helsigin yliopisto, kulttuurien tutkimuksen laitos).
MacFarlane, John M. (2011), 'Rear-Admiral Sir Johan Pitka – An Unlikely British Columbian Who Founded the Estonian Navy', *Nauticapedia.ca*, 2012. <http://nauticapedia.ca/Articles/Admiral_Pitka.php>, 2 August 2012.
Maaring, E (1968), *Viljandi rajoonis: kodu-uurijate seminar-kokkutulek 25.–28. juuni 1968* (Tallinn: Eesti NSV teaduste akadeemia).
Parbus, Ülo (2007), 'Johann von Luce ja tema kaaslaste jälgi meie kultuuriloos', in *Saaremaa muuseum. Kaheaastaraamat 2005–2006* (Kuressaare: Saaremaa muuseum).
Pesti, Olavi (1995), 'Saaremaa muuseum 1920.–1930. aastail', in *Saaremaa muuseum. Kaheaastaraamat 1993–1994* (Kuressaare: Saaremaa muuseum).
Postimees, <http://www.postimees.ee/leht/96/05/04/krimi.htm>, 23 August 2012.
Püüa, Endel (1995), 'Saaremaa Uurimise Selts kui Saaremaa muuseumi rajaja', in *Saaremaa muuseum. Kaheaastaraamat 1993–1994* (Kuressaare: Saaremaa muuseum).
Raadik-Cottrell, Jaana (2010), *Cultural Memory and Place Identity: Creating Place Experience* (Fort Collins: Colorado State University).
Rein, Kaarina (2007), 'Johann Wilhelm Ludvig Luce üliõpilasaastad 18. sajandi Saksamaal', in *Saaremaa muuseum. Kaheaastaraamat 2005–2006* (Kuressaare: Saaremaa muuseum).
Russwurm, Carl (1855), *Eibofolke, oder die Schweden an den Küsten Ehstlands und auf Runö: Eine historisch-etnograpische von der Kaiserlichen Akademie der Wissenschaften zu St. Petersburg mit einem demidowschen Preise gekrönte Untersuchung*, i (Reval: Fleischer).
Saarlane, <http://saarlane.ca/sut.htm> 25 April 2012.
Saaremaa ülestous 1919 (1989) (Tallinn: Eesti raamat).

Saks, Edgar (1960), *Studies in the ur-European history*, i: Aesti: an analysis of an ancient European civilization (Montreal: Vôitleja).
— (1966), *Studies in the ur-European history*, ii: *Esto-Europa: a treatise on the Finno-Ugric primary civilization in Europe* (Montreal: Vôitleja).
Sooväli, Helen (2004), *Saaremaa waltz: Landscape imagery of Saaremaa Island in the twentieth century* (Tartu: TUP).
Steffensson, Jakob (1972), *Runöborna och deras invandring till Sverige* (Uppsala: Verdandi).
— (1976),' *Livet på Runö: en berättelse om hur 300 människor levde på den lilla svenskön Runö i Rigaviken från 1920-talet fram till andra världskriget* (Stockholm: LT).
Uustalu, Evald (1952), *The history of Estonian people* (London: Boreas).
Vinkel, Aarne (1994), *Martin Körber: elutee ja -töö* (Tallinn: Eesti Teaduste Akadeemia Underi ja Tuglase Kirjanduskeskus).
Vunk, Aldur (2010) (ed), *Pärnumaa*, ii: *Loodus, Aeg, Inimene* (Tallinn: Eesti Entsüklopeediakirjastus).
Zetterberg, Seppo (1984), 'Die finnish-estrischen Unionspläne 1917–1919', in *Jahrbücher für Geschichte Osteuropas*, 32: 517–54.

Unpublished works

Email from Geltmar von Buxhoevden, 20 October 2009.
Family tree attached to email from Geltmar von Buxhoevden, 22 September 2009 (Geltmar von Buxhoeveden manages the family history website <buxhoeveden.net>.)

Bornholmian history-writing

Janne Holmén

Bornholm is set apart from the other islands in this research project by its location. Compared to its proximity to foreign nations, Bornholm is located relatively far from its mother country: the island is situated 135 km from the closest Danish shore, with Sweden (35 km), Germany (90 km), and Poland (95 km) all within closer range. The island Bornholm is the last remnant of what was once Eastern Denmark, since Skåne, Halland, and Blekinge were ceded to Sweden in the mid seventeenth century. At that point, the areas with which Bornholm had the closest historical and cultural ties became part of another realm. The case of Bornholm offers a possibility to study how the identity of an island is affected by the fact that it has been distanced from its 'mainland',[1] with several other nations nearby. Bornholm was a Danish *amt* until 1 January 2007, when it became part of Region Hovedstaden. This makes Bornholm the only island in this study which does not currently constitute a top-level administrative unit. Region Hovedstaden now handles issues such as health care, while Bornholm's *regionskommune* still determines regional economic development, in part by managing structural funds granted by the European Union.

Bornholm is mentioned as an independent kingdom in sources from the tenth century, but is believed to have been integrated into the Danish kingdom soon thereafter. During the Middle Ages the island was mainly controlled by the powerful archbishops of Lund in Skåne. In 1525 the island was leased to Lübeck for 50 years. Bornholm was handed over to Sweden at the Peace of Brømsebro in 1658, but the inhabitants brought their island back to Denmark after a rebellion later the same year. As a

---

[1] Bearing in mind that central Denmark also consists of islands. The Bornholmians call the rest of Denmark 'ovre' ('over there').

reward for the uprising the Bornholmians gained a number of privileges, which gave the island an independent character. As Denmark was transformed from a conglomerate state to a homogenous nation-state, the last privileges were removed in the late nineteenth century. Since Skåne remained in Swedish hands when the Bornholmians rebelled against their new masters in 1658, this was also the year when Bornholm became a distant eastern outpost of the Danish kingdom. The geographical separation from the rest of the country was to have important historical repercussions. In 1940 Denmark and Bornholm were invaded by Germany. However, contrary to the rest of the country Bornholm did towards the end of the war found itself part of the Eastern Front and was occupied by Soviet forces from 9 May 1945 to 5 April 1946.

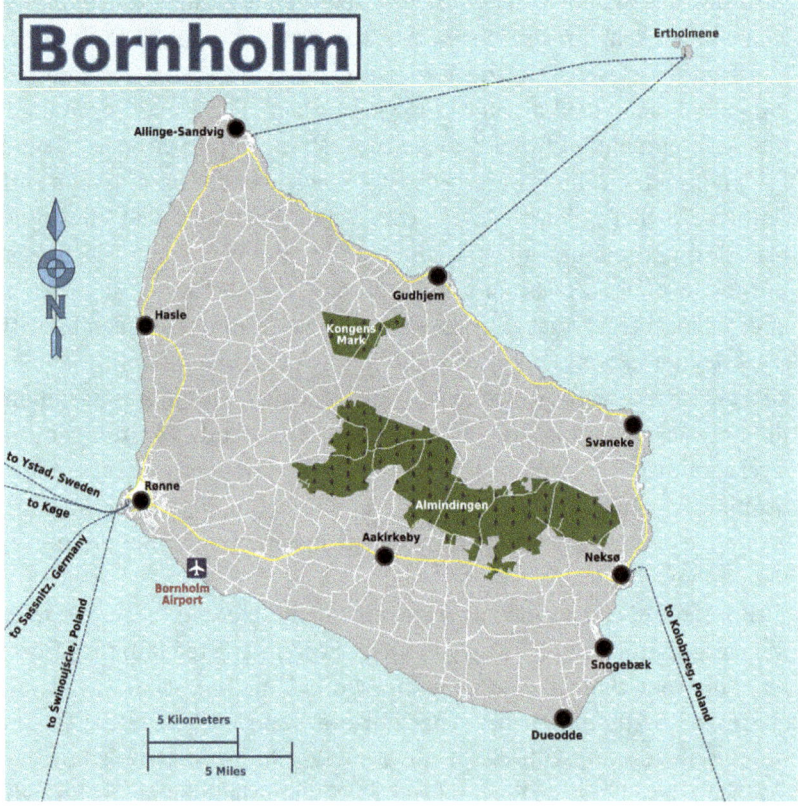

Source: Wikimedia Commons.

Uniquely among Baltic islands, Bornholm in the Middle Ages already had five urban centres with city rights: Rønne, Nexø, Aakirkeby, Hasle, and Svaneke. On 1 January 2009 Rønne had around 14,000 inhabitants and Nexø 3,769.[2] Bornholm has a population of 41,800 people. Less than a hundred of them live on the small Ertholmene (Christiansø and Fredriksø); the rest are residents on the main island.[3] Ertholmene, which was fortified in the late seventeenth century, is governed directly by the ministry of defence and is not administratively connected to Bornholm. Its lack of secondary islands makes Bornholm the most mono-insular of the islands in this investigation.

Earlier research on Bornholmian history-writing

Although a lot has been written about Bornholm's history, this regional history-writing has not been the object of much research. The few existing historiographical investigations are to a large extent focused on the depiction of the uprising in 1658, and have mainly been written by regional historians who have had an interest in how their predecessors have interpreted the event.

At the 350th anniversary in 2008, Ebbe Gert Rasmussen published an article outlining how views of the uprising had developed during the period. Rasmussen mentioned many examples of Bornholmians who in the late seventeenth century wrote their memories of the uprising, in diaries or in the margins of bibles and other books. Most prominent was Rasmus Pedersen Ravn's *Borringholms Krønike*, which was forgotten and not published until 1926, and Jens Pedersen Koefoed's 'Relation', which is only known in copies made by his family. In Rasmussen's view, Ravn's work is permeated by a strongly anti-Swedish sentiment. Koefoed's text was treasured by the circle around the Koefoed family. Rasmussen believes that the folk song *Printzensköldvisen*, which described the uprising, was also created in this environment of wealthy peasants and officers in around 1700.[4]

Rasmussen is of the opinion that the Swedish and Danish history writers of the eighteenth-century Enlightenment, such as Ludvig Holberg

---

[2] Statistics Denmark, Population, 1 January, by urban areas.
[3] Statistics Denmark, Population per Island, 1 January 2011.
[4] Rasmussen 2008b, 10.

and Sven Lagerbring, managed to break free of the bias in favour of their own realms that their predecessors had displayed in their descriptions of the uprising. The National Romanticism of the early nineteenth century was in his opinion a step backwards, and he described the Bornholmian Peder Nikolai Skougaard's *Bornholms saga* from 1834 as the absolute low-water mark. Finn Jacobsen, however, does describe Skougaard as a historian who evaluated everything realistically, and claims that he was definitely not a man given to Romanticism—this verdict is however based on his *Beskrivelse over Bornholm* from 1804.[5]

In the 1890s two writers of Bornholmian descent debated the uprising of 1658 in the Danish *Historisk tidsskrift*. The Bornholmian doctor M. K. Zahrtmann claimed that the traditional idea that Jens Koefoed was the leader of the uprising was wrong, and that the priest Paul Ancher was its true leader. G. L. Grove, a descendant of Koefoed's, claimed that this rewriting of history was based on scarce evidence—a list of names—and that all other evidence supported the old view. Rasmussen is supportive of Grove's view, and claims that it was characteristic of Zahrtmann to never be convinced by criticism. Rasmussen is also of the opinion that this locked battle over a detail delayed the essential discussion about the character of Swedish rule and the uprising's role in the context of general Danish history.[6]

Rasmussen stresses that while the uprising had been of interest to many Danish and Swedish scholars in the eighteenth and nineteenth centuries, in the twentieth century the subject was taken over by Bornholmians. He believes that the engineer Jørn Klindt-Jensen, author of a book about the uprising at its 300th jubilee in 1958, was affected by his own experiences in the resistance movement against the Germans during the Second World War. Thus Klindt-Jensen supposed that Bornholmian resistance in 1658 had been a reaction to Swedish oppression, parallel to the Danish reaction to the German occupation in 1940–5, thereby downplaying the importance of the Danish king's encouragement of the rebellion.[7]

Rasmussen considers his own most important contribution to the understanding of the uprising to be that it was not a spontaneous revolt

---

[5] Jacobsen 1975, 9; Rasmussen 2008b, 17.
[6] Rasmussen 2008b, 25.
[7] Rasmussen 2008b, 26, 28.

caused by Swedish oppression, but a result of the Danish king's intervention.[8]

The Second World War is one of the most popular subjects of Bornholmian history-writing, but it has not been the object of historiographical research. Until recently, not even the writers of the island's wartime history had reflected upon how their object of research had been portrayed by their predecessors. However, in his book *Bornholm besat* (2012), the journalist Jesper Gaarskjær argues that earlier history-writing failed to mention the many abuses committed by Soviet troops during their occupation of Bornholm in May 1945 to April 1946. He believes that this might have been a consequence of the cold war, when Danish authorities were careful not to anger Moscow. The Russians were praised for their good conduct in the Bornholmian and Danish media during the occupation, and this continued in later history-writing. Gaarskjær does not differentiate between regionally produced history-writing and other writings about Bornholm. He does however mention that professor Bent Jensen's *Den lange befrielse* was an exception, because it nuanced the old picture of the Soviets' perfect conduct.[9]

Gaarskjær is also of the opinion that the history-writing, which has explained the political processes behind the Soviet bombings and occupation of Bornholm, has helped heal the Bornholmians' wounds. Based on the interviews he made for his book, Gaarskjær believes it is nowadays difficult to find Bornholmians who still bear a grudge against the Danish government and the Danish people who celebrated the end of the war while the Bornholmians were bombed, at least among the younger generation. There is still a feeling that Copenhagen treats the island with indifference, but according to Gaarskjær this is related to recent issues such as unemployment, ferry traffic, and depopulation, not to events during the Soviet occupation.[10]

A small number of investigations have been done into Bornholmian regional identity. In the article 'Bornholmian islanders and their cultural background', Adam Pomieciński claims that despite intense feelings of regional and national separateness, the Bornholmians have been open to

---

[8] Rasmussen 2008b, 30 ff.
[9] Gaarskjær 2012, 285 ff.; Jensen 1996.
[10] Gaarskjær 2012, 322.

immigrants from outside Denmark. He concludes that newcomers are quickly assimilated in the local community.[11]

Marianne Mortensen has used interviews and locally produced tourist information to study the regional dialect's importance for the Bornholmian identity. Her conclusion is that there is a Bornholmian regional patriotism, but that the dialect does not play a positive part in it. On the contrary, many Bornholmians at times feel ashamed of their dialect. She refers to Tore Kristiansen, who has claimed that this is true of Danish regional identities in general. Kristiansen contrasts this to Norway, where dialects form an essential part of regional identity.[12]

Thus neither Bornholmian history-writing nor Bornholmian identity has been the object of detailed research. Furthermore, there is virtually no research which links Bornholmian identity and history-writing. Based on such research as does exist, however, it seems likely that there is a sense of regional identity on the island, and that the events in 1658 and during the Second World War are important in that respect.

In the absence of earlier research on the development of Bornholmian identity, a brief look at what has been written about Faroese identity might be justified. Hans Jacob Debes, professor of history at the University of the Faroe Islands, has claimed that the islands' geographical location and small size had to produce a high degree of cultural homogeneity. Debes dismissed the idea that national identity is invented or imagined; in a line of reasoning close to Anthony D. Smith's he claimed that 'Being of common origin, history, language, religion, and culture it would have been historically illogical if the Faroese were to have developed into any group but a nation'.[13] Debes's essentialist interpretation of Smith's theory is problematized by the Bornholmian example, however. In fact, most of the preconditions for nationalism which he identifies on the Faroe islands were also present on Bornholm, and still the islands developed in different directions in the late nineteenth century, the Faroe Islands towards national self-awareness and Bornholm towards deeper integration into Denmark.

---

[11] Pomieciński 2005.
[12] Mortensen 2011, 24, 31; Kristiansen 2009, 150–1, 161.
[13] Debes 1995, 64.

Methods and sources

Our studies of Gotlandic and Ålandic history-writing were facilitated by the Gotlandica and Alandica collections of regional books. Although the library in Rønne has a *lokalsamling* (local collection), it is not searchable as a separate category in the library catalogue. To find the relevant books, I have therefore combined the national (bibliotek.dk) and Bornholmian (bibliotek.brk.dk) library catalogues in order to attain as full coverage as possible. In the Danish national bibliography only books published after 2004 are searchable online. However, since the Royal Library in Copenhagen is a library of record, all entries in the bibliography since 1841 can also be found in the online catalogue of the Danish libraries, bibliotek.dk.[14] This catalogue has been the primary tool for identifying the books that can be considered part of Bornholm regional history-writing. Additional help has been found in the anthology *Bogen om Bornholm* from 1957, which contains a bibliography of works written about the island to date.[15]

Most works about Bornholm's history have been produced by writers or institutions from the island. The few exceptions are generally concerned with the two major events in Bornholm's history: the uprising in 1658 and the Second World War. One example of a borderline case is Bent Jensen's book about the Soviet bombings and occupation of Bornholm in 1945–6, which was published simultaneously by Odense University Press and in the series *Bornholmske samlinger*. Jensen was encouraged by Bornholmians to write the book, but it can mainly be considered a product of his interest in Danish–Soviet relations rather than in Bornholmian regional history.[16]

There is also a large category of books, partially aimed at tourists, describing the nature, society, and history of Bornholm. Of the islands studied in this research project, the Bornholmian production of these books is second only Gotland's. Not all of these books have been studied, but I have chosen Hansaage Bøggild's *Gyldendals bog om Bornholm* to represent this category of publications.

---

[14] The Royal Library, Denmark, <http://www.kb.dk/da/kb/service/nationalbibliografi/danskbogfortegnelse.html>, accessed 21 May 2013.
[15] Nielsen & Sørensen 1957, 640 ff.
[16] Jensen 1996, 8–9.

Authors and funders

After the Bornholmian uprising against the Swedes in 1658, the islanders sharpened their quills, and wrote what can be described as the first examples of Bornholmian regional history-writing. The most serious attempt was made by Rasmus Pedersen Ravn (1602-1677), who was a parish clerk in Aakirkeby on Bornholm at the time of the uprising. Ravn was born in Copenhagen, but moved to Bornholm as a teacher at the age of 25. The manuscript, *Borringholms krønike*, was sent to Christian V in 1671 as a plea for help for the impoverished island, but Ravn also had academic ambitions. By way of an introduction to his account of the uprising he included a description of the island's history from Noah's days until his own, with ample room for the Cimbrian and Gothic tribes. Ravn hoped that the king would publish his manuscript, but that never happened and the original manuscript was lost. *Borringholms krønike* did survive in several transcripts, however. In 1926 a commented edition of Ravn's manuscript was published by Bornholms Historiske Samfund.[17]

In 1804, Peter Nikolai Skougaard (later Peder Nikolaj Skovgaard, 1783-1838), a 21-year-old Bornholmian student in Copenhagen, published his book *Beskrivelse over Bornholm: 1. del*. Skougaard was sentenced to 14 days on bread and water because the book had denigrated Bornholm's defences and its system of taxation, as well as Denmark's constitution and past Danish kings, primarily Frederik III. According to a regulation from 1799, all writers who abused the freedom of press became subject to life-long censorship. This meant that Skougaard abandoned his studies and never published the second part of his work, which was intended to contain more about the island's history.[18]

His biographer, Christian Stub-Jørgensen, claims that Skougaard's direct, ironic criticism of authorities was typical for the way Bornholmians expressed themselves at the time. Skougaard's youth contributed to the fact that he did not know the limits of what was possible to print.[19]

Bornholm's *amtmand* (county governor) in 1866-1871, Emil Vedel (1824-1909) had a passion for archaeology, and in 1886 he published the work *Bornholms oldtidsminder og oldsager* about the island's prehistory. His assistant, the teacher Johan Andreas Jörgensen (1840-1908), was to

---

[17] Zahrtmann 1926, 1 ff.; Knudsen 1926, xii-xiii.
[18] Jacobsen 1975, 12 ff.
[19] Stub-Jørgensen 1958, 14, 36-7.

have a more profound influence upon Bornholmian history-writing. Jørgensen originated from Southern Jutland where he worked as a teacher until the Second Schleswig War in 1864, when he was fired by the Prussian authorities which took control over the province. Jørgensen worked on Bornholm's history through archaeological excavations, the foundation of a museum in 1893, and the publication of the first comprehensive work on the island's history in 1900–1901.[20]

At the turn of the last century a series of regional historical associations were formed in Denmark, and in 1905 Bornholm saw the birth of Bornholms Historiske Samfund. Since 1906 the association has published the yearly periodical *Bornholmske samlinger*.

The doctor Marius Koefoed Zahrtmann (1861–1940) was a native Bornholmian who had a deep interest in the island's past. He investigated a wide range of questions related to Bornholm's history, and toward the end of his life he collected his findings in the two-volume *Borringholmerens historiebog*. He was described by the later Bornholmian history writer Jørn Klindt-Jensen as a feisty and stubborn Bornholmian who raged like a maniac if any *førter* (Danish non-Bornholmian) dared question his theories.[21] Zahrtmann also directed heavy criticism against Bornholmians who published opinions which differed from his, which most likely reduced others' interest in voicing their opinion.[22]

In 1957 the anthology *Bogen om Bornholm* was published by Danskerens forlag, which also published similar books about two other geographically distinct Danish regions of similar size, the island of Als south-east of Jutland and the Himmerland peninsula, which is bounded by the Limfjord, the Mariager Fjord, and the Kattegatt. Like Bornholm, these regions are also renowned for their history: Himmerland has been suggested to have been the home of the Cimbrians, and Als has a high concentration of megalithic tombs.[23] Rather than attempting a complete coverage of Denmark, Danskerens forlag was apparently aiming at areas with a strong regional identity—and thereby a strong market for books on regional history.

Like the anthologies which have been so prominent in Saaremaa's history-writing, Bornholm's was a mix of articles on geography, biology

---

[20] Vensild 1993, 7 ff.
[21] Zahrtmann 1934; Zahrtmann 1935; Klindt Jensen 1957b, 273.
[22] Rasmussen 2008b, 26.
[23] Huhle 1956; Huhle 1958.

and—predominantly—history. One of the contributors to the anthology was the Bornholmian engineer Jørn Klindt-Jensen (1921–2005), who had a background in the island's resistance movement during the Second World War. His main area of interest was the uprising in 1658. To mark the 300th anniversary of the event, Klindt-Jensen published a series of chronicles about it in the local newspaper, *Bornholms Tidende*; the chronicles were anthologized the same year as *Disse danske*.[24]

The uprising in 1658 is also the main focus of Ebbe Gert Rasmussen's (1939-) writings. Rasmussen, a teacher at Bornholm Gymnasium, made an academic career of his interest and achieved a doctoral degree at Copenhagen University in 1985, based on his book *Dette gavebrev*, which had been published in *Bornholmske Samlinger* in 1982–3.[25]

After his retirement, Rasmussen wrote a book which combined the uprising on Bornholm in December 1658 with the one which broke out in Skåne shortly afterwards. The book was published by TV2/Bornholm, which also produced the documentary film that accompanied the book on DVD.[26]

Recent years have seen other attempts at writing a combined history of Skåne and Bornholm. In 1995 the director of Bornholms Museum Ann-Vibeke Knudsen together with the Swede Håkan Nilsson published *På hat med Skåne og Bornholm/På hatt med Bornholm och Skåne: Bornholmernes Hovedtöjer, Skåningarnas huvudbonader*. The book was an outcome of the Nordic Council's regional cooperation project 'Samarbetet Bornholm–Sydöstra Skåne'.

Contrary to the case on Åland, Saaremaa, and Gotland, no comprehensive overview of Bornholm's history has been published recently Zahrtmann's work from 1934–5 is the latest attempt. This means that the island's general development in the twentieth century is poorly covered. Most books published about Bornholm in the twentieth century focus on the Second World War. For example, Bornholms Historiske Samfund commissioned the Danish resistance fighter and naval historian Jørgen Barfod, director of Frihedsmuseet (the Museum of Danish Resistance) to write the history of Bornholm's resistance movement. The result was the book *Et centrum i periferien* which was published in 1976.

---

[24] Rasmussen 2008b, 27.
[25] Rasmussen 2008b p.30.
[26] Rasmussen 2008b.

In the 2000s, Erling Haagensen, a former journalist at Bornholm's local television station, wrote several books that linked the island's medieval history to the crusades and the Knight Templars. Riding on the strong, consistent interest for the Knight Templars which was further increased by the 2003 novel *The Da Vinci code*, the books were published by Danish publishers aiming at a wider audience than merely the Bornholmian.

Another Bornholmian journalist, Hansaage Bøggild, wrote a general overview of the island's nature, society, and history, which was published by Gyldendals forlag in 2004 as *Gyldendals bog om Bornholm*. Many books by the publisher have titles beginning with *Gyldendals bog om... Gyldendals bog om Grønland*[27] is the only other one which describes a region. Bøggild's book, however, an updated version of *Gyldendals egnsbeskrivelse* from 1969, which was part of a series covering the entire Denmark.[28]

Most Bornholmian history writers have published their books on the island. Several monographs have been published in the series *Bornholmske samlinger*, although most volumes consist of shorter articles. Since the beginning of the 1990s, Bornholm Museum has been a prolific publisher of works on aspects of the island's history. Sparekassen Bornholms fond which was established in 1990, has helped finance the publication of many recent books. *Østersøen gav*, a book about Bornholmian fishing published in 1993, was partially financed by the regional fishing industry.[29]

In the age of the Xerox machine, lack of funding and a publisher did not prevent enthusiasts from publishing themselves. The Bornholmian mason Tonny Pedersen Borrinjaland has duplicated booklets which are available at branches of the Bornholmian library. Pedersen Borrinjaland's writings give a strongly nationalist view of Bornholmian history, describing the islanders as a separate people. In 2011 he also published a translation of the New Testament into Bornholmian, which at 64 pages cannot yet be considered complete.[30] However, the attempt suggests an awareness of the importance bible translations have had in elevating vernaculars the status of national languages rather than local dialects.

---

[27] Gynther & Møller 1999.
[28] Rying 1969.
[29] Sparekassen Bornholms Fond, <http://sbfonden.dk/index.htm>, 23 January 2013; Rasmussen 1993, 5.
[30] Pedersen Borrinjaland 1982, 2004, 2011.

The character of the Bornholmians

Although regional history-writing emphasizes the Bornholmians' Danish patriotism, the islanders' character is described in terms of what differentiates them from other Danes. These differences are explained by the island's location, nature, and history.

Independence, liberty, and patriotism

The most ambitious attempt to describe the Bornholmians' national character has been made by the author and poet Christian Stubb-Jørgensen in *Bogen om Bornholm* (1957). Although he admitted that national characters to a large extent are constructions, he attempted to describe the Bornholmians by focusing on a number of characteristic individuals. Stubb-Jørgensen claimed that because of foreign influences, the pure Bornholmian had to be found in history. The main traits that he found were a spirit of independence, a suspicion of authority, conservatism, and a democratic trait which meant that everyone was respected according to his abilities.[31] These characteristics are also described by several other authors.

The book *Beskrivelse over Bornholm*, which Peder Nikolai Skovgaard published as a student in 1804, was full of criticism of contemporary Denmark's autocratic form of government. By contrast, he praised the golden, democratic times when peasants approved or dismissed the kings' decisions at the thing. The thing stones were memories of a time when peasants were seen as humans, not as toys or pets to be leased, pawned, or given away to bishops, Lübeckers or court favourites. He feared that the days of Nordic freedom would never return.[32] In the short term his pessimism was justified, since he was sent to jail as a consequence of the criticism he aired in the book. The mention of past, democratic times featured in the accusations against Skougaard. It should be remembered that Skougaard saw freedom as an ancient Nordic trait, not something specifically Bornholmian.

According to the teacher Johan Andreas Jørgensen, the Bornholmians were independent, headstrong, and not as easy to rule as people in other provinces. He explained this by the island's peculiar lack of nobility and

---

[31] Stub-Jørgensen 1957, 490–1, 492, 494–5, 507.
[32] Skougaard 1804, 318–19.

manors, but also by the many insults the islanders had suffered at the hands of bad officials. The doctor Marius Koefoed Zahrtmann claimed that their character, boldness, and resistance towards oppression were moulded by the nature of their island.[33]

Several authors mention the late ninth-century sources which claimed that the island was then an independent kingdom. The Bornholmians have preferred to govern themselves since the ancient days when they had their own king, according to Zahrtmann. As examples of the Bornholmians' independent mind-set he mentioned the nineteenth-century academic and politician Madvig who never became a lackey of any party, and the artillerist Johan Ancher—not at all a strict military person, but still a hero from the Second Schleswig War.[34]

Zahrtmann claimed that the Bornholmians' yearning for independence made them embrace religious sectarianism. Their sound reason, however, kept them away from the complacent, contemptible sectarian divisions which were common elsewhere. Less than 20 pages later in the same book, though, he stated that there was an unreasonable multitude of sects on Bornholm in the nineteenth century, more than elsewhere in Denmark, and that their divisions were contrary to the teachings of the bible. Jørgensen was of the opinion that isolated islands and remote areas were a fertile ground for strong religious movements, as was still visible on Bornholm in his days.[35]

Matching the descriptions of the Bornholmians' independence, there are several accounts of their Danish patriotism. The naval and resistance historian Jørgen Barfod claims that the island's isolated position in the Baltic, at the limit of the Nordic cultural sphere, never led to political separatism. Contrary to what has been the case in other border areas, its inhabitants were never shaken in their cultural and national attitudes. The journalist Hansaage Bøggild claimed in 2004 that despite its proximity to Sweden, Bornholm is the most Danish of all Danish areas; the only one which has fought its way back to Denmark from under Swedish fist.[36] These writers thus stress that Bornholm is utterly Danish *despite* its

---

[33] Jørgensen 1901, 98–9; Zahrtmann 1935, 100.
[34] Jørgensen 1900, 37–8; Halskov Hansen 2007, 60; Bøggild 2004, 44; Zahrtmann 1935, 307.
[35] Jørgensen 1901, 306; Zahrtmann 1935, 149–50, 167.
[36] Barfod 1976, 20; Bøggild 204, 18.

location, indirectly suggesting that its geographic position might indicate the contrary.

The Bornholmian spirit of independence which several authors identify can thus not be seen as political separatism. The attitude they describe is similar to the early nineteenth-century writer Baron Peter Wilhelm von Buxhöwden on Saaremaa: in exchange for their patriotism, the Bornholmians wanted to be left in control of their own island, undisturbed by the central authorities.

Several authors also quote the Swedish commander Printzenskiöld's characterization of the Bornholmians in 1658: they were uneducated, uncultivated, and obstinate 'as all islanders in general are supposed to be'. Jørgensen and Rasmussen believe this was only a first impression and that the Swedish commander later changed his opinion. Zahrtmann claimed that Printzenskiöld's opinion was influenced by the local priests: since the Bornholmians had attempted to withhold what lawfully belonged to the clergy they had become almost open enemies. The only writer who connected Printzenskiöld's initial verdict with the uprising was Klindt-Jensen. He contrasted it to two pages of praise of the islanders by the seventeenth-century teacher and parish clerk Rasmus Ravn, who among other things stressed the Bornholmians' quickness to learn. Klindt-Jensen believed that the discrepancy between Printzenskiöld's and Ravn's opinions illustrates why a conflict broke out between the islanders and the governor in 1658. This is compatible with Klindt-Jensen's view of the uprising as an inevitable national struggle between Danes and Swedes. The Bornholmian historian Ebbe Gert Rasmussen, who wrote his doctoral dissertation about the uprising and has compared it to the almost simultaneous uprising in Skåne, notes that Printzenskiöld's description of the Bornholmians is very similar to the description of the inhabitants of Skåne only nine days earlier by Ebbe Ulfeldt, a Danish aristocrat who had entered Swedish service.[37] The negative characterization of the Bornholmians is thus seen as yet another link connecting them to their Skåne peers.

Differences and divisions within Bornholm

The question of whether there was and is a particularly Bornholmian character is complicated by the existence of divisions and differences on the

---

[37] Jørgensen 1900, 181; Zahrtmann 1934, 280; Klindt-Jensen 1958, 30, 37 ff.; Rasmussen 2000, 40 ('som alle øboer i all almindelighed holdes for at være'), 2008a, 37.

island. Zahrtmann was of the opinion that the islanders' independent mind and aversion to uniformity made it difficult to find any common character. Since they had a more versatile education than other Danes their character was also more diverse. On top of that, there were also differences in character between peasants from different parts of the island.[38]

According to Zahrtmann, the old misconception that two distinct peoples lived on Bornholm was based on the coexistence of dolichocephalic and brachiocephalic individuals in Scandinavia since the Stone Age. In 1804 Skougaard believed that the northern part of the island was populated by a 'headstrong', blue-eyed, and blond people, while the southerners were brown-eyed, black-haired, and 'hasty', more Slavic than 'Gothic'. The difference, according to Skougaard, was so clear that you could deduct a person's place of birth from his physical features. Zahrtmann believed that Skougaard's observation was based on the fact that contacts between the north and south of the island were still weak in around 1800.[39] These observations are not compatible with the idea that the seclusion of an island will automatically impose a common identity upon its inhabitants. In the case of Bornholm, it seems as if the rugged and largely uninhabited interior of the island slowed the formation of a common identity well into the nineteenth century.

Bornholm's five towns also had their share of divisions. The Bornholmian towns differed from towns in the rest of Denmark in their lack of most aspects of communal administration, according to Thorvald Sørensen. In his essay in *Bogen om Bornholm* he claimed that the island's towns were controlled by a small number of merchant and skipper families. Zahrtmann wrote that the island in 1600 had 10,000 inhabitants and five towns. Royal commissions and kings suggested in the early seventeenth century that some of the towns should be abandoned, but this was never carried through. Jørgensen described how tensions between the towns surfaced when Sweden acquired Bornholm in 1658: burghers from the largest towns, Rønne and Nexø, tried to convince governor Printzenskiöld that a planned naval harbour should be placed in their town, and the delegation from Rønne even suggested that the three smaller towns should be transformed into fishing villages. Rasmussen claims that this self-sufficient attitude can be discerned in Rønne still today, as can Nexø's propensity to assert itself. In Rasmussen's view all of this is still very

---

[38] Zahrtmann 1935, 305.
[39] Zahrtmann 1934, 20 ('sindige', 'ilsindede'); Skougaard 1804, 77–8.

Bornholmian, and Jørn Klindt-Jensen considered it to be part of an ancient struggle between Rønne and Nexø.[40]

Tensions between peasants and townspeople are rarely mentioned in Bornholmian history-writing. Zahrtmann indeed claimed that there was no sharp division between town and country. A good Bornholmian should be a sailor, townsman, and peasant. Every house in town had two gates: through one the harvest from the sea arrived and through the other the harvest from the countryside. In her essay about traditional dress in *Bogen om Bornholm* the curator at the National Museum in Copenhagen, Ellen Andersen, quoted a Danish prince who in 1824 had observed that bourgeois and peasant daughters on Bornholm wore the same headgear. According to Andersen this was typical for Bornholm, which lacked the sharp division between town and country which existed in the rest of Denmark. Klindt-Jensen, however, stressed that the towns were more independent in the seventeenth century than later, and he suggests that the solidarity between town and countryside was weak. The towns had their own companies for defence, and did not form part of the militia. They only defended themselves and sometimes neighbouring towns: when Nexø was attacked by the Swedes in 1645 the town of Svaneke–Allinge[41] sent immediate help, while the militia from the countryside lingered.[42]

The early nineteenth-century scholar Skougaard did notice a rift between two categories of peasants in his time. Although all owned their own lands, the peasants near the beaches were rich while the ones in the high, heather-covered inland were poor. Skougaard believed that the rich peasants had bribed the officials who had set the taxation rates, at the expense of the poorer peasants. In *Bogen om Bornholm* the author and poet Christian Stub-Jørgensen claimed that the difference between rich and poor peasants was articulated most in the southern part of the island, whereas the peasants in the north were more evenly poor. However, even

---

[40] Jørgensen 1900, 180; Zahrtmann 1934, 204–205; Sørensen 1957, 573; Klindt-Jensen 1958, 50; Rasmussen 2000, 41.

[41] Svaneke and Allinge were originally two fishing villages that had grown together; though the conurbation never received formal rights as a *købstad* (borough), it had gained some privileges in the seventeenth century and effectively functioned as a town (Dansk center for byhistorie, <http://dendigitalebyport.byhistorie.dk/koebstaeder/by.aspx?KoebstadID=49/>).

[42] Zahrtmann 1934, 204; Andersen 1957, 202; Klindt-Jensen 1958, 34.

the poorest peasants considered it a matter of honour to be able to provide for themselves, and they tried to avoid accepting alms.[43]

Stub-Jørgensen also claimed that servants addressed their masters as equals, and that many wealthy landowners had a patriarchal feeling for their subjects. He stressed that even Martin Andersson-Nexø, the island's socialist literary giant, had admitted as much.[44]

The general picture given by Bornholmian history-writing is that the social differences have been relatively small and that the regional division between the north and south of the island has lost importance, but that there is an old and enduring rivalry between the island's towns.

Bornholm's relationship with Skåne and Sweden

In many parts of the Nordic countries there are tales of trolls who, angered by the sound of church bells, threw boulders at the churches. In Bornholmian folklore, trolls threw boulders at the island over the sea from Skåne.[45] This regional variant of the folklore narrative illustrates how important nearby Skåne has been to the Bornholmians.

In the wars against Sweden in the mid seventeenth century, Denmark lost its territory east of the Øresund strait. As a result of the uprising in 1658 the Bornholmians managed to return their island to Denmark, but the other lost areas remained in Swedish hands. Bornholm had ancient links to the province of Skåne, and the East Danish/South Swedish provinces have an important role in Bornholmian history-writing.

The nineteenth-century Swedish historian Martin Weibull, professor at Lund University in Skåne, established the term 'Skåneland', for the area comprising what is today southern Sweden and Bornholm. Skåneland was supposed to have had a common culture, followed the law of Skåne, and held a common thing in Lund. The Bornholmian historian Ebbe Gert Rasmussen considers this to be a later construction since the area cannot be perceived as a unit. There was a large discrepancy between the Skåne and poorer Halland, Blekinge, and Bornholm, which all had the character of borderlands between Sweden and Denmark.[46]

In spite of his criticism of Weibull, Rasmussen is still the Bornholmian writer who most strongly emphasizes the island's links to Skåne. He notes

---

[43] Skougaard 1804, 183 ff.; Stub-Jørgensen 1957, 506.
[44] Stub-Jørgensen 1957, 507.
[45] Åkerlund 1957, 237.
[46] Rasmussen 2008a, 28–9.

that Bornholm was not mentioned in the Treaty of Roskilde, as it was considered part of Skåne, and claims that it was fortunate for Bornholm that the island followed Skåne into Swedish hands in 1658, since a separation from Skåne would have been an even greater catastrophe. Rasmussen even states that the Bornholmians' choice of Danish nationality during the uprising later the same year was a tragedy since it severed the island's links to Skåne.[47]

Rasmussen's emphasis on Bornholm's links to Skåne is rather a new phenomenon on the island. For example, in 1934 Zahrtmann claimed that Bornholm had never been considered part of Skåne, but was seen as a separate province alongside—not under—Skåne, except in ecclesiastical matters.[48] Zahrtmann's view was probably a reaction to claims by Swedish scholars that Bornholm's close links to Skåne meant that the island should actually be considered part of Sweden.

According to Rasmussen, the Bornholmians' feeling of isolation and exclusion was new. Today, peripheral Bornholm is placed over Sweden on Danish maps, weather forecasters stand in front of Bornholm on national television, and Denmark shows little understanding for the island's needs, for example in terms of communications and education. Rasmussen does stress that in a longer, broader perspective Bornholm is situated in the middle of the Baltic, and has been Danish almost as long as that country has existed. Bornholm was part of Skåne, and the Bornholmians in the mid seventeenth century did not feel isolated.[49]

The naval historian Jørgen Barfod also emphasizes the importance of Bornholm's new position after Denmark's loss of Skåne, but rather than claiming that being a distant outpost was a catastrophe for Bornholm, he stresses that the island achieved a new, strategically important position.[50]

Present-day Skåne can also be seen as an alternative path of history, which Bornholm exited through the uprising in December 1658. Jørn Klindt-Jensen claimed 300 years later that journey around Skåne—a province where after ten generations you could still find a few touching traces of Danish culture—provided a vision of how time would have

---

[47] Rasmussen 2000, 25, 28, 29, 158.
[48] Zahrtmann 1934, 226.
[49] Rasmussen 2000, 11.
[50] Barfod 1976, 19.

altered Bornholm's Danish nature if the island had remained in Swedish hands.[51]

As the Bornholmian journalist Hansaage Bøggild noted in 2004, when Bornholmians today travel to the Danish capital Copenhagen they first take the ferry to Ystad in Skåne. He claimed that, although Sweden is a member of the European Union, the journey is not without its problems since the Swedes are suspicious. In Bøggild's opinion the Bornholmians have always had a love-hate relationship with the Swedes, who were always blamed if there was drinking and fighting on the island. Earlier it was common for islanders with Swedish names to take more Danish ones, but that trend has turned in the other direction.[52]

Several conflicts between Bornholmian and Swedish fishermen are mentioned. According to Bøggild, Bornholmians and Swedes shared the herring fisheries, but in the nineteenth century impoverished fishermen from Gudhjem on Bornholm attacked their Swedish colleagues. The legal system had to tell the Bornholmians that the Swedes were actually allowed to be there. Zahrtmann claimed that the lack of harbours for large fishing boats on Bornholm meant that fishermen from Swedish Blekinge, could rake in huge catches of herring, which they sold so cheaply in Rønne that peasants used it as fertilizer. Zahrtmann also mentioned an incident in 1562, when fishermen from Blekinge looted a Dutch ship which had gone aground on Bornholm's shores.[53]

Bøggild claimed in 2004 that Bornholmian cooking was similar to that of southern Skåne, and that it also had a lot in common with that of Germany, Zealand, and Møn. He quoted a cookbook that claimed that Bornholmian cooking had to be seen as a Baltic tradition, not the tradition of one country.[54] Bøggild was probably influenced by the interregional projects which focused to a large extent on food culture. In 1980 the Nordic Council had established the Sydöstra Skåne—Bornholm project, which in 1995 was extended to include Rügen and the Polish city Swinoujscie on the island of Wollin as an EU interregional project, the Four Corners project.[55]

---

[51] Klindt-Jensen 1958, 47.
[52] Bøggild 2004, 21, 46–7.
[53] Zahrtmann 1935, 146, 289–90; Bøggild 2004, 201–202.
[54] Bøggild 2004, 38–9.
[55] Billing & Petersen 2003, 17 ff.

This project also resulted in history-writing: in 1999 Ann-Vibeke Knudsen of the Bornholm Museum edited *Bygningskultur omkring Østersøen,* a description of 250 historic buildings in the Four Corners area which were in need of protection.[56]

There are a few examples of books that combine Skåne's and Bornholm's history. In 1995 the project Bornholm—Sydöstra Skåne published a bilingual brochure *På hat med Skåne og Bornholm/På hatt med Bornholm och Skåne,* which described traditional headgear from the region. In 2008 Ebbe Gert Rasmussen published *Bornholm og Skåne: Triumf og tragedie i skæbneårene 1658–1659,* which was an adaptation of his book *Skuddet* about the uprising on Bornholm. In it he discussed the similarities of the uprising in Bornholm and the one in Malmö, as well as the detrimental consequences of the fact that Bornholm and Skåne were now separated by a national border. Rasmussen claims that today the people of the area identify more with the state to which they belong than to the provincial context to which they belonged 350 years ago; this fact can be a source of joy or lamentation, depending on one's sentiments. Either way, Rasmussen is of the opinion that the Danish authorities should learn from the Swedish treatment of Gotland and Öland. Such a remote, secluded place as Bornholm needs special treatment and cannot be administered like an average Danish area.[57] He does not specify what about the Swedish treatment of its large islands should serve as a model for Bornholm, however.

The links to Skåne have become a more important theme in history-writing in the late twentieth and early twenty-first centuries. The European Union's encouragement and funding of interregional projects has contributed to this. The opening of the Öresund Bridge between Skåne and Zealand might also be of importance. Bornholm, Skåne, and parts of Zealand including Copenhagen, together with some adjacent smaller islands, form the Oresund region, and the construction of the bridge has strengthened the land route across Skåne as the Bornholmians' primary link to the capital, Copenhagen.

---

[56] Knudsen 1999.
[57] Knudsen & Nilsson 1995; Rasmussen 2000; Rasmussen 2008a, 164, 176.

Geographical location—a peripheral centre

A common trait in Bornholmian history-writing is the emphasis on the island's distance from the rest of Denmark. Bøggild even suggests that Bornholm should have its own time zone, since it is the only place in Denmark where the sun is exactly in the south at noon.[58] Since this illustrates that the island is situated right in the middle of the Central European time zone, the talk of a separate zone seems superfluous; however, it should not primarily be interpreted as a statement about astronomy, but as an illustration of the geographic and mental distances involved.

Bøggild also claims that Bornholm's location is so awkward that the rest of Denmark considers it 'more as a troublesome disturbance than as a part of the country with equal rights'. He points out that Bornholm is seldom shown in its correct location on Danish maps, being placed over Gothenburg or Kattegat. The Bornholmians take revenge by having maps of Bornholm with the rest of Denmark placed in the top right corner.[59]

Bøggild also claims that Bornholm has always been oriented westwards, but that being at the centre of the Baltic Sea also gives it an Eastern European heritage. In a book published by the Bornholm Medieval Centre, Lene Halskov Hansen describes the island as a central node in the Baltic during the Middle Ages, which might have made it a base for crusaders, but also for less welcome guests such as pirates. In his book about the resistance movement on Bornholm during the Second World War, Barfod repeatedly stresses the importance of Bornholm's location far from Denmark but central to the Baltic, close to foreign shores, which among other things made it an important link in the smuggling of refugees. His position is summarized in the title of the book: *Et centrum i periferien* ('A centre in the periphery').[60] Thus Bornholm is described as peripheral in relation to the rest of present-day Denmark, but centrally located in a broader Baltic perspective.

Language and dialect

The Bornholmian dialect has several characteristic traits. In 1804 Skougaard claimed that only true Bornholmians were able to pronounce

---

[58] Bøggild 2004, 20.
[59] Bøggild 2004, 16 ('mer som en besværlig størrelse end som en ligværdig landsdel').
[60] Bøggild 2004, 16; Halskov Hansen 2007, 59; Barfod 1976.

words which rhymed with *-jlnj*. He was of the opinion that Bornholmian was a separate language, not a dialect of Danish: in fact it was closer to Swedish. Because of that, Skougaard chose not to begin all nouns with capitals in his book, since he did not see any reason why he should follow the Danish orthography of the day. He also noted that there were local variations in dialect within Bornholm. His *Beskrivelse over Bornholm* also contained over 40 pages of Bornholmian–Danish dictionary.[61]

Skougaard's efforts in describing the Bornholmian language can be compared to the work done by Jens Christian Svabo in the Faroe Islands in 1781–2.[62] Both men combined the objectives of the Enlightenment and Romanticism: they wanted to bring about practical improvements to their home islands as well as document the culture, history, and language of their inhabitants. While Svabo did the groundwork for a new literary language, Skougaard's view that Bornholmian was a separate language fell out of favour. The difference between a language and a dialect is political, and in the late nineteenth century—when leading Bornholmians were in favour of Bornholm's integration into a homogenous Danish nation-state—there was no need for the idea that the islanders were speaking a separate tongue.

Two hundred years after Skougaard, Bøggild claimed that the local dialects were contaminated by Swedish—or rather it was the inhabitants of Skåne who could not speak proper Bornholmian anymore, since the Bornholmians speak the original East Danish language. Bøggild also lamented the fact that no one was doing anything to preserve the Bornholmian dialects. However, in 1935 Zahrtmann had been of the opinion that the love of local dialects was strengthened when they became endangered by contacts with the wider world.[63]

In his essay about Bornholmian dialect in *Bogen om Bornholm*, the editor H. P. Sonne expressed the opinion that the Bornholmian dialect was similar to the language spoken in Copenhagen 400 years ago. In those days the Danish spoken in the capital was affected mostly by East Danish dialects, but when eastern Denmark except Bornholm was lost to Sweden, Jutlandic dialects started to assert their influence in Copenhagen.[64] This is

---

[61] Skougaard 1804, 114, 120–1, 369–411.
[62] Debes 1995,
[63] Bøggild 2004, 47; Zahrtmann 1935, 315.
[64] Sonne 1957, 520–1.

an example of how Jutland in Bornholmian history-writing is described as Bornholm's competitor in Copenhagen.

Rasmussen claims that to most Danes the Bornholmians seem to speak in an un-Danish, sing-song manner.[65] The fact that the Bornholmian dialect sounds un-Danish or Swedish in the ears of other Danes is problematic for the islanders, who aspire to be the most Danish of all Danes. This might explain why earlier research has found that the dialect does not play a positive role for regional identity, and also why twentieth- and twenty-first-century Bornholmian writers claim that the island's dialect is the last remnant of true (East) Danish. However, Skougaard, who was writing in the early nineteenth century when Denmark was still a conglomerate of provinces rather than a nation-state, described Bornholmian as a unique language closer to Swedish than Danish.

The dialect on the island is not only described as being influenced by Danish and Swedish: Sonne also gave some examples of how the Bornholmian language was influenced by English during the heyday of sailing ships in the second half of the nineteenth century, but finds that the influence was surprisingly small outside the sphere of nautical terms. However, based on the similarities, Sonne believed that there was a connection between the Bornholmian and English languages in prehistoric times, although he is uncertain of exactly how and when the influence occurred.[66] The influence of English and of the Anglo-Saxon world in general is noticeable in history-writing from other islands which had a shipping boom in the second half of the nineteenth century—to some degree on Saaremaa, but especially on Åland.

Shipping, fishing, and harbours

European towns and cities in the nineteenth century patrolled by night watchmen, who normally shouted out the time at regular intervals. However, in Nexø on Bornholm they also shouted out the direction of the wind: 'It's 11 o'clock—the wind is north-westerly'. According to Henning Køie this illustrates the importance of the weather to the seafaring Bornholmians.[67]

---

[65] Rasmussen 2000, 159.
[66] Sonne 1957, 542–3.
[67] Køie 1957, 323.

It is not far-fetched to assume that seaborne trade formed part of the islanders' identity. Zahrtmann wrote that the Bornholmians were correctly considered a people of sailors, since they often worked the sea before they worked the land. Many Bornholmians became farsighted, resolute, and self-confident on voyages in their youth. However, he also claimed that Bornholm was and remained peasant country.[68]

Pedersen claimed in his book about Bornholmian shipping in 1850–1998 that the island was and is more dependent on shipping than any other part of the country. After the Great Northern War (1700–1720) there was peace in the Baltic region, with exception of the British (i.e. Napoleonic) Wars and the Second World War, which was an important precondition for a boom in trade and greater prosperity. The Bornholmians progressed as the number of skippers and the fleet of ships grew, securing outlets for the island's peasants, clockmakers, potters, merchants, and fishermen. The wealth can be seen in the architecture of the Florissant Age at the turn of the nineteenth century.[69] The examples Pedersen gives indicate that it was not the profits of shipping per se which made it important, however, but the fact that it connected the island to the surrounding world which allowed other trades to flourish.

The Bornholmian merchant fleet peaked in the 1870s, according to Pedersen. He connects this to a speculative trade with Iceland. After the end of seal hunting in 1863 many hunting ships were converted into merchant vessels. In Zahrtmann's opinion the peak occurred in 1850–1880, and he claimed that only smaller boats were built after that.[70]

As on Åland, Hiiumaa, and Saaremaa, Bornholmian shipping had a boom during the second half of the nineteenth century. Bornholmian history-writing contains more about this period than is the case on the Estonian islands, but less than on Åland. The reason for this is probably that, unlike Åland, Bornholm lacks an institution dedicated to the island's maritime history. Another reason why seafaring has not achieved the same central position in the Bornholmian identity as it has in the Ålandic might be that Bornholmian seafaring is not as special in a national context: Denmark, unlike Finland, is a major shipping nation with old seafaring traditions, and the capital Copenhagen has had a dominant position, reducing all other ports including those on Bornholm to minor players.

---

[68] Zahrtmann 1934, 201–202.
[69] Pedersen 1998, 7.
[70] Zahrtmann 1935, 288, 295; Pedersen 1998, 7.

In part for reasons of natural geography, the question of harbours is more central on Bornholm than on any of the other islands, since the island's seafaring has been hampered by a lack of natural harbours. In Hasle a deep harbour was created in 1834 by an original method which is mentioned by several writers: an undersea coalmine was made to collapse. The coal deposits that had been discovered during work on the harbour were valuable enough to finance its extraction, and when it was emptied its sandstone roof was removed with a saw wielded by two men on a raft.[71] The tale of the artificial harbour in Hasle combines two trades characteristic of Bornholm: shipping and coal mining, the latter not being found elsewhere in Denmark.

Many writers mention the great storm surge of 1872, which flooded and destroyed several harbours. Zahrtmann claimed that the damage to ancient monuments proved that no similar flood had occurred for 1,500 years. According to Jørgensen, the devastation was seen as an opportunity to build larger and deeper harbours, which brought important benefits for shipping and fishing. In his essay about the sea in *Bogen om Bornholm*, the artist Henning Køie stresses that the catastrophe was even more devastating in the western part of the Baltic than on Bornholm.[72] Here we notice that Bornholm is part of a maritime, archipelagic nation whose central areas are subject to the same natural forces as Bornholm. That said, the fact that Denmark mainly consists of islands is only noticeable in regional history-writing in connection to shipping and harbours. This might help explain why the maritime trades have not been thought a central part of Bornholmian identity in the same way as what in a Danish context was the exceptional position of the peasants: seafaring did not separate 'us' from 'them'.

Henning Køie was of the opinion that when daily flights began, was Bornholm came closer to Denmark, not only because of the short travel time, but above all because it meant the island was less dependent on the sea. Twisted ice may form small mountains which can stop even the strongest steamships, and in the days of the sailing ships the island could be isolated for months. Before the installation of telegraph lines there were several occasions when the islanders celebrated the birthdays of newly dead kings.[73] This illustrates that Bornholm's insular location constituted

---

[71] Jørgensen 1901, 257–8; Zahrtmann 1935, 285.
[72] Jørgensen 1901, 313 ff.; Zahrtmann 1935, 285 ff.; Køie 1957, 349.
[73] Køie 1957, 347.

an obstacle for the island's integration the Danish network of communications well into the twentieth century. It is interesting to note that it was not the speed but the reliability of aeroplanes which was welcomed most. The common notion that the sea connects is only true in good weather.

In 1993 the book *Østersøen gav* about the Bornholmian fishing industry was published in the Bornholmske samlinger series. This fishing history differs from other regional Bornholmian histories because Poland, which although geographically close to Bornholm is seldom mentioned in regional history-writing, here plays an important role as an antagonist to the Bornholmian fishermen during the cold war.[74] Poland became a neighbour of Bornholm's quite late, as a result of border changes after the Second World War, which helps explain why it is relatively invisible in Bornholmian history-writing.

Education

Skougaard claimed in 1804 that the Bornholmians could read better than Danes in general. According to him, they had an inclination for theology and were able to get into debates with the priests. Many peasants owned the Danish Lawcode of Christian V, and were so skilled at using it that they could represent themselves in court. Newspapers could be found everywhere in towns and the countryside. Zahrtmann gave a similar picture of education on Bornholm in the eighteenth and early nineteenth centuries: there was a lack of schools, but people learned to write at sea or studied on their own since they wanted to become officers in the militia or be able to represent themselves in court. Raised in the free, sound culture of the island they were not afraid to discuss theology with the priest or law with the judge. Zahrtmann believed that the Bornholmians learned what they needed in order to be able to stand up to the authorities. They did not use many schoolbooks: not even the great scholar J. N. Madvig got his hands on any. Bornholm's best administrator ever, Hans Rømer, had no formal schooling whatsoever. However, the bible, the law, and history books could be found on many farms. Ludvig Holberg's comic-heroic poem *Peder Paars* appealed to the Bornholmian mind to

---

[74] Rasmussen 1993, 79–89.

such an extent that some peasants memorized it and wove its lines into their own speech.[75]

Bornholmians travelled to Copenhagen to work as servants; the men also worked as sailors. When they came back they, according to Skougaard, had acquired experience, sense, and a civilized manner. Jørgensen—an incomer teacher—was less impressed by the islanders' manners: customs were as crude as elsewhere, but not worse, the educational level was low, and theft, whoring, and fornication were prevalent.[76]

Skougaard was of the opinion that the Bornholmians were more skilled in law than most Danes. Since they were free men with property, legal disputes easily arose which forced them to learn. Skougaard, however, did not believe that the Bornholmians were more quarrelsome and litigious than the Norwegians and others.[77]

Although Bornholmians are described as highly knowledgeable within their areas of interest, their enthusiasm for formal schooling is described as low. Zahrtmann claimed that the Bornholmians were best in class in the school of life: they were fishermen, skippers, and farmers who could create riches out of austerity and felt little need for Latin, which explained the decline of Rønne's Latin school. Both Zahrtmann and Skougaard were of the opinion that shipping created a demand for education that was not met on the island. The Bornholmians' reluctance to implement royal decrees—like the one about parish schools in 1814—slowed the introduction of schools. Zahrtmann described how the Bornholmians were fond of their guilds, which arranged drinking parties. The king prohibited all guilds in 1735, but to no avail on Bornholm. In 1739 the king proclaimed that all guild houses should be sold in order to finance parish schools. On Bornholm, Zahrtmann reports, they were sold for a trifle, and the new owners continued to arrange guild meetings.[78]

The description of education in Bornholmian history-writing is similar to what we find on Åland: the peasants are said to have been uninterested in founding formal schools, but were still highly educated in the areas which they considered practical. The difference is that in Bornholmian history-writing subjects such as theology, law, and history are described as practical. This a result of the Bornholmians' struggle to

[75] Skougaard 1804, 102–103; Zahrtmann 1935, 147 ff., 321.
[76] Skougaard 1804, 77–8; Jørgensen 1900, 123–4.
[77] Skougaard 1804, 86–7.
[78] Skougaard 1804, 103; Zahrtmann 1935, 104, 144–5, 325.

protect their privileges against priests and civil servants. The islanders' claims on privilege were founded on history, and in order to defend them they needed to know the language of power.

Bornholm's peasants

The Bornholmian peasants differed in many ways from their peers in the rest of Denmark: on this point the regional history writers are unanimous. To begin with, they did not live in villages, but spaced out in rows of single farms. Bøggild believes that the farms had been dispersed during the island's Viking Age greatness, but Halskov Hansen is of the opinion that this pattern of settlement is typical for areas with infertile soils that rely on butter production. According to Vagn Heiselberg's essay about peasants in *Bogen om Bornholm*, the single farms meant that the Bornholmians were free, unbound by the hindrance to private enterprise that villages might constitute.[79]

Another peculiarity is the island's customary system of inheritance, where the youngest son or the eldest daughter inherited the farm. In 1804 Skougaard was of the opinion that this form of inheritance was the most natural and should be introduced elsewhere, since the eldest sons had most likely already found a living somewhere else, and did not need to inherit. Vagn Heiselberg claimed that this custom was unique to Bornholm, but Zahrtmann believed that the same practice existed in limited areas in Britain, France, Germany, and Russia. He also noted that the peasants of Bornholm had voluntarily abandoned the custom in 1887. However, in 2000 Rasmussen claimed that it lived on on the island, although he felt uncertain how long it would survive. Klindt-Jensen believed that the custom created a free, strong-willed people since it forced older sons to search elsewhere for their livelihoods.[80]

The most important differences to the rest of Denmark, however, were that most Bornholmian peasants owned their land, and that there was no serfdom and almost no nobility on the island. Rasmussen describes the nobility that existed as 'Lilliputians' compared to their peers in Denmark and Sweden. Bøggild described the Bornholmian peasants as begin as free as the Vikings, and Heiselberg believes that as subjects of the archbishop

[79] Zahrtmann 1935, 217 ff.; Heiselberg 1957, 175; Klindt-Jensen 1957a, 214; Bøggild 2004, 36–7; Halskov Hansen 2007, 59, 70–1.
[80] Skougaard 1804, 123, 131; Zahrtmann 1935, 72; Heiselberg 1957, 176; Klindt-Jensen 1958, 29; Bøggild 2004, 42–3; Rasmussen 2000, 159; Halskov Hansen 2007, 59, 235–6.

for 400 years they had been able to solidify the feeling of freedom so characteristic of Viking Age peasants. Jørgensen and Zahrtmann say that since the Bornholmian peasants were not used to being submissive, they defended their rights fiercely and made life difficult for Danish officials, who were used to subjugated peasants. Zahrtmann suggests that this might have been the reason why so many officials were sent to Bornholm from Norway, where the peasants were also free and stood up for their rights.[81] The point that the Bornholmian peasants were freer than their counterparts in the rest of Denmark, who were serfs until 1800, is a central point in Bornholmian history-writing.

There was one category of Bornholmian peasants who claimed they were nobility, though: the *frimenn* (free men). In the Middle Ages they had been squires of the bishop, who had granted them freedom from certain taxes. They fought unsuccessfully for their right to be considered noblemen and exempt from all taxes well into the seventeenth century, but were eventually assimilated by the peasants. Zahrtmann pointed out that the Danish king supported their claims to be noblemen in the mid sixteenth century—when the island was leased by Lübeck. Zahrtmann believed the king simply used them to incite unrest against the Lübeckers, and when the Danish king regained control of the island in 1576 he changed tack. The Bornholmian history writers express little sympathy for the *frimenn* and agree that their writes of nobility were unfounded. For example, Zahrtmann claims that Bornholm said goodbye to the *frimenn* without any great grief.[82] The negative attitude towards nobility which is displayed in Bornholmian history-writing also encompasses the frimenn.

In 1744 more peasants than before became owners of their own farms, when all the king's lands on the island were sold. The following year Denmark was hit by a cattle plague, which did not reach Bornholm. According to Jørgensen this made it possible for the Bornholmians to sell their livestock at good prices, enabling them to pay off the debt they had incurred when they purchased their farms.[83] In his description, chance, in

---

[81] Jørgensen 1900, 120, 122 ff.; Jørgensen 1901, 101, 127; Zahrtmann 1934, 209; Zahrtmann 1935, 182; Heiselberg 1957, 173; Bøggild 2004, 36–7; Rasmussen 2000, 51; Halskov Hansen 2007, 59, 69, 74.
[82] Skougaard 1804, 213–14; Jørgensen 1900, 113; Zahrtmann 1934, 94 ff., 104, 125, 135, 169–70, 204–205; Zahrtmann 1935, 69–70; Halskov Hansen 2007, 74.
[83] Jørgensen 1901, 134 ff., 142–3.

combination with the island's insular location which saved it from the cattle plague, helped the Bornholmians become debt-free landowners.

However, in 1804 Skougaard claimed that most peasants had debts, although the rich peasants on the coast were better off than the poorer inland peasants.[84] In general, Bornholmian history-writing stresses the egalitarianism of agrarian society on Bornholm. The only real exception is Skougaard, who emphasized the differences between richer and poorer peasants.

Pirates, wreckers, privateers

In his essay about the sea in *Bogen om Bornholm* from 1957, the painter Henning Køie quoted the nineteenth-century doctor Eschricht's observations about the Bornholmians' great interest in strandings. As a newcomer to the island, the doctor at first found the ill-concealed happiness the islanders displayed when a stranding was reported as a less pleasant trait. However, he changed his mind when he saw all the riches the wrecks brought, and noticed how the entire community was involved in the salvage operation: the sailors salvaging items from the wreck, the peasants storing the goods, the merchants buying them, the doctor checking whether foodstuffs were harmless to consume, and the officials administering and supervising the whole operation. Eschricht also noted that at a good wreck no one suffered except the insurance company—and if there were no strandings no one would insure their ships, and all insurance companies would go bankrupt. The first two strandings he experienced provided him with fine writing paper, several bottles of wine, and a bag full of new books on science.[85]

Regional history-writing from Bornholm does indeed portray the islanders as eager collectors of goods from wrecked ships since time immemorial, a description similar to what we have seen on the other islands in this study. There are, however, several circumstances that make the Bornholmian discourse on strandings special.

First and foremost, the salvage of stranded goods is described as an activity that has been important to the whole island, not only parts of it, although the parish of Poulsker at the island's southern tip, Dueodde, is said to have been more blessed with wrecks than most.[86] This is probably

---

[84] Skougaard 1804, 207.
[85] Køie 1957, 353–4.
[86] Skougaard 1804, 145; Jørgensen 1901, 218–19.

a consequence of Bornholm's geography. It is a solitary island without a surrounding archipelago, situated in the midst of a busy waterway, which meant that ships could strand anywhere on the island's coastline. On top of that, the interior of the island was for a long time sparsely populated, which meant that most of the population was concentrated along the coast, close to the scene.

In addition, strandings seem to have been of greater economic importance on Bornholm than elsewhere. The Bornholmian engineer Jørn Klindt-Jensen claimed that since Bornholm lacked good harbours, strandings were the only benefits the island had of its central location in a heavily navigated waterway. Skougaard claimed that the officials who led the salvage operations profited greatly; in Poulsker they could earn several hundred *daler* in a good year. Køie also pointed out that many of the buildings on the island, which until the nineteenth century was almost deforested, contain timber from stranded ships. Jørgensen claimed that the wrecks were so numerous that they kept the island's artisans poor: potential customers did not buy their products but waited until Our Lord sent a good wreck. He added that they seldom had to wait long; in the 15-year period leading up to 1808 there were 105 shipwrecks. Zahrtmann reported that J. N. Madvig, a Bornholmian philologist and politician, had heard from his father, a scribe in the town of Svaneke in north-eastern Bornholm, that they would never have made it through the hard years if not Our Lord had sent two good wrecks.[87]

The strandings are commonly described as gifts from God. They were also linked to religion in the saying that the inhabitants of southern Bornholm 'led Christian lives and made a living from wreckages'.[88]

Several authors describe how the Bornholmian clock industry started in 1756 when local spinning-wheel makers, trying to repair broken clocks found on the wreck of an English ship, learned how to produce new ones. Zahrtmann believed that this was a myth put about in 1795 by the chamber of commerce in Copenhagen. He claimed that on Bornholm no one knew about this shipwreck, and in any case there were already clocks in Rønne which could have functioned as models.[89] This was not the only instance in

---

[87] Skougaard 1804, 145; Jørgensen 1901, 186–7; Zahrtmann 1935, 288; Køie 1957, 359–60; Klindt-Jensen 1958, 8.
[88] Jørgensen 1901, 318 ('leve kristeligen og ernære sig af vrag'); Zahrtmann 1934, 90 ('lever kristeligt og nærer sig af vrag').
[89] Jørgensen 1901, 211; Bøggild 2004, 169; Zahrtmann 1935, 138.

which Zahrtmann claimed that Copenhagen had produced myths about Bornholm. He is the only Bornholmian writer to say the shipwreck was a fabrication, however.

The night between 4 and 5 December 1678 a large Swedish fleet ran aground in Sose Bay. More than 1,000 drowned and 3,000 were taken prisoner. The writers mention that Jens Kofoed, the hero of the uprising against the Swedes in 1658, wanted to kill all the survivors, but was instead himself arrested for insubordination.[90]

Some regional history writers claim that one year later another Swedish was wrecked on Bornholm. According to Jørgensen, who relied upon de Thura's *Bornholms beskrivelse* from 1756, around 3,000 drowned immediately while 1,500 survivors made it to the shore. Jørgensen claimed they were so exhausted that they all died within a short time. Zahrtmann, on the other hand, does mention survivors: he claimed that since peace had been made with Sweden, Christian V ordered that the survivors should be treated as friends and be allowed to travel wherever they wanted. The corpses were buried in mass graves, which according to Zahrtmann might have contributed to the myth about 'the Great Swine Slaughter', an alleged mass killing of Swedes in 1658.[91] However, this second great stranding has almost certainly never took place. It is probably a misunderstanding which stems from de Thura.

The importance of wrecks in Bornholmian history-writing is highlighted by the fact that, in contrast to the other islands in this study, we find books dedicated entirely to shipwrecks. In the 1980s, Erik Pedersen published two volumes which covered all the known wrecks on the island from 1830 to 1986. He clarified that he had only included accidental shipwrecks, not old ships that had been run aground for the purpose of shipbreaking. He also treated the technological advance that reduced the number of shipwrecks and limited their consequences, such as lighthouses (1802) and salvage stations (1852). Surprisingly late in history even the most basic means of avoiding accidents were lacking. According to Pedersen, the Russian steam frigate *Archimedes* which was shipwrecked in 1850, had been using used a nautical chart that omitted Bornholm.[92]

---

[90] Jørgensen 1901, 41 ff.; Zahrtmann 1935, 54; Bøggild 2004, 194 ff.
[91] Jørgensen 1901, 43; Zahrtmann 1935, 55.
[92] Pedersen 1987, 4–5, 7 ff.; Pedersen 1988.

In wartime the Bornholmians engaged more actively in bringing the riches from passing ships to their shores. During the Napoleonic Wars, Bornholm became the home of privateers who attacked British merchant ships in 1807–1814. The privateering campaign was a Danish strategy to continue resistance against Britain after the loss of Denmark's navy during the Siege of Copenhagen in 1807. In his book about resistance on Bornholm during the Second World War, Barfod compares this campaign to other times the Bornholmians have prepared to wage 'the little war'. Henning Køie claimed in *Bogen om Bornholm* that apart from the excitement and profit, the privateers were also fired by patriotism and a thirst for revenge. He writes that since the British had robbed Denmark of its navy, it had become a private war waged by skippers and fishermen.[93] However, in most accounts of the privateers their military effectiveness, as well as their patriotism, is secondary.

The central theme in regional history-writing about privateering is instead the immense riches that it brought to Bornholm. The most colourful description is provided by Zahrtmann. Privateering was conducted as a business enterprise, 'Det Borringholmske kaperselskap'. It was divided into 44 parts which were sold to shareholders. The prize court in Rønne was handling 3 million *riksdaler* a year, and privateers were lighting their pipes with 5 *daler* notes. The influx of money in combination with the difficulty of importing food from Denmark led to a staggering inflation. The lack of coins led to the issuing of local paper money, but the government in Copenhagen stopped the attempt after one month. Since prizes could only be sold in towns, the small fishing village of Arnager with its suitably located harbour was elevated to the status of a town for the space of one month. Jørgensen claimed that the memory of the privateers was still alive almost a hundred years later.[94]

Pirater og patrioter, the first book entirely dedicated to the Bornholmian privateers, claimed that they were motivated both by patriotism and greed. The fact that the book was published in 2010 is said in the preface to reflect a growing interest in privateering following the 200th anniversary of the period in combination with the Danish navy's recent actions against Somali pirates. Privateering is also described as a resistance movement, which like other Danish resistance movements has

---

[93] Køie 1957, 341; Barfod 1976, 19.
[94] Jørgensen 1901, 220–226; Zahrtmann 1935, 198–9, 208–209.

been important not for its efficiency, but because it enabled the Danes to keep a certain amount of self-respect.[95]

As is often the case in Bornholmian history-writing, *Pirater og patrioter* balances the description of the Bornholmians' patriotism with the claim that Denmark had forgotten the island. The Bornholmians were according to the author Nils Erik Sonne, were not kept informed about what was going on in the rest of the country. The royal regulations on privateering issued on 14 September 1807 did not reach the island until 18 November. Meanwhile, the islanders had sent a delegation to the Danish Consul General in Malmö, in Sweden, to learn of the situation in Copenhagen. Based on that information the island's *amtmand* issued his own privateering regulations on 3 November 1807.[96]

The strandings and privateering illustrate how Bornholm's location— far away from central Denmark but in the midst of a busy seaway—has contributed to creating a regional historical discourse.

Ancient and medieval history

Mythological explanations about how Bornholm was settled have not gained much of a hearing among the island's regional history writers. They have, to varying degrees, acknowledged that the island was populated both by Scandinavians and by other peoples. All agree that the island was still an independent kingdom in the late ninth century. The late Viking Age is seen as a period when Bornholm became integrated into the Danish kingdom, and the Middle Ages as a period when the island, as an arena for power struggles between the king and the Church, played an important part in the development of the realm.

The origins of the Bornholmians

The early nineteenth-century writer of Bornholmian regional history, Peder Nikolai Skougaard, was very critical of earlier attempts to link the island to ancient myths. He dismissed the idea that Bornholm took its name from Beor, the servant of Tjelvar, who in the *Gutasaga* is said to have discovered Gotland, since he did not believe the Gotlandic books which were supposed to prove this had ever existed. The idea that the

[95] Sonne 2010, 5, 7.
[96] Sonne 2010, 25 ff.

Burgundians came from Bornholm was also uncertain. Neither did he believe that Gudhjem on Bornholm had got its name from the Goths or Tjelvar's father Gutho.[97]

Later writers have tried to explain the origins of the Bornholmians using the archaeological evidence. The teacher J. A. Jørgensen believed that Bornholm was populated around 2000 BC, later than Jutland and 'the islands' (meaning Funen, Zealand, and adjacent islands). They came either from the southern shore of the Baltic Sea or more probably from Skåne, which can be seen from Bornholm in good weather. He considered it undeniable that they belonged to the same people as the inhabitants of the Danish islands and Skåne.[98]

The doctor Marius Kristian Zahrtmann compared the first Bornholmians to the Eskimos, a people within the borders of Denmark who still led a Stone Age life in his day. He believed that the first Bornholmians were linguistically related to the people in Skåne. Probably the blood of the first immigrants still flowed in the Bornholmians' veins, although it had later been diluted with that of foreigners'. The Bornholmians had according to Zahrtmann always had the same sound mixture of blood as other Danes.[99]

To Zahrtmann and Jørgensen's generation it was important to stress the Danish origins of the island's first inhabitants. In regional history-writing from the period after the Second World War this is no longer the case. Academic archaeology has turned away from attempts to find the roots of modern nations in prehistory, and since the second half of the twentieth century, the regional history writers who have described Bornholm's prehistory have been professional archaeologists—it is no surprise that this trend is reflected in their writings.

According to the essay about the island's prehistory in *Bogen om Bornholm* (1957), the first evidence of human activity on Bornholm is from a period around 9,000 years ago, when the island was part of the mainland and more accessible from Skåne northern Germany than at any other time in its history. The essay was written by the Bornholmian archaeologist Ole Klindt-Jensen, later to become professor at Århus University. The Bornholmian archaeologist Finn Ole Sonne Nielsen at Bornholm Museum claimed in 1996 that some pieces of processed flint have been found in

---

[97] Skougaard 1804, 1 ff., 249–50.
[98] Jørgensen 1900, 10 ff.
[99] Zahrtmann 1934, 13, 20.

layers that might be 20,000 years old, but that the oldest settlements represented the Bromme Culture, which was found across the whole southern Baltic region in around 10,000 BC.[100] None of the archaeologists speculated as to the ethnicity of the first immigrants.

In 2004 the journalist Hansaage Bøggild claimed that the first immigrants came from the south, but he stressed that a lot had happened since then. The islanders are not exclusively Danes, but a mixed people. Eastern Europeans, Asians, Balts, Germans, and Scandinavians have influenced the island's population, whether as mercenaries on Hammershus Fortress, as foreign occupants, or as sailors who married to Bornholmians. Bøggild is of the opinion that this mixed origin is reflected in the Bornholmians' varying appearances: they are dolichocephalic and brachiocephalic, blond and dark.[101] Although Zahrtmann and Bøggild agree that the Bornholmians are Danes with a mix of foreign blood, Zahrtmann in the 1930s emphasized their Danishness while Bøggild in the early 2000s stressed the foreign influences.

Jørgensen, like Zahrtmann, believed that the first immigrants were Danes. However, he claimed that the island's isolated location had led to the development of a population that was distinctly Bornholmian, since foreign elements were seldom mixed in. Some immigration did take place: he believed the island received an infusion of power through the honest and able foreigners who married into families of Bornholmian burghers. The people who were exiled to Bornholm were a different story; although of noble birth they were not the best stock.[102] Bornholmian history-writing, like Ålandic and twentieth-century Saaremaa and Hiiumaa history-writing, is negative towards the nobility. However, on Bornholm the view of the burghers is more favourable than it was in the peasant-centred history-writing of the other islands.

Bronze Age

According to Jørgensen, Bornholm's Bronze Age culture was similar to the rest of Denmark, with some differences which can be described as a local Bornholmian style. Ole Klindt-Jensen claimed that most findings from the island had parallels in the other Nordic countries. However, one

---

[100] Klindt-Jensen 1957, 89.
[101] Bøggild 2004, 17.
[102] Jørgensen 1901, 98–9.

bronze bowl found in Østermarie had been manufactured by a hammering technique which is unknown in the Nordic countries, with the exception of one Bronze drum from Balkåkra in Skåne. Ole Klindt-Jensen considered both to be imports from Central Europe.[103] While Jørgensen saw Bornholm's Bronze Age as Danish with regional variations, the archaeologist Ole Klindt-Jensen considered it to be Nordic with Central European influences.

Several authors mention Bornholm's Bronze Age rock carvings, the only ones in Denmark. This is related to the fact that such rocky outcrops are not found anywhere else in the country.[104] Skougaard encouraged poets to visit Bornholm's rocks instead of Switzerland's; the view of the sea with British merchant ships and Russian naval ships outweighed Switzerland's advantages.[105] This was probably an indirect criticism of Denmark's inability to defend the waters around Bornholm during the Napoleonic Wars.

The Bronze Age burial mounds were in folklore believed to be mass graves where Courland pirates had been buried in the Viking Age. All the writers of regional history have considered this to be a myth. Zahrtmann believed that in turn inspired the myth of the mass slaughter of Swedes in 1658.[106]

In Zahrtmann's view, Baltic Bronze Age culture was on a level with the Mediterranean, the only difference was that the Greeks adopted the art of writing from Asia, and could make their culture immortal through the writings of Homer and Herodotus.[107]

The Iron and Viking Ages

Although the Bronze Age is seen as a key period, the Iron and Viking Ages are commonly perceived as the most important in the island's ancient history.[108]

The idea that the Goths came from Gotland has until recently been generally accepted in Gotlandic history-writing. However, Bornholmian writers have not accepted the idea that the Burgundians came from

---

[103] Jørgensen 1900, 22; Klindt-Jensen 1957, 108.
[104] Some rock carvings can be found on loose boulders on Zealand, however.
[105] Skougaard 1804, 336–7; Zahrtmann 1934, 29; Bøggild 2004, 29–30.
[106] Skougaard 1804, 264 ff.; Zahrtmann 1934, 41.
[107] Zahrtmann 1934, 27.
[108] Bøggild 2004, 34.

Bornholm. Skougaard was sceptical in 1804, as was Aage Rohmann in *Bogen om Bornholm* in 1957. Zahrtmann dismissed the theory altogether. The Swedish scholars who suggested that the Bornholmians/Burgundians had left the island around AD 300 believed that it had been repopulated by Swedes around the year AD 550. In Zahrtmann's view, the small changes in material culture that these theories were based on might as well be the result of internal development. He also stressed just how Danish Bornholm was in every respect, and that its inhabitants had fought harder than any other Danes to remain Danish.[109] Like their peers on Åland and Hiiumaa, Bornholmian history writers did not like the idea that their island had been depopulated in the past. In the Bornholmian case this was linked to their strong identification as Danes, not Swedes.

The latest archaeological evidence seems to support the view that the island was not depopulated. Finn Ole Sonne Nielsen points out that the fall in the number of graves around AD 300 reflects a general trend in the whole of Denmark. The few graves that do exist on eastern Bornholm in fact represent some of the richest graves in the whole country from that period. According to Sonne Nielsen, the many preserved settlements from across the island illustrate that the limited number of graves does not give an accurate picture of the island's population.[110]

The Bornholmian Vikings are generally described as bold and willing to make full use of their strategic situation in the middle of the Baltic Sea. Barfod illustrates the island's favourable location for trade with the fact that of the 18,000 coins from the period discovered in Denmark, 5,000 were found on Bornholm.[111] Rune stones and Christianity were late to arrive on the island, according to most writers. Zahrtmann looks askance at the arrival of Christianity; he believes that Nordic culture suffered from the Latin yoke of an immigrant clergy. In 1957 professor Ole Klindt-Jensen concluded that graves indicated a Christian influence earlier than the written sources suggested, but in 1998 the archaeologist Finn Ole Sonne Nielsen claimed that new findings of coins confirmed the late arrival of Christianity. According to the latest writer, Lene Halskov Hansen of the Bornholmian Medieval Centre, the earlier idea that Bornholm was Christianized later than the rest of Denmark was based on

---

[109] Skougaard 1804, 1; Zahrtmann 1934, 46, 49–50; Rohmann 1957, 141 ff.
[110] Sonne Nielsen 1996, 42.
[111] Jørgensen 1900, 28 ff., 35; Zahrtmann 1934, 51; Barfod 1976, 17.

Adam of Bremen, an unreliable source; coins in Christian graves from around AD 1000 tell another story.[112]

After the arrival of Christianity Bornholm's location made it a target for attacks from Wendish pirates. Bornholm came under the rule of Danish kings in the tenth century, and one of their first bailiffs was Blood-Egil, who according to legend got his name from when he drank water mixed with blood to quench his thirst after a battle. He became popular among the Bornholmians because he kept the Wends at bay, but was executed by the Danish king because of his own pirate activities. Bøggild claimed that he was hanged without trial, and Ole Klindt-Jensen believes that the real reason for his execution was that he had grown too independent. According to Zahrtmann, Egil needed to engage in piracy in order to keep his fleet fit for fight against the Wends.[113] The execution of Blood-Egil is the earliest of the many examples given in Bornholmian history-writing of how Danish authorities have mistreated the island and left it at the mercy of foreigners.

Finn Ole Sonne Nielsen pointed out in 1996 that the archaeological evidence from Bornholm's Viking Age is scarce and that the period has been neglected in the literature. He does believe, however, that the pattern of settlements and large parts of the road network on the island remained intact from the Viking Age into the early nineteenth century.[114]

Medieval rivalry between kings and archbishops

From the twelfth to the fourteenth centuries Bornholm had a central position in Danish history as an arena for the power struggles between the Danish kings and the archbishops of Lund. In 1149 the archbishop gained control of three of Bornholm's four districts (*hærad*) while the last one remained in the hands of the Danish king. The king's castle Lilleborg was burned down in 1259, after which the archbishop had de facto control of the whole island. In 1327 he also gained formal control of the last quarter of Bornholm, and the island remained in the archbishop's grip until the 1520s.[115]

---

[112] Jørgensen 1900, 29 ff., 53; Bøggild 2004, 35, 133; Zahrtmann 1934, 47-8; Klindt-Jensen 1957, 136, 139; Sonne Nielsen 1998, 16-17; Halskov Hansen 2007, 60-1.
[113] Jørgensen 1900 47 ff., 51 ff.; Zahrtmann 1934, 37-8, 56 ff.; Klindt-Jensen 1957, 139; Barfod 1976, 17; Bøggild 2004, 207.
[114] Sonne Nielsen 1996, 55.
[115] Halskov Hansen 2007, 65.

The Bornholmian history writers are divided in their views on this conflict. Jørgensen and Bøggild are critical of the archbishops, especially of the fact that Archbishop Jakob Erlandssen made an alliance with Bornholm's old enemies, the Wends, in his attack on Lilleborg. Jørgensen claimed that many complaints against the archbishop were sent to the king in the fourteenth century, both from the locals and from the Hanseatic League. He admitted that it is not certain the Bornholmians would have had an easier time as direct subjects of the Danish king, but at least it was a grave historical untruth to claim, like Zahrtmann, that the archbishop's rule ushered in a golden age.[116]

In his book from 1934 Zahrtmann did not any more describe the period as a Golden Age, and he distanced himself from Jakob Erlandsson's alliance with the enemies of the realm. His general view of the archbishops' reign was still relatively positive, however. He claimed that Bornholm was in many respects independent in legal matters, not subject to Skåne, and that the island probably had its own thing (*landsting*). Furthermore, since Bornholm belonged to the archbishop, the island did not come under Swedish rule as Skåne did for 28 years in the fourteenth century, when the Danish king used the province as pawn.[117]

Most recently, Lene Halskov Hansen puts the conflict into a larger perspective by mentioning that there was strife between Church and Crown across the whole of Europe in the mid-thirteenth century. She also notes, however, that Archbishop Erlandssen was said to be fighting as much for himself as for the Church, and that the pope sent a furious letter to Erlandssen after the burning of Lilleborg.[118]

The differences in the Bornholmian history writers' evaluation of the Middle Ages, although they generally agree in their judgements of other periods, are probably related to the fact that this was a time of war between two rival Danish seats of power. In conflicts between Denmark and foreign threats, the writers—as Danes—support Denmark, and in conflicts between Bornholm and the Danish central authorities they—as Bornholmians—generally side with the islanders, although a few exceptions can be found. This simple identity-based compass does not give much guidance in the complex feudal political landscape of the Middle Ages. It is telling that the only thing there is complete agreement

---

[116] Bøggild 2004, 70–1; Jørgensen 1900, 60, 66, 71, 80.
[117] Zahrtmann 1934, 66, 75 ff., 81, 90–1.
[118] Halskov Hansen 2007, 64.

about is that it was unsuitable for Archbishop Jakob Erlandsson to invite the foreign Wends to attack the king's troops on Bornholm.

Churches

The writers agree that the first wooden churches on the island were built around 1170 and that they were replaced with stone churches a century later. The origin and function of Bornholm's peculiar round stone churches is hotly contested, however. Most authors believe they were defensive towers. Zahrtmann also claimed that they were built by a Bornholmian master, and that their round shape represented a genuinely Nordic architecture connected to sun worship.[119]

In 2003 a former journalist at TV Bornholm, Egil Haagensen, suggested in a book that Bornholm's churches were not defensive structures but built as magazines for the crusades, probably by the Knights Templar. Furthermore, he believed that the churches were placed in a deliberate geometrical pattern. A slight deviance between the ideal pattern and the actual placement of the churches was explained as a compromise between geometry and practical considerations. Haagensen developed his theories in later works, bringing the Holy Grail into the equation. In *Sigtet for tavshed* ('Indicted for silence', 2007) he suggested that the round churches formed a great astronomical observatory, which enabled the Knights Templar to disprove the heliocentric worldview as early as in the twelfth century. The Church kept this discovery secret, delaying the Copernican revolution by 400 years. The book is structured as a trial where the Church is accused of crimes against humanity, and Haagensen himself is a witness. Two figures known from Galileo Galilei's *Dialogue of the two world systems*, Simplicius and Salviati, are among the spectators. While the simpleton Simplicius in Galileo's book uses the pope's arguments for the heliocentric world view, in *Sigted for tavshed* he puts his trust in archaeologists from Lund University and Danish medieval historians who have criticized Haagensen's theories. The reasonable Salviati, meanwhile, is as sceptical of professors as journalists and writers.[120]

Although criticized by scholars at universities in Sweden and Denmark, Haagensen's theories have had an impact in the Bornholmian

---

[119] Skougaard 1804, 241 ff.; Jørgensen 1900, 54 ff.; Zahrtmann 1934, 55–6, 61, 63, 68; Christiansen 1957, 377, 381–2, 396 ff.; Bøggild 2004, 134.
[120] Haagensen 2003, 112, 2006, 2007, 86.

community and among tourists.[121] He has spread his ideas through books, newspaper articles, documentary films, an adventure film, and his homepage. Recent regional history-writing has also suggested that the churches might have played a role in the crusades.[122] No other writer than Haagensen, however, mentions the possibility that the Knights Templar might be connected to Bornholm.

Finn Ole Sonne Nielsen, archaeologist at the Bornholm Museum, claimed in a newspaper article in 2006 together with other scholars that Haagensen's theories lacked all kinds of evidence. He also stated that the Bornholmian tourism industry was in a froth of excitement over Haagensen's theories about the Knights Templar and their hidden treasure, and was planning to arrange a treasure hunt. According to Sonne Nielsen, Bornholm Museum and the Bornholm Medieval Centre were going to take part, but only because they wanted to prove that there was no connection between the Knights Templar and Bornholm.[123]

The treasure hunt, which was first arranged on Bornholm in 2012, is based on the testament of Eskil, who became bishop of Bornholm in 1137. The testament, which is a fictive creation by Haagensen but based upon what he believes are the facts of medieval and biblical history, was divided into 24 parts which were dispersed at historical sites around the island. Families and tourists could buy a backpack needed to find all the missing pieces, a task estimate to last two to five days. The last piece was to be found at the Bornholm Medieval Centre, which was indeed one of the organizers of the treasure hunt.[124] The centre is also the publisher of Halskov Hansen's book about the island's Middle Ages.

Not all Bornholmian churches are round; several have a rectangular shape. One of them is the island's main church, Aa kirke in Aakirkeby, which was constructed around the turn of the twelfth century and is thus probably also the oldest. According to Bøggild, Adolf Hitler considered it

---

[121] *Kristeligt Dagblad*, 16 May 2006, <http://www.kristeligt-dagblad.dk/artikel/38476:Kirke---tro--Fantasteri-og-forskruet-vroevl>, accessed 14 December 2012.
[122] Bøggild 2004, 134; Halskov Hansen 2007, 66 ff.
[123] *Kristeligt Dagblad*, 16 May 2006, <http://www.kristeligt-dagblad.dk/artikel/38476:Kirke---tro--Fantasteri-og-forskruet-vroevl>, accessed 14 December 2012.
[124] Erling Haagensen, <http://www.merling.dk/Eskilstestamente1.html>, accessed 14 December 2012; Skattejagt Bornholm, <http://www.skattejagtbornholm.dk>, accessed 14 December 2012.

such a masterpiece of Germanic architecture that he wanted to move it to Berlin.[125]

Early modern Bornholm

For most of the sixteenth century, Lübeck dominated Bornholm. The second half of the century and the whole of the seventeenth century was characterized by wars between Denmark and Sweden, which often left the Bornholmians on the front line.

The age of Lübeck, 1525–75

For fifty years, from 1525 to 1575, the Danish king leased Bornholm to Lübeck. The Bornholmian history writers give slightly different descriptions of how this came about. According to J. A. Jørgensen the Lübeckers helped Frederick I come to power, and they received Bornholm because the king did not have the funds to pay his debts. Marius Kristian Zahrtmann instead emphasized that Bornholm was given to the Lübecker in return for Gotland, which they had occupied. In his interpretation this meant that the king had traded Danish Bornholm for originally Swedish Gotland, which exercised Zahrtmann greatly: 'Bornholm was regarded as a chattel, which could be sold, not as an indispensable limb of the body of Denmark'.[126] To Zahrtmann, who was in favour of Bornholm's integration as a normal part of Denmark, this was a historical disaster.

The first Lübecker governor, Berendt Knop, is generally described as cruel and greedy in regional history-writing. During the Count's Feud 1534–1536, when Lübeck tried to reinstate Christian II as king of Denmark, the Bornholmians revolted against Knop. He was however able to crush the revolt. Both Jørgensen and Zahrtmann wrote that Christian III promised the Bornholmians support, but then extended the Lübeckians lease of the island by 50 years. Jørn Klindt-Jensen considered it ironic that the Lübeckers during the Count's Feud acted as proponents of democracy and freedom of religion. He believed the Bornholmian

---

[125] Christiansen 1957, 384; Bøggild 2004, 21.
[126] Jørgensen 1900, 80–1; Zahrtmann 1934, 111–14 ('Borringholm regnedes som et Stykke Løsøre, der kunde sælges bort, ikke som et umisteligt Lem af Danmarks Legem').

uprising was an effect of 'poor communications: the Bornholmian peasants were not informed about Skipper Clement's peasant uprising on Jutland, which was directed against the other side in the conflict.[127]

Later Lübeckian governors are described more positively. Schweder Kettingk, who defended the island against the Swedes during the Northern Seven Years War (1563–1570), is even portrayed as a hero. Zahrtmann, Jørgensen, and Klindt-Jensen describe him as the man who first taught the Bornholmians to defend their island—something Jørgensen claimed the Lundensians (aka the archbishops) had never taught them. Klindt-Jensen went so far as to claim that Kettingk thereby laid the foundation of 'the island's independence as a Danish country'.[128]

Schweder Kettingk learned Danish, was made a Danish nobleman by the king, and asked for reduced taxes on Bornholm because of the sufferings during the war.[129] However, for many centuries Kettingk was remembered as a wicked governor. Jørgensen gave Zahrtmann the credit for having cleared his name. According to Zahrtmann, Kettingk became a victim in the power struggle between the king and the council in Lübeck, and the accusations raised against him in the process gave him a bad reputation. He believes that Kettingk's objections to the king's heavy war taxes were the main reason why he was deposed.[130]

Zahrtmann believed that Kettingk tried to maintain better relations with the Danish king than his predecessors since he realized that Lübeck's power was dwindling, and Denmark's rising.[131] An important circumstance that made it possible for Schweder Kettingk to become popular in Bornholmian history-writing is that Denmark and Lübeck were on the same sides in the Northern Seven Years War.

The Danish king Frederick II demanded Bornholm back in 1575, although Lübeck wanted to extend the lease. Frederick II dismissed the Lübeckians' claim that Christian III had extended the period with 50 years in 1535, on the grounds that the Danish council had not consented to the decision. Zahrtmann also recounted the legend of how the Danish king

---

[127] Jørgensen 1900, 84–5; Zahrtmann 1934, 118–19; Klindt-Jensen 1957b, 267; Bøggild 2004, 72–3.
[128] Jørgensen 1900, 275; Zahrtmann 1934, 150, 160–1; Klindt-Jensen 1957b, 269, 271 ('øens selvstændighed som dansk land'); Bøggild 2004, 73–7.
[129] Zahrtmann 1934, 138, 155, 160–1.
[130] Jørgensen 1900, 109, 115; Zahrtmann 1934, 175; Klindt-Jensen 1957b, 269.
[131] Zahrtmann 1934, 147.

had danced with the Lübecker mayor's wife, whereupon she persuaded her husband to give the island back to Denmark.[132]

Zahrtmann claimed that the long period of foreign rule was an enforced schooling which left the Bornholmians self-reliant and quick-witted. The Lübeck period has been called the Peddler Regime, but Zahrtmann considered that infantile; although not all of them became a Schweder Kettingk, peddlers were a respectable estate.[133] This reveals a more positive view of burghers than is found in Ålandic and Saaremaa history-writing.

After the Lübeckian period, Bornholm returned to Denmark like a chicken chased out of the nest, according to Zahrtmann. He claimed that, although Bornholm was now reunited with Denmark and the islanders knew of their Danish decent, the Danes did not fully accept the Bornholmians as countrymen. The laws of the kingdom did not apply to Bornholm, which like the Faroe Islands was treated as something of an exception. Although Bornholmian history after 1576 to a large extent followed Danish history, it also had some separate developments. The Bornholmians even had a chronology of their own; while the rest of Denmark used regnal years, the islanders used the governors residing at Hammershus Castle for gubannatorial years instead.[134]

It is noteworthy that Bornholm's relative independence after 1576 is described in such negative terms, a parallel to how Martin Körber on Saaremaa considered the periods in the Middle Ages when the island had been governed more independently to regrettable. For writers who strongly identify with mainland nations, historical periods when the islands enjoy relative independence are not always welcome.

The Swedish invasion of 1645

The Swedish admiral Carl Gustav Wrangel invaded Bornholm in 1645. Bornholm was defended by a militia, which threw down its arms almost without a fight. This event is seen as shameful in Bornholmian history-writing, and responsibility for it is placed on the officers in the militia.

The invasion came during the peace negotiations between Sweden and Denmark in Brømsebro, and was intended to increase the Danes' willingness to make concessions. The Swedes landed near Nexø, took the city

---

[132] Zahrtmann 1934; Jørgensen 1900, 116; Zahrtmann 1934, 182–3.
[133] Zahrtmann 1934, 184.
[134] Zahrtmann 1934, 185.

quite easily, and in short order all drunk. Several regional history writers believe that if the militia had attacked at this point they could have won. The men were eager to fight, but their own officers forbade them to do so. According to Jørgensen and Zahrtmann, the officers even threatened to shoot at their men with cannons if they attempted to attack the Swedes.[135]

The naval historian Jørgen Barfod gave a slightly different picture in 1976. He too believed it was the officers who encouraged the Bornholmians to surrender at Nexø, but added that at Hammershus Castle the situation was reversed: the men gave in, leaving their officers no other choice but to surrender.[136]

Zahrtmann claimed that it was the Danish king who saved Bornholm from becoming part of Sweden in 1645: he preferred to give away two Norwegian counties and two 'un-Danish' islands, Gotland and Saaremaa.[137] As in his description of why Bornholm was leased to Lübeck in 1525, Zahrtmann divided the Danish realm into Danish and un-Danish parts.

Since it was decided at the peace negotiations that Denmark would get Bornholm back, the Swedish governor John Burdon tried to extort as much as possible from the island in the short time available. According to Jørgensen, the events of 1645 instilled a hatred of Swedes among the Bornholmians.[138]

Jørgensen and Zahrtmann claimed that the militia officers who had surrendered without a fight feared the day Bornholm would be returned to Denmark and asked Wrangel for help. Jørgensen wrote that they were sentenced to death, but were pardoned and exiled instead. He believed that Wrangel had influenced the Swedish government to stand surety for their lives, and that most of them fled to Sweden.[139]

The description of events on Bornholm in 1645 are similar to the Ålandic descriptions of the uprising against Russian forces in 1808 in one respect: the lower and middle stratum of the population are described as patriots who were willing to fight against the foreign invaders, while members of the elite are seen as cowards and collaborators.

---

[135] Skougaard 1804, 26 ff.; Zahrtmann 1934, 238–250; Jørgensen 1900, 134–155.
[136] Barfod 1976, 17–18.
[137] Zahrtmann 1934, 251.
[138] Jørgensen 1900, 162, 171; Zahrtmann 1934, 249–50.
[139] Jørgensen 1900, 167 ff.; Zahrtmann 1934, 251.

The uprising of 1658

The uprising against Swedish rule in 1658 is the historical event which has left the deepest traces in the Bornholmians' consciousness, according to Ebbe Gert Rasmussen. The fact that the islanders managed to defeat the Swedes by their own efforts has caught the imagination of generations, and is still today used as an example of the Bornholmians' Danishness.[140]

Zahrtmann wrote that the generation which in 1645 had put their homeland in the hands of the Swedes died in the plague of 1653–5, which killed between two-thirds and a half of the island's population: the heroes of 1658 were a new, young generation.[141]

Under the Peace of Roskilde 1658, Denmark ceded its provinces east of the Öresund—including Bornholm—to Sweden. On 20 March the Danish king sent instructions to Bornholm that the island was to be handed over to Sweden, but the message was delayed since difficult ice conditions isolated the island from the rest of Denmark until a month later. Not before 29 April did the Swedish governor Johan Printzenskiöld arrive on the island. Jørn Klindt-Jensen believes the governor alone came to represent the Swedish regime, without having proper contact with his country.[142]

Skougaard claimed in 1834 that Printzenskiöld attempted to introduce a more just system of taxation on the island. Richer peasants had acquired land from poorer peasants without any alterations being made to their taxes, and they wanted to maintain their advantage. The attempted tax revision, according to Skougaard, was the root of the growing animosity towards Printzenskiöld.[143] This emphasis on the differences between rich and poor peasants can only be found in Skougaard's writings.

Skougaard is far from the only Bornholmian history writer who has something positive to say about the Swedish governor, however. On the contrary it is a widespread opinion that earlier Danish history-writing has given a biased, anti-Swedish picture of Printzenskiöld and the uprising, largely based upon *Borringholms manifest*, a document written by the participants in the uprising in order to legitimize their deeds.[144]

---

[140] Rasmussen 2000, 7.
[141] Zahrtmann 1934, 276–7.
[142] Jørgensen 1900 p.177; Zahrtmann 1934, 279; Klindt-Jensen 1958, 43; Rasmussen 2000, 31.
[143] Skougaard 1834, 46 ff.
[144] Jørgensen 1900, 191–2; Zahrtmann 1934, 282–3; Ramussen 2000, 91.

Printzenskiöld is thus portrayed relatively positively in regional Bornholmian history-writing. He is said to have tried to ease the burdens of the Bornholmians. Jørgensen wrote that he attempted to alleviate the king's strict demands; Zahrtmann claimed that 8 of the governor's 13 letters to the Swedish king contained pleas to reduce taxes, and, according to Rasmussen, Printzenskiöld tried to limit the conscription of troops from the island.[145]

But if Printzenskiöld was not an oppressor, how do the regional history writers then explain that the Bornholmians rebelled against him? Jørgensen claimed that the islanders were full of hatred against the Swedes since 1645; therefore it was impossible for them to understand that the Swedish commander was in fact a man of honour. Like Zahrtmann, he believed Charles X Gustav's renewed attack on Denmark in the autumn of 1658 sealed Printzenskiöld's fate, and Klindt-Jensen claimed that when their new motherland attacked Denmark, their old country, the Bornholmians had to side with the latter. However, he noticed that there had been some resistance already in June, when soldiers from Bornholm refused to serve elsewhere than on their home island. The title of Klindt-Jensen's book about the uprising is a quote from one of Printzenskiöld's letters, *Disse Danske* ('These Danes'), indicating that the governor himself realized that the Swedification of Bornholm had failed. Klindt-Jensen also quotes a claim by the bookkeeper of the Swedish administration that the islanders openly declared they were good Danes, and would remain so. Klindt-Jensen stated that although it is fashionable among historians to deny that broader layers of the population harboured patriotic feelings, the uprising of 1658 is incomprehensible if the Bornholmians' patriotism is not taken into account.[146] Klindt-Jensen was thus aware that contemporary professional historians doubted the existence of a Danish nationalism in the seventeenth century, but he believed the Bornholmian uprising proved them wrong. As Ebbe Gert Rasmussen has pointed out, Klindt-Jensen was probably affected by his own experiences in the resistance movement, and projected the national feelings of the Second World War back into the seventeenth century.

---

[145] Jørgensen 1900, 178, 184, 189–90; Zahrtmann 1934, 281–2; Rasmussen 2000, 81, 84, 91.
[146] Jørgensen 1900, 194 ff., 199; Zahrtmann 1934, 286; Klindt-Jensen 1958, 55, 66, 99–100.

Rasmussen, who has written a doctoral dissertation on the uprising, explains its causes differently. He claims that the Bornholmians initially remained loyal to their new masters, even after the Swedish attack on Denmark. However, in November they changed their minds, since by that time a letter from the Danish king Frederick III which encouraged them to rebel had become widely known. Jørgensen mentioned the letter back in 1900, but claimed that it was not decisive and merely increased an already existing determination to rebel.[147] He was writing in an era when the national feelings of the Bornholmians were taken for granted.

A small group of conspirators planned to kidnap Printzenskiöld, but ended up shooting him instead. Regardless of their different opinions in other respects, the Bornholmian history writers are all critical of the killing. In Bøggild's words, they slew the rightful representative of the Swedish king. Zahrtmann believed half a dozen men should have been able to capture him alive, and Jørgensen is of the opinion that if Printzenskiöld could have been taken to Copenhagen the rebellion would have had a lustre it now lacks. [148]

With the Swedish commander dead, the rebels had no choice but to launch a full-fledged rebellion. The Swedish troops at Hammershus Fortress were made to capitulate by an act of deception—a rebel was dressed in Printzenskiöld's clothes and paraded outside the walls as a prisoner. Skougaard claimed that the soldiers were from Skåne, and therefore unwilling to shoot at their former countrymen. All writers except Skougaard agree that the Swedish defenders numbered less than 100 men; Rasmussen, who has investigated the matter most thoroughly, claims they were no more than 60. On the basis of these figures they dismissed the myths which claimed that a thousand Swedes were taken prisoners and later killed with axes in their beds, an event known as 'the Great Swine Slaughter'. Skougaard, who based his account on the folk song *Printzenskiöldsvisen*, believed the slaughter was a historical fact. Jørgensen says that the treatment of the Swedes was a dark chapter in the island's history, but that the rumours were grossly exaggerated. He believed that people gave them credence because Bornholmians were considered hard and cruel. Zahrtmann believed the myth originated in Copenhagen, and that it

---

[147] Jørgensen 1900, 199; Rasmussen 1982, 138; Rasmussen 2000, 102–103.
[148] Jørgensen 1900, 218; Zahrtmann 1934, 289–90; Bøggild 2004, 139.

marked an entire people. He did however admit that the Bornholmians themselves had passed the tradition on until our time.[149]

Skougaard published his book on the uprising in 1834, when the Romantic movement inspired scholars all over Europe to study and publish folk songs. For example, the Finnish national epic *Kalevala*, mainly based on Karelian folk songs, was published in 1835. It is in this context we might understand Skougaard's decision to rely so heavily upon *Printzenskiöldsvisen* in his description of the events in 1658.

The myth about the Great Swine Slaughter proved hard to kill. Klindt-Jensen wrote that Swedish and Danish scholars believed they had buried it in the nineteenth century, but that it unexpectedly resurfaced at the 300th anniversary of the uprising in 1958.[150]

What makes the uprising so important in the Bornholmian historical consciousness is primarily not what took place between the islanders and the Swedes before and during the uprising, but between the islanders and the Danish king afterwards. In what according to Zahrtmann was an attempt to create a legal foundation for the uprising, the Bornholmians held what they labelled a meeting of the Estates. In Rasmussen's view this was a temporary Bornholmian government: the island had opted out of Sweden but not yet opted back into Denmark. 'Bornholm was to be considered an independent island'.[151] In this respect he differs from the earlier, Danish nationalist regional history writers Zahrtmann and Jørgensen, who did not describe Bornholm as independent.

The Bornholmians decided to turn to the Danish king and offer him the island as a gift. The king accepted, and promised the islanders some privileges and that Denmark would never again allow the island to slip into foreign hands. The idea that the islanders liberated themselves, and secured their connection to Denmark forever by voluntarily offering Bornholm to the king is the cornerstone of Bornholmian regional history-writing. This idea was most clearly articulated by the late nineteenth- and early twentieth-century history writers Jørgensen and Zahrtmann. According to Jørgensen this meant that centuries of shifting sovereignty were now over, and that Bornholm was like a separate republic with

---

[149] Skougaard 1834, 74 ff., 81 ff.; Jørgensen 1900, 222, 227 ff., 231 ff.; Zahrtmann 1934, 291 ff., 295, 299; Rasmussen 2000, 117, 121.
[150] Klindt-Jensen 1958, 113.
[151] Zahrtmann 1934, 293; Rasmussen 2000, 123 ('Bornholm var at regne for en selvstændig ø').

Frederick III as lord. Zahrtmann wrote that the rebels achieved their goal that the land (Bornholm) would forever follow the motherland (Denmark), and that the Danish flag had fluttered over Bornholm ever since the Swedish flag was lowered on 9 December 1658. The Bornholmians and all Danes hoped that the king's promise would never be broken.[152]

Later writers of regional history also stress the importance of the uprising, but from the mid twentieth century they have a more cynical attitude towards Denmark's interest and ability to keep Bornholm Danish. Klindt-Jensen wrote that because of the uprising Bornholm became Danish anew 'for better or worse', and he found it astonishing that the Danish king Frederick III asked the Swedes to help his heirs defend Bornholm in the event of a *Danish* attack. This is less surprising in light of the research by Rasmussen, who has shown how the Danish king used the uprising to stage a *coup d'état* and introduce autocracy on Bornholm, two years earlier than in the rest of Denmark; the Bornholmians did not understand the importance of the fact that they had given Bornholm to the king as a personal, hereditary gift. The idea that the king fooled the Bornholmians has become generally accepted and was given greater currency in Bøggild's book from 2004. In addition, Rasmussen noted that the islanders were unaware that Frederick III had used Bornholm as security for supplies the Lübeckers delivered to Copenhagen, which was besieged by the Swedes.[153]

In his book about the uprisings on Bornholm and in Skåne in 1658–9, Rasmussen claimed that the rebels in both cases had similar, multiple purposes. In part they were motivated by their Danishness, but also by economic motives, as they hoped to gain privileges and to get rid of customs duties. Rasmussen also noted that the leaders in both cases were merchants, and that the uprisings thus can be seen as an attempt by the merchants to revolt against the established authorities. He considered it a weak parallel to other bourgeois movements in early modern Europe.[154]

The most important difference between the authors who were writing before the Second World War and the ones active after it is that the latter continuously repeat that Denmark had abandoned Bornholm. Both

---

[152] Jørgensen 1900, 255; Zahrtmann 1934, 299–300.
[153] Klindt-Jensen 1958, 133, 136 ('på godt og ont'); Rasmussen 1982, 274; Rasmussen 2000, 139; Bøggild 2004, 140.
[154] Rasmussen 2008a, 160–1.

Bøggild and Rasmussen mention the withdrawal of troops from Bornholm, the most Danish and defence-friendly part of Denmark. To Rasmussen, 1658 is not, as it was for Jørgensen and Zahrtmann, the year when Bornholm was forever tied to Denmark. Instead he stresses that the generation of 1658 knew Bornholm could manage itself, and acted accordingly. In his book about the uprising in 1658 Rasmussen also mentions the Russian bombings in 1945 as an example of how Denmark turned its back on the island; since it was 'only' Bornholm that was bombed no one even bothered to answer the phone in Copenhagen.[155] It is probable that the bombings meant the end to the enthusiastic patriotism and faith in 300-year-old royal promises that were expressed by Jørgensen and Zahrtmann.

Isolation, integration, alienation

In the eighteenth century, Bornholmians defended the privileges they had gained as a result of the 1658 uprising with relative success. In the nineteenth century a process of normalization and integration into Denmark took place, which meant that the island administratively had become an ordinary part of the kingdom by the late nineteenth century. This process was lauded as a desirable modernization by the late nineteenth and early twentieth-century history writers. However, after the Second World War, faith in Denmark's ability and willingness to take care of Bornholm's interests dwindled.

The Bornholm militia

After the uprising in 1658 the Bornholmians gained the privilege of not being excused military service outside Bornholm. Instead they were to defend their own island in the Bornholm militia, where all men from the island served.

The two most prominent Bornholmian history writers in the late nineteenth and early twentieth centuries, the teacher J. A. Jørgensen and the doctor Marius Kofoed Zahrtmann, claimed that it was considered an honour to serve in the militia. According to them the islanders were good soldiers, but disliked formal discipline and exercises. They connect this to

---

[155] Bøggild 2004, 42–3; Rasmussen 2000, 159 ff.

the difference between free Bornholmian peasants and the subjugated Danish peasants. Zahrtmann called the eighteenth century the 'century of whipping', but claimed that the Bornholmians stayed outside it: the free Bornholmians would not stand for it, and less than anyone to have needed patriotism whipped into them. He noted that the militia's commander Kruse in 1741 wanted to enforce corporal punishment as in the rest of the army, but that the ministry of war in Copenhagen, who knew the Bornholmians better, answered that it was better to punish them with fines 'Since the people on Bornholm are of their own mind, and it does not seem expedient to use to much rigour'.[156]

The early nineteenth-century scholar Peder Nikolai Skougaard also opposed military exercises, but on the practical grounds that he believed the militia should be used as light troops. Field exercises made the troops better at harassing the enemy and making use of the terrain without getting involved in battles. He also claimed that the militia's armament a motley collection of rifles that had just one thing in common—they were no good for shooting. On top of that, he described how one officer was almost beaten to death by his men, and spent several pages criticizing other officers.[157]

Skougaard's sharp and ironic criticism of the militia was raised during his trial for exceeding press freedoms with *Beskrivelse over Bornholm*. Christian Stubb-Jørgensen believes that Skougaard got his detailed information about the militia's flaws from his father, who was a lieutenant in the Bornholm Dragoons.[158]

When the Bornholm militia was dissolved in 1867, the islanders started to go to the mainland for military training. Contemporary Bornholmian history writers were quite positive of this change, Zahrtmann because it brought the island closer to the motherland, Jørgensen because it allowed the islanders to widen their horizons. He was of the opinion that the militia's officers had long understood they needed military training, and that the new freedom[159] brought enlightenment, which made them willing to accept the change without referring to Bornholms privileges, as had always been the case in the past. Zahrtmann claimed that since 1867 a

---

[156] Jørgensen 1901, 162, 166; Zahrtmann 1935, 99–100, ('Som nu Folket paa Borringholm er af en egen Genie, og det ikke synes tjenligt att bruge for megen Rigeur'), 184.
[157] Skougaard 1804, 159, 166, 168.
[158] Stub-Jørgensen 1958, 37–8.
[159] Absolute monarchy was abandoned in 1849.

more Danish and less Bornholmian breed had grown up on the island.[160] His observation corresponds well with the common assumption that conscription has been one of the most effective ways for the nation-state to create national identity and cohesion.

How best to understand that Zahrtmann described the Bornholmians in the eighteenth century as the most patriotic of all Danes, but still claimed that they became more Danish after the introduction of military service? We need to remember the difference between patriotism in the old, autocratic Danish conglomerate state and nationalism in the Danish citizen state that emerged in the mid nineteenth century. This difference is best illustrated by Skougaard, the only regional history writer who experienced the eighteenth century and early nineteenth century himself. By historical happenstance, the Bornholm Dragoons happened to have the arms of Jutland on their banner. Skougaard considered this wrong, since they would never have fought for Jutland, but only for their *fødeland* (native land, meaning Bornholm) and their king.[161] Loyalty was thus restricted to their own island and to the king.

The Bornholmian journalist Hansaage Bøggild claims that the Bornholmians maintained their military pride well into the twentieth century; peasants even used their military titles in the phonebook. He links this to a sense of freedom and pride as well as consciousness that serfdom had never existed on the island.[162]

In his essay about peasants in *Bogen om Bornholm*, the journalist Vagn Heiselberg highlighted one consequence of the militia's existence which paradoxically diminished the Bornholmians' freedom: it lessened their chances to move away from the island, since they were not allowed to abandon the militia. It was easy to get a dispensation, especially since the authorities wanted to reduce the pressure on the island's agricultural lands in the eighteenth century.[163]

Defending Bornholm's privileges

The Bornholmians' problems did not end after the uprising. The Swedish commander Printzenskiöld is described quite positively in Bornholmian history-writing, but many of the subsequent Danish commanders are

---

[160] Jørgensen 1901, 306; Zahrtmann 1935, 238–9.
[161] Skougaard 1804, 178.
[162] Bøggild 2004, 42–3.
[163] Heiselberg 1937, 188, 193.

portrayed as villains. Worst of them all was August Deckner. Eventually the Bornholmians managed to get him punished, and he died in hard labourer in 1691.[164]

Most important of the privileges the Bornholmians received as a reward for their efforts during the rebellion was a reduction of certain taxes. Skougaard, who wrote when the privileges were still in place, found them highly reasonable: taxes were paid in order to maintain security, order, and defence, and since the Bornholmians handled these matters themselves without recompense from central government, it would be unjust to demand Danish levels of taxation from them.[165]

It was when the islanders also refused to pay new taxes introduced by the king that conflicts arose. The king could not use the Bornholm militia to extract taxes, since it consisted of the island's male population—the taxpayers. According to Zahrtmann, 1,000 Danish soldiers were about to be sent to Bornholm in 1770, but the Bornholmian Peder Koefoed Ancher—descendant of the two main leaders of the 1658 uprising—managed to avoid an armed conflict. Instead he saw to it that the privileges were clearly specified, which made future conflicts easier to avoid. Jørgensen claimed that this was an important turning point in the island's history, since it put an end to the many false and unreasonable interpretations of the privileges. Zahrtmann is of the opinion that the Bornholmians' by dint of their successful defence of their privileges, had shuffled themselves to the edge of Denmark's map into a position similar to that of the Faroe Islands. Denmark's laws were not enforced on the island, and the peasants opposed all progress such as roads, measures against sand erosion, and the regulation of home stills.[166]

Several writers describe the effect that home distillation had on the Bornholmians' drinking habits. Skougaard claimed in 1804 that the Bornholmians considered home distillation to be one of their privileges, and that it would not be abolished without a rebellion. Distillation had increased on the island since its prohibition in Sweden in 1768. According to Bøggild, they drank twice as much as other Danes, and Skougaard claimed they consumed even more alcohol than other heavy drinkers such as the Icelanders, the Faroese, and the inhabitants of Northern Norway

---

[164] Jørgensen 1901, 95–6; Zahrtmann 1935, 61, 79
[165] Skougaard 1804, 135–141.
[166] Jørgensen 1901, 159; Zahrtmann 1935, 45, 175, 177, 180 ff.

and Finnmarken.[167] Here too Skougaard's parallels were drawn between Bornholm and peripheral Danish possessions, and not with Jutland, Funen, and Zealand.

Bøggild claimed that when Denmark's first elected government abolished this privilege the delegates from Bornholm raised objections on the grounds that spirits were necessary for hardworking family men in quarries and coalmines.[168] These particular occupations were probably mentioned because they were unique to Bornholm: there were no quarries and coalmines elsewhere in Denmark, whereas hardworking peasants and fishermen could be found elsewhere, and were not enough to justify an exception.

In Zahrtmann's opinion, the Bornholmians were more royalist than the government and the king himself in their defence of their privileges. He believed this bold loyalty made the king refrain from intervening against the Bornholmians even when they were clearly violating the law.[169] In other words, the Bornholmians' expressions of royalism and patriotism delayed the island's integration with the rest of Denmark. To such Danish nationalists as Jørgensen and Zahrtmann there was nothing good about that.

Heroes of progress in the nineteenth century

Hans Rømer and Peder Dam Jespersen are two figures who in Bornholmian history-writing are used to illustrate how the modern world impinged the island, despite resistance from its conservative inhabitants. Jørgensen described Rømer, forester (*skovrider*) on the island in 1800–36, as a Bornholmian oborn and bred from old peasant family who was educated by his mother. While his predecessors had been mainly preoccupied with supplying the royal kitchens with game, Rømer worked all his life planting forests on Bornholm. The Bornholmian journalist Hansaage Bøggild claimed that it was thanks to Rømer that the island became Denmark's most forested *amt*. The forests are concentrated in *Allmindingen* (The commons) at the centre of the island. In his essay about Allmindingen in *Bogen om Bornholm* from 1957, the teacher Frede Kjøller described how peasants, angry that their livestock were not allowed to graze in the forest, sabotaged Rømer's fences, and lured pigs to feed on the small tree plants. According

---

[167] Skougaard 1804, 86–7; Bøggild 2004, 87.
[168] Bøggild 2004, 87.
[169] Zahrtmann 1935, 183.

to Zahrtmann, Rømer was also the representative of the Danish Commission of Antiquities (Oldsagskommissionen) on Bornholm, and he did investigations of the old castles Gamleborg and Lilleborg which are situated in Allmindingen.[170]

The west coast of Bornholm consists of sandy beaches, and according to Jørgensen the local population had caused severe erosion in the eighteenth century by allowing their animals to graze and by cutting heather peat for fuel. After storms, roads and farmlands were covered with sand. The Danish government issued a regulation against beach erosion in 1792, but the Bornholmians stubbornly opposed it and managed to delay its implementation—until the Bornholmian administrator and large landowner Peder Dam Jespersen was employed as Sandflugts kommissær (Beach Erosion commissioner) in 1819. Patiently, he planted a forest which offered protection against the devastating sand. Jørgensen claimed that locals were so ignorant that they shot at Jespersen and Rømer. In Jørgensen's days almost a century later the islanders were instead full of gratitude to Rømer and Jespersen.[171]

Zahrtmann dwelt on Rømer and Jespersen in his book since he believed that the transition between old and new was reflected in their lives. Unlike Jørgensen he also described the conflicts that arose between the two. Jespersen started to plant forests on the island, something Rømer for decades had considered his prerogative, and that might have sparked animosity. Zahrtmann, however, mainly considered the cause to be that they were both typical Bornholmians. He referred to the old saying that went that you should never take more Bornholmians on board than there are masts to bind them to, and claimed that the infighting between Rømer and Jespersen meant that Copenhagen was unwilling to install native Bornholmians as officials on their own island.[172]

However, the Bornholmians did not meet all aspects of Denmark's modernization with conservative resistance. According to the author Christian Stubb-Jørgensen, the new constitution which Denmark acquired in 1848 suited the Bornholmian culture in many ways. He believed democracy was the system which provided the best possible opportunities for free spirits like the Bornholmians. In addition, Stubb-

---

[170] Jørgensen 1901, 261; Bøggild 2004, 51, 56 ff.; Zahrtmann 1935, 255; Kjøller 1957, 365.
[171] Jørgensen 1901, 267 ff.
[172] Zahrtmann 1935, 253–4, 284.

Jørgensen claimed that the Bornholmians were fast learners and therefore adapted well to cultural changes.[173]

In K. H. Kofoed's meticulous investigation of Bornholm's political history covering 1848–1913—which spans five volumes of *Bornholmske samlinger*—it is mentioned that Bornholm was allowed to keep its tax privileges after 1848 only because the island's isolated location made it impossible for its inhabitants to fully enjoy the benefits of the Danish state. However, in 1896 a Danish minister claimed their isolation had ended now there was regular steamboat traffic and the island had recently become equipped with better harbours than any other part of the realm. He also used the planned construction of a railway on the island as a reason why the Bornholmians should now be taxed like other Danes.[174] The end of Bornholm's privileges was thus seen as a natural outcome of the perceived end of the island's isolation.

Kofoed's writings describe the very period in Bornholm's history when the island was integrated into Denmark and regional history-writing started to express a strong Danish patriotism. Simultaneously, on the Faroe Islands, to which Bornholm was often compared (and which had its own Skougaard in Svabo) sentiment instead turned in the direction of a separate Faroese nationalism. The late nineteenth century might thus be described as truly decisive for the development of Bornholmian identity. With the exception of Kofoed's work, however, the period is poorly covered in regional history-writing. Although equally important, the gradual transformation of Bornholmian society brought on by industrialism and nationalism does not form as tantalizing a topic for regional history-writing as the uprising in 1658 and the Second World War. The lack of any recently written general history of Bornholm probably contributes to the fact that the period is relatively neglected.

The Schleswig wars, 1848–51 and 1864

In the mid nineteenth century Denmark fought two wars over the sovereignty of Schleswig and Holstein, two duchies in the Danish realm with a substantial German population. The wars proved important for Denmark's and Germany's development into nation-states. However, the Bornholmians were left outside of this nationally decisive war. Jørgensen

---

[173] Stubb-Jørgensen 1957, 519.
[174] Kofoed 1940 p.35–6.

wrote that the national movement which accompanied the first war did not become as strong on Bornholm as in the rest of the country. Since the militias obligations were limited to defending the island, Bornholmians did not need to follow the events as anxiously as other Danes. Jørgensen did however stress that they might still have been patriotic and nationalist in their minds and thoughts. Zahrtmann believed that the Bornholmians during both wars considered it wrong that they were mere spectators to Denmark's struggle.[175]

In 1957 the engineer Jørn Klindt-Jensen took the fact that there were Bornholmian volunteers in the war as a sign that the islanders had finally begun to feel affinity with other Danish provinces. Although the number of Bornholmian volunteers was small, the artillerist Johan Andreas Peter Ancher managed to become a national hero in the Second Schleswig War. Zahrtmann stressed that Ancher was a son of Bornholm's militia, and thus allowed that organization to bask in the reflected glory. Jørgensen wrote that the whole Denmark contributed to an honorary sabre that was awarded to Ancher after the war and that he managed to achieve hero status even on the enemy side.[176] To Zahrtmann and Jørgensen, who welcomed Bornholm's integration as a normal part of Denmark, it was important to highlight the few Bornholmians who had taken part in this nationally decisive struggle.

To the nationalist regional history writers in the early twentieth century, and even for Klindt-Jensen in the middle of the century, it was natural to assume that the Bornholmians were at least emotionally engaged in the conflict. However, in 2004 Bøggild wrote that the war took place far from Bornholm, that the islanders had no relationship to it, and that they were not even obliged to take part.[177] In the twenty-first century it is no longer self-evident for regional history writers to assume that Bornholmians have always been Danish patriots.

Perhaps Bøggild's view of the Bornholmians' sentiments during the wars was influenced by Lourents Peter, who was originally from Southern Schleswig but worked as a teacher on Bornholm during the Schleswig wars. In 1966 Bøggild published a compilation of Peter's letters, in which it was claimed that the Bornholmians did not care whether the island

---

[175] Jørgensen 1901, 277–8; Zahrtmann 1935, 237.
[176] Jørgensen 1901, 282 ff.; Zahrtmann 1935, 238; Klindt-Jensen 1957b, 315.
[177] Bøggild 2004, 214.

became Danish, Swedish, or German, as long as it remained Bornholmian. Peter also believed Bornholmian peasants would rather become Swedish subjects than pay the war taxes.[178]

Bornholm's isolation from the rest of the country is illustrated by Peter's description of how the islanders learned about the outbreak of the Second Schleswig War in February 1964. They did not receive any information from Copenhagen, and since the mail was delayed five days—normally it arrived once a week in wintertime—the first confused information came from English and Russian ships. The Bornholmians decided to telegraph Copenhagen for a clarification, which required them to send a boat to Ystad in Sweden.[179] Although Lourents Peter's account might be coloured by resentment at the fact that the Bornholmians were not as engaged as himself in the war which was taking place in his native Southern Schleswig, his observations illustrate that in the 1860s Bornholm's low level of integration into the Danish kingdom was still equalled by low levels of national sentiments among its inhabitants.

Bornholm in the Second World War

Zahrtmann described attitudes on Bornholm in the early twentieth century as being quite anti-German, and judging by the tone of his writings Zahrtmann himself shared these feelings. He claimed that the beautiful northern Bornholm was made ugly by German names such as *Hotell Strandschloss*. When German entrepreneurs planned to create a *Neu-Berlin* on Bornholm, patriots collected money to buy the land and raised the Danish flag on the spot. The First World War ended the threat from German tourists as they disappeared across the sea.[180]

However, in 1940 Bornholm became occupied by Germany, one day later than the rest of Denmark. The Bornholmian resistance movement published a justification as early as 1945, in which it explained it had held a low profile during the war in order to lull the Germans into a feeling of security. This strategy had enabled them to smuggle refugees to Sweden via Bornholm.[181]

Two decades later the prominent Danish resistance fighter and naval historian Jørgen Barfod was commissioned by Bornholms Historiske

---

[178] Bøggild 1966, 34.
[179] Bøggild 1966, 32–3.
[180] Zahrtmann 1935, 319–20.
[181] Frihedbevægelsen 1945, 4.

Samfund to write a book about the Bornholmian resistance, which he completed in 1976. Barfod stressed that the island's position far to the east and distant from the rest of Denmark created other circumstances for the resistance than elsewhere in the country. For example, the German forces on the island were subject to naval command in Kiel, not to the German command in Denmark.[182]

Many writers draw a parallel between the Second World War and the island's seventeenth-century history. Jørn Klindt-Jensen pointed out that the Soviet attack on Bornholm took place 300 years after the Swedish attack in 1645, and that it begun in the same place, Nexø.[183] It is however the uprising against the Swedes in 1658 which is most commonly linked to the island's situation in 1940–1945.

Barfod mentions that the Bornholmian resistance used the freedom fighters of 1658 as role models, and that the first edition of their illegal paper *Pro Patria* had a seventeenth-century fighter on the front page. The leader of the civil administration on Bornholm, *amtmand* Paul Christian Stemann, towards the end of the war invoked the memory of the uprising in his negotiations with the German commander Captain Gerhard von Kamptz. Stemann said that the Bornholmians were normally calm and reasonable, but could get violent if they lost patience, and had once shot a Swedish commander who was sent to the island.[184]

In spite of this, Barfod describes Stemann as basically German-friendly, which caused him difficulties in the local community, which held a more negative view of the occupants. According to Barfod, the Bornholmians were politically moderate, and extremist parties such as the Nazis and communists gained little support on the island.[185]

Initially, Kamptz was given the blame for the Soviet bombings of Bornholm in May 1945, both internationally and in regional Bornholmian history-writing. He has been described as a madman who continued to fight after the German capitulation. For example, the resistance movement claimed in 1945 that Germans fired on Soviet planes, which caused the bombings on 7 May, and that von Kamptz's refusal to surrender resulted in the major bombardment the following day. Barfod was however of the opinion that the German fire on the planes, was

---

[182] Barfod 1976, 9.
[183] Klindt-Jensen 1957, 317.
[184] Barfod 1976, 108, 237.
[185] Barfod 1976, 44, 70, 332.

insignificant. According to him, events on Bornholm were reminiscent of what happened in most of Europe; it was Denmark that was a peaceful exception. Klindt-Jensen, Barfod, and Bøggild wrote that Bornholm was an important link in the German rescue of refugees across the Baltic Sea, which meant that Kamptz's continued resistance enabled a mass evacuation. Barfod also pointed out that since the military forces on the island were under the direct command of the German navy, they were not included in the capitulation of German forces in Denmark: Bornholm was in effect part of the Eastern front. In spite of that, Kamptz declared himself willing to surrender to British forces, but they did not arrive.[186]

The fact that Bornholm was bombed while the rest of Denmark was celebrating the end of the war—and particularly that the regional resistance movement was unable to get the ministers in Copenhagen to answer their telephones while bombs were falling over Rønne and Nexø—led to strong sense of abandonment on the island. In his book, the Bornholmian journalist Børge Kure used the headline 'Abandoned and betrayed by their country' to describe the sentiments. According to Rasmussen, the foreign minister did not have time to come to the phone, since it was 'only' Bornholm which was being bombed. Klindt-Jensen, who was writing in 1957, noted that even then no one had explained why the Danish government acted as it did. Professor Bent Jensen has thoroughly investigated whether the image that Copenhagen abandoned Bornholm is true. His conclusion is that all initiatives for contact came from Bornholm, and that the central authorities in the capital made no effort whatsoever to inform themselves about the situation on the island.[187]

Although regional Bornholmian history-writing in general stresses the island's Danish patriotism, the descriptions of the 1945 bombings give a unique example of how rapidly the dramatic events of war might affect feelings of affinity and identity. Both the Bornholmian journalist Børge Kure and Barfod state that the islanders were so disappointed with the Danish government's inability to help during the Soviet bombings and occupation of the island that they were contemplating joining Sweden

---

[186] Frihedsbevægelsen 1945, 5–6; Klindt-Jensen 1957b, 317; Barfod 1976, 264–5, 336; Bøggild 2004, 181 ff.
[187] Kure 1981, 13, 15, ('Forladt og svigtet av deres fædreland'); Knudsen 2000, 16–17; Rasmussen 2000, 159; Bøggild 2004, 179; Klindt-Jensen 1957b, 319; Jensen 1996, 112.

instead.[188] This brief shift of sentiment was influenced by the fear that Bornholm would become permanently occupied by the Soviet Union.

However, most of the writers agree that the generous aid the Bornholmians received from Denmark after the bombings lessened the feelings that they had been abandoned. Sweden also helped by erecting 300 wooden houses in the bombed towns Rønne and Nexø. Although this kind of architecture is described as something completely new and foreign to Bornholm, the writers agree that they have been very popular and fit well into the surroundings. According to Klindt-Jensen this was a nice ending to the tale of Swedish attempts at conquering the island.[189] The Swedish wooden houses have thus been more easily accepted than the German tourist hotels were in the early twentieth century. This reflects the fact that Sweden was no longer perceived as a threat to Bornholm.

Back in January 1944, *amtmand* Stemann was negotiating directly with Sweden about the possibility of sending Swedish troops to the island, without contacting either the resistance or Danish politicians. Barfod considered Stemann's attempt to conduct his own policy a fatal political blunder. Kure claimed that Swedish troops were indeed ready to seize Bornholm if the Germans had not surrendered.[190] Politically wise or not, Stemann's independent actions are however far from unique; we have seen several examples of how Bornholmian governors, while isolated in wartime, have been forced to inform themselves about the political situation and independently develop strategies to best handle it.

After the Soviet landing on Bornholm there was great uncertainty of the island's future. The local committee of the resistance movement contacted a number of Danish dignitaries, including the king, in order to ensure that the island would remain Danish. Kure wrote that an attempt to bring in Danish resistance fighters trained in Sweden to the island—in order to stress the island's connections to the rest of Denmark—failed since the Soviet troops had already closed all traffic to Bornholm.[191]

The first Soviet troops to arrive on the island are described as *fremmedartede* (strange, alien) by Barfod and Kure; the latter also called them Mongols. He claimed they were so damaged by the war that they

---

[188] Kure 1981, 17; Barfod 1976, 327.
[189] Frihedsbevægelsen 1945, 6; Klindt-Jensen 1957b, 319, 321; Petersen 1957, 489; Bøggild 2004, 180.
[190] Barfod 1976, 277; Kure 1981, 88.
[191] Barfod 1976, 314; Kure 1981, 17, 21.

were considered impossible to readapt to civilian life; therefore they were sent to Bornholm where heavy fighting and high casualties were expected. Fortunately the Germans surrendered on their arrival. The book published in the first years after the war by the Bornholmian resistance movement described this first wave of Soviet soldiers as shock troops which did not make a happy impression. The Soviet troops for their part trusted the resistance fighters who they called '*partisanski*', and a close cooperation began. According to Kure, the Soviet officers even put their soldiers in a camp and asked the resistance to guard the entrances, not allowing anyone to get out without permission. Kure's book also contains the reminiscences of a Kirgizian officer 30 years afterwards. He described his arrival on Bornholm as similar to getting into paradise: suddenly the war was over, and they were surrounded by beautiful, friendly people.[192]

The resistance movement claimed in 1947 that the Russians committed surprisingly few crimes, and many of the incidents were caused by Danes who sold spirits to the Russians. Barfod also mentioned this commerce. The Russians, according to the resistance, were good-natured, but generalizations were hard to make since they represented different races: Mongols, Kirgizians, Belorussians and so on. All of them, however, liked animals and children. The resistance movement did also stressed that the Soviet troops contained many female soldiers and officers, and their brochure contains several pictures of them.[193] The description of the Soviet troops has remained fairly constant down the decades. However, the female soldiers—who seem to have fascinated contemporary Bornholmians—have disappeared from later descriptions of the Soviet occupation.

Although the resistance movement emphasized its close cooperation with the Soviets, it did admit that the fact that the foreign troops lingered long on the island, in combination with the rising foreign interest in the matter, made many Bornholmians feel nervous about the future. Bornholmian history-writing does display a certain resentment against the harsh comments about the Soviet occupation in Swedish newspapers: the resistance movement described the Swedish press as misleading and negative, contributing to the fears on the island, and Barfod quoted Anthony Eden's remark that Sweden had done little for the Allied cause

---

[192] Høgh 1947, 5; Barfod 1976, 302–303; Kure 1981, 23, 37.
[193] Høgh 1947, 5, 8; Barfod 1976, 324.

and that the relationship between the Soviet troops and the local authorities were cordial.[194]

Most writers claim that Bornholm was liberated on 5 April 1946, when the Russians left the island, not 5 May 1945 which the rest of Denmark considers its day of liberation. The resistance movement in its 1945 booklet *Bornholm: besatt, bombet, befriet* ('Bornholm: occupied, bombed, liberated'), instead indicates that Bornholm had already been liberated by the Soviet troops—with help from the resistance. The departure of the Soviet troops meant that Bornholm was against left to itself, still Danish but once again an outpost, as Jørn Klindt-Jensen described it.[195] This position as an eastern outpost of Denmark and NATO made Bornholm an important military base during the cold war.

Current relations with Denmark

The Bornholmian history writers' depictions of the decades around the turn of this century are full of grievances about Denmark. It is commonly stated that Denmark neither understands nor cares about Bornholm's needs. One example is transport, which is an area that both Bøggild and Rasmussen claim is handled without understanding by the Danish authorities. They also criticize the withdrawal of military forces from Bornholm after the end of the cold war. Bøggild writes that the dissolution of the regiment on Bornholm in 2000 stung the islanders, 90% of whom had supported the parties that were in favour of Danish NATO membership in 1949. He describes how 12,000 people formed a circle around the barracks as a protest in support of the regiment. This was in Bøggild's words a punch on the nose for the politicians, and led to the establishment of Bornholm's local defence region, the only one in the country under the direct command of the army.[196] However, on 1 January 2007 the local defence region was also dissolved.[197]

Another grievance is the lack of autonomy and the integration of Bornholm into Region Hovedstaden in 2007. Three years prior to the reform, Bøggild wrote that the Bornholmians feared being brought under

[194] Høgh 1947, 4; Barfod 1976, 316–17.
[195] Frihedsbevægelsen 1945; Barfod 1976, 326; Kure 1981, 89; Knudsen 2000, 188; Klindt-Jensen 1957, 321.
[196] Bøggild 2004, 16–17, 41–2; Rasmussen 2000, 159.
[197] Bornholm's Home Guard, <http://www.hjv.dk/HHV/TRSJ/DET%20BORNHOLMSKE%20HJEMMEV%C3%86RN/Om%20distriktet/Sider/Almegaards%20Kaserne.aspx>, 23 November 2012.

Copenhagen's control. Rasmussen claimed a year after the reform that the island was now administered from the town of Hillerød on Zealand, and that local autonomy was a mere memory.[198]

Rasmussen explains the Bornholmians' weak influence in Copenhagen with the fact that unlike the Jutlanders they do not have a strong mafia at Christiansborg, the home of the Danish Parliament and the prime minister's office. When the Jutlanders sneeze, the capital vibrates, Rassmussen claims, but the Bornholmians only have two members of parliament and are not taken seriously.[199] One example of this is given in *Østersøen gav*, where it is claimed that large Jutlandic trawlers have depleted the Bornholmians' cod fisheries, and that the responsible minister responsible sided with the big players.[200] The islanders' continued grievances have against their national government are an important factor in explaining why Bornholmian history-writing is still centred on episodes where it is felt that Copenhagen betrayed the island.

Conclusions

There is a remarkable consistency in the themes of Bornholmian history-writing. Already in the late seventeenth century locals were writing about the uprising in 1658, and this event is still one of the most dominant in the early twenty-first century. From the start, the Second World War has challenged the uprising as the most popular theme in Bornholmian history-writing. However, regional historians who write about the Second World War often refer to the uprising in 1658, and vice versa. The two events are linked by the master narrative of Bornholmian history-writing: how the Bornholmians have loved Denmark and fought harder than anyone else to be Danish, but how they have repeatedly been let down by the authorities in Copenhagen.

In spite of this consistency, a clear development can be seen in Bornholmian history-writing. The first writer in this study, Peter Nikolai Skougaard, who wrote his *Beskrivelse over Bornholm* as a student in 1804, cannot be said to have stressed the island's strong bonds to Denmark. Most often he emphasized the differences between Bornholm and other

---

[198] Bøggild 2004, 16–17; Rasmussen 2008a, 177.
[199] Rasmussen 2000, 161.
[200] Rasmussen 1993, 127.

Danish areas, and when he found similarities it was with the free peasants of Norway rather than with the serfs in Denmark proper. Skougaard found most of Bornholm's privileges reasonable. Since the Bornholmians were taking care of the defence of the island themselves, it was only fair that they did not pay as much in taxes as other Danes. Skougaard wrote in the era before nationalism, just like his contemporary Peter Wilhelm von Buxhöwden on Saaremaa. Both of them identified primarily with their home island, although Buxhöwden defended the privileges of the nobility while Skougaard identified with the peasantry, particularly its poorer members.

The only general surveys of Bornholm's history have been published by the teacher Jørgen Jørgensen in 1900–1901 and the doctor Marius Kristian Zahrtmann in 1934–1935. These two authors were both Danish nationalists, who were pleased to see that Bornholm became more integrated into Denmark in the second half of the nineteenth century. Thus they also welcomed the end of Bornholm's privileges, and particularly the replacement of the militia by military service in Denmark, since these were important steps in the formation of a more Danish generation of Bornholmians. Jørgensen and Zahrtmann thought Denmark had let Bornholm down many times in the past, with the lease of Bornholm to Lübeck in 1525–75 as the most blatant example. However, they saw the Bornholmian uprising in 1658 as a major turning point in its history, since they believed that it forever tied the island to Denmark. They also used it to illustrate the point that since the Bornholmians had delivered their island back to the king of Denmark by their own efforts, they were the only Danes who had chosen their nationality—the most Danish of all Danes.

It could be added that at the time when Zahrtmann wrote his book another area had indeed chosen to become part of Denmark, since Northern Schleswig was reunited with the country through the plebiscite of 1920.

Bornholmian history-writing from the period after the Second World War was less optimistic about Denmark's ability to defend Bornholm and safeguard its interests. The Soviet bombings of Rønne and Nexø in May 1945, which took place while the rest of Denmark was celebrating the end of the war, were together with the subsequent Soviet occupation an important turning point. Jørgensen's and Zahrtmann's belief that the uprising in 1658 had forever tied the island to Denmark was now questioned. Several authors claim that the islanders for a brief period of time contemplated to joining Sweden instead, although Sweden had earlier been portrayed as the island's arch-enemy in regional history-writing.

It would be wrong to assume that the return to more negative attitudes towards the Danish government was solely a consequence of the events in 1945. Attitudes seem to have hardened in recent decades, probably as a consequence of a combination of factors: economic difficulties, shrinking population, the removal of the military from the island, and grievances about poor communications. The point is also made that Bornholm is treated as an average Danish municipality in spite of the fact that its geographic situation demands special solutions. It is ironic that the Bornholmians, who claim to be the most Danish of all Danes, are even more critical towards their national government than the Ålanders are, who barely consider themselves Finns at all. The decisive difference probably arises from the increased autonomy that made Åland less and less dependent on decisions made in Helsinki, while the Bornholmians feel that their influence over regional affairs has been diminished.

It could be argued that although the Bornholmians emphasize their Danishness, the others against whom they define themselves are other Danes—Jutlanders in particular. As a vociferous periphery, Jutland is seen as competitor to Bornholm. Sometimes the Bornholmians are seen as the last representatives of an old Danishness which was lost when the rest of Eastern Denmark was conquered by Sweden in the mid seventeenth century.

Regional history-writing also emphasizes the Bornholmians' free and independent mind-set. This is frequently connected to the fact that Bornholmian peasants, in contrast to their peers in the rest of Denmark, were never subjected to serfdom. The Bornholmians are described as a people who down the centuries have wanted to rule themselves and have made life hard for unpopular governors, Danish or foreign. The Bornholmians' Danish patriotism is evoked to demand better support and protection from the Danish motherland, but it does not mean that government interference in local affairs is welcome. The privileges that the Bornholmians received after the uprising in 1658 are also connected to the image of the islanders as a free people. They were exempted from some taxes and were not obliged to serve in the military outside their home island, which they were responsible for defending with the Bornholm militia, where all males were members.

More than on any of the other islands in the Baltic Sea, Bornholmian history writers have had to fight against widespread popular myths. Bornholm is situated in the midst of a busy sea route at the inlet of the Baltic, a strategic location which has attracted many foreign attackers: Vends, Lübeckers, Swedes, Germans, and Russians. The island's exposed position distant from the rest of Denmark—in combination with the fact that its defence has most often been left in the hands of the islanders themselves—may have contributed to the popular myths about the Bornholmians' mass slaughters of foreigners. Bronze Age mounds were interpreted as mass graves of Courland pirates, and the graves of shipwrecked Swedes from the great strandings in 1678–9 were remembered as the last resting place of the Swedes murdered in the Great Swine Slaughter, which allegedly took place after the uprising in 1658.

These myths might have functioned as a warning to foreign aggressors boosting the islanders' belief in their own ability to ward off foreign threats. The Bornholmian history writers—with the exception of Peder Nikolai Skougaard who believed in the Great Swine Slaughter—put no faith in these myths. Since they were widespread among the island's population, writers of regional history did however need to address them. The myths were connected to a quite negative stereotype of Bornholmians as violent and unruly, an image that the late nineteenth- and early twentieth-century regional history writers wanted to counteract. Marius Kristian Zahrtmann claimed that the myth of the Great Swine Slaughter, as well as the one about the Bornholmian clock industry's origins in a wrecked ship loaded with clocks, were invented in Copenhagen. However, Zahrtmann also himself contributed to the picture of an unruly breed of islanders, for example by claiming that the early nineteenth-century reformers Rømer and Jespersen were unable to cooperate since they were both Bornholmians. Later writers claimed that Zahrtmann was himself a prime example of a stereotypically unruly Bornholmian.

Another set of myths which regional history writers have struggled with are the attempts by Swedish nineteenth-century scholars to integrate Bornholm into their history-writing, either by claiming that the Burgundians emigrated from Bornholm whereupon the island was repopulated from Sweden, or by linking the island to the *Gutasaga*. These theories have at best been received with scepticism on Bornholm, but most often with rejection. Since the Bornholmians have always emphasized their Danishness, these Swedish national myths have not been compatible with the islanders' historical consciousness.

A third set of myths has arisen since the turn of this century. A former journalist at Bornholm television, Erling Haagensen, has launched theories which link Bornholm's medieval round churches to the Crusades, the Knights Templar, the Holy Grail, a conspiracy by the Catholic Church, and other paraphernalia of modern popular history culture. So far, Bornholmian regional history-writing has handled this new myth cautiously, making small adjustments in their descriptions of the round churches with intimations of the possibility of alternative interpretations. However, they have so far avoided the wilder ingredients of Haagensen's theoretical edifice. Bornholm's tourism industry, however, has made use of Haagensen's narrative skills. Haagensen's view of history links Bornholm directly to a greater Western European cultural sphere, bypassing the national Danish dimension which has been so important in earlier Bornholmian history-writing.

Bornholm's geographic location, as a peripheral island situated closer to foreign countries than to the Danish motherland has had a profound effect on its regional identity and regional history-writing. The island's position has made it both vulnerable to foreign attack and susceptible to being forgotten by the central authorities. The Bornholmians have embraced the dual strategy of expressing patriotism towards Denmark in hope of assistance—during the cold war combined with NATO-friendliness—while remembering that in times of crisis they might ultimately have to rely upon their own resources. This explains the characteristic trait of Bornholmian history writers to simultaneously emphasize the islanders' Danishness and their independence. The balance between these two strategies has shifted over time, of course. In the early twentieth century, Bornholmian writers believed that the geographical disadvantages of Bornholm's peripheral location might be overcome by normalization and national integration. In the late twentieth century, however, regional history writers have returned to the idea that the island's special geographic position makes it impossible to fully integrate as a normal part of Denmark, and instead calls for special solutions and increased autonomy.

References

Bornholm's history-writing

Åkerlund, Carl J. E. (1957), 'Sagn og overtro', in Nielsen & Sørensen 1957.
Andersen, Ellen (1957), 'Klædedragt', in Nielsen & Sørensen 1957.
Barfod, Jørgen H. (1976), *Et centrum i periferien. Motsandsbevægelsen på Bornholm* (Rønne: Bornholms Historiske Samfund).
Bøggild, Hansaage (1966), *Sønderjyde på Bornholm: Uddrag og referat af Breve fra lærer Lourents Petersen, Østermarie, til hans fynske ven Rasmus Nielsen* (Rønne: Sonne).
— (2004), *Gyldendals bog om Bornholm* (Copenhagen: Gyldendals).
Christiansen, Tage (1957), 'Kirker', in Nielsen & Sørensen 1957.
Frihedsbevægelsen (1945), *Bornholm: Besat – bombet – befriet*, i (Rønne: Frihedsbevægelsen paa Bornholm).
Haagensen, Erling (2003), *Bornholms rundkirker: Middelalderens største kompleks* (Lynge: Bogan).
— (2006), *Tempelherrernes skat* (2nd edn., Lynge: Bogan).
— (2007), *Sigtet for tavshed* (Hellerup: Documentas).
Halskov Hansen, Lene (2007), *Velkommen til middelalderen og til Bornholms Middelaldercenter* (Gudhjem: Bornholms Middelaldercenter).
Heiselberg, Vagn (1957), 'Kongens frie bønder', in Nielsen & Sørensen 1957.
Høgh, Børge, (1947), *Bornholm: Besat – bombet – befriet*, ii: *Russerne og Bornholm* (Rønne: Frihedsbevægelsen paa Bornholm).
Jensen, Bent, (1996), *Den lange befrielse* (Bornholmske samlinger, 3/9; Rønne: Bornholms Historiske Samfund).
Jørgensen, Johan Andreas (1900), *Bornholms historie*, i: *Fra Oldtiden til 1660* (Rønne: Sørensen).
— (1901), *Bornholms historie*, ii: *Fra 1660 til nutiden* (Rønne: Sørensen).
Kjøller, Frede (1957), 'Allmindingen', in Nielsen & Sørensen 1957.
Klindt-Jensen, Jørn (1957a), 'Byggeskik', in Nielsen & Sørensen 1957.
— (1957b), 'Urolige tider', in Nielsen & Sørensen 1957.
— (1958), *Disse danske* (Rønne: Bornholms Tidendes Forlag).
Klindt-Jensen, Ole (1957), 'Oldtiden', in Nielsen & Sørensen 1957.
Knudsen, Ann-Vibeke & Nilsson, Håkan (1995), *På hat med Skåne og Bornholm: Bornholmernes Hovedtöjer/På hatt med Bornholm och Skåne: Skåningarnas huvudbonader* (Rønne: Samarbetet Bornholm/Sydöstra Skåne).
— (1999), *Bygningskultur omkring Østersøen* (Rønne: Four corners/Bornholms museum).
— (2000) (ed.), *Bornholm i Krig 1940–1946* (Rønne: Bornholms museum).
Kofoed, Kristian Hansen (1940), *Bornholms politiske Historie fra 1848 til vore Dage*, vi: *1894–1913. Venstrereformpartiets Periode* (Bornholmske samlinger, 27; Rønne: Bornholms Historiske Samfund).

Køie, Hening (1957), 'Hav og havn', in Nielsen & Sørensen 1957.

Kristiansen, Tore (2009), 'Mig og de danske dialekter – En fortælling om baggrunden for mine fortællinger', in Asgerd Gudiksen et al. (eds.), *Dialektforskning i 100 år* (Copenhagen: Copenhagen University, Nordisk Forskningsinstitut, Afdeling for Dialektforskning).

Kure, Børge (1981), *En ø i krig: Bornholms besættelses-historie baseret på en række avisartikler i dagbladet Bornholmeren i 1980* (Rønne: Bornholmeren).

Nielsen, Richard & Sørensen, Thorvald (1957) (eds.), *Bogen om Bornholm* (Haderslev: Danskerens forlag).

Pedersen, Erik (1987), *Bornholmske strandinger: Strandinger ved Bornholms och Christiansøs kyster 1830–1986*, i: *1830–1919* (Rønne: Bornholmerens forlag).

— (1988), *Bornholmske strandinger: Strandinger ved Bornholms och Christiansøs kyster 1830–1986*, ii: *1920–1986* (Rønne: Bornholmerens forlag).

— (1998), *Med Sejl Damp & Motor: Bornholmske skibe ca. 1850 till 1998* (Rønne: Bornholmerens forlag).

Petersen, Poul (1957), 'Vort land Bornholm', in Nielsen & Sørensen 1957.

Rasmussen, Alan Hjorth (1993), *Østersøen gav: trekk av Bornholms og Christiansøs fiskerihistorie 1880–1993* (Bornholmske samlinger, 3/7; Rønne: Bornholms Historiske Samfund).

Rasmussen, Ebbe Gert (1982), *Dette gavebrev. Det politiske spil omkring den bornholmske opstand og Peder Olsens indsats i løsriveIseverket 1658–59* (Bornholmske samlinger 2/15–16; Rønne: Bornholms Historiske Samfund).

— (2000), *Skuddet: En bog om Villum Clausen og de dramatiske hændelser under den bornholmske opstand i 1658* (Nexø: Editio).

— (2008a), *Bornholm og Skåne: Triumf og tragedie i skæbneårene 1658–1659* (Åkirkeby: TV2 Bornholm).

— (2008b), *Den berømmelige action: Bornholm 1658 gennem 350 år* (Bornholmske samlinger 4/2; Rønne: Bornholms Historiske Samfund).

Rohmann, Aage (1957), 'Stednavne', in Nielsen & Sørensen 1957.

Rying, Bent (1969), *Gyldendals egnsbeskrivelse*, i: *Bornholm med Ertholmene* (Copenhagen: Gyldendal).

Skougaard, Peter Nikolai (1804), *Beskrivelse over Bornholm*, i (Copenhagen: Andreas Seidelin).

— (1834), *Bornholms saga* (Aalborg: Lundt).

Sonne, H. P. (1957), 'Sproget', in Nielsen & Sørensen 1957.

Sonne, Niels Erik (2010), *Pirater og patrioter* (Rønne: Dam).

Sonne Nielsen, Finn Ole (1996), *Forhistoriske interesser* (Rønne: Bornholms Amt, Teknisk Forvaltning).

— (1998) *Middelalderens Bornholm* (Rønne: Bornholms Amt, Teknisk Forvaltning).

Stub-Jørgensen, Christian (1957), 'Bornholmerne', in Nielsen & Sørensen 1957.

Sørensen, Thorvald, (1957), 'By og erhverv', in Nielsen & Sørensen 1957.

Zahrtmann, Marius Kofoed (1934), *Borringholmerens historiebog: Første og anden bog* (Rønne: Colberg).
-- (1935), *Borringholmerens historiebog: Tredje og fjerde bog* (Rønne: Colberg).

Other works cited

Bornholm Home Guard, <http://www.hjv.dk/HHV/TRSJ/DET%20BORN HOLMSKE%20HJEMMEV%C3%86RN/Om%20distriktet/Sider/Almegaar ds%20Kaserne.aspx>, accessed 23 November 2012.
Billing, Peter & Petersen, Tage (2003), *På egne ben i nye omgivelser: Sydöstra Skåne og Bornholms möjligheter i Öresundsregionen. Udarbejdet for samarbejdet Sydöstra Skåne/Bornholm* (Nexø: CRT).
Dansk center for byhistorie, <http://dendigitalebyport.byhistorie.dk/koebstaeder/by.aspx?KoebstadID=49/>, accessed 21 May 2013.
Gaarskjær, Jesper (2012), *Bornholm besat: det glemte hjørne af Danmark under Anden Verdenskrig* (Copenhagen: Gyldendal).
Gynther, Bent & Møller, Aqigssiaq (1999), *Gyldendals bog om Grønland* (Copenhagen: Gyldendals).
Haagensen, Erling <http://www.merling.dk/Eskilstestamente1.html>, accessed 14 December 2012.
Huhle, Robert (1956a) (ed.), *Bogen om Als* (Haderslev: Danskerens forlag).
-- (1956b) (ed.), *Bogen om Himmerland* (Haderslev: Danskerens forlag).
Jacobsen, Finn (1975), 'Efterskrift til Beskrivelse over Bornholm', in P. N. Skovgaard, *Beskrivelse over Bornholm: Genudgivet med en efterskrift af Finn Jacobsen* (Copenhagen: Rosenkilde & Bagger).
Knudsen, Johannes (1926), introduction, in id. (ed.), *Rasmus Pedersen Ravns Borringholms krønike 1671* (Rønne: Bornholms Historiske Samfund).
Kristeligt Dagblad, 16 May 2006, <http://www.kristeligt-dagblad.dk/artikel/ 38476:Kirke---tro--Fantasteri-og-forskruet-vroevl>, accessed 14 December 2012.
Mortensen, Marianne (2011), *Den bornholmske dialekt dør - og hvad så? - Om forholdet mellem dialekt og identitet i en bornholmsk-københavnsk kontekst*, Roskilde University digital archive, available at<http://rudar.ruc.dk :8080/bitstream/1800/6898/1/Projekt%20dialekt%20Marianne%20Mortense n.pdf>, accessed 7 November 2012.
Pedersen Borrinjaland, Tonny (1982), *Bornholms historie* ('Borgundaland': Tonny R. J. P. Borrinjaland).
-- (2004), *Bornholms historie* (n.p.: Tonny R. J. P. Borrinjaland).
-- (2011), *Bibel - Det nya Testamente. Bibelinj auersat tee ded bornholmska sprog* (n.p.: Tonny R. J. P. Borrinjaland).
Pomieciński, Adam (2005), 'Bornholm Islanders And Their Cultural Background', *Sprawy Narodowosciowe-Seria Nowa*, 27.

Royal Library, <http://www.kb.dk/da/kb/service/nationalbibliografi/danskbog fortegnelse.html>, accessed 21 May 2013.
Skattejagt Bornholm, <http://www.skattejagtbornholm.dk>, accessed 14 December 2012.
Statistics Denmark, <www.dst.dk>.
Stub-Jørgensen, Christian (1958), *Peter Nikolai Skovgaard og hans bøger om Bornholm* (Rønne: C.E.B).
Vensild, Henrik (1993), 'Bornholms Museumsforening 1893–1993, Træk af Foreningens og Bornholms Museums historie', in Ann-Vibeke Knudsen (ed.), *Bornholms museumsforening 1893–1993* (Rønne: Bornholms museumsforening).
Zahrtmann, Marius Kofoed (1926), 'Rasmus Pedersen Ravn og hans Boringholms krønike', in J. Knudsen 1926.

Comparative conclusions
General lessons regarding islandness and collective identities

Janne Holmén

In this concluding essay we will compare the history-writing from the Baltic islands, investigate common denominators in how identity is expressed, and analyse how differences are related to the islands' varying geographical locations and historical circumstances. Finally we will discuss how insights from our study can contribute to the two academic fields which have been our theoretical point of departure: island studies—particularly the notion of islands as being at the same time secluded and connected—and theories about the historical development of collective identities.

The rise of regional history, 1804–2013

The regional history-writing carried out on the islands in the Baltic Sea has undergone several phases, each of them related to different patterns of identification. During the first half of the nineteenth century, Northern Europe had not yet entered the age of nationalism. The regional history writers active in this period—such as the student Peder Nikolai Skougaard on Bornholm and Baron Peter Wilhelm von Buxhöwden on Saaremaa— were motivated by a determination to defend the privileges of the groups with which they identified, and to indirectly criticize autocratic rulers. Ideologically, writers such as Skougaard and Johan Ludwig von Luce on Saaremaa combined the traditions of the Enlightenment and Romanticism, promoting practical knowledge and improvements while describing the history and popular culture of the peasant population. During this period, there was no regional history-writing at all on the two smallest island regions, which at the time still lacked towns: Åland and Hiiumaa.

The period from the mid nineteenth century up to the First World War was characterized by a process of nation-building in Sweden, Denmark, and Finland. Members of the regional elite on Gotland, Bornholm, and Åland—which with the founding of Mariehamn in 1861—started associations, museums, and periodicals. They wrote books and articles about history in order to integrate their regions into the national culture. Towards the end of the nineteenth century, Åland was drawn into the battle between the Svecoman and Fennoman versions of Finnish nationalism, and sided decisively with Swedish-minded Svecomanism— although this ideology probably never developed deep roots outside the small elite which to a large extent had its origins on the mainland. However, on Saaremaa, regional research was carried out in a feudal setting, and was entirely restricted to the Baltic German elite. There was no history-writing informed by Estonian nationalism—or even written in the Estonian language—on the island during this period. The most prominent history writer on the island, the pastor Martin Körber, instead displayed what might be described as an emergent Livonian nationalism.

In the inter-war period, the process of national integration continued on Gotland and Bornholm, and it also took off on Saaremaa, where the island was written into Estonian history as a volume in *Eesti*, which covered the entire county. However, on Åland events took a different turn since the islanders in 1917–18 shifted from Finnish to Swedish nationalism. This happened during a struggle for reunification with Sweden, which was fuelled by security concerns caused by the Russian Revolution, and eventually led to autonomy for Åland within Finland in 1922. On Åland and Saaremaa, the regional museums which had been in the hands of associations dominated by the elite were taken over after the First World War by the new regional governments, which mainly represented the peasant class.

The Second World War brought changes to most of the Baltic islands, with the exception of Gotland, where history-writing continued down the same path as before, centred on the Middle Ages and with the island's political affinity to Sweden never brought into question. The Soviet annexation of Estonia meant that regional history-writing on Saaremaa split into a Soviet branch carried out on the island, often in cooperation with the commission for local history at the Estonian Soviet Republic's

Academy of Science, and a national Estonian branch which continued the inter-war tradition in exile in Canada or Sweden. The two branches similarly took as their main focus the fate of the peasant population. However, the Soviet regional history writers wrote more negatively about the Danish and Swedish periods in Saaremaa's history, blaming problems during the Russian period on the feudal Baltic German nobility, not the Russian rulers, who they claimed brought peace and order to the island. In the early 1970s, the first Hiiumaa regional history-writing was produced in exile in Sweden.

On Åland, the early 1950s brought a new orientation in regional history-writing, emphasizing Åland's independence rather than its links to Sweden. This was in line with the new political orientation on Åland, where the hopes of reunification with Sweden had been replaced by an urge to achieve an improved Autonomy Act, which was accomplished in 1951. The Second World War meant that Bornholm was bombed and occupied by Soviet forces. The Danish government's inability to assist the Bornholmians during these events led to disappointment on the island. Regional history-writing from the period after the war was less positive towards Bornholm's integration into Denmark, and the criticism of Copenhagen has increased since the turn of this century.

In the late twentieth and early twenty-first centuries, the islands have seen a wave of greater critical uses of regional history-writing. One more academic strand of research emerged on Åland and Gotland questioned or problematized many of the myths of regional history-writing and history culture. On Åland this was clearly connected to the moralizing tendency in contemporary—particularly Swedish—history-writing, criticizing racist, and nationalist tendencies in the island's early twentieth-century society. On Saaremaa, the collapse of the Soviet Union was followed by a period of intense criticism of Soviet crimes, which was succeeded in the early twenty-first century by a more nuanced and varied history-writing. Crimes committed by other parties in the Second World War were by then also acknowledged, and sometimes it was even admitted that the Soviet period had had a lasting impact on certain areas of Estonian society.

Wars and uprisings

The extent to which an island is isolated or connected to the surrounding world is not exclusively a consequence of geographic factors. Political and historical circumstances influence the balance between the separating and the connective properties of the surrounding sea. For example, border changes, custom regulations, and developments in shipping affect the islanders' propensity to interconnect with the surrounding world. However, it might be argued that war is the factor that has the greatest potential to disrupt existing patterns of trade and communication. During periods of war and unrest, the Baltic islands have become more secluded from the mainland—by piracy and privateering, travel restrictions, minefields, and so on. The geography of the islands has often meant the islanders' experience of war differs from that of the mainlanders—fortifications, foreign occupations, great influxes or exoduses of refugees etc. These experiences have played a pivotal role in the formation of regional identities on the islands.

It has been said that small island states are exceptionally vulnerable to unconventional security threats: there are several examples of islands that have been captured by a few dozen mercenaries.[1] Our studies indicate that as a parallel to this, small military forces on islands are exceptionally vulnerable to popular uprisings, as has been repeatedly illustrated in the history of the Baltic islands. These uprisings have influenced the formation of collective identities.

The memory of how the islanders took collective action to liberate and briefly take control of Bornholm in 1658 and Åland in 1808 has played an important role in the construction of identity on these islands. It has been used as evidence of the islanders' patriotism and their self-determination at one and the same time. The memory of the Great Uprising on Saaremaa in 1343–5 has served a similar function, with the important difference that Estonian regional history writers have linked it to simultaneous uprisings on the mainland, so emphasizing Saaremaa's links to the mainland rather than the island's uniqueness. In contrast, the uprising on Saaremaa in 1919 against the national Estonian government is considered a tragic accident by the Saaremaa history writers with a national Estonian point of view. However, in Soviet Age history-writing the uprising was used to

---

[1] Bartmann 2007, 300.

illustrate the revolutionary spirit of the islanders, and it was seen as a reaction to ruthless feudal and capitalist oppression as well as an act of solidarity with the proletariat in Estonia and Russia. Recently, the Bornholmian uprising in December 1658 has been linked to the one in Skåne early the following year, a link made at a time of transnational region-building around the Öresund strait.

Often the islands' isolation from the mainland has been described as a factor which contributed to the uprisings. This explanation has had a special appeal to regional history writers who have been against the uprisings. With the exception of the Soviet Age history writers, writers on Saaremaa have explained the 1919 uprising against the Estonian national government by the island's isolation. The Ålander Otto Andersson, who wanted Åland to remain part of Finland, considered the Åland movement's attempt to reunify the island to Sweden a consequence of misinformation and fear, caused by the island's isolation. Similarly, the Bornholmian Jørn Klindt-Jensen, who believed that the Lübeckians represented the 'democratic' side during the Counts Feud in 1534–1536, considered the lack of communications to be a reason why the Bornholmians rebelled against them, ending up on the opposite side in the conflict of the rebellious peasants in Jutland. Thus the islands' isolated locations have been used to explain why islanders have acted against what the history writers perceive as their own interests.

However, the islands' isolation cannot be reduced to a mere metaphor which writers can choose to include in their narratives whenever it fits their purposes: it is also a geographic reality which has fundamentally affected regional history. It can be argued that the outcomes of the above-mentioned uprisings to a large extent depended upon the islands' degree of isolation. The relative isolation made it possible for the Bornholmians to take over their island in 1658 without noticing the Swedish forces on the mainland, and melting ice made it impossible for the Russian forces on Åland in 1808 to receive reinforcements. An exception which confirms the rule is the swift failure of the uprising on Saaremaa in February 1919. It can be explained by the fact that the island was not isolated at the time; on the contrary the ice formed a convenient highway for the punitive expedition which the Estonian government sent out from the capital. Isolation has thus influenced collective identities both through direct influence over political events and as a factor referred to in uses of history.

The Baltic as a front line

Most invasions of the Estonian islands until the twentieth century took place over the ice. It could be argued that ice has been a more important political factor in the Baltic Sea than anywhere else in the world, contributing to a seasonal variation in the power balance between maritime and continental powers. On Åland, geography and politics contributed to a recurring pattern in the eighteenth- and early nineteenth-century wars between Sweden and Russia. Generally, the ice over the open water between Sweden and Åland melted earlier in the spring than the ice in the archipelago between Åland and Finland. In the days before motorized shipping, there was a period in spring when Åland could be reached by boat from Sweden while ice still obstructed travel to Finland. This meant that Åland was repeatedly invaded by Russians troops in the winters, which then withdrew before they became isolated on the island, vulnerable to an attack from the Swedish navy.

In general, it can be argued that the kingdoms along the western shores of the Baltic have been maritime powers, while the realms in the east—Russia, the German Order, and Poland–Lithuania—have been predominantly land-based. This has contributed to the fact that Denmark's and Sweden's influence on the islands in the eastern Baltic have been much more profound than the eastern influence on Bornholm and Gotland. As a consequence, the islands of the Baltic Sea share similar Nordic cultural traits, the Lutheran religion, and, in the cases of Saaremaa and especially Hiiumaa, historically a significant population of Swedish peasants. However, Peter the Great's determination to transform Russia into a naval power in the early eighteenth century brought Saaremaa, Hiiumaa, and Åland under Russian influence.

After a period in which the Baltic Sea had been the central Sea of Sweden, Peter the Great turned it into a front line. This meant that the Baltic islands now became more strategically important, a position which they maintained until the end of the Cold War; as a consequence, the islands in this study have repeatedly been garrisoned and fortified. During the First World War, Åland and Saaremaa were isolated from the mainland due to travel restrictions imposed by the military. It is possible that this relative isolation during the formative period that preceded the Finnish and Estonian declarations of independence might have contributed to the fact that islanders from Åland and Saaremaa ended up on a collision course with the new national governments in Helsinki and Tallinn. The stress that the billeting of troops placed on the local society has been brought forward as an important factor behind the development of Ålandic identity as well as the 1919 uprising on Saaremaa.

Especially on Bornholm, but to some extent also on Gotland, the garrisons were looked upon benevolently, and it was their withdrawal at the end of the cold war that has been considered the problem. This is linked to the fact that the garrisons represented nations—Denmark and Sweden—with which the islanders identified, and until the second half of the nineteenth century the Bornholmians garrisoned their island themselves. Although Ålanders are in general described as antimilitaristic in regional history-writing, the Swedish troops which arrived on Åland in 1918 are seldom described as anything other than welcome. The exception is Otto Andersson, who claimed that their actions were less popular in the eastern parts of Åland.

Security as the root of identity

A comparison between the islands makes it evident that expressions of loyalty towards a nation-state might be altered in times of war, if the state seemed incapable of providing security. When Finland in 1917–1918 seemed to be slipping into civil war and bolshevism, Ålanders turned their eyes to Sweden, just as some Bornholmians did when the Danish authorities seemed to have abandoned the island during the Soviet bombings in May 1945. After Estonia was erased from the map in 1940, the prospect of a Greater Finland seemed attractive to many on Saaremaa.

Of these shifts in allegiance, only the Ålandic turn away from Finland became permanent. An important explanation for this is Åland's autonomy in 1922. The new local authorities consciously attempted to defend their autonomy by developing the islanders' Ålandic, Swedish-oriented identity, and they used history-writing as a means to this end.

On Åland and Bornholm, exceptions from military service—and on Bornholm also reintegration into the national military in 1867—have affected national identity. Resentment about military service also played an important role in the outbreak of the uprising on Saaremaa in 1919.

The military history of Saaremaa, Åland, and Bornholm illustrates how identity has been formed in the interplay of geographical and political factors. Although identity on the islands is influenced by their geographical insularity, which has been heightened in times of war, identity is by no means static. Expressions of identity and national affiliation have been heavily influenced by the islanders' shifting security concerns. It is illustrative that the island in this investigation which displays the greatest consistency in terms of national belonging—Gotland—is also the one which has remained longest in the hands of one and the same state, Sweden, since the emergence of a regional history-writing in the nineteenth century. Since Sweden has been able to provide relative security, there has been no need to contemplate any alternatives. The sense of security experienced on Gotland is illustrated by the fact that the brief Russian invasion of Gotland in 1809 is seen more as a picaresque incident than as a serious threat.

The social roots of regional identity

Regional history-writing cannot only be understood in terms of identification with the home island and nearby states; the writer's identification with different social classes is also important. In the case of Saaremaa, this factor is especially prominent. During the nineteenth-century, history-writing on the island was done by, and to a large extent focused upon, the Baltic German aristocracy and clergy. To a certain degree even the burghers were excluded from this elitist version of history, as the pastor Martin Körber did not consider trade to be an honest occupation. After Estonia's independence, history-writing came to be dominated by the Estonian peasant class, and the peasants continued to be at the centre of Soviet Age history-writing too.

Åland offers an interesting parallel to Saaremaa. Its nineteenth- and early twentieth-century history writers also represented the national elite, but after the First World War the peasant class took control of regional history-writing. In both cases, regional authorities mainly representing the peasants took over the museums from private organizations representing the elite: Ålands vänner and Verein zur kunde Oesels. In twentieth-century history-writing, 'real' Ålanders and Saaremaa islanders were equated with peasants. In the case of Åland, the working class was also excluded, being described as Finns. A tendency to distance itself from the proletariat can also be seen in some examples of Hiiumaa and

Saaremaa history-writing, where they are described as being non-existent, or—by the Saaremaa branch of the Memento Association—as people mainly interested in other activities than work.

As on Åland and the Estonian islands, Bornholmian identity excludes the aristocracy. However, on that early urbanized island the burghers of the towns are also seen as true Bornholmians. As was the case with the Finns on Åland, on Bornholm the blame for drinking and fighting was often placed on the Swedish proletariat. Regional history-writing on Gotland is also clearly anti-aristocratic. Unlike Bornholm, which has an equally old urban culture, Gotlandic history writers display an ambivalence towards the burghers in Visby, who are sometimes described as the enemies of the Gotlandic peasants.

Geography and identity

It has been argued that island communities are conservative and traditional. In this investigation we have seen examples of two old traditions described as extinct by nineteenth- or early twentieth-century history writers, but which other regional historians almost a century later claimed were still practised: the Bornholmian inheritance custom whereby the youngest son acquired the farm, and the Saaremaa custom that agriculture was a female enterprise, while men had to go to sea or look for work overseas. In the Saaremaa case, it can be argued that the geography of the island offered the potential for the custom to reoccur at different times under similar economic circumstances. Agricultural land is scarce and meagre, and it has been rational to supplement agricultural production with other incomes. Good economic opportunities elsewhere, such as the peasant shipping boom in the late nineteenth century, have naturally increased this tendency, while serfdom and the economic regulation of the early nineteenth century reduced it to such a degree that it was declared extinct.

Similarly, it can be argued that the islands' geographic locations have the potential for certain patterns of collective identities to reoccur under the correct political circumstances. This is the case with Bornholm's location as a distant Danish island close to Skåne in southern Sweden and Åland's location equidistant between Finland and Sweden. Bornholmian history writers of recent years are critical of Copenhagen, want more political power devolved to the regional level, demand special solutions tailored to their island's needs, and emphasize their links to Skåne, just as Peder Nikolai Skougaard did in 1804. However, in the late nineteenth and early twentieth centuries, Bornholmian history writers saw the old, existing regional independence and the island's privileges as conservative hindrances to its development, which they believed would be best assisted by the normalization of the island as an integrated part of the Danish nation-state. As a consequence of this ideology, the links to Skåne and Sweden were played down. Likewise, Ålandic history writers today emphasize Åland's independent nature, in the same way as Karl August Bomansson in 1852 claimed that the islanders considered themselves neither Finns nor Swedes, but Ålanders. However, from 1917 until after the Second World War, regional historians firmly declared that Ålanders had always considered themselves Swedes.

Nationalism can be used as an ideology that promotes modernization in the sense of economic and social development, removing internal barriers which hinder the dispersion of improvements and wealth within the nation-state. However, nationalism can also be used to strengthen external barriers, defending the regions within the nation-state against external threats. The modernizing aspect of nationalism was a prominent factor behind the Danish nationalism of Bornholmian history writers such as J. A. Jørgensen and M. K. Zahrtmann, while on Åland the shift to Swedish nationalism in 1917 was prompted by security concerns as a result of the Russian Revolution. Today Bornholmians perceive that the streamlining of their island as a normal Danish region is transforming it to a forgotten periphery, without proper consideration of its special needs. The Soviet bombings in 1945 also diminished the Bornholmians' faith in Denmark's protective capabilities. On Åland, the advantages of autonomy within Finland, in terms of the economy and the chance to decide questions of regional importance, have become so obvious that the alternatives no longer appeal. The island has achieved the status of an entrepôt as described by Warrington and Milne: it has been able to exploit its strategic position for its own benefit.[2]

It is also interesting to note how differences between island and mainland—for example in Bornholmian Bronze Age culture or Saaremaa architecture—are at times described as variations on a national culture

---

[2] Warrington & Milne 2007, 413 ff.

developed in the isolation of the island, but at other times, when nationalism is less important and the connective properties of the sea are emphasized, they are seen as the result of international influence. Although the idea of a united Baltic region has become more popular after the end of the Cold War, this theme has still not become very important in history-writing on the islands studied in this research project. In recent decades, interregional cooperation projects have resulted in a few works which connect the islands' histories to that of other areas, one of them being Søren Sørensen's book about the history of the large Baltic islands. However, this kind of interregional history-writing has still not much of an impact upon the mainstream of regional history-writing on the islands in the Baltic Sea.

Differences and divisions within the islands

Not on a single island in this study do history writers describe their regional identity primarily as an effect of ethnic or racial differences to the surrounding world, although especially on Gotland the islanders are described as having been a separate people in the past. This contradicts the suggestion that ethnic identity has been more persistent in a regional setting than is the case at a national level.[3] History writers on all of the islands consider the islanders to be descendants of immigrants from adjacent areas, primarily from Sweden, Denmark, and Estonia, acknowledging various degrees of genetic influence from other directions. In the case of Bornholm and the Estonian islands, the mixed origin of the population is stressed more than on Åland and Gotland. The nineteenth-century Baltic German history writers in particular considered this mix to be a strength, which made the islanders superior to the mainlanders. A parallel can be made to Winston Churchill's description of the Britons in *The Island Race*.[4] Pure-bloodedness was most strongly emphasized in Ålandic history-writing from the first half of the twentieth century.

However, in early nineteenth-century sources in particular, inhabitants of different parts of the *same* island are described as having highly disparate customs and physical features; sometimes they are even described as different races. This underlines regional identity as an imagined

---

[3] This suggestion is for example discussed by Nordlund 2001.
[4] Churchill & Baker 1984.

community, the formation of which did not begin until quite late in many of our islands. The identity-forming power of islands is illustrated by the fact that most of the local (sub-regional) history-writing on Åland and Saaremaa has taken place on secondary islands which are either relatively large (Muhu) or distant from the main island (Ruhnu, Kökar, Brändö).

On Bornholm, which has several urban centres, there is evident rivalry between them. In Gotlandic history-writing it is instead the rivalry between Visby and the countryside which is emphasized. Although towns might have a divisive influence, the comparison between the islands does indicate that the existence of an urban centre was crucial for the rise of regional history-writing. Bornholm and Gotland had towns and cities in the Middle Ages, and Arensburg on Saaremaa grew into a town in the sixteenth century, and these three islands also had an early start in regional history-writing—the medieval *Gutasaga* and the *Chronica Guthilandorum* from 1633, the Bornholmian descriptions of the 1658 uprising from the end of the same century, and Luce's pioneering work on Saaremaa's history in the early nineteenth century. Åland and Hiiumaa, however, consisted entirely of countryside at the beginning of our period of research. Mariehamn on Åland was founded in 1861, and Kärdla on Hiiumaa gained city rights in 1938. No regional history-writing was produced on these islands before the rise of the regional towns. The only exception, Bomansson's writings about Åland's history in the 1850s, confirms the rule, since at that time the short-lived conurbation of Skarpans flourished around Bomarsund Tortress.

From early on, towns functioned as places for interaction in which a sense of regional community could develop, at least among the regional elite. In the nineteenth and twentieth centuries, the advent of newspapers in the towns helped form a community of readers who shared the same regional news. The printing presses also made it technically possible to print books regionally. In the first half of the twentieth century, Åland's regional newspaper and its political power were in the hands of Julius Sundblom. The paper *Åland* thus became an important tool for a deliberate campaign of identity formation, and its influence helps explain how the Ålanders could rapidly shift from Finnish to Swedish nationalism in 1917–18.

On Hiiumaa, the formation of regional identity only gained momentum in the last decades of the twentieth century. The lack of an urban centre is probably not the only explanation. Until after the Second World

War, Hiiumaa was part of Lääne County, and has sometimes been included in the history-writing of that region. This is most likely related to the island's proximity to the mainland. Hiiumaa also has the smallest population of the islands in this study, but the fact that a community is small does not necessarily mean that it has a weak collective identity or lacks history-writing. After all, the minuscule island of Ruhnu, which prior to the Second World War only had a few per cent of Hiiumaa's population, experienced an earlier and more extensive production of local history-writing, albeit entirely written in exile.

One explanation for the late start of identity formation on Hiiumaa might be that its emergent collective identities have repeatedly been broken down. In the seventeenth century, Hiiumaa's Estonian and Swedish peasants together rallied against the landowning nobility. The nobility reacted with a strategy of divide and conquer which split the peasants' shared identity.[5] Given it has been pointed out that population transfers might hamper the formation of regional identities,[6] the expulsion of Swedish peasants from Hiiumaa to Ukraine in the late eighteenth century may have been of importance, and similarly the mass flight and deportations during and after the Second World War. Saaremaa faced similar problems in the 1940s, but there regional history-writing and the construction of a regional identity had begun in the early nineteenth century. However, until the First World War, Saaremaa history-writing was a Baltic German identity project, and the Estonian version of the Saaremaa identity was established quite late. In a striking manner, Saaremaa and Hiiumaa resemble 'the fief' in the typology of island governance established by Warrington and Milne: islands heavily exploited by a colonial power or a domestic elite.[7] Warrington and Milne argue that in a fief both dominant traditionalism and radical utopian minorities—the latter on Saaremaa represented by the 1919 insurgents and the strong inter-war Communist Party—counteract the formation of nationalism.

---

[5] Jansson 2000, 441–2.
[6] Kurantowicz 2001.
[7] Warrington & Milne 2007, 404.

Free and egalitarian islanders?

One common denominator which can be found on all of the islands is that the islanders are considered to be a particularly freedom-loving breed. on all of the islands, this is to some degree associated with a maritime lifestyle and their Viking heritage. With the exception of the Estonian islands, it is also connected to the absence of serfdom and the a regional nobility.

In the absence of an elite, Bornholm, Gotland, and Åland are described as egalitarian societies with small social differences. In recent history-writing from Saaremaa, it has been acknowledged that the island nobility were poorer than the mainland nobility, and that to some degree they had been influenced by the peasants' language and customs, thereby indicating that the social differences in this case too were smaller than on the mainland.

It would be premature to conclude that freedom and egalitarianism are typical island traits, however. We have chosen a sample of Nordic islands, and Nordic history is characterized by a relatively free, egalitarian peasant class. The free peasant has also been a central character in the nationalism of the Nordic countries. The free and egalitarian properties were more pronounced in marginal areas without a strong nobility, such as the islands, but the same was true of Norway and the sparsely populated areas in the northern parts of Sweden and Finland, which have contributed to making some of these areas central in national history-writing. It is no coincidence that Bornholmian history writers often compared their island to Norway and Denmark's Atlantic islands, rather than to Denmark proper where peasants were subject to serfdom.

Freedom and equality cannot be reduced to a Nordic trait, either. The nineteenth-century Saaremaa history writer Martin Körber claimed that islanders and mountain-dwellers shared a love of freedom. In his great work about the Mediterranean in the age of Philip II, Fernand Braudel included a chapter about the freedom of the mountains, in which he concluded that feudalism had left the mountainous regions outside its political economic, social, and legal system. He extended this to all areas where the expansion of the state, dominant languages, and civilization was slowed by a sparse population. Braudel claimed that the absence of feudal justice on Sardinia was as much a consequence of its mountains as its insularity. Braudel saw the mountains as physical barriers which offered protection from the submission brought on by civilization with its socio-political order and monetary economy.⁸

It would be tempting to draw a parallel between the lawlessness of Sardinia described by Braudel—'I make my own laws and take what I need'⁹—and the propensity of Baltic islanders to consider stranded ships their property, sometimes even gifts of God. However, we need to remember some important differences between the Mediterranean and the Baltic areas.¹⁰ In contrast to its Mediterranean counterparts, the Nordic states managed to expand their influence into relatively sparsely populated areas. In addition, the 'free' islanders of the Baltic archipelagos inhabited such poor land that they could not support themselves without a monetary economy, or at least marketplaces where they could acquire necessities they were not able to produce themselves. Furthermore, the islands and coasts of the Baltic Sea are relatively flat, which means that Braudel's notion that mountains are as important as insularity in explaining isolation is not applicable. On the other hand, while ice is a rarity in the Mediterranean, in the Baltic it is an important factor affecting communications, capable of isolating islands for months. This periodic isolation undeniably imposed a certain freedom on the islanders; when the central authorities could not reach them, whether with help, demands, or instructions, the islanders had to make best use of their own resources according to their own judgement.

Regional identity, a threat to national unity?

In the case of Gotland, Hiiumaa, and Saaremaa, regional history-writing does not emphasize tensions between island and mainland, whether Sweden or Estonia. In fact, on these islands it is very difficult, if not impossible, to draw a line between regional and national history-writing. Gotland's history, and especially its Middle Ages, is seen as an important part of Swedish history. Similarly, Saaremaa is considered to have played an key role in what is described as a national Estonian struggle against

---

⁸ Braudel 1976, 38–9.
⁹ Braudel 1976, 39.
¹⁰ An interesting discussion of these differences can be found in Gerner & Karlsson 2002, 28–9.

invaders in the early thirteenth century. The cultural and historical landscapes of Gotland and Saaremaa have also become national icons, perceived as relics of how Sweden and Estonia looked in the past. A substantial number of the books about Saaremaa's and Gotland's history have been produced in cooperation between writers and institutions from the islands and the mainland, and in 2008 large parts of the Swedish National Heritage Board were relocated to Gotland. On these three islands, the formation of a regional identity has not been connected to political separatism.

Åland and Bornholm have developed differently. On these two islands, with a few exceptions a clear distinction can be drawn between regional and national history-writing. In the early twentieth century, both Åland and Bornholm bade fair to become well-integrated parts of the Finnish and Danish nations. Ålandic history was written by Svecoman Finnish nationalists, who emphasized Åland's important role in Finland's history; some of them in fact were pioneers of Finnish national history-writing. If the process had continued, Åland might have approached the same central position in Finland's historical consciousness as Gotland acquired in Sweden's.

However, this was interrupted by the Russian Revolution and the Ålanders' quest for security by attempting to unite their island with Sweden. As a counter-strategy, the Finnish authorities invented Ålandic political regionalism by offering the islanders autonomy. Finland's presidents—often in opposition to short-sighted, populist sentiments in Parliament—have consistently, far-sightedly, and successfully played the autonomy card throughout the twentieth century, eventually completely removing the Ålandic dreams of reunification with Sweden from the political agenda. Autonomy within Finland is now the favoured alternative for a majority of Ålanders, while the party favouring complete independence attracts the support of a minority—10% of the vote in public elections.

The Danish government has acted very differently towards Bornholm. We must remember that today's Denmark is the remnant of what once was a vast conglomerate state of loosely bound provinces stretching from Greenland to Estonia. As long as Denmark was a dominant power in the Baltic, these provinces were bound together by the sea. However, from the late sixteenth century onwards Denmark's might dwindled. First Sweden, then Russia, and from the late eighteenth century Britain took control over the Baltic waterways, which came to divide the Danish provinces from one another. One by they went their separate ways.

The Danish nation-state that took shape in the mid nineteenth century was, in contrast to the old, loose conglomerate state, highly centralized. In a country which had lost region after region since the sixteenth century, regionalism was not encouraged. In a multi-volume work about the history of Danish identity, regional identities are barely mentioned.[11] Equally, as Denmark is divided by waterways, the idea of the sea as a natural boundary was not favoured—especially since natural boundaries has been a common Swedish reason for its conquest of Skåne in the seventeenth century. Since the mid nineteenth century, Bornholm has lost all of its special privileges, and since 2007 is administered as part of Region Hovedstaden, which also encompasses parts of Zealand including Copenhagen. It might be argued that the Danish regional reform of 2007 serves to counteract the formation of strong regional identities, as the new regional borders divide and connect areas without consideration for geographic entities or traditional provinces.

In recent decades, the reactions on Bornholm towards the long-term effects caused by the removal of political power from the regional level have become increasingly negative. Bornholmian history writers write that they as a forgotten periphery in the east have no friends in Copenhagen, while Denmark's western periphery, Jutland, rakes in political support and benefits. Thus, while the regional authorities on Åland have successfully used the international agreements regarding Åland's status in their power struggles with the Parliament in Helsinki, the Bornholmians, lacking autonomy, have to compete with other Danish areas for the favour of the central authorities in Copenhagen. To make their voices heard in this competition, the Bornholmians still refer to their strong Danish patriotism, claiming to be the most Danish of all Danes.

The complementarity of islandness

The surrounding sea secludes islands from the rest of the world and provides them with natural boundaries. However, it is equally true that the sea can act as a medium for communication and trade. This seemingly paradoxical aspect of islandness is often mentioned, but has so far not

[11] Feldbæk 1991–1992.

been satisfactory investigated empirically. Clarke and Clarke describe isolation and connection as complementary rather than mutually excluding properties of an island.[12] If we want the concept to explain the circumstances under which island communities have evolved, it needs to be complemented with more empirical underpinnings. By describing what seclusion and connection has meant for the formation of collective identities on the Baltic islands, we hope to advance the general understanding of this complementarity.

Maritime communications have historically been faster and more efficient than land routes, but they also pose substantially higher risks and are more sensitive to weather and other disturbances. The sea can carry dramatic novelties and exceptional events from distant lands—fleets of invaders, waves of refugees, stranded ships, even stranded fleets—to the shores of the islands. They have also enabled the islanders to take part in Baltic, European, and even global trade networks. However, the sea has until recently been unable to function as a safe and reliable medium of uninterrupted communication with the mainland. Although the Baltic islands are situated quite close to the mainland, difficult weather conditions periodically isolated them, especially in early winter or in springtime when the fragile ice could neither be crossed by foot nor by boat. In several instances, slow communications meant the islanders ended up proclaiming different monarchs than the mainlanders, as when in the spring of 1658 the Bornholmians learned they were subjects of the Swedish king after a month's delay. In the nineteenth century, mainland communities were connected by the expansion of railways and regular train services, which have been seen as one important factor in the rise of the nation-states and national identities. The islands of the Baltic had to wait for an equally reliable means of everyday communications.

It can be argued that the sea's possibilities and limitations as a means of communication have thus contributed to making the islands—because of irregular daily communications—somewhat less connected to their neighbouring regions than is the case with mainland regions. At the same time, through potentially fast and efficient long-distance communications, they have been better connected to distant areas. This of course has had consequences for how well the islands have been integrated into the nation-states. On Åland, peasant ships were crossing the Atlantic half

---

[12] Clarke & Clarke 2009.

a century before daily, reliable steam-boat connections to the mainland were established—or all children had access to primary schools, for that matter. To various extents Saaremaa, Hiiumaa and Bornholm also took part in this international shipping boom. The fact that in these cases globalization *preceded* national integration might have contributed to making national identity weaker.

Common heritage, invented traditions—or geography?

In our study of regional history-writing on Baltic islands, it is difficult to find support for Anthony D. Smith's idea that nationalism is based upon a primordial 'ethnie' with an origin myth, a common history, a distinct common culture, a territory, and a sense of solidarity. On the contrary, we have shown that even in an island setting, the idea that the inhabitants shared a common territory arose quite late, with local divisions overriding the regional identity well into the nineteenth century. Although these divisions are described as having been reduced in recent history-writing, writers still refer to some internal differences as persisting to this day—think of the rivalry between Rønne and Nexø on Bornholm, between Visby and the countryside on Gotland, and between the archipelago and main Åland. It is thus appropriate to describe the island regions as imagined communities that have gradually developed since the nineteenth century—or in the case of Hiiumaa, the late twentieth century.

Gotland is perhaps the island which best fits the description of an ethnie, with truly ancient myths of origin, a much-vaunted common culture, and a view of its history that has remained basically unchanged down the centuries. However, political separatism which resembles nationalism cannot be seen on the island.

The only example we have found of an island where regional identity has developed into micro-nationalism is Åland in the second half of the twentieth century. However, that only happened after attempts had been made to embrace Finnish and Swedish nationalism. Åland is a poor fit with the standard model of an ethnie. Compared to Gotland, Bornholm, and Saaremaa, Åland is—if we use Anthony D. Smith's terminology—quite 'depleted' in terms of origin myths and a documented common history. In fact, the notion of a common territory is also less clear on Åland with its fragmentized archipelago. The attempts in the 1950s to 1980s to invent a history worthy of Åland's autonomous status—by expropriating the past of richer ethnies such as Iceland—were met with ridicule from the surrounding world and have now been abandoned on the island. This is one of the few examples of a plainly invented tradition (in the sense of Hobsbawm and Ranger) that we have found on the Baltic islands, which illustrates that adaptions and constructions upon firmer historical ground constitute a more common and durable form of identity formation.

In contrast to the multi-ethnic countries without historical precedents which Smith advances as examples of depleted ethnies, Åland's difficulties in rooting its autonomy in culture and history are a consequence of the fact that for at least 600 years it was a well-integrated, centrally located province of the Swedish kingdom, which then also encompassed present-day Finland. As a result, the island's history and culture are to a large degree shared with the Finnish and Swedish mainland. As in a multi-ethnic depleted ethnie, history and culture alone are not capable of defining what separates Åland from the surrounding world.

In accordance with what Smith expects of a depleted ethnie, Åland was governed virtually without an opposition or party politics until the 1970s, resembling a single-party state. Since then a party system has been introduced, but at the same time the veneration of Åland's autonomy and demilitarization has increased, amounting to what Smith describes as a political religion, another avenue by which depleted ethnies can strengthen national identity.

One might ask whether all the Baltic islands can be considered part of a Nordic super-ethnie, based on real or imagined cultural similarities such as a Viking heritage, a free peasants, the Lutheran religion, and a Western orientation. Can this common culture and history explain why the islanders have been so swift to shift allegiance to other Nordic countries when threatened by outside powers such as Russia/the Soviet Union and Germany, which might be seen as representing a foreign ethnicity, 'the others'? Possibly, but in the nineteenth century, Russia seems to have been looked upon benevolently, as shown by the many mixed marriages on Åland in the mid nineteenth century, and the roughly simultaneous mass conversions of peasants to the Orthodox faith on the Estonian islands. The fear that on Åland in 1917 and Saaremaa and Bornholm during the Second World War made islanders contemplate a shift of nationality, was not caused by a mythical Russian cultural otherness, but by the tangible danger posed by the new communist regime.

Benedict Anderson is of the opinion that national identities in European colonies were strengthened by the fact that bureaucrats could make careers within the colony, but could not take the step overseas to the career ladder in the metropolis.[13] In most of the islands in this study, the sea separating them from the mainland is no impediment to a career leading up to the highest positions in the state. Indeed, the islands' histories are full of individuals who have done just that. However, on present-day Åland, a mechanism is in place which hampers the islanders' career opportunities on the mainland: a public officials in Finland have to display proficiency in both national languages, Finnish and Swedish. Since Åland is the only area in Finland where it is not compulsory to learn both at school—compounded by the fact that Ålandic pupils, unlike many mainland Finno-Swedes, do not get everyday practise in Finnish outside school—very few Ålanders master Finnish sufficiently well to be qualified for these positions. If Anderson's model is applicable, this might contribute to a continued strengthening of Ålandic-ness as a separate national identity.

Åland, Gotland, Bornholm, and Saaremaa display strong regional identities, illustrated by the rich production of regional history-writing, and in recent decades regional identity has been strengthened on Hiiumaa too. The fact that most of the islands have been administrative units for long periods of their history, and that their borders correspond with old provincial borders, is most certainly of great importance for the development of regional identity. It cannot be denied, however, that the blueprint for these administrative borders is geographical, and has surrounded the islands with water. The islands' insularity has meant that although they have been impacted by the same historical processes as the mainland, they have experienced the effects in a slightly different way. In the nineteenth and early twentieth centuries, industrialization transformed life in the entire Baltic region, but while it brought with it factories and railroads on the mainland, on many of the islands it took the form of peasant shipping, globalizing rather than nationalizing the identity of the islanders in the process. Times of war and unrest, too, affected the islands differently than the mainland; depending upon the belligerents' ability to make use of the sea, the islands could be hit exceptionally hard or entirely spared from hostilities. These differences meant that crucial events in

---

[13] Anderson 2006, 55 ff.

national history have been remembered differently on the islands than on the mainland, a phenomenon which is most accentuated on Bornholm and Åland. To borrow from the terminology of Ernest Gellner, islandness can be described as an 'obstacle to social entropy', a barrier which prevents all parts of the nation from becoming identical under the homologizing pressure of industrial society.

However, the most important factor in creating a difference between the islands and the mainland is the islands' strategic locations, which have repeatedly ensured their exceptional status. It has been argued that the placement of the border between Sweden and Denmark through Öresund strait—and perhaps their very existence as two separate nations rather than one—is a consequence of the unwillingness of great powers to leave any one country in control of that important seaway. In a similar manner, Åland's demilitarized, neutralized, and autonomous status is a result of great power politics aimed at avoiding any state's unhindered use of the island for military purposes. The Ålanders have been able to take advantage of this situation in order to expand their autonomy. In the regional government's struggle to strengthen its autonomy, regional identity has been intentionally heightened, in part with the aid of history-writing. A strong regional identity was thus not a cause of autonomy, but instead was the last link in a chain of events: the point of departure was the island's geographic position, which in a certain political setting became of strategic importance, leading in turn to an exceptional legal status and, eventually, autonomy. Autonomy was the result of a 'popular uprising' (the Åland movement), which was in part fuelled by tensions caused by Åland's geographic insularity. Ålandic history-writing and identity-building can thus be seen as an attempt to make best use of the situation into which geography and history had thrust it.

In the case of Bornholm, things have headed in the other direction. The regional reform of 1 January 2007 integrated Bornholm into Region Hovedstaden, and although Bornholms Regionskommune has some privileges compared to an ordinary Danish municipality, the reform removed regional influence from important areas such as health care. However, regardless of how the administrative borders of Denmark's regions are drawn, Bornholm's geographic location as a peripheral island cannot be denied, and the identity-forming forces which it implies are very much at work today, not least in the form of vivid regional history-writing. In the words of Fernand Braudel, a 'mere' geographical expression is far from insignificant, being 'a representation of a historical entity within which events had similar repercussions and effects'.[14] It is not the geographic borders per se, but the shared historical experience that they impose on the people living within them, which constitutes the basis of a common identity. It might be argued that the unpopular reshaping of regional borders constitutes yet another shared experience around which this identity can take form.

Our studies have brought us far from the simple geographically deterministic model that islands, being neatly delimited by natural borders and often relatively small in size, automatically impose a common sense of identity on their inhabitants. However, we have not relegated the idea of islandness to a mere metaphor, implying that the physical geography of islands is completely irrelevant to the formation of collective identities. Instead we have reached the conclusion that islandness *does* influence regional identity, but through a series of complex historical processes, which are summarized in the figure on page 413. Throughout history, the islands' geographical locations have given them strategic importance and good access to international trade networks, but also have complicated and delayed their communications with the mainland states to which they belong.

Their strategic locations have left the islands subject to fortifications, troop billets and occupation. This has contributed to the outbreak of regional uprisings or protests, which, aided by the islands' relative isolation from the mainland, have sometimes been successful. The islands' strategic locations have also brought them exceptional status. Because of their fortifications, Saaremaa and Hiiumaa were subject to travel restrictions during the Soviet period. The uprising in 1658 brought the Bornholmians a number of privileges, and the Åland movement in combination with international interest in the strategically important Åland Islands resulted in autonomy in 1921. This kind of exceptional status is perhaps the most important factor in the formation of a strong political identity, manifested in the shift in Ålandic regional identity in the direction of a national identity in the late twentieth century.

The islands' relative isolation from the mainland has made it practical to maintain them as administrative units, which in the long term has been

---

[14] Braudel 1976, 164.

of importance for the formation of a regional identity. Their isolation also contributed to a relatively slow start for the national movement on most of the islands. The national movements' difficulty in getting traction on the islands might also be linked to their good access to international trade networks, which in the second half of the nineteenth century meant that Åland, Saaremaa, Hiiumaa, and Bornholm were deeply involved in the international shipping boom, which connected them to an international network—and especially to Great Britain—rather than to their closer national surroundings.

COMPARATIVE CONCLUSIONS

The relationship between islandness and regional identity on the Baltic islands

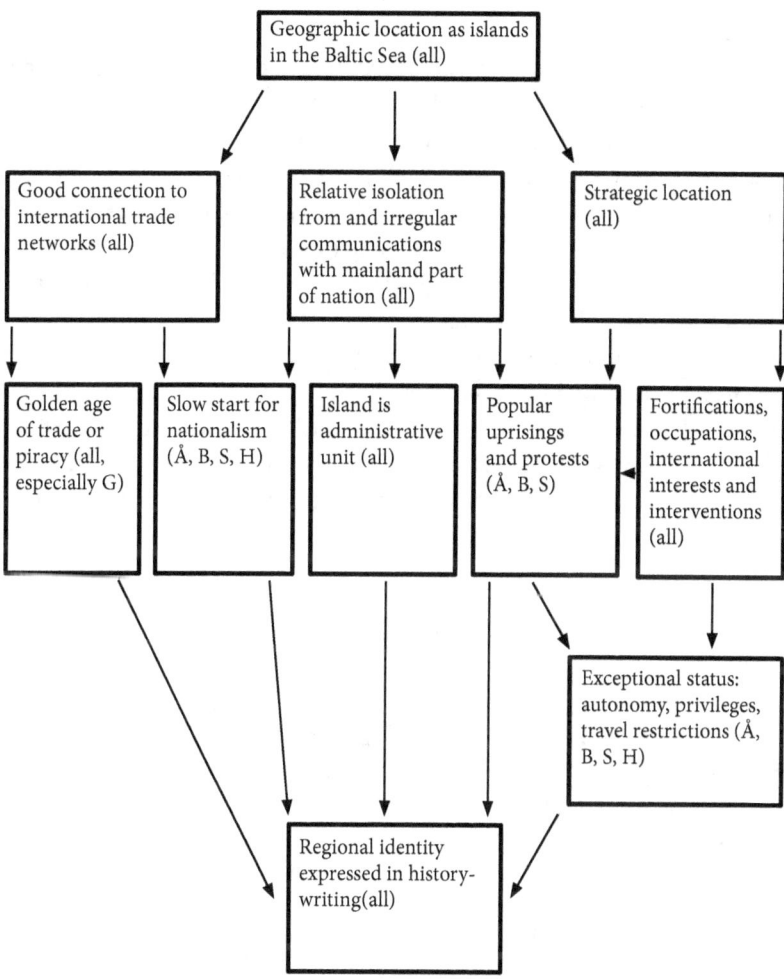

All of the islands studied in this project have experienced periods when they have benefited greatly from their locations close to international trade routes, through trade, piracy, or privateering. On all of the islands these 'golden ages' form an important part of the regional history-writing and regional identity, but on Gotland—where regional history-writing is centred on the island's medieval history—this theme is completely dominant.

It must be emphasized that although the islands share many traits, their individual characteristics regarding location, size, and political affiliation have influenced the construction of regional identity in turn, making every case special. However, these unique identities have all been formed through different combinations of geographical and historical factors, as discussed. It has to be remembered that this model of island identity formation is based on studies of islands in the Baltic, and we would not argue that it will be applicable to all islands, regardless of size, location, and political circumstance. We would hope, however, that the conclusions reached in this research project might advance the field of island studies by clarifying in some detail the mechanisms by which islands form strong regional identities. Likewise, we hope that our findings will help historians and other scholars interested in collective identities rediscover geography as a crucial parameter in identity formation.

Works cited

Anderson, Benedict (2006), Imagined Communities: Reflections on the Origin and Spread of Nationalism (rev. edn., London: Verso).

Bartmann, Barry (2007), 'War & Security', in Godfrey Baldacchino (ed.), *A World of Islands: An Island Studies Reader* (Charlottetown: Institute of Island Studies).

Braudel, Fernand (1976), The Mediterranean and the Mediterranean World in the Age of Philip II, i (New York: Harper).

Churchill, Winston & Baker, Timothy (1985), The Island Race: an abridgement by Timothy Baker of the four volumes of 'A history of the English-speaking peoples' (Exeter: Webb & Bower).

Clarke, Erik & Clarke, Thomas L. (2009), 'Isolating connections—connecting isolations', *Geografiska Annaler: Series B, Human Geography*, 91 (4): 311–23.

Feldbæk, Ole (1991–2), *Dansk identitetshistorie* (4 vols., Copenhagen: Reitzel).

Gellner, Ernest (1983), *Nations and Nationalism* (Oxford: Blackwell).

Gerner, Kristian & Karlsson, Klas-Göran (2002), *Nordens medelhav. Östersjöområdet som historia, myt och projekt* (Stockholm: Natur & Kultur).

Jansson, Torkel (2000), 'Estlandssvenskhet före estlandssvenskheten. Kustbornas identifikation före nationalmedvetandets födelse', in Torkel Jansson & Torbjörn Eng (eds.), *Stat—kyrka—samhälle. Den stormaktstida samhällsordningen i Sverige och Östersjöprovinserna* (Stockholm: Stockholm University, Department of Baltic Studies).

Kurantowicz, Eva (2001), 'Local Identity of Small Communities. Continuity or Change', in Michael Schemmann & Michal Bronn Jr (eds.), *Adult Education and Democratic Citizenship IV* (Cracow: Impuls), 187–194.

Nordlund, Christer (2001), *Det upphöjda landet. Vetenskapen, landhöjningsfrågan och kartläggningen av Sveriges förflutna, 1860–1930* (Umeå: Umeå University).

Södertörn Academic Studies

1. Helmut Müssener & Frank-Michael Kirsch (eds.), *Nachbarn im Ostseeraum unter sich. Vorurteile, Klischees und Stereotypen in Texten*, 2000.
2. Jan Ekecrantz & Kerstin Olofsson (eds.), *Russian Reports: Studies in Post-Communist Transformation of Media and Journalism*, 2000.
3. Kekke Stadin (ed.), *Society, Towns and Masculinity: Aspects on Early Modern Society in the Baltic Area*, 2000.
4. Bernd Henningsen et al. (eds.), *Die Inszenierte Stadt. Zur Praxis und Theorie kultureller Konstruktionen*, 2001.
5. Michal Bron (ed.), *Jews and Christians in Dialogue*, ii: *Identity, Tolerance, Understanding*, 2001
6. Frank-Michael Kirsch et al. (eds.), *Nachbarn im Ostseeraum übwer einander. Wandel der Bilder, Vorurteile und Stereotypen?*, 2001.
7. Birgitta Almgren, *Illusion und Wirklichkeit. Individuelle und kollektive Denkmusterin nationalsozialistischer Kulturpolitik und Germanistik in Schweden 1928–1945*, 2001.
8. Denny Vågerö (ed.), *The Unknown Sorokin: His Life in Russia and the Essay on Suicide*, 2002.
9. Kerstin W. Shands (ed.), *Collusion and Resistance: Women Writing in English*, 2002.
10. Elfar Loftsson & Yonhyok Choe (eds.), *Political Representation and Participation in Transitional Democracies: Estonia, Latvia and Lithuania*, 2003.
11. Birgitta Almgren (eds.), *Bilder des Nordens in der Germanistik 1929–1945: Wissenschaftliche Integrität oder politische Anpassung?*, 2002.
12. Christine Frisch, *Von Powerfrauen und Superweibern: Frauenpopulärliteratur der 90er Jahre in Deutschland und Schweden*, 2003.
13. Hans Ruin & Nicholas Smith (eds.), *Hermeneutik och tradition. Gadamer och den grekiska filosofin*, 2003.
14. Mikael Lönnborg et al. (eds.), *Money and Finance in Transition: Research in Contemporary and Historical Finance*, 2003.
15. Kerstin Shands et al. (eds.), *Notions of America: Swedish Perspectives*, 2004.
16. Karl-Olov Arnstberg & Thomas Borén (eds.), *Everyday Economy in Russia, Poland and Latvia*, 2003.

17. Johan Rönnby (ed.), *By the Water. Archeological Perspectives on Human Strategies around the Baltic Sea*, 2003.
18. Baiba Metuzale-Kangere (ed.), *The Ethnic Dimension in Politics and Culture in the Baltic Countries 1920–1945*, 2004.
19. Ulla Birgegård & Irina Sandomirskaja (eds.), *In Search of an Order: Mutual Representations in Sweden and Russia during the Early Age of Reason*, 2004.
20. Ebba Witt-Brattström (ed.), *The New Woman and the Aesthetic Opening:Unlocking Gender in Twentieth-Century Texts*, 2004.
21. Michael Karlsson, *Transnational Relations in the Baltic Sea Region*, 2004.
22. Ali Hajighasemi, *The Transformation of the Swedish Welfare System: Fact or Fiction? Globalisation, Institutions and Welfare State Change in a Social Democratic Regime*, 2004.
23. Erik A. Borg (ed.), *Globalization, Nations and Markets: Challenging Issues in Current Research on Globalization*, 2005.
24. Stina Bengtsson & Lars Lundgren, *The Don Quixote of Youth Culture: Media Use and Cultural Preferences Among Students in Estonia and Sweden*, 2005.
25. Hans Ruin, *Kommentar till Heideggers Varat och tiden*, 2005.
26. Ludmila Ferm, *Variativnoe bespredložnoe glagol'noe upravlenie v russkom jazyke XVIII veka* [Variation in non-prepositional verbal government in eighteenth-century Russian], 2005.
27. Christine Frisch, *Modernes Aschenputtel und Anti-James-Bond: Gender-Konzepte in deutschsprachigen Rezeptionstexten zu Liza Marklund und Henning Mankell*, 2005.
28. Ursula Naeve-Bucher, *Die Neue Frau tanzt: Die Rolle der tanzenden Frau in deutschen und schwedischen literarischen Texten aus der ersten Hälfte des 20. Jahrhunderts*, 2005.
29. Göran Bolin et al. (eds.), *The Challenge of the Baltic Sea Region: Culture, Ecosystems, Democracy*, 2005.
30. Marcia Sá Cavalcante Schuback & Hans Ruin (eds.), *The Past's Presence: Essays on the Historicity of Philosophical Thought*, 2006.
31. María Borgström & Katrin Goldstein-Kyaga (ed.), *Gränsöverskridande identiteter i globaliseringens tid: Ungdomar, migration och kampen för fred*, 2006.
32. Janusz Korek (ed.), *From Sovietology to Postcoloniality: Poland and Ukraine from a Postcolonial Perspective*, 2007.

33. Jonna Bornemark (ed.), *Det främmande i det egna: filosofiska essäer om bildning och person*, 2007.
34. Sofia Johansson, *Reading Tabloids: Tabloid Newspapers and Their Readers*, 2007.
35. Patrik Åker, *Symboliska platser i kunskapssamhället: Internet, högre lärosäten och den gynnade geografin*, 2008.
36. Kerstin W. Shands (ed.), *Neither East Nor West: Postcolonial Essays on Literature, Culture and Religion*, 2008.
37. Rebecka Lettevall & My Klockar Linder (eds.), *The Idea of Kosmopolis: History, philosophy and politics of world citizenship*, 2008.
38. Karl Gratzer & Dieter Stiefel (eds.), *History of Insolvency and Bankruptcy from an International Perspective*, 2008.
39. Katrin Goldstein-Kyaga & María Borgström, *Den tredje identiteten: Ungdomar och deras familjer i det mångkulturella, globala rummet*, 2009.
40. Christine Farhan, *Frühling für Mütter in der Literatur?: Mutterschaftskonzepte in deutschsprachiger und schwedischer Gegenwartsliteratur*, 2009.
41. Marcia Sá Cavalcante Schuback (ed.), *Att tänka smärtan*, 2009.
42. Heiko Droste (ed.), *Connecting the Baltic Area: The Swedish Postal System in the Seventeenth Century*, 2011.
43. Aleksandr Nemtsov, *A Contemporary History of Alcohol in Russia*, 2011.
44. Cecilia von Feilitzen & Peter Petrov (eds.), *Use and Views of Media in Russia and Sweden: A Comparative Study of Media in St. Petersburg and Stockholm*, 2011.
45. Sven Lilja (ed.), *Fiske, jordbruk och klimat i Östersjöregionen under förmodern tid*, 2012.
46. Leif Dahlberg & Hans Ruin (eds.), *Fenomenologi, teknik och medialitet*, 2012.
47. Samuel Edquist, *I Ruriks fotspår: Om forntida svenska österledsfärder i modern historieskrivning*, 2012.
48. Jonna Bornemark (ed.), *Phenomenology of Eros*, 2012.
49. Jonna Bornemark & Hans Ruin (eds.), *Ambiguity of the Sacred: Phenomenology, Politics, Aesthetics*, 2012.
50. Håkan Nilsson, *Placing Art in the Public Realm*, 2012.
51. Per Bolin, *Between National and Academic Agendas: Ethnic Policies and 'National Disciplines' at Latvia's University, 1919–1940*, 2012.

52. Lars Kleberg & Aleksei Semenenko (eds.), *Aksenov and the Environs/Aksenov iokrestnosti*, 2012.
53. Sven-Olov Wallenstein & Brian Manning Delaney (eds.), *Translating Hegel: The Phenomenology of Spirit and Modern Philosophy*, 2012.
54. Sven-Olov Wallenstein and Jakob Nilsson (eds.), *Foucault, Biopolitics, and Governmentality*, 2013.
55. Jan Patočka, *Inledning till fenomenologisk filosofi*, 2013.
56. Jonathan Adams & Johan Rönnby (eds.), *Interpreting Shipwrecks: Maritime Archaeological Approaches*, 2013.
57. Charlotte Bydler, *Mondiality/Regionality: Perspectives on Art, Aesthetics and Globalization*, 2014.
58. Andrej Kotljarchuk, *In the Forge of Stalin: Swedish Colonists of Ukraine in Totalitarian Experiments of the Twentieth Century*, 2014.
59. Samuel Edquist & Janne Holmén, *Islands of Identity*, 2014.
60. Norbert Götz (ed.), *The Sea of Identities: A Century of Baltic and East European Experiences with Nationality, Class, and Gender*, 2015.

www.ingramcontent.com/pod-product-compliance
Lightning Source LLC
Chambersburg PA
CBHW051554230426
43668CB00013B/1848